While the Gods Were Silent

Growing up Under Fascists and Communists

An Autobiographical and
Historical Narrative by
Julius Scherzer

PublishAmerica
Baltimore

First printing

ISBN: 1-4241-0285-5
PUBLISHED BY PUBLISHAMERICA, LLLP
www.publishamerica.com
Baltimore

Printed in the United States of America

To my grandchildren:

Benjamin,
Daniel,
and Michael

Table of Contents

Acknowledgments

I want to thank the following for assisting me in writing this book: Barbara French, whose class on creative writing helped me develop the skills required to write this narrative; Loretta Foster, for helpful criticism, comments and suggestions made after reading the manuscript; Prof. Meinhard Mayer, for helpful suggestions and corrections; Sally Wechsler and my cousin Fidelia Lang-Gillman, for carefully proof reading my manuscript; My son Gabriel Scherzer, as well as Jane Horvat and Michael Fischer, for their valuable assistance in overcoming the difficulties encountered in some computer operations; Dr. Michael Berenbaum, for his encouragement to publish this work; Rory Vaughan from Publish America, for working patienly and diligently with me during the production phase of this volume. To all of them, I am very grateful.

ROMANIA

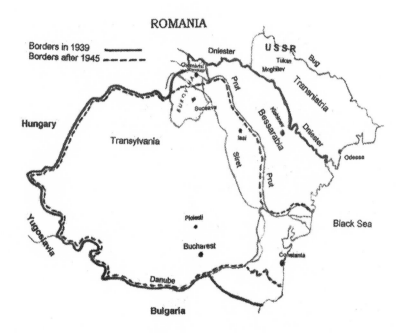

Borders in 1939 ——————
Borders after 1945 - - - - -

Hungary

Transylvania

Yugoslavia

Danube

Bulgaria

Dniester

Cernivtsi

Suceava

Prut

Bessarabia

Siret

Prut

Ploiesti

Bucharest

U S S R

Tulcin

Moghilev

Bug

Transnistria

Dniester

Odessa

Black Sea

Constanta

Those who cannot remember the past are condemned to repeat it.
—George Santayana

The author at age 18

Preface

My father often used the Latin proverb: *Verba volant, scripta manent* (Spoken words fly away, but written words remain). I remember him using these words when I was still a child, and I carried them in my mind all my life. As I grew older, I perceived this Latin expression as Father's early advice to put on paper the experiences and feelings from my past. Now, at an advanced age, I have finally decided to follow his suggestion and write about my experiences while growing up as a small Jewish boy under fascism, and later, as a teenager and as a young adult, under communism. I want to share my memories before they are lost. This book will shed light, not only on my personal experiences during a very difficult period of history, but will also illuminate the life-shattering events that took place under divers dictators, be they of the right or of the left.

I decided to write this narrative also with another objective in mind: to memorialize those members of my family who perished during World War II. Their names are not inscribed on a tombstone, nor are they engraved on a memorial plaque. Their grave sites are unknown. By describing their life and fate in this book, I try to honor their memory and keep it alive.

This account covers the first 35 years of my life. Little is known in the West about the history and events that occurred in that corner of Europe where I spent my early years. I have therefore combined the autobiographical narrative with a brief description of the historical events that took place in the countries where I lived during that time span, refracted through the lens of my own and my family's experience. I have lived in the midst of a variety of peoples, cultures and languages; have experienced and survived many of the tempests of war and revolutionary changes that have scarred Europe—and my soul—during the twentieth century.

The story I have written recounts my life under different dictatorships. When I started writing about my childhood and adolescence, I was not sure how much I still remembered from those years long gone. However, when I began to rake the furrows of my aged brain in search of ancient memories, I discovered that traumatic experiences from a turbulent past have not been forgotten. They emerged from the fog of forgetfulness, often in stark and vivid details. The patient recollection of my memory helped me revive these images from the distant past, to give them concrete shapes and colors, and bring them back to life. I discovered how valid Faulkner's saying is that "the past is never dead, it is not even past." The passage of time had not erased the images of those experiences from my memory. I was able to recreate and to relive the past.

Those were years of great upheaval in my personal life, the life of my family, and the world in which we lived. I had lived in the Age of Evil. The suffering and violent death of innocent people had shadowed the world throughout a large part of my life. As a child, as a teenager, and later as a young adult, I had known dictatorships of the right and of the left. Under Romanian rule I lived through the fascist regime of Goga-Cuza, the autocratic reign of King Carol II, and the military dictatorship of Marshall Ion Antonescu. I had known the dictatorship of Joseph Stalin under Soviet rule and that of Gheorghiu-Dej under Romanian communist rule. It was a harsh world, where decency seldom thrived, where fairness was unknown, and where bias and prejudice prevailed. I had seen how war and dictatorships—be they of the right or the left—poison the human soul and bring out its darkest impulses. More benign political regimes, such as parliamentary democracy, constitutional monarchy, and social democracy, had also played a role in my life. In the process, I became familiar with most political systems that Europe had seen in the twentieth century.

Not much is known in the West about Romania and its history. Even less is known about life in Bukovina, a region annexed by Romania from Austria after World War I, where a clash of cultures had been played out between the two World Wars. What is known to the older generation about that country is the bombing of the Ploiesti oil fields by American bombers during World War II. A more recent political event known in the West is the overthrow and execution of communist dictator Nicolai Ceausescu. Scant are the publications describing the events that occurred in Germany-allied Romania during the war, especially in the provinces formerly occupied by the Soviets. Little had been written about the early years of the communist regime in post-war Romania.

For a better understanding of my personal experiences and to see them in context with the world I lived in, I have added in many chapters of this narrative a brief description of the political, economic and social conditions that prevailed at that time.

The persons described in this work are all real. In some instances, the names of non-family members have been changed, in order to protect their privacy. In other instances, only first names were used.

I hope the reader will find my account interesting and instructive. A Bibliographical Note at the end of this volume offers the reader a short list of books that describe in more detail the different historical events discussed in this narrative. For those unfamiliar with the Yiddish and Hebrew terms used in this text, I have attached a glossary of such terms.

1. Early Childhood in "Little Vienna"

When I think of my childhood, I see the city of my birth, like a long-lost Atlantis, emerging from the ocean of memories and slowly returning to life. There is still a town with that name (or a similar one) sitting in the same place. Even some of the buildings and streets may be the same. The two towns, however, are very different. The city of my childhood exists only in my memories. It is a city of yesterday that belongs to the past.

Where was I born? I'm not sure how to answer this question. It is not that I don't know where I arrived in this world. I hesitate because that place has had numerous names in the past, and I don't know which one to use.

Why the variety of names? During the twentieth century, the city belonged to different countries at different times. This may seem strange to an American, but is a well known fact in many parts of Europe. Throughout the century, diverse masters had ruled my place of birth, and each gave it a new name. The city is now called Chernivtsi (the Ukrainian name), formerly Chernovitsy (the Russian name), formerly Cernauti (the Romanian name), and formerly Czernowitz (the Austrian-German name).

When I was born there, the city belonged to the Kingdom of Romania, and its official name was Cernauti. My mother was born in the same area before World War I, but her documents show that her place of birth is Austria. One of my cousins came into this world in that region after World War II; at that time, however, that territory had become part of the Soviet Union. Today, the city belongs to Ukraine. It may seem confusing, but life itself in that part of the world had often been confusing.

In this narrative I shall call the city Czernowitz, the name always used by my parents.

Czernowitz was the capital of the province Bukovina. The city is located at the foothills of the northern Carpathian Mountains, on the right bank of the Prut River. Old history books claim that it was founded in the 12th century. It was the administrative, economic and cultural center of Bukovina until 1940. In that year, Czernowitz had a population of about 100,000. Between the two World Wars, the city's inhabitants were a motley mixture of Ukrainians (we also called them Ruthenians), Romanians, Jews, Swabian-Germans, and Poles, with a sprinkling of Russians (the Lipovan sect), Hungarians, Armenians, Slovaks, and Gypsies. Fate—or history—had brought together all these ethnic groups and placed them in that corner of Europe, turning it into a modern Babel. Jews made up about half the city's population.

Bukovina had a turbulent history. Being close to major empires— Austria, Russia, Turkey—that shaped the history of Central and Eastern Europe, the province had been a crossroad of history throughout the centuries. Kiev-Russian princes, Polish nobles, Turkish sultans, Austrian emperors, Romanian kings, and Soviet dictators had ruled this province. Life in that part of the world had never been dull. The Austrians ruled Bukovina from 1775 until the end of World War I, when the Austrian Empire ceased to exist. The Kingdom of Romania annexed the province in 1919, and was its master until 1940, when it was forced by the Soviet Union to give up the northern part of Bukovina, including Czernowitz. In 1941, following the invasion of the Soviet Union by the German armies and their Romanian allies, Northern Bukovina came again under Romanian rule. In 1944, the advancing Red Army re-occupied the province. The Soviet Union again annexed Northern Bukovina, and incorporated it into the Soviet Republic of Ukraine. Southern Bukovina remained under Romanian rule. Following the collapse of the Soviet Union, Northern Bukovina became part of Ukraine in 1991.

All these changes kept the people of our city on their toes. Just when they got used to one ruler, a new one arrived. And the process of adjustment started all over.

From its location on the hills next to the Prut River, Czernowitz dominates the surrounding fields and the Prut valley. To the west of the city are the Tsetsina woods. Two steel bridges, built at the beginning of the 20th century, connect the city with the left bank of the river. One is a railroad bridge, while pedestrians, horses, and automobiles use the other one.

The road from the Prut valley to the city is quite steep. As a child, I often watched the sweat-covered, panting horses, foam dripping from their mouths, pulling the creaking, heavy carts loaded with potatoes, onions, firewood and other goods for the market. The horses were enticed to climb the steep hill with shouts and much whip cracking by cursing peasants. The demeanor of these screaming peasants frightened me, but I kept watching them. The perspiring horses and the cracking of the whips fascinated me. While looking at that scene, I enriched my vocabulary. The curses, shouted in Romanian or Ukrainian, were the first words I learned in those two languages. Years later, as a schoolboy, I watched smoke-belching trucks and automobiles climb the same hill with much less effort. Still, I found the image of the sweat-covered horses and whip-cracking peasants much more interesting.

My parents got married in 1920. Two years later my sister was born, and in 1928 I came into this world. They named my sister Bertha, after her paternal grandmother, and named me Julius, after my paternal grandfather. Already in her childhood, my sister was serious and had a mind of her own. In contrast to me, she was a quiet child, but extremely stubborn. It was easier to make a dog moo than to change her mind. She also had a sharp tongue. When I was in grade school, after having a fight with my sister, I told her that I didn't like her and wanted to know why I didn't have a brother.

"After you were born, our parents took a close look at you and decided not to have any more children," was her reply. That is why, according to my sister, I have no other siblings.

The memories from my early childhood take me back to the 1930s. My parents had to show great patience with me. I was not *artig* (well behaved).

19

I was a wild and disobedient child, impulsive, and full of energy. I found mischief more fun than obedience. I preferred to run rather than walk, fidgeted in my chair at the dinner table, and enjoyed doing things I was told not to do. I liked to run into the middle of the street, touch stray dogs, and was inclined to break china and glassware. My behavior often upset my mother and made my father resort to his Germanic method of discipline: applying his walking stick or leather belt to my backside.

The conversation between my parents and myself consisted more often than not in them giving me orders, in laying down the rules. "Wash your hands!" "Finish the soup!" "Brush your teeth!" There were lots of "don't" in those rules: "Don't mess up your shirt!" "Don't slurp your soup!" "Don't kick the ball in the kitchen!" "Don't run. You'll fall!" "Don't touch that dog. He'll bite you." Whenever I wanted to have fun by doing something that elicited a "don't do it" from my parents, I felt like a dog jerked to a halt by the leash. I came to the conviction, so strong in many children, that the things you most want to do are rarely attainable.

During those years we lived on the fourth floor of the Chamber of Commerce Building in the center of the city. Father warned me repeatedly not to run up and down the stairs or slide down the handrail. I was sure, however, that if I'm warned not to do something, it must have some pleasant side to it, like all the other fun stuff I wasn't supposed to do. I decided to ignore Father's warning. I did run up and down the stairs, and did slide down the handrail.

The smooth, shiny wooden handrail that topped the metal railing was very tempting. One summer's day, I decided to slide down the handrail that separated the staircase from the four-story-deep abyss. When I reached the 3d floor the rail made a curve. At that point, sliding at fairly high speed, I fell off the railing and hit the stairs hard with the back of my head. I felt a sharp pain, saw stars in front of my eyes, and started to cry. Touching the back of my head with my hand, I felt a sticky fluid. I looked at my red hand and realized that I was bleeding profusely. Mother heard my cries and came running. When she saw my bloody head, she panicked.

"Oh, my God, how did this happen?" she cried out. I didn't answer; just kept crying. I was sure she would figure it out without my explanation.

Mother swabbed the wound with her handkerchief that turned quickly deep red. But the flow of blood didn't stop, while I was hurting and crying. She ran down the stairs with me, jumped into one of the horse-drawn carriages standing in front of our house, and rushed to our family doctor, Dr. Noe. It was a long ride to the doctor. Too long. I whimpered all the way there. Once in the doctor's office, Dr. Noe washed the wound with alcohol and dabbed it with iodine—a very painful experience; he shaved the hair around the injury, stitched together the gash on my head, and then covered it with gauze and adhesive bandage. All the while, Mother watched apprehensively. I left the doctor's office with a bulky bandage on my head.

I had been lucky. Had I fallen off the other side of the railing, I would have dropped three floors through the air before touching the ground. Needless to say, that would have been the end of my mischief making.

Although I was shocked by the accident, I was more scared by what would follow. The thought that Father would find out what had happen frightened me. He had warned me repeatedly not to run down the stairs or slide down the handrail. I knew what the penalty for my unruly behavior would be. On the way home from the doctor's office, I begged Mother not to tell Father about the accident.

"Please, Mother, don't tell. Please."

Mother said she wouldn't tell if I promised not to slide down the railing or run down the stairs anymore. To make sure Father wouldn't find out, I was ready to promise anything.

"I promise, I promise," I replied with the most convincing voice I was able to muster.

For the next several weeks, I wore my beret in the presence of my father, in spite of the summer heat. I wanted to make sure that he wouldn't notice the bandage on my head. Luckily, he didn't find out about the accident, and my back was spared an encounter with his leather belt.

When I started attending kindergarten many months later, I showed off the scar on my head to the other children.

"What a nice scar!" they said with admiration.

I was proud of my scar and of having won their attention. I almost felt it was worth getting that gash on my head.

Several times a week Mother took me to the Schillerpark, located not far from the National Theater. To reach the park, we had to cross a large square named Elisabethplatz (Piata Vasile Alexandri in Romanian). In the center of the square was a small sunken garden, adorned with rows of gladiolas, geraniums and irises. For some mysterious reason, the town's people called it "The English Garden." After crossing the square, we passed the impressive building of the National Theater. Its façade was decorated with allegorical figures, and classical Greek columns guarded its arched entrance. I often stopped in front of the theater and admired the ancient Greek heroes gazing into the distance.

Across the square was the imposing structure of the *Jüdisches Nationalhaus*, the Jewish Community Center, and next to it the *Musikverein*, the Music Conservatory building. Both were built in the neoclassical style that prevailed at the turn of the century. A short walk behind the National Theater, along the Schillergasse, led to the Schillerpark, a large park that sloped down towards the suburb of Kaliczanka. The park was named after the nineteenth century German poet Friedrich Schiller.

On the way to the park, I occasionally noticed an interesting event. There were many stray dogs that roamed the city's streets in the vicinity of the park. On several occasions I saw a pair of dogs copulating in the middle of the street. Afterwards, however, they were unable to part, regardless of how hard they tried. Watching the dogs' futile attempt to separate from each other caused much amusement among the bystanders. After awhile, a merciful soul poured a bucket of water over the coupled dogs, forcing them to run. That did the trick. They ran in different directions and thus separated from each other. The people who watched laughed. They had their fun, and so did I.

While walking to the park, Mother always held my hand. She had good reasons to hold on to me. If she let go, I would run into the street and try to catch one of the numerous pigeons that inhabited the city, or try to touch a stray dog. On one occasion, when Mother let go of my hand for a moment to take out a handkerchief from her handbag, I ran into the middle of the street to chase a small dog. An oncoming car blew the horn, screeched, veered, and just missed me. Frightened, I forgot the dog and ran back quickly to the sidewalk. Mother was horrified. That event scared the wits out of my mother and me. From then on, she always held my hand firmly. No more dog chasing.

In the park, Mother kept a close eye on me, to make sure I didn't disappear among the bushes or get into a fight with other children. Most of the time, however, I played by myself. I had a few toys: a small rubber ball, a small tin bucket, a shovel, and a wooden hoop, which I rolled with a short stick. I felt happy in the park and looked forward to playing there.

When I grew older I started to make my own toys. I enjoyed making "things" to play with, using my own hands. My favored toy was a rifle. Part of it I had carved from a piece of wood, using my mother's kitchen knife as a carving tool. With a wire I attached to it a metal pipe that I had found in a heap of discards. That was supposed to be the barrel. A nail served as a trigger. It did not look as nice as the rifles sold in toy stores, but I liked it since it was my own creation, my handiwork. I also made a soccer ball from an old sock tightly packed with rags and sewn by my mother in the form of a ball. It did not bounce, but rolled and could be kicked. During one of my soccer practices in the kitchen, I found out that kicking the ball into a windowpane would crack it. (Learning that lesson cost me a slap on my behind.) I also had a few picture books and colored pencils.

I never had any fancy toys. Later, I watched with envy as other children rode their tricycles and bicycles. When I asked Father why I couldn't have a bike, he replied: "I'll buy you one later." But he didn't buy it. The future set other priorities to my father.

On Fridays my father took me to the city's steam bath. We called it the "Turkish bath" or, in Yiddish, *shvitzbood.* Nowadays such a steam bath is called a sauna, like those I saw in later years in Finland. Our steam bath was located on Russischegasse, in the Jewish section of town. In those days, few Jews could afford a bathing place of their own. On Friday afternoons, Jewish men, who wanted to cleanse and refresh themselves before the Sabbath, visited the bath. The steam bath was open to women Friday mornings.

The bath had three large rooms: one for dressing and undressing, with hooks along the wall to hang the visitor's clothing and underwear; another room held a small cold-water pool and wooden benches for relaxing; and a third room was the steam bath proper. Naked men would sit or lie down in the steam bath room on wooden benches at different heights, perspiring profusely. The steam was generated by pouring buckets of water periodically over rocks heated by burning wooden logs in a special oven. The more courageous people sat on the top benches, where the temperature was higher and perspiration more intensive. Being less courageous, I sat on the lowest bench.

Never have I seen so many different naked men in one place. There were tall men and short men, hairy men and bald men, big-bellied, fat men and gaunt, skinny men, smooth-skinned, muscular young men and wrinkled, flabby old men. All these men-folks were covered with sweat that oozed from every pore of their shiny skin. When not sitting on one of the wooden benches, they moved lazily in the hot, steamy atmosphere.

What amazed me most was to see some of these men take bundles of birch twigs and beat their own backs and limbs until the skin became hot red. Then they poured buckets of cold water over their heads and bodies to cool off. I could not understand why they were doing that. I would not have wanted to beat myself—I got enough beatings from others. I was convinced that if somebody else had beaten these men with twigs, they would have complained bitterly. Besides, why did they stay in that hot, steamy room if they could not stand the heat, and had to cool off by dousing themselves with buckets of cold water? Did they do that for religious reasons? I remembered my sister saying that in some distant countries deeply religious people submit their bodies to all kinds of pain to proof their devotion to God. I had to find an explanation for that strange behavior.

."Why do these men beat their bodies with twigs?" I asked my father. "Have they done something wrong, have they sinned, and now they punish themselves so that God will forgive them?"

Father smiled, his face shining with sweat. "No, they don't do this to punish themselves. Beating the hot, perspiring body with bundles of twigs helps stimulate blood circulation and cleanses the skin. It helps people stay healthy. The people of northern Europe practice this custom for many centuries." Thus I discovered that people do sometimes-unpleasant things to stay healthy. It also reminded me of what my sister would say to me when I upset her: "A thorough spanking would do you good."

After spending some time in the steam room, Father and I took a dip in the cold-water pool located in the resting room. Then we relaxed briefly on the wooden benches before getting dressed and leaving. We arrived home refreshed and hungry.

On Saturday afternoons my father took me for a walk. From our house it was a short walk to the main square of the city, the Ringplatz (Piata Unirii in Romanian). Three- and four-story buildings, erected in the neoclassical style, surrounded the square. On the ground floor the buildings had spacious stores with big display windows, of which those of a chocolate and candy store attracted most of my attention. In the summer Father would buy me a vanilla-and-chocolate ice cream cone for one leu (Romanian currency) from a peddler, who sold *Lodi* ice cream from a two-wheeled cart in the middle of the square. It was the highlight of our walk, and I always looked forward to the delicious treat.

The Ringplatz was dominated by the imposing, three-story city hall, with Greek columns on its façade and a tower clock at its top. When the clock rang and we were in the square, Father stopped, took his gold watch from the vest pocket, opened its engraved lid, and adjusted the time. He then slid the watch back into his pocket, and we continued our walk. Below the clock was a number, changed daily, which showed the noontime temperature in the city. In the summer the temperature could reach a stifling high of 35 degrees C (95 degrees F), while in winter it could drop to a bone-chilling low of -30 or even -35 degrees C (-31 degrees F).

In the center of the square was the bronze statue of a Romanian soldier. He stood on a stone pedestal, gazing into the distance. With one arm he held a dying comrade, and with the other a rifle at the ready. The statue was dedicated to the Romanian soldiers who had died in World War I. It fascinated me. Whenever I was on the Ringplatz I gawked at the sculpture and studied every detail of it—the contorted face of the dying soldier, the helmet on the head of the other soldier, his rifle, the pouch with bullets—until my father pulled me away.

Behind the soldier's statue was the elegant hotel *Zum Schwarzen Adler*, To the Black Eagle, where important or wealthy visitors resided.

Sometimes I sneaked in and admired the beautiful objects on display in the lobby. The large hotel lobby was adorned with stately crystal chandeliers, brocaded curtains, huge oil paintings of pastoral scenes in gilded frames, bisque porcelain cherubs on black marble bases, and large, thick Persian rugs with intricate patterns.

"Why are there so many paintings, statues and carpets in the hotel lobby?" I wanted to know.

"All these decorations are supposed to give the visiting guest the flavor of Old Vienna," replied my father.

I did not know what "Old Vienna" was. With some effort of my imagination, however, I created a wondrous image of that distant, fairytale-like city. I imagined it shining in the sun, with majestic towers and richly decorated homes, each of them having huge oil paintings in gilded frames, marble statues, sparkling chandeliers and multicolored rugs.

On Saturday night I went with Father sometimes to Druckmann's wine cellar. Mr. Druckmann, the owner, was a religious Jew with a long, black beard and side locks, who always wore a black *yarmulka* on his head. At the wine cellar, Father got together with a few friends once a week to discuss politics over a glass of wine. On those occasions I sat on a bench next to him, but was often attracted by the noise at the neighboring tables. Jewish university students, sitting at those tables, were drinking wine and beer. Father told me that they belonged to the Jewish student organizations *Hasmonea* or *Zephira,* because the Romanian student organization *Junimea* did not accept Jews. They wore their organization's embroidered cap and sash, gave speeches, and sang *Gaudeamus igitur* and other student songs in Latin and German. Many of them displayed small, trimmed mustaches that gave them a more assertive, manly appearance. The students' embroidered sashes, their dashing student caps, and their boisterous songs captivated me. Secretly I wished to be a student and have a cap like theirs.

As time went by the revelers became more and more rowdy. Their songs resonated through the cavernous room, through the damp air loaded with the odor of tobacco and alcohol. The drinking and singing lasted late into the night, until Mr. Druckmann clapped his hands and said with a loud, firm voice, "Closing Time!" At that point we all got up and left. Everybody was in good spirits, including my father. Some of the customers had to be helped to make it to the door.

Later I learned that the students gathered at Druckmann's wine cellar to be out of public view. In the late 1930s, Romanian students and hooligans often attacked Jewish students, forcing them to meet in secluded places.

On Sunday, in fair weather, my parents went for a walk in the Volksgarten, a park located at the southern end of the city. They took me along, while my sister spent time with her friends. In the summer, one could find many of the city's inhabitants in the park, trying to escape the heat and stuffiness of their apartments. Dressed in their finest clothes, the men wearing felt hats and the women elegant headgear, they walked leisurely on the neat, gravel-covered alleys, exchanging polite greetings with passers-by. Some sat on green-painted benches in the cool shade of an oak, acacia, or chestnut tree, reading a book or newspaper. From the trees came the chirping of sparrows and warblers, while the soothing fragrance of blooming lilacs filled the air. In the evening, young couples walked in the shadows, holding hands, and talking in subdued voices.

On Sunday afternoons, a military band gave a free concert in the Volksgarten, which always attracted a large crowd. I loved to listen to the band, but was even more impressed by their adorned uniforms and shiny instruments. Pushing my way through the crowd of grownups surrounding the band, I tried to get close to them, to have a better look at the ornaments, insignia and ribbons on the players' uniforms. Secretly I wished I could have such an outfit. The music was mostly by Strauss and Lehar, alternating with military marches and Romanian folk songs. Most of all I liked the marches, and often tapped the ground with my foot to the rhythm of the vivid music.

During the summer, on weekends, the whole family took the tramcar to the Prut River for an outing. I loved the ride in the tramcar. I can still hear the screeching noise made by the vehicle rounding a curve, the bell ringing as the conductor warned pedestrians, and the hissing sound accompanied by sparks when the movable rods on top of the tramcar made contact with the power line which was strung out overhead. For the outing, Mother carried a shopping bag filled with bread, vegetables and fruits, while Father carried a blanket. There were swimming and picnic areas on both sides of the river, between the pedestrian bridge and the railroad bridge. We crossed the pedestrian bridge and went to the *Volksbad* beach, where families with small children used to gather. Across the water was the *Venezia* beach, where the city's younger people met.

There were many children at the *Volksbad* beach. Under the watchful eyes of their parents, some were wading, some jumping, and some were carrying small buckets with water from the river. Other children played with pebbles near the water's edge or rolled in the grass. Their voices and laughter reverberated through the fresh, clean air.

I took my first swimming lessons in the Prut. Father was a good swimmer, and he taught me how to do the breaststroke. In the process I swallowed a lot of water, and more than once Father had to grab my hand and pull me to the shore. Once, after splashing around not far from the shore, I tried to stand up in what I thought was shallow water. My feet, however, could not touch the ground. In an instant I sank into the bottomless stream. I panicked! Frantically, I began treading water and splashing, while water was rushing up my nose. For an instant I opened my eyes. I saw myself immersed in a bluish-green, fluid world, surrounded by countless tiny air bubbles generated by my frantic movements. All that underwater experience may have lasted only seconds, but to me it seemed an eternity. Suddenly I felt a strong hand grab my arm and pulling me to safety. Father had noticed my frantic movements, realized what was happening, and rushed to my rescue. I gasped for air. Once I had my feet on solid ground, I started coughing, rubbing my burning eyes, blowing my nose, wheezing and spitting water that I had swallowed. It took me awhile to breathe normally.

Everybody was upset. Mother was upset with Father for not watching me, Father was upset with me for not staying close to him, and I was upset because I almost drowned. It took me some time to calm down. Later I learned that there were many invisible, deep holes at the bottom of the river, made by exploding artillery shells during World War I. I had stepped into one of those holes.

One of my favored activities at the beach was skipping stones across the water. I carefully picked a smooth, flat stone, and held its edge between my thumb and index finger. When I threw it with all my force, it hit the surface of the water at a low angle with the flat surface. It was fun to watch the stone bounce repeatedly and happily on the surface of the river before disappearing in its depth. I honed my skills by throwing stones repeatedly. First, the stone skipped on the water twice, then three times and finally it skipped four or even five times. This accomplishment made me proud and gave me great satisfaction. I bragged about it to whoever cared to listen.

As a little boy, I tried all kinds of experiments, some of which had painful consequences for me. Once, having nothing else to do, I decided to pour salt into Mother's sugar bowl. I wanted to see what would happen when sugar and salt were mixed together. It was probably the early chemist in me that made me do it. Since I didn't notice any change, I did not bother to empty the sugar bowl, and went on to other important things.

For the following day my parents had invited several of my father's colleagues and their spouses. It was one of those rare occasions when we had guests in our house. For the occasion Mother had baked one of her delicious chocolate cakes. She hoped it would impress her guests. After the visitors arrived and made themselves comfortable, Mother served each of them a cup of coffee and a slice of cake. As soon as the first guest took a bite of the cake, he made a grimace and promptly spit it out. Mother was horrified. She tasted the cake and discovered that it was loaded with salt. Mother had used the sugar from the bowl to make the cake. It did not take long to find out who the culprit was. Mother apologized profusely to our guests. When they left, my behind took some serious punishment.

My father's first name was Joseph, and my mother's, Fanny. We children called our father, Tata, and our mother, Mama. Once I asked my father to tell me about his childhood, about his past.He was born in Suceava, a town in Southern Bukovina. He told me that his mother died at childbirth and that his father died in a fire at the Vienna Burgtheater at the end of the nineteenth century. An aunt raised him. When Father was five years old, his aunt sent him to *cheder*, an elementary Hebrew school, where he learned the *aleph-bet*, the Hebrew alphabet. He went on to attend the Austrian elementary school, then middle school, high school and eventually studied law at the University of Vienna. While in Vienna he supported himself by tutoring high school students in Greek and Latin. After receiving his diploma, he started practicing law in Czernowitz.

Mother told me about her past. She was born in Molodia, a small town near Czernowitz. Her Yiddish name was Fayge, an abbreviation of the Yiddish word *Faygele* (Little Bird). Her father was a bookkeeper. Her mother raised five children: four girls and a boy. My mother's sisters were named Anna, Jetty, and Tzili; her brother was named Joseph. Mother went to the Austrian elementary and middle schools in Molodia. After World War I, her family moved to Czernowitz, and Mother was sent to attend a school of commerce. After graduation, she worked as a bank clerk and later as a secretary in a law office in Czernowitz.

During my father's visit to the law office, he met my mother. She was a very pretty, young woman, with short-cropped, chestnut-brown hair, bright eyes, delicate features, and milk-white skin. That is the way she looked in the picture that used to sit on her night table, taken when she was in her early twenties. She was much younger than my father, and he fell in love with her. In 1920 they were married at the Temple in Czernowitz. They rented an apartment on Elisabethplatz on the fourth floor of the building that also housed the city's Chamber of Commerce. Father set up his law office in one room of the apartment. Mother helped out with secretarial work, mostly taking stenographic notes and typing. My sister and I were born in that apartment.

Father's sister, Laura, was raised by another relative and took on the name Sternlieb. In her late teens she married Joseph Weich and had four children: Bertha, Rita, Szigu, and Martin. When World War I broke out, her husband was drafted into the Austrian Army and sent to the Russian front. Shortly afterwards, he was taken prisoner by the Russians and spent the rest of the war in captivity. While Joseph Weich was a prisoner of war, my father took care of his children. When the front moved dangerously close to Suceava, where the children lived at the time, Father took them to Vienna. They spent together the rest of the war in that city. Only afterwards did the children return to Suceava.

When the war ended, Joseph Weich also returned to Suceava. Soon after, he emigrated to Canada together with his older son, Szigu. In the early 1920s, Laura and the other children also went to Canada and settled in Montreal. Years later, when the children grew up, they got married (except for Martin) and raised their own families .

During my childhood, Father was no longer a young man. When I attended elementary school, he was already in his late fifties. Father was short of stature, but had a strong and sturdy body. He was bald, with gray hair near the temples. He had green, penetrating eyes, bushy eyebrows, toothbrush mustache, and sharp features. For reading, he wore wire-rimmed glasses. The deep furrows on his forehead were mute testimony of a difficult life. He was always serious, rarely smiled, and was a disciplinarian. He was also a very orderly, neat person, and always dressed impeccably: carefully pressed dark three-piece suit, crisp white shirt with stiff collar and white, hard cuffs, monogrammed gold cufflinks, and dark striped silk tie. I can still see the flowery letters JS engraved on his cufflinks. The tip of a white linen handkerchief stuck out always from his breast pocket. He kept his watch in his vest pocket, with the golden watch chain hanging loosely from the vest's buttonhole. His elegant, black shoes were always shiny and spotless. Father's presence inspired respect, mixed with a touch of fear.

Father was a heavy smoker, in spite of his frequent coughing. The daily rolling of tobacco into cigarettes had left yellow-brown stains on his thumbs, index, and middle fingers. He always carried in his pocket an elegantly designed cigarette case made of Tula silver, bearing his initials and engraved with delicate flourishes. In the morning Father splashed some *Kölnischwasser,* eau-de-Cologne, on his face and filled the air with its aroma. After smoking several cigarettes, however, the smell of tobacco prevailed. Even his clothes smelled of tobacco.

Like many assimilated, westernized Jews, Father went to Temple only on the High Holidays. On those occasions he was elegantly dressed: he wore top hat, black tailcoat, black bow tie, white, starched shirt, and shiny, black shoes. Besides fasting on *Yom Kippur* and eating matzoth on Passover, Father ignored most Jewish religious practices. Having grown up in a German-speaking environment, Father admired German efficiency and was strongly attached to German culture and customs. He revered the names of Goethe, Schiller and Heine, of Bach, Beethoven and Mozart. Except for the short time he went to *cheder*, his education and reading were exclusively limited to the German cultural sphere. He had no interest in Yiddish literature, theater, or newspapers. Only upon my mother's insistence did he hire a young man to instruct me in Hebrew.

At home we all spoke German, although occasionally my parents would sprinkle their German with Yiddish expressions, such as *weiss der reech* (the devil knows), *loss mech up* (don't bug me), or *er is ah gahnev* (he is a thief). The rise to power of Adolf Hitler eventually changed my father's opinion about the Germans.

Father and Mother were an ill-matched pair. They had very different personalities. Father was stern, irascible, pedantic, precise in word and deed, and strict with us children—especially with me! He showed a loathing for slovenliness of any kind. In other words, he was very "Germanic" in his behavior. Mother, on the contrary, was easygoing, had an even temperament, was orderly but not pedantic, and was kind to us children. However, she had certain opinions, which under attack she would defend vigorously.

Mother was more inclined to celebrate the Jewish holidays than Father was—especially the culinary part. For Passover she made excellent *latkes*, potato pancakes, and for Purim tasty *hamantashen*, triangular sweets with a poppy seed filling. Father was interested exclusively in German-Austrian culture. Mother, however, enjoyed not only German novels and poetry, but also Yiddish songs and theater. In her younger years she was slender and walked with poise. Mother liked to dress well, although she avoided excessive elegance. The only makeup she used was face powder. Even so, she often attracted the glances of strangers. As a child, when I walked with her on the street, I remember passers-by turning their heads and staring at Mother.

My parents loved me, but they showed it in their own fashion. Father tried to instill in me discipline, honesty, obedience, and to give me a good education. He taught me that nothing great, nothing of value, and nothing that will last can be achieved without effort, without knowledge. Mother told me fairy tales, recited poetry, baked delicious pastries, and sang beautiful songs. I had to earn my father's love by behaving properly—according to his definition of "properly"—by being neat and orderly, and in later years, by getting good grades in school. When dealing with me, his voice was often stern and commanding: "do this!" or "don't do that!" There was no room for excuses. Father's love was hard and conditional. He would not hesitate to use his belt or walking stick to discipline me. By contrast, Mother's love was unconditional. She loved me regardless what I did or failed to do. Her love was warm and always present. Her gaze was filled with softness and tenderness that I feel to this very day. She admonished me when I misbehaved, but did that in a kind way. She never meted out physical punishment. Mother handed out tenderness, while Father was there for the discipline.

I do not remember being kissed, embraced, or caressed by my parents. There was very little touching in our family, except for holding my hand during a walk, mostly for reasons of safety. Nor was there any verbal expression of affection. The words, "I love you," were never uttered in my family. I learned early to keep my feelings to myself. The tightly controlled feelings of affection were restrained by my father's strict upbringing, and hampered my ability to express emotions in open, outgoing ways. It took me years to overcome this impediment.

At times, my parents quarreled. The quarrel was about my father coming home late from Druckmann's wine cellar after spending an evening with friends, or about my mother's opinion of my father's friends. On other occasions they argued about my father's opinion of members of my mother's family. Father kept his distance from Mother's family, due to deep differences in their outlook toward religious matters and Judaism in general. When my parents argued, they often switched from German to Yiddish. Apparently, it was easier for them to quarrel in *mame-loshen*, their mother tongue.

Sometimes the subject of their disagreement was one of my father's clients. In these arguments, legality and morality were at loggerheads.

Mother was always the champion of morality. Over the years, she had taken a dim view of some of my father's clients—crooks, cheats—whom she considered scoundrels, and she was not happy when Father represented them in court.

"He should go to jail," she used to say whenever she learned that Father had agreed to defend one of these outlaws.

A heated argument erupted once when Father came home from the courthouse and announced that he had been engaged by Mr. Rudenko to represent him in his divorce case. Rudenko, a wealthy landowner in his early fifties, was known for his rudeness, his heavy drinking, and the frequent beating of his wife, Milka. After twenty-three years of marriage to Milka, he had decided to divorce her. Mother had heard rumors that Rudenko had a young mistress and wanted to marry her.

When Father said he agreed to represent Rudenko, Mother became upset. There was a sharp exchange between them.

"How can you represent such a low-life and protect his interests? Everybody knows that he is a brute, a drunkard, and a wife-beater," Mother charged.

"He is entitled by law to be represented in court by a lawyer, to protect him and his interests," Father replied with some irritation.

"To protect him and his interests?" said Mother bitterly. "It means that you'll present that brute to the judge in the best possible light. You'll do your utmost to have him pay only a pittance to the poor woman he beat regularly, who suffered and slaved for him for over twenty years!"

"A lawyer has to defend and protect his client," Father replied, his voice loaded with annoyance. "In court I will present Rudenko's side of the case, the same way as Milka's lawyer will present hers. That will allow the judge to get an objective view of the whole case, and enable him to make the right decision."

Hearing that, Mother became really fired up. "Since when do lawyers care if judges get an objective view and make the right decision? For a lawyer, the right decision means a decision in his client's favor! When you represent a client, you're just interested in winning the case, not in seeing that justice is done. You care about justice only when you lose the case!" She then added with a sharp edge in her voice, " Lawyers are always willing to manipulate the law, to use every technicality and every trick in the book to win the case."

Father naturally resented such a characterization of the practitioners of the legal profession. "I do not manipulate the law and I don't use any tricks in court. I always act in accordance with the law."

Mother was not ready to concede. "If Milka had asked you to represent her in court, you would have accepted, wouldn't you? In that case, you would have exposed Rudenko as a scoundrel and wife-beater, and would have asked the judge to make him pay through his nose. But when a lawyer represents a scoundrel, a robber, or a murderer, he does his best to have the judge find his client not guilty or give him a light sentence, regardless how heinous the crime. Is that fair? Is that just?" Mother stopped for a moment to catch her breath, then continued: "Don't you see how immoral it is, even if the law allows you to do that? Are lawyers supposed to give up their own moral principles once they start practicing law?"

Now Father felt offended. "I did not give up any of my moral principles. I was and I am an honest man. All I am doing is acting within the framework of the legal system of the society we live in. Naturally I will do my best to protect the interests of my client, just as the lawyer of the opposing party will do for his client. Listening to both parties, the judge can reach a fair conclusion and pass judgment according to the law." Then he added: "Would you rather live in a lawless society, where people did not have the right to be represented in a court of law? That would lead to chaos and anarchy!"

Mother did not give up easily. "I am not saying that a society without laws or without a judicial system would be better. What I am saying is that a lawyer is willing to represent either party in a dispute, and will do it for the party that pays him, regardless how guilty that party is. By shielding an individual who has done a vile deed, the lawyer ignores basic moral principles."

"In a civilized society, even a vile individual has the right to be defended in a court of law," replied Father at his wit's end. Then he took another tack he knew would bring the debate to a close. "If I would not defend Rudenko, another lawyer would do it, and I would not have the money you need to put bread on the table. Would you rather see the children go hungry?"

"That still does not make it right." Mother muttered. "I just hope the judge will see through all the legalistic tricks, and make that scoundrel Rudenko pay poor Milka plenty."

Father went on to represent Rudenko in court. In the end, the judge decided that Rudenko had to pay a significant amount of money to Milka. Father and his client were not happy with the judge's decision, but Mother was very pleased with the outcome.

Listening to those discussions and similar debates in our house, made me somewhat skeptical about the ethics of the practitioners of the legal profession.

Mother spent a good part of her time in the kitchen. Wearing that same house dress and apron, she spent the day cooking dinner, baking *challah*, making fruit preserves from sour cherries, or putting together one of her delicious *Torte*, cake, for Sabbath. Mother was a very good cook and could prepare some excellent dishes. I often stood next to her, watching how she worked skillfully with her delicate hands, without notes or a cookbook.

One of Mother's specialties was pot roast braised in a delicious sauce that she served with boiled potatoes and carrots. I also liked the borscht she made from red beets, which she served with boiled potatoes and sour cream. Another delicious dish was *pirogen* that consisted of little triangular pies made from flattened dough and a filling. She used a variety of fillings: cottage cheese mixed with eggs, mashed potatoes with brown onion flakes, or, during the summer, pitted sour cherries. Mother knew that I loved *piroshky* filled with sour cherries, and she made them often. Occasionally, she made the Romanian dish *mamaliga*—the same as Italian *polenta*—by boiling cornmeal in water to make a paste, spreading it on a plate and covering it with butter and *feta* cheese. At times she served *mamaliga* with *sarmale*, stuffed cabbage. How delicious it was! I can still remember the smell of the steamy *sarmale* tickling my nostrils.

Best of all were Mother's pastries and cakes. In the mid-1930s, when she could still afford to buy all the necessary ingredients and they were still available in the market, Mother made some delicious cakes. I remember her *Nusstorte*, nut cake, and her *Schokoladetorte*, chocolate cake. For Purim, she made delicious *hamantashen*, filled with poppy seeds, honey and raisins. In the corner of the kitchen she had an icebox, where she kept the foodstuff in the summer. The "iceman" arrived with a block of ice once a week to replace the melted ice.

Although Father was not a religious man, Mother prepared special meals for the Sabbath—Friday night and Saturday. Those were the best dinners of the week. The meal consisted of soup, meat or poultry, and fruit or a baked dessert. On Friday nights Mother also served baked fish, usually carp. There was always *challah* on the table, as well as wine for my parents and soda water for us children. Mother prepared the braided *challah*—in Yiddish we called it *koilitsh*—on Friday morning. Wearing an apron and with her sleeves rolled up, she kneaded the dough into a soft paste on her kitchen board, and let it set to rise. She then divided the dough into three equal parts, rolled them into strips of equal length, and braided them together. She put the raw challah into a baking pan, let it set again to rise, brushed it with egg yolk using a small bundle of goose feathers, and baked it in the oven. The taste of freshly baked, fluffy challah, covered by a gold-brown crispy crust, was delicious. It even looked mouth watering.

While watching my mother, I often wondered how she could remember so many recipes to make all that tasty food. Only years later did I realize that Mother had an excellent memory.

While Mother was cooking or cleaning house, she liked to sing. She had a soft, pleasant voice, and I enjoyed listening to her songs. I think that I inherited my joy of singing from her. She sang in German and Yiddish, songs she had learned early in her life, in Austria. Most of the songs were sad, but those from operettas were cheerful. One of her songs, I remember, was called *Sonia*. It is about the musing of a convict sent to Siberia for killing his love, Sonia, when he caught her in the arms of another man. Another song she used to sing was *Seemans Loos* (Sailor's Fate), about a doomed sailor, trapped on a sinking ship on the high seas. She often sang arias from Lehar's *Die lustige Witwe* (The Merry Widow), from Strauss's *Die Fledermaus*, and Joseph Schmidt's *Ein Lied geht um die*

Welt (My Song Goes 'Round the World).

Mother's favorite song was *Die Lorelei*, a highly popular German song based on the lyrics by the baptized, nineteenth century German-Jewish poet, Heinrich Heine. It is a fairytale about a young sailor, who, distracted by the fascinating song of a beautiful blond woman sitting on a rock near the Rhine River, doesn't pay attention to the rocks in the water and drowns. In later years, in Nazi Germany, the author of these lyrics had been claimed to be "anonymous," in order to render Heine a non-person.

Toward the end of the day, when Mother had finished her daily chores, she would sit with me at the kitchen table and read aloud children's stories or poetry. *Max and Moritz,* by Wilhelm Busch, is the first story I remember her reading to me, in German. It is the story of two little pranksters who played tricks on adults, but were severely punished in the end. The story is well known in German-speaking countries.

Mother also recited poems she had learned when she was a young girl in *gymnasium,* the secondary school. Having an exceptional memory, Mother could recite long poems she had learned in her youth, such as Friedrich Schiller's *Die Glocke,* (The Bell); *Der Taucher,* (The Diver); and *Die Kraniche des Ibicus,* (Ibicus' Cranes). Two poems of unknown origin to me, that she learned in grade school, were *Der Bettler,* (The Beggar), and *Die Bäume,* (The Trees). I was fascinated by these poems, and learned them by heart. Sometimes she sang or recited a poem for me while she was preparing food or mending my socks. I stood near her, enchanted by her soft voice and lovely songs. Mother was happy when I was quiet and listened to her, since my other activities often were noisy or caused damage in the house.

Sometimes Mother would tell me about events in her life when she was young. I remember her telling me about experiences during World War I. She and her three sisters—Anna, Jetty, and Tzili—were young, pretty girls at the time. They attracted the attention of soldiers and officers of the armies that moved through the village of Molodia, where the girls lived with their parents. Officers were frequently quartered in their house, and, as the fortunes of war changed, so did the officers. First came the Austrians, then followed the Russians, the Germans, and then again the

Russians. Regardless what uniform they wore, regardless to whom they pledged allegiance—the Kaiser, the Emperor, or the Czar—they had one thing in common: they all liked young, pretty girls.

When the officers got drunk, which happened quite often, they went from room to room looking for the girls. In those situations, my worried grandfather sent his daughters to hide in a barn next door. The girls climbed into the hayloft, pulled up the ladder, and hid under the hay. They trembled and clung to each other. They were terribly afraid of the drunken brutes in uniform. When the drunks could not find what they were looking for, they started smashing glasses, dishes, furniture, and anything in the house that could be broken. When they finally fell asleep on the floor, on a couch, in a chair, or sometimes in bed, my grandfather went to the barn and gave the "all clear" signal. With hay in their hair and skirts disheveled, the girls climbed down from the loft, left the barn, and tiptoed to their rooms. In the morning, having slept off their drunkenness, the officers displayed again their usual polite behavior, as if nothing had happened the night before. Sometimes they apologized for wrecking their rooms, but usually they just ignored the chaos they had created. The Germans and the Russians were the worst of the bunch. They never apologized, and behaved like true masters. When the situation on the front changed and they were forced to retreat, they left their rooms in shambles.

There were evenings when Mother used to read aloud to my father from a German novel. On such occasions I sat on the floor, played with my picture books, and listened to the story, while Father sat on the couch. At the time, I did not understand much of what my mother read. Still, I was listening. I remember Mother reading *Die Buddenbrocks* and *Der Zauberberg* (The Magic Mountain), by Thomas Mann; *Die Jüdin von Toledo* (The Jewess from Toledo), by Lion Feuchtwanger; and *Joseph Fouché* by Stefan Zweig. The last author, who excelled in writing historical and psychological novels, was Mother's favorite writer. He was an Austrian Jew who later fled from the Nazis to Brazil. In 1942, when he learned about the atrocities perpetrated against the Jews by his former German and Austrian compatriots, he and his wife committed suicide.

The reading of stories and novels in our home planted the seeds for my future avid interest in books. During my teenage years, reading books felt like magic. They opened a whole new universe for me. Depending on what I was reading, I experienced a whole gamut of emotions. I was held in suspense by an adventure story, scared when I read a thriller, amused by a funny episode, saddened by a drama, and dreamy when it was a romance. Books also gave me much intellectual gratification. When I grew up, they led me into the world of poetry, philosophy, psychology, history, and science. They also became an escape from a depressing reality. Reading good books became one of my most cherished leisure activities.

Many of the books I devoured as a teenager, and later as a young adult, were embedded in my mind for decades. They molded my literary taste and I continued to treasure literature of the same kind in later years. Still, I didn't ignore the riches of contemporary literature and enjoyed reading many vibrant works of modern writers.

As in many other middle-class Jewish homes in Czernowitz, we had a fairly good library. There were books everywhere: on shelves, on the table, on the dresser, and on the floor. There were luxury editions bound in brown or red linen embossed with gilded letters, hardcover books with leather backing, and paperback books. The works of German-language Jewish novelists, poets and playwrights were well represented in our home. The shelves were lined with the works of Heinrich Heine, Jakob Wassermann, Arnold Zweig, Stefan Zweig, Lion Feuchtwanger, Emil Ludwig, Arthur Schnitzler, Hugo von Hofmannsthal, Franz Kafka, Franz Werfel, Max Brod, Kurt Tucholsky, and many other Jewish men of letters. These authors had made an enormous contribution to German and Austrian culture.

The works of great German writers and poets, such as Johan Wofgang Goethe, Friedrich Schiller, Gotthold Lessing, Johann Hoelderlin, Thomas Mann, Rainer Maria Rilke and others were also represented in our library. So were the works of great writers of the universal literature in German translation. As I found out later, German had been the language in which Jewish writers made their most significant contribution to a nation's culture during the nineteenth and early twentieth century.

The fascination with culture was not limited just to our family. The members of the Jewish middle-class in our city had an insatiable thirst for culture. They called Czernowitz "Little Vienna"—*Kleinwien des Ostens,* in German—and were proud of the cultural life in their city. People of every age read voraciously, went to the theater, attended concerts, and participated in literary evenings. Some poor students would go without a decent pair of shoes and freeze their feet in winter, but they would buy a book or a ticket to a concert. At literary evenings, fabulist Elieser Steinbarg read from his collection of fables, and poet Itzik Manger recited his latest poems in Yiddish. The *Hasamir* chorus performed regularly to a full house. Dr. Rammler, a psychiatrist who was a strong supporter of the arts, organized weekly musical evenings at his apartment. There were numerous Jewish writers, poets, artists, art critics, journalists and publishers, whose prodigious work created a vibrant cultural life in the city. Some of them, such as Rose Auslaender, Paul Celan, Moses Rosenkranz, Karl Emil Franzos and Selma Meerbaum-Eisinger, became famous in the German-speaking world. There were also, of course, non-Jewish writers and poets who had lived at different times in the city and contributed to its literary fame, such as Gregor von Rezzori—Austrian-German writer, Ol'ha Kobiljanskaia—Ukrainian poet, and Mihai Eminescu—Romanian poet. Jewish actors and actresses, who grew up in Czernowitz, performed regularly at the Burgtheater and Volkstheater in Vienna.

One of the Jewish artists, born and raised in Czernowitz, who became world famous in the late 1920s and early 1930s, was Joseph Schmidt. He came from a poor family, sang in the Temple chorus, and later, with the help of a wealthy supporter, perfected his voice at the conservatory in Vienna. He became the most famous singer in the German-speaking world, and sang frequently on radio Berlin until 1933. He also gave numerous concerts in major European cities. During one of his performances in Germany in early 1933, Hitler's propaganda minister, Joseph Göbbels, who was in the audience, applauded enthusiastically. He reportedly said that he was going to have Joseph Schmidt declared an honorary Aryan. The singer apparently was not impressed. With the rise of Hitler to power, he fled first to Austria, and then to Belgium. When World War II started and the Nazis occupied Belgium, Joseph Schmidt fled to Switzerland. The Swiss put him into a refugee camp, where he died of tuberculosis in 1942.

As a child, I felt very comfortable at my grandparents' apartment. Mother and I visited them every Friday night after dinner. They lived on Karolinengasse, not far from us. My grandfather was a tall, stout man with a short beard and dreamy, watery eyes. He had spent a good part of his life studying the Bible and Talmud, and had become knowledgeable in religious matters. He went daily to services in the small Orthodox *shul* located next to the building where my grandparents lived. Once a week, a group of Jewish men got together with my grandfather in the *shul*, read a page from the Talmud, and discussed its meaning. Grandfather lead the discussion, and explained some of the more intricate points to the rest of the group. The rabbi and the congregation respected my grandfather for his knowledge and wisdom.

The grandchildren called grandfather Dziadziu, and grandmother, Baba. Mother said that grandfather's parents had chosen a wife for him— an old Chassidic custom. Although he spoke Yiddish at home with his wife and children, he also spoke German fluently and was quite knowledgeable in German literature. Having grown up in Austria, he spent a considerable amount of his spare time reading German and Austrian literature. Grandfather was an avid reader, and much of his knowledge he acquired through self-education. He was also familiar with German poetry, drama, and prose. Mother told me that when she was a young girl, Grandfather had her sit next to him while he read poems by Friedrich Schiller and Heinrich Heine, in German. Mother claimed that it was this reading that awoke her interest in poetry, an interest she maintained throughout her life. Later on, when I visited my grandfather, he also read to me some of those German poems.

Grandfather was an unusual man for his time. He was familiar with both religious Jewish literature, as well as with secular German literature. In the years preceding World War I, most Jews living in Austria were interested either in religious or secular matters. Religious Orthodox Jews studied the Torah and Talmud, while emancipated, secular Jews studied German literature and philosophy. Those knowledgeable in one area did not know and did not care much about the other area. Grandfather was an exception.

I recall Grandmother as a quiet person, with gray hair and a pale, gaunt face. She always wore a dark dress and had her hair covered with a scarf, as was customary among Orthodox Jews. She had raised five children, not an easy task in those days. Whenever I visited my grandmother she asked me if I had been a good boy, and after my invariable "yes" answer she treated me with a slice of *leikah* (honey cake) or a *kichle* (cookie). Since Grandmother treated all the grandchildren with cake and cookies, we all loved her and liked to visit with her. Grandmother spoke Yiddish with us, as she did with the rest of the family, and my first words of Yiddish I learned from her. She always called me *shein yinga'leh* (nice little boy), while stroking my head with her thin, bony hand.

My mother's oldest sister, Aunt Anna, lived with my grandparents. She had raven-black, slightly undulated hair, a very pale complexion and a frail body. What impressed me most were her large, dark eyes. In a way, she was quite different from the rest of the family. She was very quiet, the quietest person in the whole family. She spoke little, and even her movements through the house were ghostlike, her steps inaudible. I had the feeling that she tried to be invisible, not to draw anybody's attention. In the winter, when walking from a cold room into a warm room, she opened the door barely enough to squeeze through—there should be no loss of warm air because of her. She also ate very little, presumably not to be a financial burden to her parents. She had no friends and rarely ventured outside the house.

Aunt Anna didn't have much luck in her life. She had married David Agatstein, with whom she had a son, Eddie. The marriage did not last. After the divorce, Eddie stayed with his father, while Anna moved in with her parents. Because of her failed marriage, she felt that she was a failure, and assumed that everybody saw her that way. She was withdrawn, rarely smiled, and her dark eyes were always sad. She did most of the chores in the house. When the family gathered Friday nights at my grandparents' apartment, she was the one who served everybody with sweets and tea. After having served the family, Anna sat quietly at the edge of her chair and listened to the conversation, rarely saying a word. She often reminded me of Cinderella.

A younger sister of my mother, Aunt Jetty, was married to Bernhard "Berl" Rosenbaum. They had a little girl, Gusta, who was three years younger than I was. Uncle Bernhard owned a hardware store, where he worked late into the night. He had a high-strung personality, and rarely seemed to rest. He suffered from asthma, coughed frequently, and spoke with a raspy voice. That did not deter him from being a heavy smoker. Aunt Jetty came often to the store to help out with bookkeeping. On those occasions she brought along little Gusta, who sat next to her quietly, playing with her doll. Uncle Bernhard and Aunt Jetty were well off. Initially they lived in a small, one-family house. Later, in the mid 1930s, they built an apartment house near the outskirts of the city, on Wolangasse, and moved into one of the apartments. They rented out the other units.

I loved to visit Uncle Bernhard's store. He let me play with the metal chains, dip my hands into boxes with shiny screws, climb on the ladder, and touch the different tools and gadgets on display. I always looked forward to a visit at his store.

Aunt Tzili was my mother's youngest sister. Her actual first name was Cecilia, but everybody called her Tzili. A halo of red curls surrounded her freckled face. A soft curl dangled over her forehead. When she was in her teens, her parents sent her to the *Morgenroit* School, a Jewish trade school in Czernowitz. She finished school and became a skilled seamstress. With other young seamstresses, Aunt Tzili worked in the shop of Mrs. Axelrod. It was a well-known shop that served the ladies from the Czernowitz high society. She used to sing and play the mandolin, and often entertained me with her songs when we visited her. I was fascinated by the beautiful sounds Aunt Tzili was able to generate with the instrument, using her long, delicate fingers.

Uncle Joseph was my mother's only brother. He was nine years younger than my mother. Like his sisters, he was born in Molodia, near Czernowitz. When he was in his teens, he came under the influence of socialist ideas, and became a member of the *Bund*, a Jewish-socialist organization. In the 1930s, he joined his father in running the stationery store that my grandfather had set up after World War I in Czernowitz.

44

In the late 1930s, Uncle Joseph married Ruchel Schauer, a quiet, shy person. In 1939 they had a child, Elli. Both Joseph and Ruchel loved the outdoors, and were avid hikers. In the summer, they hiked almost every weekend in the woods of Tsetsina, or went swimming in the Prut. Often they took me along on their hikes. With knapsacks on our shoulders and in high spirits, in the early morning hours we walked energetically next to the Schillerpark, past the Kaliczanka suburb, towards the Tsetsina woods. Before reaching the tree line, we had to walk over a wide-open green field. It felt like walking through an emerald sea of grass leaves that waved gently in the mild breeze. In some places the field was dotted with daisies, lilies and pansies, forming a symphony of colors in the bright sunlight. It was a splendid sight.

Once in the woods, we would spend the day walking for hours on narrow, meandering trails, collecting blackberries, and picnicking in the shade of tall oak and beech trees. Afterwards we would quench our thirst in the icy water of a mountain spring, inhale the cool, fresh air, and listen to the chirping warblers. The gurgling of the stream, the smell of the dark soil, the rustling of the leaves in the trees, the play of shadows and light beneath the tree branches gave me an invigorating, uplifting feeling. I felt enchanted by the beauty that surrounded me.

During those walks in the woods I discovered the immense diversity of nature. The variety of trees, the different shapes of leaves, the numerous shades of green, the gamut of colors among the delicate flowers, the silky touch of their petals—all that charmed and amazed me. I learned to enjoy the beauty of nature, and later became an avid hiker myself.

This was my family during early childhood. It would not take long for that graceful family to be torn apart.

2. Jewish Life in My City

Before the war Czernowitz had a vibrant, dynamic life, full of energy and creativity. Western culture and mores had left their mark on "Little Vienna." Most inhabitants of our city had a secular world outlook, and were steeped in Austrian-German erudition. Still, there was no shortage of houses of worship. Near the center of the city stood the dome-capped Eastern Orthodox cathedral, which served the Romanian population. There were Catholic churches with neo-Gothic towers, Protestant churches built in the Baroque style, and an Armenian Church with Moorish decorations, all serving the Ukrainian, Polish and German population. At the edge of the city, the palace of the archbishop of the Eastern Orthodox Church dominated the scene. It was a very large, imposing, redbrick structure, with towers, domes, and glazed, colored roof tiles. The palace was the largest building in the region. In later years, under the Soviets, it became the seat of the city's university.

I never entered any cathedral or church in my childhood. Mother warned me that I might be thrown out or even beaten up, if people in the church recognized that I was a Jew. I didn't quite understand why I would be beaten up, but I decided not to take the risk. I already knew that not following my parents' advice could have painful consequences.

The Jews had their own places of worship. The largest one was the Jewish Temple. It was an imposing structure and stood on a hilltop that dominated the city. The tall, massive walls of the Temple were topped by a row of small turrets, and the deep, arched windows were decorated with stained glass brought from abroad. A large dome, visible from every corner of the city, crowned the massive structure. Inside, firmly planted into the Temple's stone floor, gray stone columns ascended towards dizzying heights. Mostly secular and moderately religious Jews attended the services at the Temple. During the service, the men sat on benches on the ground floor, facing the *Aron Hakodesh*, the Ark of the Law, on the eastern wall. About twenty feet in front of the Ark was the *bimah*, a platform, with an elevated table, on which the Torah scrolls were unrolled and read to the congregation. That was also the place where the *chazzan*, the cantor, stood and led the prayer. Both the Ark and the elevated table were covered with blue velvet, embroidered with golden thread.

The women sat on benches in the balcony. Tradition required that men and women be separated during worship. (Otherwise, I was told later, lewd thoughts may creep into some men's mind during prayer.) Still, these were considered at the time "modern" services, and were similar to those held today in an American conservative synagogue.

Whenever I entered the Temple with my parents, usually during the High Holidays, I felt small and insignificant as I gazed up at the enormous dome, at the multicolored stained glass windows, and at the tall walls that enclosed the spacious prayer hall. The imposing structure, the sober atmosphere that prevailed during the service, the solemn attitude of the congregation, the beautiful chanting of the cantor—all impressed me.

In the 1930s, until the invasion of the Soviet Union by the Nazis in 1941, the service at the Temple was officiated by Rabbi Dr. Abraham Mark. He was a graduate of the Vienna University with a doctorate in philosophy, and completed his rabbinical studies at the Jewish Theological Institute in the same city. I learned later that he was the author of several books on Jewish theology, had given numerous lectures on Jewish and Zionist topics, and was an ardent supporter of organizations dedicated to the teaching of Hebrew to Jewish children and adults.

Besides the Temple, there were several other Jewish places of worship. The major one used by Orthodox Jews was the Great Synagogue. On some Saturday mornings, I went with my grandfather to that synagogue. It was an old, massive, stone building, much older than the Temple, and was located in the Jewish quarter of the city. With its thick, time-blackened walls, solid wooden gate and small, narrow windows, it gave the impression of an old fortress. Whenever I passed the Great Synagogue on Sabbath, I could hear the murmur of prayer coming from inside the building, which was packed to capacity.

Then there was the *Chorshul* and several smaller Orthodox houses of worship, *shuls*, spread throughout the city. In smaller *shuls* that did not have balconies, both men and women prayed on the ground floor, separated from each other by a *mechitzah*, a partition. Some of the pious worshipers, with beards and corkscrew side locks, wore Chassidic garb: fur-trimmed hats—*shtreimels*, long black overcoats—*caftans*, black pants, white or black socks, and black shoes. The Orthodox women wore dark dresses, and had scarves wrapped around their heads. They never wore makeup. On Friday night one could see the worshipers rushing towards the synagogues, with prayer book and *tallit* under their arms.

There were three days every year when every Jew, religious or secular, went to a synagogue. These were the High Holidays: two days of *Rosh Hashana*, the Jewish New Year, and *Yom Kippur*, the Day of Atonement. My parents also went to the Temple on those holidays—and only on those holidays. It was the occasion when those assimilated, Germanized Jews like my father practiced a Jewish ritual. Mother used to call them "the three-day Jews."

During the High Holidays, the Temple was filled to capacity. On that occasion, leading Christian personalities of the city—the prefect, the mayor, judges, leaders of churches—were invited to the services, and given seats of honor. (This was the case before the spread of fascism in the country. Afterwards, even moderate Christian notables refused such an invitation.) Many intellectuals and secular Jews, including my parents, who rarely set foot in a place of worship during the year, attended services in the Temple during those holidays. All the synagogues in the city were also filled with worshipers.

From my grandfather I learned that the Day of Atonement is the holiest day of the year. Already in my early childhood the observance of that holiday left a deep impression on me. On the eve of the holiday the Jews of Czernowitz stopped their everyday activities. In a city where nearly half the population was Jewish, where many stores and shops were owned by Jews, the arrival of *Yom Kippur* eve brought the city nearly to a standstill. As evening approached, the hustling and bustling of this lively city ceased. The Jews locked their stores and shops, and rushed home to prepare for this important holiday. My parents and sister put on their finest clothes. Before getting dressed, Mother washed me thoroughly from top to toes. Only afterwards could I wear my nice navy-blue suit, white socks, and black lacquered shoes. Father lit memorial candles "in memory of his deceased parents," Mother told me in a subdued voice. Then the whole family sat down for the holiday dinner. Mother served food that was to suffice for the next twenty-four hours. After eating we rushed to the Temple, Father holding his *tallit* and prayer book under his arm. We wanted to arrive on time to hear the *chazzan* intone *Kol Nidre*, the ancient prayer that opens the celebration of this holiday.

Occasionally I spent *Yom Kippur* eve with my grandparents. In their home the ritual was more "Jewish." Before starting the meal, Grandmother covered her head with a scarf and lit the candles held by two silver candlesticks. She then covered her eyes with her hands and recited a blessing. Grandfather said another blessing, *kiddush*, over a cup of wine. Grandmother served dinner and after lighting the memorial candles we all went to the *shul* next door. My grandparents never went to the Temple. In their view, the service at the Temple was much too "modern," not a traditional service.

Grandfather wore a dark hat and caftan girded with a black cord. His dark clothing contrasted with his white beard and pale face. At the *shul* there was a noisy gathering of Chasidim with long beards and side locks, dressed in black caftans, white socks, and buttoned-up white shirts without tie. Some of them wore *shtreimls* on their heads, while others wore black hats. Little boys with *yarmulkas* and side locks sat next to their fathers, fidgeting and moving restlessly in their seats. The women were separated from the men and were sitting in the balcony. The Orthodox married women, who had their heads shaved and wore *sheitls*, had their heads covered with a modest, dark scarf.

People who only a few hours earlier, dressed in their everyday clothes, were still haggling, quibbling, arguing, and doing their last minute preparations for the holiday, were now in their houses of prayer wearing their holiday finery. Once the evening service started, the city fell silent, the streets almost deserted. For the worshipers gathered in synagogues, the solemnity and awe inspired by the holiest of the holidays felt like the heavy atmosphere loaded with electricity before a thunderstorm. A hush settled over the congregation. Religious or secular, rich or poor, they all listened in awe to the age-old chanting of *Kol Nidre* by the *chazzan*, whose powerful voice seemed to rise to heaven. Even the little boys stopped fidgeting and listened to the chanting. At the end of the evening service, after Grandfather said *git yom-tov* and shook hands with the people around him, we returned home. Other people also shook hands and wished each other the best before leaving. Grandfather told me that on *Yom Kippur,* even people who had argued with each other during the year, shake hands and make up with each other.

The next day was a long, difficult day. It was a day of fasting and praying, a day of repentance. Since I couldn't eat anything, the day appeared to me also very long. Part of the day I spent with my parents in Temple, and part in Grandfather's *shul.* In Grandfather's synagogue the pious worshipers, wrapped in their *kittels* and prayer shawls, prayed to the Almighty the whole day without interruption, as if summoned to the Last Judgement. Swaying back and forth in their shroud-like garments, they cried out loud to God, faces turned towards heaven, eyes shut as in trance, pleading and begging forgiveness, while beating their chests in repentance. With prayer shawls drawn over their heads, they raved, they murmured, they wailed, they sobbed, drowning out the *chazzan's* wailing voice. They drove themselves into frenzy. I watched with fascination how some of the Chasidim threw themselves to the ground, touching the floor with their foreheads while whispering a prayer with eyes closed. Then suddenly they jumped to their feet, their bodies wrapped in *tallitim* swaying again, while heart-felt pleas and lamentation came from their parched lips that no drop of water could touch. In the women's gallery the wailing and weeping was heartbreaking. It was a soul-baring, gut-wrenching worship.

"Why are people wailing and crying?" I asked Grandfather. I was baffled and couldn't understand what was going on.

"They are praying to God that their sins be atoned, and that their names be sealed in the book of life," explained Grandfather in a subdued voice.

I was amazed, fascinated and somewhat frightened by the ecstasy and lamentation that surrounded me. What a contrast between the daily behavior of these people—the arguing, the haggling, the hassle of the daily chores—and their fervent, uncontrolled emotional outburst in their pleading with God for forgiveness!

After the conclusion of the evening service, the physically and emotionally drained worshipers packed their *tallitim*, wished their family, friends and acquaintances the best, and returned home to break the fast. When we got home, Grandfather first had a shot of *schnapps* with a slice of honey cake, while I had only a slice of cake. Afterwards we had an elaborate meal. Food had never tasted so good as it did after a day of fasting.

How different the service was at the Temple where my parents prayed! The observance of *Yom Kippur* by secular, modern Jews seemed a world apart from that in the Orthodox synagogue. Many of the modern, middle-class Jewish men wore top hats and black tailcoats, outfits similar to those worn by middle-class West-European Jews on this occasion. Those of lesser means wore a simple black felt hat and a dark suit. Most of them were clean-shaven, with some of them displaying a small mustache. The women wore their best dark dresses for this event, and their stylish hair was covered with a silk scarf or hat. Wearing no *kittels* and only a small prayer shawl, these mostly middle-class, westernized worshipers prayed in a more restrained, more formal way. They kept their feelings under control. There were no outbursts of emotions, no dropping to the floor, no loud crying or wailing. Only in the women's gallery one could hear subdued crying.

Cantor Gurmann, who was the main cantor at the Temple in the 1930s, wore a long *kittel*, and his head was crowned by an imposing white miter. The cantor's powerful and melodious voice reverberated through the temple like that of an opera singer. His expressive lyrical chants stirred the emotions in some worshipers, while others admired the vocal splendor of his voice. A small chorus dressed in white, as well as an organ player, accompanied the cantor. The ceremony was solemn and formal,

51

not ecstatic; praying by this westernized congregation was subdued.

Before the start of the *yizkor* service, my father told me to go outdoors and play until that part of the service was over. I noticed that other parents also sent their children out. I realized that this prayer was only for adults. Naturally, this arose my curiosity. Why couldn't children be present during that part of the service? What were the adults doing in the absence of children? Many years later, when I said *yizkor*, the prayer for the dead, after my father's death, I realized how lucky I had been not to have to say that prayer during my childhood.

After the concluding evening prayer, the members of the congregation shook hands politely with each other, exchanged a few friendly words, and then rushed home to break fast. The long, hard day was over.

For a little boy like me, the long hours of prayer in a language I did not understand put my patience to the test. An empty stomach did not help. I must admit that most of the times I failed the test. While sitting next to my father or grandfather, I fidgeted in my chair, looked at the lions decorating the A*ron Hakodesh* where the *Torah* scrolls were kept, listened to the chanting of the cantor, and thought about fresh, crispy rolls with butter and jam. Instead of looking into the prayer book, I often observed the people in the congregation and the way they prayed. I couldn't quite understand why during certain prayers, some people showed considerable emotions and fervor, while others appeared calm and composed. Were those who put their emotions on display "better" Jews than those who kept their emotions under control? Or had they committed more sins and therefore had to ask God more fervently to be pardoned? In later years I found out that neither of these assumptions were correct.

When the Jewish holiday of *Sukkot* arrived shortly after *Yom Kippur*, a *sukkah* was built next to Grandfather's *shul.* The *sukkah* was a flimsy booth with walls made of wooden boards and a roof of widely spaced slats covered with green tree branches. Inside the *sukkah* was a long wooden table and two benches. Ever curious, I asked Grandfather why he had that booth built. He told me that the *sukkah* was meant to be a reminder of the hastily set-up shelters used by the ancient Israelites during their forty years of wandering in the wilderness. For seven days my grandparents ate their meals in the *sukkah*. When I visited, I loved to eat the evening meal with my grandparents.

After the meal, I sat in the *sukkah* by myself, listened to the quiet of the night and looked through the roof of green branches at the star-studded dark sky. I was wondering: is there any life in the distant universe? If there is, do the beings of those other worlds look like me? Or are they totally different? If there are, in the cosmos, creatures similar to me, do they also look at distant stars and ask the same questions? I thought that it would be fun to shake hands someday with somebody from another part of the world.

I sat in the *sukkah* meditating about the universe, until I heard Grandmother calling. I went indoors, still thinking about life on some distant planet.

Twice a year, Mother did grand housecleaning: before Passover in the spring, and before Rosh Hashanah in the fall. Most of the city's Jews, rich or poor, religious or secular, kept the custom of thorough housecleaning in the spring and fall. Religious Jews did it to comply with tradition, while secular Jews did it for hygienic reasons. Spring-cleaning started a week before Passover. Mother cleaned our apartment from top to bottom. She polished the furniture, wiped the stove and kitchen shelves clean, dusted the pictures on the walls, and went down on her knees to scrub the kitchen floor with a stiff-bristled brush. She took the rugs outdoors and beat them furiously with a rug beater made of braided reeds. The silver candlesticks and brass door locks were polished with a soft cloth until they gleamed.

Mother gave a special thorough cleaning to the dishes, pots, and pans she intended to use during the eight-day holiday. She called the cleaning of dishes for Passover *kashern*. Mother told me that some people had an extra set of dishes that were stored during the year and used only on this holiday. Since we did not have an extra set, Mother had to *kashern* some of our everyday dishes. I am not sure how those dishes differed from other clean dishes, but mother said that according to tradition only *kashered* dishes might be used on this holiday. On the last day before Passover, she removed all the *chametz* from the house. Not a single crumb of bread was left in a drawer, on a shelf, or on the kitchen table. I also turned the pockets of my pants inside out, to make sure that no crumb from a crumbled cookie was left in my pants. For the next eight days, instead of ordinary bread we ate matzoth, potato latkes, and matzo-meal pancakes. From Mother I learned that the unleavened bread was meant to be a reminder of the hasty departure of the ancient Israelites from Egypt.

Passover is a joyous festival, since it commemorates the Exodus from Egypt and the liberation from slavery. The holiday starts in the evening with the Seder. With his ambivalent attitude toward tradition, Father did not participate in the Seder, although he liked the Passover food. On the evening of the first Seder, Mother took us children to our grandparents. Aunt Anna and Aunt Cilli, as well as Uncle Joseph, were also present. For that occasion, everybody wore his or her best clothes. I had been washed and scrubbed clean by my mother and was dressed in my navy-blue suit. We sat around a long table covered with a white, embroidered tablecloth. In the middle of the table were Grandmother's two silver candlesticks, each crowned by a tall, lighted candle. Next to the candlesticks was a stack of three matzoth, covered with a colorful embroidered matzoth-cover. Close to the head of the table was a Passover plate filled with symbolic foods used during the Seder ritual: a shank bone of roast lamb, hard-boiled egg, bitter herbs, sweet *charoses*, honey, and horseradish.

Grandfather presided over the table, sitting in a large armchair with a pillow behind his back for greater comfort, as required by tradition. He wore a *kittel*, the white shroud-like garment worn by Orthodox Jews on this occasion. With his white beard, white *kittel* and a *yarmulke* on his head, he looked like a biblical figure. In front of him was the Haggadah, the Hebrew book with illustrations that described the Exodus of the Jewish people from Egyptian bondage. The Haggadah was worn and discolored, proof of its repeated use for many Seders in the past. Every member of the family also had a Haggadah placed next to his or her plate, and a glass filled with wine. A special cup of wine was set aside for the prophet Elijah, just in case he decided to drop in.

Being the youngest family member present, I asked in Hebrew the traditional *kashes*: why is the night of the Seder different from all other nights of the year? Grandfather replied by reading to us from the Haggadah about the events of the Exodus. He read the story with an old, traditional chant, that I found sometimes stirring, other times somnolent. Again and again the others at the table joined him in chorus. Since Grandfather chanted in Hebrew—which I did not understand—it seemed to me a very long story. What I found more interesting were the colorful illustrations of the Haggadah: Moses facing Pharaoh, Moses slaying the Egyptian, the Israelites leaving Egypt, Moses parting the sea, and the Egyptians drowning in the sea. When Grandfather recited the names of the ten plagues God visited upon the Egyptians, he dipped the little finger of his right hand into his wineglass for each plague, each time spilling the drop of wine that clung to his finger. I found this ritual interesting and also puzzling. I remembered that at home, whenever I stuck my finger into the soup—let alone spilled any of it—I was promptly admonished. I concluded that it is acceptable to do it with wine, but not with soup.

At certain passages in the Haggadah, Grandfather served each of us little pieces of the symbolic food from the Passover plate. Of those I liked best the sweet *charoses* made from groundnuts and fruit. Matzo dipped in honey was also tasty, although it made my fingers sticky. Everybody— except for me—drank generous amounts of wine. Tradition requires that each participant drinks four glasses of wine. To keep everybody sober, Grandmother had made sure that it was served in small glasses.

While Grandfather and the rest of the family were reading the Haggadah, I was busy doing something else. At the beginning of the Seder, while everybody was watching, Grandfather concealed a piece of matzo, called the *afikoman*, behind the pillow he was leaning on in his armchair. Tradition has it that if a child can "steal" the *afikoman* during the Seder, he can "ransom" it at the end of the meal. It is said that the rabbis devised this game to prevent the children from falling asleep during the lengthy ceremony. Naturally, I was interested in getting that piece of matzo, and I had already made plans as to how I would spend the ransom money in the candy store. But first I had to steal the *afikoman*. While Grandfather was reading aloud the Haggadah, I sneaked twice behind his armchair and tried to grab the matzo from behind the pillow. But Grandfather noticed it and stopped me. Only toward the end of the Seder did Grandfather cease to pay attention to what I was doing—or made me believe so—and I was able to steal it. I could barely wait for the end of the evening to cash in the ransom.

When Grandfather finished reading the lengthy Haggadah story, Grandmother and Aunt Anna began serving an elaborate meal. It started out with matzo-ball soup, and was followed by boiled chicken with *kaizelach* and apple-*tzimmes*. There were also potato *knaidlach*, *kugel* and honey carrots. For dessert, Grandmother made fruit compote. The wineglasses were constantly refilled during the meal, so that soon everybody was cheerful and in high spirits. Mother gave me a glass of club soda instead of wine. Only occasionally did she allow me to have a small sip of wine. The meal was concluded with a glass of tea. I gave Grandfather the stolen matzo, and received five *lei* as ransom money. The whole family closed the Seder service with the cheerful singing of *Chad Gadya*, a traditional Passover song.

At the end of the long evening, after Grandfather had said the after-meal Grace, my belly was full, I had five *lei* in my pocket, and I was very sleepy. The excitement of the *afikoman* hunt and the few sips of wine may have been the culprits. Holding on to my mother's hand, half-asleep, I was barely able to walk home.

The city's inhabitants formed a vivacious, colorful, sometimes cynical, often antagonistic, mixture of diverse ethnic and religious groups. Life in the city was a strange amalgam of culture, snobbery, joie de vivre, prejudice, cynicism, obstinacy, religiosity, atheism, extremism and moderation. The different ethnic groups of the city had their own houses of culture and social gatherings. There was the Romanian *Casa Poporului*, the German *Deutsches Haus*, the Ukrainian *Narodni Dim*, and the Polish *Dom Polski*. The Jews usually met in the *Jüdisches Nationalhaus* or in the *Toynbeehalle*. The facades of some of these buildings were decorated with allegorical figures, such as a strong, bare-breasted woman holding a sword, a book, or wheat sheaves—symbols of strength, culture, and prosperity. In these houses of culture the members of different ethnic groups gathered in the evenings or on holidays to socialize, to watch artistic performances, or to listen to speakers in their native tongue.

The people of Bukovina, both Gentiles and Jews, who had lived under

Austrian rule for one-and-a half centuries and had been exposed to western culture, felt that they were more advanced, more sophisticated and more "civilized" than those from the Romanian Old Kingdom. Even the Romanian intellectuals, who had grown up and been educated under the Austrians, shared that opinion. The new Romanian rulers became aware of this attitude and naturally resented it. A gap developed between the two populations, a gap created by differences in history and culture, which would not be bridged for decades. The local population, especially in urban areas, maintained the feeling of superiority towards the new masters, although they did not display it in public. The rulers, in turn, remained suspicious of the loyalty of their new subjects. During World War II, those suspicions proved to be disastrous for the Jewish population of Bukovina.

In later years I learned that until the mid 1930s, the different ethnic and religious groups that made up the population of this cosmopolitan city, tried to hide their prejudices towards each other behind a façade of civility and propriety. But in fact, many Romanians and Poles disliked the Germans, while the Ukrainians disliked the Poles. The Germans, in turn, felt superior to the Poles, disliked the Ukrainians, and felt contempt for the Romanians. Catholics did not care much about Protestants, and Protestants kept their distance from Catholics. Both Catholics and Protestants felt superior towards the Russian Orthodox. Of course, Catholics, Protestants, and Russian Orthodox, be they Poles, Ukrainians, Germans, Russians or Romanians, were not exactly fond of the Jews in their midst. This became obvious especially when an Orthodox Jew, with long beard and side locks, wearing a black felt hat and black *caftan*, rushed to the synagogue or to his place of business. The catcalls and laughter of the less-restrained youngsters, the derogatory smiles and disdainful glances of the seemingly respectful adults, betrayed their true feelings toward this man. Still, until the rise of nationalist chauvinism and the spread of Nazi ideology, people with different ethnic or religious affiliations usually displayed courteous behavior toward each other and got along fairly well. Those better educated and more refined among them often hid their prejudices toward each other behind a façade of excessive friendliness and politeness.

Considering the not-too-friendly attitude of the city's non-Jewish population towards its Jewish neighbors, one would have expected that the Jewish community would be a cohesive block, fostered by the surrounding animosity. Nothing could be farther from the truth. The Jewish irrepressible love for argument led to noisy, heated disputes that occasionally resulted in conflicts within their own congregation. I remember Jews arguing with each other wherever they happened to meet: on the street, at the *shul*, in a café, at the *Kultusgemeinde,* at Jewish cultural events. They spoke with passion and gesticulated energetically to make their point.

The Jewish community of Czernowitz was splintered into numerous factions, and each faction had its own divisions. The fissures were along social, political, cultural, linguistic, and religious lines. There were Jewish communists, social democrats, Bundists (no relation to the German-American Bund), Zionists, liberals and conservatives. Each of these groups, in turn, was also splintered. There were communists of the Stalinist stripe and communists of the Trotzkyite stripe. There were left-wing Zionists, right-wing Zionists, and middle-of-the-road Zionists. When people belonging to different groups met, there were heated discussions among them. Communists argued with social democrats, Bundists with Zionists, liberals with conservatives, Stalinists with Trotzkyites, left-wing Zionists with right-wing Zionists. Of course, there was also antagonism between rich and poor.

Along religious lines the Jews were divided into ultra-Orthodox, moderate-Orthodox and Conservatives. Secular Jews usually displayed their Judaism only on the High Holidays, when they showed up at the Temple. There were also Jewish agnostics and atheists. Culturally the Jews were divided into Yiddishists, Hebrewists, Germanists, and Esperantists. The latter were convinced that Esperanto, the artificial language created by the Polish Jew Zamenhof, would become the universal language of the world.

Since every Jew considered himself an *oberchochem*—Yiddish slang for "super-smart"—and believed that his opinion was the right one, there were heated debates, discussions, and endless arguments, dampened occasionally by a cynical remark. The arguments and discussions, however, rarely took on a hostile character, and just contributed to a lively exchange of ideas and opinions. Only later, during the dark years of fascist oppression, were the debates of lofty ideas replaced by the immediate, down-to-earth preoccupation of daily survival. Persecution and hatred forced the Jews of Czernowitz to unite and stick together.

A large segment of the Jewish population lived in poverty. The *Kultusgemeinde,* the Jewish Community Council, set up soup kitchens for those in need. Jewish-American charitable organizations, such as the American Joint Distribution Committee (AJDC), OSE and ORT, also assisted the poor with food, clothing, and training.

The city had a large number of Jewish beggars, who knew how to organize their activities. The beggars set themselves up into groups, and each group had its own section of the city where it was active. Most of the begging was done from Jewish store owners. On a certain day of the week a beggar would appear in the store and collect alms. The same beggar always appeared on the same day of the week. On other days other beggars would show up to collect their alms. It was a well-organized enterprise. At my grandfather's stationery store a different beggar would appear every day of the week to collect his alms. Grandfather gave each a coin or two. When one beggar happened to intrude into the territory of another one on the same day and the two met, one could hear an exchange of curses and obscenities that would have made a street sweeper blush. They cursed each other in Yiddish, and the curses tumbled from their mouths like grains from a torn sack. On such occasions, I found out how rich and colorful the Yiddish language is.

One of the exciting events in my childhood was accompanying my mother to the open-air market on *Austriaplatz,* Austria Square. Monday and Thursday were market days. On those days Mother bought produce from the farmers, and I tagged along.

In the wee hours, horse-drawn carts loaded with produce left the city's suburbs—Rosch, Kaliczanka, Klokuczka, Monastiriska—and delivered the goods to the open-air market. Some of the German women-farmers from the suburb of Rosch, who lived closer to the city, walked from their home to the market, skillfully balancing the goods on their heads.

The market was a motley, noisy mixture of farmers, housewives, street vendors, and domestic animals, intermingled with a variety of colorful characters such as gypsies, beggars, loafers, music makers and pickpockets. The market also mirrored the hodgepodge of the city's ethnic makeup. One could hear a cacophony of German, Romanian, Ukrainian, Polish, Russian, and Yiddish. The Romanian peasants, dressed in their colorful national costumes, hawked chickens and eggs, while the Schwabian-German women, wearing their traditional *"Dirndl,"* offered fresh butter, cheese and vegetables. The Lipovans, dressed in Russian *"rubashkas,"* sold fresh corn on the cob. Ukrainian laborers haggled over used pants with Jewish *handeles,* used clothes vendors, and cobblers hammered away diligently at worn out boots, while their customers waited barefoot or in their socks. Gypsy girls, in colorful dresses, with flowery scarves over their raven-black, shiny hair, read the palms of illiterate peasants, predicting their future.

Through the din one could hear the neighing of horses, the barking of dogs, the crowing of roosters. The whole market was enveloped in the odor of cheap tobacco, onion, garlic, tanned sheepskins, and horse droppings. There was a whiff of *rakiu,* a cheap alcoholic drink made from distilled prune juice, preferred by the peasants. Occasionally, a peasant who had too much of this stuff, started a fight with his neighbor. That provided temporary entertainment for the crowd that quickly formed a circle around the combatants. While the jostling crowd watched the brawl and cheered-on the fighters, the pickpockets in their midst were busy plying their trade.

I was always eager to see the people fighting with each other, and tried to squeeze through the crowd to get a better view. But Mother held my hand firmly and pulled me away, in spite of my protest. Eventually, a policeman arrived and carried off the drunk, berating and cursing him. It was a colorful scene.

In spite of the strict upbringing by my father, the early years of my childhood were carefree. They were years of innocence. In the park I ran on the grass and among shrubs, feeling free like a bird. I caressed the petals of flowers and the bark of trees. I played with the pebbles on the soil. I touched a passing dog or a cat that curled at my feet. I listened to the chirping of sparrows, to the gurgling of brooks. I inhaled the perfume of flowers. Occasionally, I ran after a squirrel that crossed my path. Other times, I tried to catch one of the countless pigeons that had made our city their home. I watched the beautiful clouds in all their changing shapes and sizes, and in all their shades of white and gray. In the evening, I stretched out my hand trying to touch the moon and the stars, or listened to the twitter of grasshoppers. I was a happy little boy.

But as time passed, I learned that life is not carefree. When I was six, my mother took me to the kindergarten. It was run by *Safa Ivriya*, an organization dedicated to the cultivation of the Hebrew language. The kindergarten was located on the first floor of the Jewish Community Center, in a room with white walls and several wooden benches. There were pictures of King Carol II and of Theodor Herzl on the wall. The teacher was an elderly lady who wore dark-rimmed glasses, and her gray hair was partly covered by a small black hat. She was obviously of the Orthodox persuasion. She and the children spoke German. There were about a dozen children who played together, listened to stories from the Bible, learned the Hebrew alphabet, and sang Hebrew songs. I recall one song I learned in those days:

Al chalon, al chalon
Hinei tzippor yaffah,
Yelled ratz al challon
Tzippor, tzippor affah.
(On the window, on the window
Sits a pretty bird,
The boy runs to the window
But the bird flies away)

If I was a difficult child at home, I was even more difficult in kindergarten. First I could not get used to being away from my mother and cried through most of the sessions. Naturally, that disrupted everybody's activity. Exasperated, the teacher sent me to an adjacent empty room, where I could cry as much as I pleased. Sometimes I spent a whole hour by myself in the empty room. It took awhile until I grew accustomed to the kindergarten. Only then did I stop crying. But even then, I did not make life easy for the teacher. I could not sit quietly while the teacher taught us a song, or read us a story. As my mother would often say to me, I did not have *Sitzfleisch*, meaning I could not sit still in one place. I fidgeted with my colored pencils, tried to catch a fly buzzing around my head, or attempted to take the colored pencils from the boy next to me. This led to shoving and eventually one of us started to cry. Again, I was dispatched to the empty room. Gradually, after several weeks of disrupting the class, I got finally used to the other children as well as to the teacher, and started to enjoy the activities.

One of the happiest times in kindergarten was the celebration of Purim. It was a joyous festival, commemorating the salvation of the Jewish people from Haman, the wicked minister of King Ahasveros in ancient Persia. The teacher told us the story of Purim as described in the *Megillah* (the biblical book of Esther).

While the well to do Jewish families celebrated Purim with sumptuous meals, generous amounts of wine, and masquerade balls, we children celebrated in our own way. On Purim day, all the children came to kindergarten dressed in costumes, improvised from a variety of old clothes and objects. Some of the children wore masks. I was dressed as an American Indian, with feathers supplied by my mother as a headdress. I wore an old white peasant shirt over my shoulders, held around my waist by one of my sister's colored belts. In my hand I held a homemade bow and arrow. On my face I had painted red lines with one of my crayons. The other boys were dressed as pirates, cowboys, and clowns. The pirates had their hair tightly wrapped with a scarf, wore a black patch over one eye and brandished a wooden sword. The cowboys had borrowed their fathers' wide-brimmed hats, wrapped small scarves around their necks, and carried big wooden revolvers. The clowns had red-painted cheeks, big, round rubber noses and their father's top hats. The girls were dressed as gypsies, ballerinas, angels, and princesses. We all looked like characters from a fairy tale.

Our teacher gave each of us a *grogger*, which according to tradition is used as a noisemaker to blot out the name of Haman each time it was mentioned. It was a noisy, cheerful celebration. We sang the Hebrew songs we had learned in previous months, danced in a circle, and filled the room with the noise of rattling *groggers*. We quickly became boisterous. We laughed loudly, jumped up and down, pushed each other, and ran around the classroom grinding our rattlers. The teacher tried in vain to contain our celebration. Through the din of rattling, laughing, jumping, and stomping, we could hear her exclamation, "Children, no jumping! Children, no running!" Eventually, we quieted down. During the lunch break I ate the traditional *hamantashen*, little triangular pastries filled with poppy seeds. Mother had made them especially for this holiday and put them in my lunch box. At the end of class, we were a bunch of happy, tired children. It was a day of great fun.

Early in my childhood, being curious, I continuously asked questions of my parents, sister, and kindergarten teacher, until I drove them to despair. I wanted to know why the grass is green and the sky blue; why dogs swim and cats don't; why the leaves on oak and beech trees turn yellow in the fall, while pine trees keep their needles green; why bird-droppings are white, while dog-droppings are brown; why my sheep-wool sweater when left in the rain shrinks, but a sheep standing in the rain doesn't. I was also curious why my buttered slice of bread always drops to the floor buttered-side down. I wanted to know why I have two nipples on my chest and what they are for. Are they for decoration? Why do I have two arms and two legs, but only one *petzle* (little penis)?

After watching a Jewish wedding celebrated by the rabbi in my Grandfather's courtyard, I asked my mother why everybody was happy and congratulated the groom when he deliberately stomped on a glass and broke it, whereas when I broke a glass by accident I got a slap on my behind. When my father took me to the communal steam bath for the first time and I saw many naked men, young and old, I wanted to know why old men get wrinkles on their faces, but not on their behinds. My sister told me that I asked too many *klotzkashes*—Czernowitz-Yiddish for "dumb questions"—and that I was driving people nuts. Perhaps it was my curious nature that made me choose, in later years, the career of a scientist.

Before becoming a scientist, however, many tumultuous events still awaited me down the road.

My Mother Fanny, sister Bertha, me (Julius, age 1),
and my father Joseph. 1929

Returning from Temple at the End of the Holidays:
Mother, Bertha, Julius and Father; 1939

My Grandparents, Aunt Ruchel and her baby Elli;
1941 (Note the star of David on Grandmother's chest)

Left to right: Uncle Josef, Aunt Ruchel, Fanny, Julius, in Bucharest; 1963

3. The First School Years

After one year in kindergarten, my parents decided to send me to a public elementary school. I looked forward to this encounter with a mixture of anticipation and anxiety. But it turned out to be not a pleasant experience. I faced a world that was alien, bewildering, and—as I quickly discovered—more often hostile than friendly. It was my first contact with a teacher and children who spoke Romanian, a language I neither spoke nor understood.

The school was attached to a Pedagogical Institute that trained girls to become schoolteachers. There were about twenty children in my class, three or four of them Jewish. The Jewish children sat in the back of the classroom. Our school uniform was a gown made of black chiffon, with starched, white collar and red bow tie. Girls in their late teens from the Pedagogic Institute, who attended our teacher's lessons, usually took up the last row of benches.

The first few weeks in school were not a happy time for me, to put it mildly. I could not understand what the teacher or the children were saying, and why the children were poking fun at me. At the end of the first day of school, when I walked out of the building and saw my mother, I ran towards her and started to cry. I told her that I didn't understand anything that was being said, that the other children were making fun of me, and that I didn't want to go back to school. Mother tried to console me. In a soothing voice she said, "The first day of school is already over. Just another nine months and you will have vacation." I didn't know exactly what nine months meant, but Mother's soft voice and the word "vacation" calmed me down and I stopped crying.

The teacher, Miss Constantza, was a young Romanian woman, who did not speak any German. She decided that the best method of teaching me the language was to ignore me and to let me struggle on my own. At home, my sister, who was older and had also struggled to learn Romanian, helped me.

After several weeks, I began to understand certain words, then whole sentences and, after a few months, I was finally able to understand what the teacher and the children were saying. It took me, however, more than a year to speak the language, albeit far from perfect. You can imagine how much fun the other boys had with my imperfect Romanian and me, as well as with my funny accent. The ridicule never stopped. Even in later years, when I spoke Romanian fluently, a slight German accent would crop into my speech.

At the end of my first school year, Miss Constantza decided to put our knowledge on display. It was the final examination day, and the teacher invited parents and other family members to attend. The children were dressed in their black gowns, with starched white collars, and bright red bow ties. We were sitting on our classroom benches, backs straight, and hands clasped behind our backs. The parents were sitting on chairs placed along the white walls. It was a festive atmosphere. The room was decorated with Romanian tricolor flags and colored-pencil drawings made by the children throughout the year. On the wall above the blackboard hung the picture of King Carol II in military uniform. The teacher was eager to show what the children had learned in school, while the parents were prepared to take pride in their children's knowledge.

We started singing the Romanian anthem, *Traiasca Regele* (Long live the King), then sang several songs we had learned during the year. Finally each of us, individually, had to answer the teacher's questions. Many of the questions dealt with identifying animals or different objects from pictures, and describing them. We also had to identify the letters of the alphabet, and write simple numbers.

When my turn came, the teacher asked, "Tell me, Scherzer, what covers the body of a dog?"

I knew that the correct answer in German was *Haar* (hair), but I did not know the corresponding word in Romanian. So I answered using a word

I thought was the right one.

"Feathers, Miss Teacher."

Needless to say, my answer caused much amusement among the adults gathered in the room. The teacher, however, was not amused. Realizing that I had made a blunder, I blushed and dropped my head. I wished I could have fallen through the floor. After all these years, I still remember the scene in the classroom, my embarrassment, and even today, when I look at a dog, I sometimes think what he would look like if he were covered with feathers instead of hair.

The following years in grade school were not much fun, to put it gently. The teachers were strict, and the penalties for disobedience severe. Not paying attention in class, talking during the lecture, not doing the homework, were all penalized. The penalty usually consisted of standing in a corner of the classroom until recess, facing the wall. Troublemakers were expelled from the room for the rest of the hour. A repeat offense was penalized more severely: kneeling in the corner, facing the wall. If these penalties did not help, the teacher used other means. The malfeasant would be given a lash with a belt or a wooden ruler on the outstretched hand. The most painful punishment was being in a corner, kneeling on hard corn kernels.

The worst incident, however, happened to me after class. While most children could barely wait for the bell to ring, announcing the end of class, I dreaded that moment. During the recess, the Romanian, Ukrainian, and German children organized "games" that gave them much pleasure, but frightened me. One of the games they liked to play was called "War between Christians and Jews." The outcome was predictable. The few Jewish children were thoroughly beaten and left with marks on their bodies. On those occasions I took more punches than I can remember. In another game, of the "cop-and-robber" type, the Jewish children had to play the role of robbers. As expected, the "cops" always captured the "robbers" and beat them up.

Such "games" were also played at the end of the school day, on the street in front of the school. When I walked out of the school building, the bullies were already waiting for me like a pack of hungry dogs, looking for a treat. It did not help that the bullies were taller and stronger than I was.

It was in the first grade that I found out that, in addition to my real name, I had another name: *jidan*, kike. As time went by, I heard that name more and more often, sometimes with variations, such as *pui de jidan* (kike brat), or *jidanash* (little kike).

For the first time, I became aware that I was different from other children. In kindergarten I had been grouped together with Jewish children that behaved and were treated by the teacher the same way I was. Now, the non-Jewish children made me rudely aware that I am a Jew, that I am somehow inferior. Their hostility made me perceive that my Jewish identity, without any other reason, was the sole fact that gave others a license to harass, mock, beat me up, spit in my face and call me names.

It was my first encounter with blind hatred and prejudice. I suddenly felt like an outcast among the other children; as if I had some terrible, shameful disease that made me the target of their contempt and animosity. It was the moment in my childhood, never to be forgotten, when I realized that I had entered this world as a second-class citizen. I felt that as long as I lived in that society, no personal accomplishment, no personal virtue would change that fact.

It was a bewildering feeling. When an adult has felt injustice, he protests; a child just cries. At night, alone in my bed, I cried. It was so unfair! Why did they bully and beat me? Why so much disdainful hostility from children that I barely knew and had never hurt? I was too young to understand, but old enough to hurt.

There was one kid, Johan, who tried to protect me from the bullies. He was German, and sometimes he spoke to me in German. Maybe the reason he tried to protect me was because we shared the same native tongue. He was not strong, but swift and agile. When things got hot, he managed to interpose himself between the bullies and me, and tried to separate us. But he did not always succeed. There were too many of them.

At the beginning I did not say anything at home about the "games" played at school. I did not want to be perceived as a coward. But one day, something happened to me that I could not hide from my parents. It was at the end of class, and I was running down the hallway to escape from one of the bullies who was trying to catch me. He was taller and stronger than I was. I knew that if he caught me, he would hurt me. When he got close, he tripped me. I fell, hitting the stone floor with my face. I felt a sharp pain, and my nose and lower lip started to bleed profusely. I had hurt my nose bone and my teeth had cut into my lower lip. I started crying in pain, while blood was dripping on the white collar of my uniform. Satisfied with his accomplishment, the bully laughed and walked away.

I came home in tears, and told my mother what happened. Seeing my bloody face and clothes, Mother became very upset. She washed my face, removed my uniform, and tried to comfort me. She promised that from now on she would pick me up from school every day. She also promised to talk to the teacher about the incident.

Indeed, after Mother talked to the teacher, the "games" stopped during the intermission. But the harassment did not stop. The pushing, stepping on my toes "by mistake," spilling of ink from my inkwell on my schoolbooks, name calling, all continued. Sometimes I pushed back or punched the most aggressive bully, but more often than not I ended up the loser. At the end of the school day, I always walked out of the building with trepidation, never knowing what to expect. When I saw my mother waiting for me, I ran towards her and embraced her. Anxiety turned into happiness. How good it felt to walk home, my hand in Mother's hand, feeling her protective presence!

While in elementary school, I had to cope not only with harassment from the school bullies, but also with the disparaging remarks made by students from the Pedagogical Institute. While sitting on my back-bench, I was close to those students who sat in the last row of benches. Although they knew my name, they always called me "Moishe" or "Itzik," typical Jewish names that had a ring of derision in those days. When they used those names, they always laughed, as if they had said something very funny. I could not understand why the names of Romanian children, such as Gheorghe or Nicolai, were not funny, but Moishe and Itzik were funny. They also mocked my German accent, and thoroughly enjoyed seeing me embarrassed and close to tears. On those occasions I discovered that not only children, but also some grownup people showed contempt and hostility towards me, for reasons that I could not understand. I was baffled and frightened.

In school I had a single friend, Josy. He was skinny, pale and very quiet. He also was Jewish, and was similarly harassed. The surrounding hostility brought us together. During recess we stayed near each other, feeling safer this way. But the friendship did not last. After the first year of school, his parents discovered that he had tuberculosis, and decided to keep him at home. He did not return. I felt more alone in school after that.

The continuing harassment and mocking took its toll. I became withdrawn, trying to put up an invisible wall between the hostile world and myself. I became extremely sensitive and was easily offended, like someone with a horrible deformity. But I also felt guilty, the guilt of being cursed by fate. Guilty for belonging to a lower order of human, guilty of being a despised creature. I felt safe only at home, although even at home I had to be *artig,* to "behave properly." That insular condition gradually generated a feeling of alienation and isolation. I became dispirited and turned inward, trying to shut out the poisonous hostility that surrounded me. I became shy. I did not play with other children, and, after Josy's departure, did not make any friends in school. I was denied a basic human relationship—friendship with other boys. I played by myself and withdrew more and more into my inner world.

Even in later years, when I met young people who were not hostile towards me, I had difficulty establishing bonds of friendship. I felt awkward in society. During my adolescence, I found escape in books, music, and in the beauty of nature. The dreary experience in my early childhood had left an indelible mark on my mind and soul.

The daily torment at school followed me into my sleep. Harrowing nightmares began to torment me. Night after night I dreamed of being chased and attacked by big, strong bullies. Sometimes it was a single bully, other times it was a whole gang. In my dream, I ran as fast as I could to escape, but they closed in on me—and kept laughing. It was a monstrous, bone-chilling laughter. When they grabbed me, I screamed in terror— and awoke. My whole body was wrapped in cold sweat. I was trembling. The screams awakened my mother, who came running to my bed and tried to calm me with soothing words. Still, I was afraid to go back to sleep, afraid of some other horrible dream. The nightmares that started in grade school tormented me into my adolescence.

After school, in addition to doing my homework, I had to sit down with my father three times a week and take lessons in German spelling and grammar. I found out quickly that learning German grammar was no easy task. I had to memorize the gender of each noun in order to use the appropriate definite article. While in English all nouns use the same definite article regardless of gender, in German there are three definite articles—*der, die, das*—corresponding to nouns of masculine, feminine, and neuter gender, respectively. But I quickly discovered that there was not always a rational correlation. I could not understand why one says *das Weib* (the woman), or *das Mädchen* (the girl), using the neuter article, but one says *die Bank* (the bench), or *die Wand* (the wall), using the feminine article.

"Is a bench or wall more feminine than a woman or girl?" I asked my father.

"It doesn't make sense," he replied, "but that's the way the German language is. Just try to memorize it."

I concluded that German grammar is not always rational. Years later I found out that most of the German people would act in ways that the civilized world considered anything but rational. After all, can you expect rational behavior from a people that uses the neuter article for the word "woman" and the feminine article for "wall?"

The interminable length of convoluted German sentences, with subject at the beginning and predicate far away near the end, made comprehension not too easy. The verbs, however, were the most difficult part of German grammar. There are numerous irregular verbs, and I had to remember the conjugation of each of them. Not an easy job for a nine year old! In addition, I had to struggle with the Gothic alphabet that my father taught me, to enable me to read and write German with those letters.

Father was impatient and would tolerate no wrong answer. He was strict and demanding. An error in the conjugation of some irregular verb, or the wrong case used with a preposition, resulted in a sharp admonition. I found out quickly that I had to prepare myself well for each lesson.

Those lessons were not much fun at the time. Later, however, I began to appreciate the effort made by my father to teach me German. Due to his effort, I was able to read and write in that language, and to acquaint myself with German literature and philosophy. In later years, when I started learning English grammar, I was surprised how much simpler it was compared to German grammar.

My father also taught me a number of German and Latin proverbs. He sprinkled his conversations with these proverbs, in order to emphasize a point. He frequently used the German proverbs, *"Schmiede das Eisen solange es glüht"* (Work the iron as long as it is hot), and *"Zu einem groben Klotz gehört ein grober Keil"* (To crack a tough wood block you need a tough wedge). The English equivalent of the latter one is "Fight fire with fire." This proverb Father often used in later years, when the discussion turned to Hitler and Nazi Germany.

Father's favored proverbs were in Latin. *"Summum jus, summa injuria"* (Extreme justice is extreme injustice), he used to say when a judge handed down a sentence that my father considered too harsh. *"Ubi bene, ibi patria"* (Where I feel good, that's where my fatherland is); *"Quod licet Jovi, non licet bovi"* (What Jupiter may do, an ox may not do); and *"Homo homini lupus"* (Man is a wolf to man, i.e., man is inhumane to other men) were proverbs that my father used frequently. He often used the last proverb during the war years, when man's inhumanity to man was so prevalent in our society. One of Father's preferred proverbs, *"Verba volant, scripta manent"* (Spoken words fly away, written words remain), inspired me to write this book.

When I was nine years old, I had an experience that, although it may seem trivial, made a deeply disturbing impression on me. It was a warm day in late fall when Mother decided to take me along for a walk to Kaliczanka, one of the city's suburbs. Mother knew a peasant who had a small vegetable garden, where he planted tomatoes, cucumbers, and radishes. He also had several apple, pear, and plum trees. She had come to buy fresh fruits and vegetables for the weekend. When we arrived at the peasant's house, Mother walked inside, while I stayed in the garden. I walked around among the plants and trees, admiring the large tomatoes and ripe, reddish-gold apples. I also smelled the roses planted along the wall of the house, and caressed their delicate petals.

While walking in the garden, I suddenly heard loud squealing coming from the neighboring yard. Curious, I approached the wooden fence, and peeked between the weather-beaten planks into the adjoining area. The scene I saw is still etched in my memory. A peasant, sweating profusely, was struggling with a squirming, squealing pig, trying to hold him down to the ground. Another peasant, holding a long knife, was stabbing the pig repeatedly in his underbelly, trying to find the heart under the thick layer of fat. The sharp squeal of the pig in agony filled the air. It was a sound of harrowing suffering, of terror, of excruciating pain. It was a heart breaking sound. When the peasant's knife finally found the heart, the sharp squeal turned into a gurgling sound that became weaker and weaker until it stopped. The pig was now motionless, while blood was spurting from the stab wounds and running from his snout. I was transfixed and at the same time sickened by what I saw. I felt a knot in my stomach, but could not take my eyes off that scene.

The two peasants dragged the slaughtered animal by its hind legs, leaving a trail of blood behind in the dirt. They stopped under a raised wooden beam. Next they tied the pig's hind legs with a thick rope, threw one end of the rope over the overhead beam, and pulled at the rope until the pig was suspended in the air, its belly facing me. They tied the rope's end to one of the two supporting beams, and went to work on the slowly swaying carcass. With one move of his sharp knife one of the peasants slit the pig's underbelly, from front legs to hind legs. A stream of blood gushed from the open belly, rapidly filling the empty bucket the peasant shoved hurriedly underneath. The gushing blood also splattered on the sweating peasants, leaving large, red-brown blotches on their white linen shirts. Their knife and hands too were covered with blood. When they opened the carcass and started cutting out the blood-dripping heart, liver, and other organs, my stomach could not take it anymore. I turned just in time to throw up in the garden on a yellow-green cucumber. I then ran to my mother and asked her to take me home quickly. I was in tears, was shaking, and had a sick feeling in the pit of my stomach.

At first Mother thought I had fallen ill; then I told her what I had just seen. It was the first time I had witnessed the cruelty of man towards an innocent, helpless animal. I was outraged and distraught. Why did those peasants commit such a horrible deed? Mother tried to explain that they would use the slaughtered pig to feed themselves and their families. That the flesh of the slaughtered pig will be the roasted meat in the peasants' dinner plate, the ham in their sandwiches, the bacon in their breakfast dish. It was the first time I realized that people raise and kill animals in order to eat them, to satisfy their taste for meat. I had discovered the cruelty of humans toward other living beings. In later years I was to discover the cruelty of humans toward each other.

Never did I go back to that house. Even now I can hear the sharp, desperate squeal of the pig in agony. I think what I witnessed on that late-fall day was the reason I avoided eating pork even as an adult. Religious considerations played only a secondary role.

During my early childhood, I often fell sick in the rainy season or during the winter. I was a scrawny, skinny, little boy, with ribs clearly visible through my pale, transparent skin. Often I caught a nasty cough that wouldn't go away. Coughing all day, coughing all night, coughing so intense, it felt as if my lungs were coming out. Yellowish phlegm, lots of it, coming out of my throat and lungs, was clogging my windpipe. The coughing wouldn't stop. Mother's treatment with a mixture of aspirin, chicken soup and hot tea with lemon, made the cough eventually stop.

I was also engaged in a constant struggle with my large tonsils—still have them—which became easily inflamed in the cold weather. My throat hurt, I had difficulty swallowing and ran a fever. Mother promptly decided that I should stay in bed, drink warm milk with honey, or hot tea with lemon. Hot chicken soup, of course, was part of the treatment. When my tonsils were seriously inflamed, Mother applied an additional treatment: she heated some dry cornmeal on the stove, poured it on a scarf, made a roll of it, and wrapped it around my neck. The hot cornmeal was supposed to heal my tonsils faster. Sometime it did.

When the fever persisted, Mother called Dr. Noe. The doctor, a middle aged man with graying hair and lively, dark eyes, came with his small, brown suitcase of medicine and instruments. The doctor took out one of his instruments—he called it a stethoscope—and stuck one end of it into his ears. The other end he pressed first to my chest, then to my back, and listened to the sounds in my body. He then shoved a thermometer into my armpit, checked the temperature, had me open my mouth and say "aaah," smiled at me, and prescribed some bad-tasting medicine.

I was not thrilled with the idea of swallowing bitter medicine.

"If I swallow the medicine does it know where to go and what to do?" I wanted to know.

"Sure it does," the smiling doctor comforted me, "it goes to work immediately and takes away the pain."

"It never goes the wrong way?" I asked, hoping somehow to avoid taking that bitter liquid.

"No, it doesn't," replied the doctor soothingly.

I was wondering. How can that dirty-green liquid, after being swallowed, find its way in my dark stomach? I was sure it was dark, since neither sunlight nor electric light could get there. I knew I couldn't find my way in darkness, especially in a place where I had never been before. Furthermore, how did that bitter, ugly liquid know what to do once it reached the place it was supposed to reach? It would have to be very smart to be able to take away the pain and cure my illness. To me, it didn't look smart at all. Still, I concluded that the doctor knew better, and I followed his advice. Reluctantly, I swallowed a tablespoon of the bitter medicine.

Being sick also had some advantages. First of all, I did not have to go to school. When I stayed home I did not have to hear the taunting from my classmates, or fear the bullies. Nor did I have to do any homework. Sickness also carried the advantage of being coddled by everybody in the family. Mother, always concerned, would fuss around me, arrange the pillows, tuck me in under the blanket, check my temperature, and ask repeatedly if I wanted something to eat or drink.

Father, who was usually pre-occupied and distant, sat by my bed in the evening, and told me some of the stories he knew best: stories from ancient Greek and Roman mythology. He told me about the war between the ancient Greeks and the Trojans, how the Greek warriors sneaked into Troy in the belly of a giant wooden horse and conquered the city.

"Why did the Greeks go to war against Troy?" I wanted to know.

"Because of a pretty woman," replied my father. "Her name was Helen. She was a Greek woman who was kidnapped by a Trojan shepherd named

Paris. The Greeks wanted her back and went to war against Troy to get her."

"Do people always go to war because of pretty women?"

"Not anymore," replied my father with a smile. It was one of the rare occasions that I remember him smiling. "They did this in ancient times. Not only the Greeks, but the ancient Romans also fought for their women. When their neighbors, the Sabines, abducted a large number of Roman women and married them, the Romans went to war against the Sabines. Nowadays, however, people are more likely to fight for their women with their fists or knives."

I didn't quite understand why people would fight with their fists or knives for a woman, but upon further inquiry Father told me not to ask so many questions and just listen to his stories. Father then told me the story of Ulysses' odyssey on his return to Greece, of his encounter with the giant, one-eyed Cyclops, and of the sorceress, Circe, who turned Ulysses' men into swine. (At that point, Mother, who was listening to the story from the other room, interjected, "Some men behave like swine even in the absence of a sorceress." Father ignored the remark.) Father also described Ulysses' faithful wife Penelope and the punishment meted out to her suitors. I found those stories fascinating, and temporarily forgot my illness.

My sister was also kind to me. She brought me picture books from the library, where she went frequently to get books for herself and for our parents. When Aunt Tzili came to visit, she brought me a toy, or, more important, an orange. Oranges were rare and expensive in those days, and receiving an orange was a rare treat. While I delighted myself with slices of orange, Mother took the peels, sprinkled them with sugar, and let them dry. These dried, sweet orange peels were another delicious treat.

When the doctor came to see me, I did my best to look as sick as possible, even when I already felt better. After checking my temperature and looking into my throat, he readily realized what I was doing. He smiled at me and patted me on the head. Although the fever was gone and my tonsils had recovered, the doctor told my mother that I should stay home a few more days. I think he said this to make me happy.

Sometimes my sister took me to the movies. They were mostly French or German movies, but occasionally English or American ones were also shown. They all had Romanian subtitles. I liked the *Tarzan* movies. Watching the handsome and agile hero of that movie made me wish to have his looks and skills when I grow up. Most of all, however, I enjoyed the Laurel and Hardy shows. They always made me laugh and made me feel good. Charlie Chaplin's movies were also among my favorites. Sister tried to explain that behind the funny movements and hilarious accidents in which Chaplin was involved, there was always a serious social subject. I, however, didn't care much about the social subject, and just enjoyed watching the bumbling, funny-looking tramp.

The movies I saw played at the cinema *Scala* or *Savoy*. I still remember watching *The Hunchback of Notre Dame* and crying. The cracking of the whip on his bare back, the bloodied streaks on his skin, the face contorted in pain, his outcry like that of an animal in agony—that horrible scene was too much for me to bear. I left the cinema deeply distraught.

"Why were people so cruel to the poor hunchback, Quasimodo?" I asked my sister, wiping my tears.

"Because there are bad people in the world who make good people suffer," she answered philosophically.

"Are they like the bullies in school?" I wanted to know.

"Yes, they are," she replied.

Then I understood. To stop me from crying, she told me that Quasimodo in the movie was not a real hunchback, but a normal-looking man named Charles Laughton, who only pretended to be a hunchback.

"Laughton is an actor," she said, "and he was only acting in the role of Quasimodo."

I became fascinated with that kind of acting. I think the movie planted in me a seed, which in later years developed into a keen interest in acting.

There was also cinema *Roxy*, where only cowboy and cop-and-robber movies were shown. Mostly working class youngsters went to see them. Middle-class people were too snobbish, and ignored the *Roxy*. Neither my parents nor my sister took me to any of those movies.

"They are not for you," I was told.

"Why?" I wanted to know.

"Because there is a lot of shooting and killing in those movies," came the curt reply.

Case closed. There was no point in arguing. I could not change my parents' minds, and surely could not convince my opinionated sister to change hers. I could never win. From my classmates, I knew that in cowboy movies there was shooting by people that wore wide-brimmed hats, carried revolvers and rode fast horses. I would have liked to see such a movie, but I never saw one in my childhood.

Later, during my teenage years, the political system changed. The new rulers were fascists or communists, and none of them allowed the showing of cowboy movies. The first time I saw such a movie was in America, at age 35.

Occasionally, my mother took me to the Yiddish theater. She liked to attend performances given by well-known visiting theater ensembles that came from different parts of Europe. One of the ensembles that gave frequent performances in our city was the Yiddish Theater from Vilna. From Mother I learned that this was the best Yiddish Theater in Europe. I did not understand much of what was happening on stage, why people argued, laughed, or kissed each other. However, I liked to watch the actors dressed in outlandish costumes, their strange makeup, and their acting. It reminded me of Purim. Years later, under the Soviets, I went to the Yiddish Theater regularly, never missing a performance.

One place I looked forward to visit was my grandparents' house. Since I was always at the very bottom of the pecking order at school and at home, the attention and kindness my grandparents focused on me was very comforting and pleasing. They lived in a ground floor, two-bedroom apartment, facing a paved courtyard bordered by shrubs. The bedrooms were small and the kitchen was semi-dark. Strips of flypaper hung from the ceiling in each room. The daylight came into the kitchen through the panes of a window that separated the kitchen from a small hallway. The hallway also had a window facing the courtyard. There was a windowless toilet. When the toilet smelled, so did the hallway.

On Saturday night, after dinner, while Father met with his friends at Druckmann's restaurant and my sister got together with her girlfriends, Mother took me to her parents. Her sisters and Uncle Joseph were also there. In the summer we sat on the porch, while in winter the family sat around the stove in the kitchen. Grandmother spread sunflower seeds on the cast iron plate on top of the stove, and let them roast until they turned brownish. Then everybody ate some of the roasted seeds, while discussing the latest events in the family and in the world. The warm, roasted seeds were delicious. Their pleasant aroma tickled my nostrils.

On those occasions I met cousin Gusta, Aunt Jetty's little girl, who also visited her grandparents on Saturday night. Gusta and I liked to play "hide and seek" when we got together. I still remember her black locks, her dark, sparkling eyes, and the crystalline, carefree laughter. We got along very well and looked forward to playing together.

When I came to my grandparents and Gusta wasn't there, I usually went into the courtyard to play with my little rubber ball. In the same courtyard was a small, Orthodox *shul* where my grandfather used to pray every day of the year, morning and evening. On Sabbath, Grandfather went to *shul* for services in the morning and prayed there until noon. He then came home, washed his hands, and sat down for his *Shabbes* (Yiddish for Sabbath) meal at the table that Grandmother had covered with a clean, white cloth. After he said the *Kiddush* blessing over a cup of wine, Grandmother served him *cholent*, a dish of meat, potatoes and beans. Since cooking on the Sabbath was forbidden by Jewish tradition, she prepared the *cholent* on Friday and kept it in the warm oven until noon the next day. The *cholent* was followed by fruit compote, usually made of prunes or cherries. The meal always concluded with a glass of tea and a slice of honey cake. In those days it was common to drink tea from a glass and not a cup. When I was there, I did not care much about the *cholent*, but enjoyed eating the fruit compote and the slice of honey cake.

Next to the *shul* was a small apartment, where the rabbi and his wife, the rebetsin, lived. Originally the family came from Sadagora, a small village near Czernowitz, and belonged to the Friedman-dynasty of Chasidic rabbis. It was said that the rabbis of that dynasty had performed many miracles. The rabbi's followers considered him a *tzaddik*, a "righteous man." He wore a *shtreimel* and a long, black caftan. I remember him having a long gray beard, side locks, bushy eyebrows and dark eyes partially covered by heavy eyelids. The people surrounding him called him *the Rebbe.* There was always a crowd inside and outside his apartment. Some people came with petitions asking help for a dying mother or a sick child. Others begged the Rebbe for help, because they had barren wives and wanted a son. There were people who asked for advice when threatened by authorities, and others for whom a business deal went sour and who blamed one another.

Then were those who liked to spend their time just milling around in the crowd. The latter Grandfather called *leidiggehers,* a Yiddish word for those who have nothing to do. The Rebbe helped, mediated, provided guidance, and settled disputes. Regardless of how difficult the case was, he always helped with a word of wisdom, a word of advice, or a word of consolation. His followers considered him a wise and knowledgeable man.

In this crowd was a nitwit named Feivl. He lived on the meals the rebbitzin served him daily in her kitchen, and his not-so-dumb remarks amused the crowd. Once I assisted at a small incident between Feivl and the Rebbe. It happened after the rebetsin had given Feivl his meal, and he asked for more food. The Rebbe, who happened to be present, didn't like the tone of Feivl's request, and he showed him the door. Feivl slouched out through the door, but then turned around and said, in Yiddish: "*Veil mir zeinen narronim, kent ihr zein rabbonnim!*" (Only because we are dummies can you be our Rebbe!). People who heard the remark were amused. After all, Feivl was not as dumb as he appeared to be. The next day, forced by an empty stomach, Feivl became friends again with the Rebbe and the rebetsin.

Only the people milling around my grandfather's courtyard knew Feivl. There was, however, another queer character, known as the town fool. He was Bubby the Red, a name given to him because of his wild, red hair. Everybody knew him. He walked the streets in a torn-up overcoat, tattered pants, without a shirt, and barefoot. On his head he wore a crushed, black bowler hat that a compassionate soul had given him to cover his wild hair. Still, his red, curly hair hung in tangles over his gentle, childish eyes that shone with unjustified cheerfulness. He had the mind of a child, and was always laughing. Even when children threw pebbles at him or pulled at his rags, he kept laughing. He was a fixture of the city.

Everybody poked fun at him, but at the same time people liked him. When he was hungry, he went to the basement of the Jewish Community Center, where he got a bowl of soup and a slice of bread. When the war broke out in 1941, he was one of the first to be shot and killed by the Germans.

We lived in a rented apartment on the fourth floor of the Chamber of Commerce building until 1938. The building was known by that name because the city's chamber of commerce occupied one of its floors. We had an assortment of neighbors in that building.

The Kolnik family lived on the third floor. Mr. Kolnik was an oil painter, who was struggling to make a living. I was one of the admirers of his artwork. He rolled up and stored in the attic some of his finished paintings that he did not like. When Mother went to the attic to hang freshly washed linen to dry, usually I tagged along. While Mother was hanging the linen on a clothesline, I enjoyed myself by unrolling Mr. Kolnik's paintings, shaking off the dust, and staring at the animals and human heads on the canvases. There were heads of fat people and skinny people, bald people and bearded people. There were monkeys, birds, and donkeys. The style of his paintings was not "realistic," and many of the painted figures appeared distorted. From my sister I learned that people called such paintings "modernist." Still, I liked them. Many years later I realized that some of the paintings were similar to those used by Mr. Kolnik to illustrate the collection of Yiddish fables by Eliezer Steinbarg. In the early 1930s, Mr. Kolnik went to Paris, where he became well known for his modern paintings. I wish I had the paintings he left in the attic!

On the second floor of our building lived Judge Popescu, an elderly bachelor gentleman known for his sharp mind and his integrity on the bench. Serious and distant, he was highly respected by everybody who knew him. A Romanian peasant, whose legal case was to be handled by Judge Popescu, once brought him a live chicken as a "gift." The judge almost threw the peasant down the stairs, and threatened to call the police if he would not leave immediately. His rectitude was impeccable. He belonged to the city's Romanian elite. When the Soviets occupied the city in 1940, he was promptly arrested. Later, he was exchanged for a high-level Communist from a Romanian jail.

On the first floor of our building were the offices of the Chamber of Commerce, whose functionaries had rarely any contact with the residents of the building. On the ground floor was the elegant café "Astoria," with its large chandeliers, wide windows, and shiny parquet floor. Waiters in white jackets, black bow ties and black pants served coffee and Viennese pastry.

Of all the tenants in our building, our immediate neighbors were the most colorful. Next to us, on the fourth floor, lived Mr. Beniuk with his wife and dog. He was a low-level clerk in a small, private office. He had been a member of the old Hapsburg *"Hoch- und Deutschmeister"* regiment, had fought in World War I, and loved to sing his favorite Austrian military march, the "Deutschmeister Marsch." Mr. Beniuk longed for the old days of glory. He had a small, toothbrush mustache, kept a military posture and talked with a raspy voice. Mrs. Beniuk was a homemaker who always had a complaint: one time it was her head that ached, another time it was her back, yet another time her feet. Still, there was one part of her that never hurt—her mouth. In the presence of other people she talked incessantly, rarely giving them a chance to express their opinion. She spoke in a rapid-fire, loud voice.

Mr. Beniuk was Ukrainian, while his wife was Polish. They had a German shepherd, Wolfi, whom he loved and she hated. He would let the dog eat from his dish and sleep in his bed, while she would not even touch the animal. Mrs. Beniuk often said to my mother, "Mrs. Scherzer, if someday I divorce my husband, you should know it's because of the dog."

When Mr. Beniuk came home drunk, which happened quite often, his wife became angry and started berating him. He got even by giving her a thorough beating. All the neighbors knew what was going on because the whole building reverberated with her screams. Between screams, we could hear them heaping abuse on each other. Things quieted down only after both were exhausted from the beating and screaming.

The verbal clashes between Mr. and Mrs. Beniuk enriched my knowledge as well as my vocabulary. During such heated exchanges, Mrs. Beniuk would often call Mr. Beniuk "Ukrainian swine," while he, in turn, would call her "Polish whore." I knew what a swine was, but I didn't know what a whore was. I decided to inquire.

I went to see my sister. She had read all kinds of books and was more knowledgeable than I was. I found her sitting on the sofa in the living room, reading a book.

"Sis, what is a whore?"

Sister raised her eyes from the book, turned her head slowly toward me, and looked at me with a frown.

"Where did you pick up this word?" she inquired with annoyance in her voice.

"I heard Mr. Beniuk calling Mrs. Beniuk a whore," I replied innocently

"It's a bad word; you shouldn't use it!" she said in a commanding tone. She always spoke with that tone when she wanted to cut a conversation short.

"But Mr. Beniuk uses it. "

"You are not Mr. Beniuk," was her clipped reply.

Now that sister had awakened my curiosity, I was not to give up my inquiry.

"I want to know what that word means," I insisted.

With a deep sigh, sister put the book in her lap. She paused briefly to find the right explanation.

"A whore is a bad woman. She's one who becomes intimate with men to make them feel good; in return, the men give her money."

Sister had the peculiar habit of explaining one strange word with another strange word.

"What does it mean she becomes intimate with men?" I wanted to know. I could see a scowl on my sister's face. She was becoming more annoyed with me.

"It means that they get physically close to each other, they caress and kiss each other, and may even lie down together in bed."

Now I was puzzled. What was wrong with caressing and kissing each other? I was often caressed and kissed by my grandmother when I visited her. Besides, why would a man feel good with a woman in bed? I knew that I wouldn't have liked to have anybody in my bed, man or woman. It would have been very uncomfortable.

"Why is it wrong for a man and a woman to be close to each other, to be intimate? You said she makes them feel good, and they give her money—which makes her feel good. Moreover, why can't a woman be intimate with several men and make all of them feel good, then take money from each of them? This way everybody would be happy."

Sister rolled her eyes. She realized she could not get rid of me, and had to do some more explaining. "If a man and a woman like each other very much, when they love each other, they get married and live together. Then they can both enjoy being intimate. But if a woman doesn't love or even like a man, and becomes intimate with him only for the money, that is a bad woman. Some people call such a woman a whore."

I mulled over my sister's explanation. That raised another question in my mind.

"The other day Father said to Mother that her sister, our Aunt Jetty, had married Uncle Bernhard for his money; that she would have never married an older man if he wouldn't have had plenty of money. Does that mean that Aunt Jetty is a bad woman, a whore?"

"Absolutely not. How can you say such a stupid thing? Aunt Jetty is a very nice lady. She loves Uncle Bernhard, even if occasionally she argues with him."

"Does she make him feel good?"

"Of course—well, most of the time, when they don't argue."

"Does Uncle Bernhard give her money?"

"Sure he does. He loves her. He gives her money to buy herself nice clothes and shoes. He also buys her rings, and bracelets, and pearls to please her, and she in return is nice to him. They have been married for many years and they try to keep each other happy."

I gave some more thought to what my sister said. Eventually, I came to the following conclusion: long-term intimacy in return for money is good; short-term intimacy in return for money is bad. It was not clear in my mind why the difference, but I accepted sister's explanation.

My sister's patience had come to an end. "Now go play ball and let me read my book." With a vigorous gesture she picked up the book from her lap and started reading.

I went to the door. Before leaving I turned around. "Sis, are Polish whores different from other whores?"

"Enough questions for one day. Go play ball!" It was an order.

I left the room, not completely satisfied. At least, I had learned something about the relationship between men and women.

In 1938, the Jewish tenants were evicted from the Chamber of Commerce building. The owner decided not to have "undesirable elements" in its building. We had to move. My parents found a two-bedroom apartment on the Postgasse—strada Bucurestilor in Romanian—on the second floor of a three-story building. The owner was Dr. Simche, an attorney, who lived across from us on the same floor. The doorman, Nicolai, a tall Ukrainian with a big, black mustache and dark, wild eyes, guarded the entrance to the building. The main entrance was in a courtyard that was also a passageway connecting two streets: the Postgasse and the Bahnhofstrasse. Down the street was the Post Office, which in those days also housed the city's telephone and telegraph exchange.

Across the street from our building was the Stock Exchange. There were always people milling around that building: traders, speculators, and moneychangers. In 1938, after the government prohibited private trading in foreign currencies, there were frequent police raids on our street. The police cordoned off the street and searched the people milling around in front of the Stock Exchange. Anybody found carrying foreign currencies was arrested and the currency confiscated. Those arrested had to pay a heavy fine before being set free. A significant bribe to the chief of police could also do the trick.

When the soles on my shoes were worn out, my mother took them to a cobbler who lived in the Jewish quarter. Although there had never been a Jewish ghetto in the city until 1941, there was a Jewish quarter. It was located in the northern part of the city, not far from the Prut valley. Its main street was the Judengasse. It was one of the poorest sections of the city, with old, neglected, one- or two-story buildings, squalid backyards, and foul-smelling alleys. Noisy, bedraggled children played next to stinking trashcans. That's where poor Jewish tailors, cobblers, tinsmiths, old-clothes traders, and junk dealers lived and worked. Some of them had their shops at street level, while others lived and worked in dark basements. In the summer, a reeking odor pervaded the whole area.

The small, dark shops were filled with all sorts of things: a jumble of used household goods, old furniture, worn hats and shoes, and old clothes of all sizes and colors. A lot of decrepit and unusable stuff could be found there, waiting for a buyer who could still make use of some of that junk. Then there were the street peddlers, hawking their wares from flimsy stands: old books and magazines, buttons and threads of different colors, handkerchiefs, brushes, shoemaker's wax, and matches. Little boys in threadbare short pants and torn shirts were hawking Yiddish newspapers, shouting the latest headlines. On warm days one could see the junk dealers and old-clothes traders standing in front of their shops, talking in Yiddish, gesticulating energetically with their hands, and shouting across the street to one another.

During the week the streets were crowded with people. Throngs of shabbily dressed buyers, *leidiggaiers,* beggars, and urchins jostled each other. Some were looking for bargains, others were browsing, while still others were hustling or begging. From the tailor's airless tenement one could hear the rattling sewing machine, from the tinsmith's shop the hammering of brass, from the cobbler's semi-dark cellar room the pounding of nails into shoe soles. Only on Saturday, the holy day of rest for these harried people, did the Jewish quarter quiet down. Among the Jewish poor, poverty rarely bred crime, but rather effort and ingenuity.

The Jewish hospital, old-age home, and orphanage were also located in the Jewish quarter. In front of the old-age home one could see white-bearded men with pale, weathered faces, leaning on canes while standing on the sidewalk. Others were sitting on a wooden bench near the building's entrance, hunched forward and gazing into space or at passerby.

Well-to-do Jews lived in the more prosperous areas of the city, next to the middle-class Christian population. Only rarely did they venture into the Jewish quarter.

I outgrew my clothes quickly, and Mother had to buy fabric periodically for a new suit. We went then to the tailor to have the suit made. In those days, ready-made suits were expensive and only the rich could afford them. Most people had their clothing made by a tailor. My visit to the tailor's shop was my first encounter with true poverty, and left a lasting impression on me.

The tailor and his family lived in the Jewish quarter of the city in abject poverty. He had only one room in the basement of a dilapidated building, where he worked and lived with his wife and four children. To reach the room, we had to walk through a dark passageway, pass a smelly lavatory used by several families that lived in the building, and descend into the darkness down a flight of stairs to reach the basement. The room where the tailor lived and worked was semi-dark, even in daytime. It had two small windows close to the ceiling at the level of the sidewalk. Occasionally, a few sun rays entered the darkened room through the dirty windows. The floor was partially covered with a few cracked, worn out, wooden boards, that showed some traces of brown paint near the walls. The rest of the floor was bare, hard soil. The bleak walls glistened in the dim light because water was seeping through in small blobs, and running in tiny rivulets to the floor. A single dusty bulb hung from the socket in the middle of the ceiling. The air was damp and stifling, and there was a whiff of urine from the lavatory next door.

The tailor's workshop was in one corner of the room. It held a rickety wooden table and stool next to an old Singer sewing machine. In another corner stood an iron stove, on which the tailor's wife cooked the meals and boiled water. In the other two corners of the room stood two beds, one for the tailor and his wife, and the other for the four children. An old wooden table stood in the middle of the room and was flanked by two benches. There was one wooden chair in the room, reserved for the visiting customer.

The tailor, dressed in old trousers and wearing a dirty, gray shirt, was a feeble, skinny man with a gaunt face and eyes reddened by the strain of sewing in half-darkness. His wife, disheveled, with a sullen face, barely talked to us, and kept busy with her boiling pots. The kids, ranging in age from two to seven, were unkempt, barefoot, and had dirty hands and feet. The younger ones had snot running from their noses. The youngest one was crying, because the rag that served as a diaper was wet and dirty. In the winter, the children spent most of the time in bed under a goose-down comforter, the warmest place in the room.

When the tailor took my measurements, he tried to smile at me. His bloodless lips were twisted into a painful, miserable grimace—the smile of a man who was not used to such an expression. Whenever we went to the tailor, Mother took some candy in her handbag, and I gave it to the children. It was a rare treat for them, and their happy faces showed it. Seeing their happiness also made me feel good. I was glad to be able to cheer up these dirt-poor children.

At the age of nine I made my first trip to a foreign country. My grandfather had relatives in Zaleshchiki, Poland, and I went with my mother to visit them. Zaleshchiki was very close to the Romanian border, across the River Dniester. Czernowitz was a mere thirty miles from Zaleshchiki. We traveled by train—another first for me. Mother and I took our seats in a third-class carriage. The train moved out of the station slowly, the steam-driven locomotive belching black smoke and white steam. The huge engine that pulled the long train looked to me like a mighty iron monster spewing hot vapors through its nostrils. It fascinated me. As we gained speed, I listened to the rhythmic clicking of the iron wheels, racing over the rail tracks, and to the periodic whistling of the locomotive. I enjoyed watching the scenery go by the window of our carriage: the fields of golden wheat, the modest houses of the peasants, the orchards filled with apple and pear trees, and the bluish hills in the distance. Occasionally, a little boy standing in front of his house waved at the train. I waved back at him. Leaning out through the window, I let the wind rush through my hair, and inhaled the cool air filled with the aroma of freshly cut grass. I found traveling by train magical.

It took about thirty minutes to reach the border. Before crossing the steel bridge over the Dniester, we spent an hour for passport and customs control. The Romanian customs inspection was very strict. The inspector searched each of our suitcases and Mother's handbag. Women from the customs office took my mother to a separate compartment and, as she told me later, submitted her to a body search. Each passenger was thoroughly searched. The inspector also searched my pockets, but didn't find anything, except for the neatly folded handkerchief that my mother had given me before the trip.

After completing the individual inspection, the custom inspector searched our train compartment. He used a powerful flashlight to check under the benches for hidden objects. I tried to help him in his search, crawling on the floor and under the bench. A sharp tug from my mother brought me to my feet. She lifted me with both hands and put me down firmly into my seat. "Sit here," she said to me in a sharp, commanding tone. Intimidated, I obeyed. After the inspector left, I asked my mother what he was looking for. Had he lost something? Mother said that the inspector hadn't lost anything, and that he was looking for foreign currency as well as illegal merchandise that some people may try to smuggle across the border. The illegal merchandise consisted mostly of items made of silk. A pair of silk stockings or a silk blouse was a highly valued gift in Poland. I also found out why Mother had pulled me out brusquely from under the bench when the inspector started the search. She had seen the lady sitting next to us hiding a pair of silk stockings under the seat, and she did not want me to help the inspector find them. The lady would not have been pleased.

Across the bridge, at the Polish side of the border, the search was less strict. Men in uniforms checked our travel documents, made a cursory inspection of my mother's suitcase, and let us pass. In the meantime, I was gawking at Polish soldiers with their khaki uniforms and four-cornered hats. I also listened to them speaking Polish, a language that I could not understand. It was very different from Romanian or German, but sounded soft and melodic. Many words had the sounds *sz* and *shch*, which I could hardly pronounce.

At the railroad station in Zaleshchiki, my mother's two cousins were waiting for us. When we stepped off the train, there was a lot of embracing, kissing and talking in Yiddish, everybody speaking at the same time. One of my mother's cousins, Shaindl, a cheerful, energetic woman who showed a golden tooth when she smiled, almost squashed me with her embrace. A Yiddish-speaking coachman, with horse and carriage, took us from the rail station to our relatives' home. They lived in the Jewish quarter of the city, in a cramped apartment. Everybody was friendly to me, patted me on the head, and gave me candy. Friends and neighbors came, and soon the place was full of people, chatting, laughing, and drinking tea that Shaindl served with a smile, showing her golden tooth.

Before World War II, Zaleshchiki had a large Jewish community. The Jews living there eked out a living as tradesmen, craftsmen, or small shopkeepers. They lived in small, cramped houses, poorly lit and badly in need of a coat of paint. Many were strictly Orthodox Jews. In the Jewish quarter I saw men with long, black overcoats and black caps, with beards and side locks, talking lively to each other, gesturing with their hands, or rushing toward some unknown destination.

Next to the house where my relatives lived was a *cheder*, where a bearded, old rebbe taught little children the *aleph-bet* and read the Torah with them. It was the first time that I saw an East European *cheder*. There were about a dozen little boys, between the ages of four and six, some sitting on a bench next to the rebbe at a long, wooden table in the dimly lit room, trying to read in a singing voice from a thick, well-worn book. Other children played in the small, dusty courtyard. They wore *yarmulkes* over their curly hair, had side locks, and their raggedy shirts were sticking out from torn short pants. Some of the children wore a *tallit katan,* a sleeveless undershirt, the four corners of which ended in *tzitzit,* tassels of twined cord.

Their youthful energy and passion for play animated the whole yard. The smallest among them had snotty noses, but were happy and cheerful. They ran around barefoot, side locks flying, laughing and shouting at each other in Yiddish, while their little feet kicked up the dust. It was a lively scene of poor, small children having fun on a warm, sunny day. The image of the old rebbe and the little boys hunched over the worn book in the semi-dark room, chanting together from the ancient text, became a lasting memory. It was the image of a world very different from my own.

We spent three days with our relatives before returning home. What I remember from that trip was the crowd of Yiddish-speaking people in Shaindl's apartment and on the street, the poverty in which people lived, and the little boys with side locks and torn pants chanting from a holy book or playing barefoot outside the *cheder.* Only a few short years later this world disappeared.

In the mean time, in Romania, the situation was turning from bad to worse.

4. My Early Teens

Hitler's rise to power in Germany led to an increase in power and influence of anti-Semitic, ultra-nationalist political parties and movements in Romania. The most extreme movement was the Iron Guard, under the leadership of Corneliu Zelea Codreanu. He was a man filled with hatred. He hated democratic ideas and those who believed in them; he hated liberal politicians and intellectuals; he hated the King; but most of all, almost pathologically, he hated the Jews. He considered the Jews to be the greatest misfortune that had befallen the Romanian people. As could be expected, he was a great admirer of Adolf Hitler and had his demagogic talent. Codreanu's speeches could electrify a sympathetic crowd.

The official name of his organization was *The Legion of Archangel Michael*, and the members of the Iron Guard called themselves *Legionaries*. Codreanu, the leader of the Legionaries, was called *Capitanul*, The Captain. Their paramilitary units wore green shirts, leather belts around the waist and across the chest, and black trousers tucked into high, black boots. People also called them "The Green Shirts." When they did not wear their uniform, the Legionaries and other nationalists often wore the Romanian national costume: short, sleeveless sheepskin jacket with colorful embroidery, long, white linen shirt over coarse, white linen trousers, held together by a black or blue-yellow-and-red cotton sash worn at the waist. The Legionaries marched in tight formation, singing about their coming victory over Jews and bandits. The lyrics of their songs proclaimed that, "we shall rid the country of all the bloodsucking *jidani* (kikes) and criminals."

All together, the Legionaries were not exactly a kindhearted bunch. In December 1933 they assassinated the Romanian Prime Minister I. G. Duca, whom they accused of being "a friend of the Jews." Codreanu was also a sworn enemy of King Carol II, and attacked him openly in his public speeches.

Aware of the strong influence of right wing ideology in the country, at the end of 1937 the King appointed a nationalist, anti-Semitic government, under the leadership of Octavian Goga and Alexandru C. Cuza. The new masters had close ties with the Nazi representatives in Romania. The link that united the Romanian fascists with the Nazi masterminds was rabid anti-Semitism. The Cuza-Goga government acted under the slogan "Romania for Romanians."

Not surprising, the first act of the new government was to issue a host of anti-Jewish legislation. The new laws were designed to limit drastically Jewish economic activity in the country. In January 1938, a decree was issued that requested the verification of the citizenship of the Jewish population of Romania. The objective was to deprive a significant number of Romanian Jews of their citizenship, to be followed by expulsion from the country.

A large segment of the Romanian press picked up the Cuza-Goga slogans and began spreading vitriolic accusations against the Jews. The drumbeat of anti-Semitic propaganda was led by the fascist Romanian newspaper, *Porunca Vremii.* The Jews were accused of enriching themselves by deceit. The significant Jewish contribution to the development of Romania's economy and commerce was ignored. Jews were described as a malignant, foreign element—they were demonized. The incitement spread by Goga's fiery anti-Semitic speeches and by a virulent anti-Semitic press had the effect one could expect. When preaching hate, one reaps violence. Jews were beaten in public, and their property was confiscated or destroyed. Theology students, who were enthusiastic supporters of Goga and Cuza, excelled in acts of brutality against Jews. (It is ironic that those who were supposed to become priests and preach love and kindness toward their fellow men displayed such thuggish behavior.) Jewish students, who tried to attend university lectures, were beaten and ejected from the building. Hoodlums beat up Jewish children on the street. The Jewish population lived in the grip of fear.

The fascist government did not last. The economy deteriorated quickly, and the King realized that the country was sliding into chaos. In February 1938, the monarch dissolved the Cuza-Goga government, suspended the constitution, and installed royal dictatorship. He appointed the head of the Romanian Orthodox Church, Patriarch Miron Cristea, as head of government.

To protect his throne, the King acted decisively. Zelea Codreanu was arrested, accused of subversive activities against the state, and sentenced to ten years in prison. Carol II dissolved all political parties, proclaimed a new constitution, and invested himself with dictatorial powers. In March 1939, after the death of Patriarch Miron Cristea, the King appointed Armand Calinescu as Prime Minister. Calinescu was a foe of the Legionaries, and his political views were more moderate.

In September 1939, as Calinescu was driven to the office, a horse-drawn cart loaded with firewood blocked his car. As soon as the car came to a halt, several individuals with drawn pistols ran toward the vehicle and raked it with gunfire. Then the assailants fired point blank at the passengers through the vehicle's windows. Armand Calinescu died instantly. The murderers were captured and interrogated. It turned out they were members of the Iron Guard. Another group of Legionaries tried to occupy the Bucharest radio station and was able to enter the building, but was eventually arrested.

The King acted with vengeance. The assassination of the Prime Minister was followed by a blood bath against the Iron Guard. Calinescu's assassins were executed at the place of their crime, and were left lying on that spot for twenty-four hours next to a sign with the word "Traitors." Zelea Codreanu was shot dead, supposedly as he tried to escape from prison. Many leading Legionaries were arrested and executed. Some members of the Iron Guard fled to Germany.

Carol II had a friendlier attitude towards the Jews, since he profited handsomely from his association with the wealthiest among them. One of those with whom the King had a very profitable association was Max Ausschnit, the founder of the largest steel trust in Romania, at Resita. Moreover, it was widely known that the monarch had a Jewish mistress, Magda Lupescu. With her flaming-red hair, green eyes, milk-white complexion and sharp mind, she had captivated the King's heart when he was still the Crown Prince. It was said that she exerted considerable influence on Carol II. The Romanian people resented that relationship. Not so much for the King having a mistress, since that was to be expected from a monarch, but for the fact that she was Jewish. The King, however, maintained his relationship with Mme. Lupescu, in spite of the discontent it generated in the country.

In September 1939, shortly before Calinescu's assassination, World War II broke out in Europe.

In the late 1930s, life had become more difficult for my family. The slew of anti-Semitic legislation issued by a succession of rightwing governments made it increasingly difficult for my father to practice his profession. The anti-Jewish atmosphere also penetrated the halls of justice. Once Father came home from court very agitated, pale, and barely able to speak. Questioned by my worried mother, he finally told us that the judge had made mocking remarks about him during the proceedings, in the presence of his client and the public. The mocking remarks referred to my father's German-Jewish accent when he spoke Romanian. Father felt insulted by an insensitive, anti-Semitic judge. Under those circumstances, what client would want to be represented by a Jewish lawyer? Moreover, my father's difficulties with the Romanian language, which he had not been able to master, exacerbated the situation. He had fewer and fewer clients during the last years before the war, and it became increasingly difficult for him to support the family. Sometimes, after a long, hard day, Father would go to Druckmann's restaurant, and try to drown his frustration and anger in a glass of wine.

On occasion, without my father's knowledge, Mother had to borrow money from Uncle Joseph to make ends meet. He ran his stationery business together with my grandfather and was better off than my father in those days. I was the courier who took the money from my uncle. Mother sent me to the store to ask him discretely for some money. Uncle opened the drawer underneath the counter, took out two shiny, silvery coins and gave them to me. The coins had on one side the effigy of King Carol II and on the other side the inscription "100 lei." Clenching the coins in my fist, I ran home and gave them to my mother. Although she never told me to keep it a secret, I felt instinctively that I should not tell Father about my mission. If he knew, he would have been very upset. Still, I relished my "conspiratorial" role.

Father had few friends, most of them non-Jewish. His best friend was professor Olariu, a Romanian intellectual who used to teach philosophy. He grew up in Austria, attended Austrian schools, and felt more comfortable with the old Austrian intelligentsia than with the new Romanians. Every Saturday evening my father met Professor Olariu and a couple of other friends at Druckmann's cellar restaurant. Over a glass of wine they discussed politics and the latest developments in the world. Father and Olariu were very close. They remained close friends even during the years of rising anti-Semitism, when many Romanians distanced themselves from their Jewish friends. Father and Olariu parted in the summer of 1940, when the Soviets occupied Czernowitz, and the professor left for Romania.

The tensions in society affected also the atmosphere at home. There was rarely any laughter when we were together. I stopped playing in front of the house, afraid of being beaten up by hooligans. But it was Father who was mostly affected by the outside events. The difficulties of making a living, the uncertainty about the future, the loss of some non-Jewish "friends" who started avoiding him, all that took its toll. He became more irritable and less patient with me. Due to frustrations experienced in the outside world, he came home in a foul mood and often yelled at me. I ran into another room crying, believing that it was my fault that he was upset. He rarely walked or played with me anymore. Any disobedience on my part was punished, usually with harsh words, sometimes with the walking stick or belt. As usual, Mother kept her cool, but struggled to manage the family with a shrinking income. Bertha and I went to school, where we had to cope with the hostile attitude of some of our classmates and teachers. During the demonstrations organized by the Legionaries or by supporters of the Cuza-Goga government, we stayed home behind locked doors. Jews caught on the street during those demonstrations were brutally beaten. Most of the time we lived in fear.

On a warm summer day in 1938, while we were having dinner, Father turned to me and said: "You have finished grade school and now you have to get ready for secondary school. There are only a few weeks left before school starts. You better begin preparing yourself for the admission exam to the *lyceum.*"

The lyceum combined middle and high school. It was structured after the French *lycée* and required eight years of studies. The Romanians had adopted the French school system due to historical and cultural bonds between France and Romania, both being Latin countries. In addition to year-end exams, there were comprehensive exams after the first four years and after the eight years of school. These exams were called the minor and major baccalaureate, respectively. There were separate lyceums for boys and girls. To be admitted to the lyceum, the applicant had to finish grade school and pass an examination in reading, writing, and arithmetic.

I did not feel like studying during the hot summer days. I preferred to play with my picture books or with my ball. Besides, I felt that preparing myself a few days before the exam would be sufficient to pass it.

"At what lyceum shall I apply?" I inquired.

"This morning I met the director of the lyceum No.1, named *Aron Pumnul*. We went to school together and are good friends. When I told him that you will start attending a lyceum this year, he insisted that I send you to his school. It is one of the best in the city, with good teachers and tough discipline. Such a school will be good for you. It will give you a good education and will teach you how to behave."

When I heard the name of the lyceum, my heart sank. I knew that *Aron Pumnul* was one of the toughest schools, with one of the most difficult admission exams. There were several other *lyceums* in the city, most of them far less demanding. But Father wanted me to attend the best school. I realized that my days of vacation were over.

I started preparing myself for the exam. I worked on countless arithmetic exercises, practiced reading, wrote short stories, and memorized grammar rules. In the process I chewed up several pencils, since I was in the habit of chewing my pencil while studying. My sister helped me with the math problems. When the day of the exam arrived, I was ready.

The day following the exam I stood, with my mother, in front of the school's bulletin board, waiting for the posting of the list of those who passed the exam. Along with other parents and children, we waited for the results with trepidation. Time passed very slowly and some of the children became unruly. Finally, a young teacher approached the bulletin board, and attached the list with a thumbnail. There was a lot of pushing and shoving, everybody trying to get close enough to the list to read it. When I saw my name on that sheet of paper, I jumped with joy. I was among the top third of those accepted. I had made it!

My hard work had paid off. It was the first time that I felt deep satisfaction that comes with the accomplishment of a difficult task. I had been rewarded for a job well done. I felt exhilarated. When school started, however, my exhilaration quickly dissipated.

What my parents did not know or ignored at that time was that this school, considered the best in Czernowitz, had become the most nationalistic and chauvinistic school in our city in the late 1930s. In those days, strong nationalism was easily identified with strong anti-Semitism. Many of the teachers were supporters of the Cuza-Goga regime, and some of them sympathized with the Iron Guard. Most of the senior Romanian students had also adopted right-wing political ideologies. The students were mostly Romanian and Ukrainian, with only a sprinkling of Jews among them. As soon as school started, I realized that my non-Jewish classmates would not care to become friendly with me.

The school required almost military discipline. When the teacher entered the classroom, the students jumped to their feet as a sign of respect. They sat down only after being told by the teacher to do so. Talking in class during the lecture was prohibited. Any breach of discipline resulted in ejection from the classroom. All the teachers gave us a heavy load of homework. We had to solve arithmetic problems, write essays, memorize poems by the Romanian poets Eminescu and Cosbuc, remember the years when a succession of kings ruled and what battles they fought. Any student caught without his homework done or otherwise unprepared, was given a failing grade that weighed heavily in the computation of the year-end grade.

Unannounced 15-minute written tests—*extemporals*—were given frequently to the whole class. There were monthly tests and quarterly tests, mid-year tests and year-end tests. There were written tests and oral tests. The grade varied from one to ten, one being the worst grade and ten the best. Four or less was a failing grade. Any student caught cheating during a test got the grade one. This made it almost impossible to get a year-end passing grade, and the student had to repeat the class.

The teachers were always formal, serious, rarely smiled, and never joked. They commanded both respect and fear. The treatment of the boys was harsh, the punishment quick. Each teacher had developed his own method of persuasion to make us study harder. The history teacher, Mr. Teodoreanu, used a wooden ruler to punish the unlucky boy who could not remember the date of some long forgotten battle. He ordered the boy to stretch out his hand, palm up, and hit it hard with his ruler. He then applied the same treatment to the other hand. To make the punishment more painful, he sometimes used a thin, green branch instead of the ruler. While he meted out punishment, he smiled—the smile of a sadist. The teacher for arithmetic, Mr. Bujdei, had developed a more original method. He punished the wrong answer by pinching the boy's sideburns, and pulling up on them until the boy was standing on his tiptoes with tears filling his eyes from pain.

This treatment created latent hostility towards the teachers. Not to give them any satisfaction during the application of punishment, the boys tried to hold back their tears. But it was hard not to cry. My geometry teacher, Mr. Trofim, dispensed punishment by slapping the boy on the back of his head with a heavy hand. If the boy happened to be Jewish, the slapping was accompanied by name calling, such as *pui de jidan,* kike brat, or *jidanash,* little kike. The teacher's mocking remarks aimed at Jewish boys always caused much laughter among my non-Jewish classmates. Such remarks planted the seeds of contempt and aversion in the minds of the non-Jewish children toward the few Jews in their midst. No wonder that during recess, Christian children felt free to punch or kick their Jewish colleagues.

The natural sciences teacher, Mr. Dragan, was an exception among the teachers. He was tall, with an athletic build, and looked quite eccentric in those days. In the highly formal environment of *Aron Pumnul,* he never wore a tie. Mr. Dragan was the only teacher who came to class dressed in slacks, sport shirt, and a short sport jacket. During the warm season he wore sandals, a unique deed at *Aron Pumnul* for both teachers and students. He had traveled over several continents—an unusual feat in those years. He accompanied his zoology lectures about exotic animals with vivid stories about the countries where the animals lived. The lectures were often sprinkled with funny episodes that made us laugh. He never meted out physical punishment, and did not make any derogatory remarks to any of us.

Mr. Dragan was the first teacher whose lectures I enjoyed. He knew how to make them interesting and was friendly with the children. He told us about trees that are over one hundred-meter tall and over one thousand years old that grow in a distant land named California. He described how during World War I home pigeons were used to transmit messages to and from the front, since phone lines were often damaged by exploding bombs and artillery shells. But how did the pigeons find their way over long distances? Were they guided by the geomagnetic field of the earth? Or was it the sun that helped them reach their destination? This, he said, scientists were still investigating. He told us about his scientific work in Yugoslavia on rivers that disappear suddenly in the ground, travel though a maze of invisible underground caves, only to resurface many miles from the place of their disappearance. How he and his teammates dumped tons of paint into the disappearing river and watched the paint reappear in the emerging water, thus proving that it was the same river.

I recall a lesson in which Mr. Dragan discussed the importance of water for life on earth. At some point during the presentation, he mentioned that ice floats on water because it is lighter than water. Then he asked the class, "What would happen if ice were heavier than water?"

One of the boys raised his hand. "The ice would fall to the bottom and we could not ice-skate in the winter on the Prut." The class laughed.

"That is correct," replied the teacher, "but what would be the more important consequences for life on earth?" There was silence in class.

"If ice would fall to the bottom of the river," explained Mr. Dragan, "the river would eventually freeze solid during the long winter months and all the fish in it would die. However, since ice is lighter than water, it stays on top of the river and the fish can swim happily under the ice until spring arrives."

Then he concluded: "What seems to be an insignificant fact of nature—that ice is lighter than water—makes the difference between life and death for millions of fish. Moreover, if ice were heavier than water, all the ice accumulated during the winter could not be melted during the summer months. The sun rays could not reach and melt the ice accumulated at the bottom of seas and oceans. As a result, the whole earth would be a much colder place, and life would have evolved quite differently. You, my boys, would have had to walk wrapped in fur coats and wearing fur gloves summer and winter."

I found such lectures fascinating. They provided not only knowledge in a vivid form, but also stimulated my imagination. Later I realized how important it was to have teachers like Mr. Dragan at this fragile age, teachers who knew how to convey knowledge in an interesting, enjoyable way.

When it came to grading, all teachers were very stingy. As a principle, some of them never gave the top grade, ten. "Ten is for God only," my math teacher used to say. In Mr. Trofim's class, a Jewish boy never saw a grade better than seven, even if he answered the question correctly. A Jew was required to perform twice as good to be considered half as good. If you were Jewish, you had to deserve a ten in order to get a seven.

During the religion classes, given by an Eastern Orthodox priest, the Jewish boys had to leave the classroom. They had to attend the lessons given by Rabbi Wolfsohn. He was a modern rabbi, with a short goatee, large, sad eyes, and a pale complexion. He always wore a dark suit, white shirt, and black tie. In contrast to other teachers, the rabbi was always kind and friendly with us. He kept apart from the other educators, who rarely spoke to him. Sometimes there was no classroom available for the Jewish religion class. In that case the rabbi gathered the Jewish boys at the end of a hallway or in the corner of the spacious schoolyard, had us sit on the ground, and read aloud a chapter from the Bible. The reading was followed by discussion.

I enjoyed the religion class, since it was much more relaxed than other classes. I liked to listen to the beautiful stories from the Bible, especially from Genesis and Exodus. I was impressed by the story of Moses, by the miracles he performed, and by his rescue of the Israelites from slavery. I wished secretly that Moses would live in our midst and bring the plagues of Egypt on some of my teachers. But most of all I enjoyed the easygoing and friendly attitude of the rabbi. There was no military discipline; there was no physical punishment. There were no tests during the school year, and the year-end exam was a breeze. It was the only class in which a Jewish boy at *Aron Pumnul* could get ten at the final exam.

There were times when the discussions with the rabbi became very lively. It so happened that the religion class followed the natural science class taught by Mr. Dragan. In the natural science class we learned that plants and animals had been on earth for millions of years, and that many animal species had appeared and disappeared within that time. We learned about fossils, about evolution, and about Darwin's theory of natural selection. We also learned that man had evolved from the animal kingdom over millions of years.

With the lessons of Mr. Dragan still fresh in our mind, the rabbi read to us a different version about the creation of the world. According to the book of Genesis, God created the world in six days. We were not shy and started to ask questions.

"Which is the true version?" I wanted to know.

The rabbi smiled and did his best to bridge the two very different views of the world. "The Bible often uses figurative descriptions in its narrative. The Hebrews, who lived 3000 years ago, could easier understand such descriptions. Some modern Biblical scholars interpret the word "day" used in the description of Creation as a "period of time." One day in God's creation may be, from man's point of view, a very long time period, and does not necessarily correspond to one day in our calendar."

We could see, however, that the rabbi did not feel comfortable. At the same time, being mischievous, we children enjoyed asking questions that made the rabbi uncomfortable, although we did not always succeed.

One of the kids raised the following question, "Why did God use only one of Adam's ribs to make a woman; why didn't He use some of the other ribs to make several women—a blond, a brunette, a read head—to give Adam a choice."

The rabbi smiled and replied: "God in His infinite wisdom had decided that one woman was enough for Adam." (Later on I understood. Even with one woman, Adam got into trouble.)

Another boy wanted to know why God did not create woman first and man afterwards. The rabbi explained that God created man first because he needed a man's rib to make a woman. (Years later I heard another explanation: God made man before woman because He did not want any advice on how to make man.)

On one occasion, when we discussed the creation of the world as described in the book of Genesis, I raised my hand.

"Rabbi," I wanted to know, "isn't it true that during the day we get the light from the sun, and at night we get it from the moon and from the stars?"

"Of course," replied the rabbi, "every child knows that."

"But you told us, Rabbi, when God created the world, He created light on the first day, whereas the sun, the moon, and the stars He created only on the fourth day. Where did the light on the first day come from?" I wanted to know.

I thought it was a tricky question and gloated at the thought of seeing the rabbi embarrassed. The last thing I expected was a scientific answer. But the rabbi had one ready.

"Scientists," he replied, "have established that the universe was filled with bright, hot gases long before the stars, the sun, and the moon were born. Therefore, science supports the Biblical claim that the existence of light preceded that of the heavenly bodies. Moreover, the order of creation described in the Bible—creation of water and land, followed by the creation of plants, then of animals, and finally of man—is the same order as the one recently established by science."

I liked the answers, and I liked our rabbi. He was a wise and knowledgeable man. He convinced us that science and religion can go together. In later years, however, I learned that throughout history there had been many clashes between science and religion; that ultimately scientists as well as theologians have concluded that it was best to keep the two areas of human endeavor apart.

When I was in the second year at *Aron Pumnul,* my parents hired a young man to teach me Hebrew. His name was Mandel. He made a living teaching the language of the Bible to Jewish children. Poor children he taught without tuition, since he felt that every Jewish child should know the language of Zion. Since I had already learned the alphabet in kindergarten, I now started to learn Hebrew grammar and vocabulary with Mandel, once a week. I made slow progress, since it was a language very different from German and Romanian. Furthermore, I did not have much enthusiasm for the study of this difficult language, and was more interested in playing ball than studying Hebrew. Still, after one year of study, I had acquired some basic knowledge of the language.

In May 1940 I finished the second year of lyceum.

While I was at the lyceum for boys, my sister, Bertha, was in the seventh year at the lyceum for girls. The school she attended had a large number of Jewish pupils. Her wit, sharp mind and sharp tongue made my sister quite popular among her classmates. She made many friends in school, and some of those friendships lasted a lifetime.

As a teenager, my sister joined *Hashomer Hatzaïr* (The Young Guard), a left-of-center Zionist youth organization. My father, who had no political affiliations, was against any leftist movement and opposed such an affiliation. He also felt that it was risky in those times to join such an organization. Bertha, however, was strong-willed and independent. Once she had made up her mind, nobody could change it. She ignored my father's advice and joined Hashomer Hatzaïr, along with several of her classmates.

Bertha attended meetings at Hashomer several times a week, usually in the evening. Encouraged by her, I tagged along, despite misgivings by my parents. They did not like to see me away from home in the evening, at a time when it was dangerous for Jews to be on the street. I, however, was happy to be among other Jewish children with whom I could talk and play, unafraid of being beaten or harassed. I felt comfortable and relaxed in that environment.

The organization was located in the Jewish quarter, where it had rented several rooms in a rundown house. The whitewashed walls were

WHILE THE GODS WERE SILENT

decorated with pictures of Theodor Herzl, Josef Trumpeldor and other Zionist leaders. There were also pictures of sun-tanned *chalutzim* (collective farm workers) from some distant *kibbutz* (collective farm) in Palestine. Over the entrance, posted on the wall, was a large cardboard square with a quote from Herzl: "If you want, it will not be a dream."

The members of the organization were intelligent, energetic, and had a thirst for knowledge. Their leader was Abrasha Gimpelmann, a young man with a sharp mind and vast eclectic knowledge. He had a big, imposing figure, with black curly hair and dark lively eyes, glancing at the world from behind black-rimmed glasses. Abrasha was an idealist, and in his eyes was a glimmer of the lofty dream to which he had dedicated himself. He always spoke in a calm, deep voice, with much self-confidence and authority. It sounded very convincing to his audience.

At one of the meetings I attended, I recall him saying, "Jews are accused of having simultaneous and opposite faults. They are capitalists and communists, they are clannish and assimilated, they are materialists and excessive intellectuals. For the native Gentiles, the Jew is an alien and a vagrant; for the property holders—a beggar; for the poor—an exploiter and a millionaire; for patriots—a man without a country; for all classes—a hated rival." The solution to this situation, Abrasha said, was for the Jews to become a free people in their own land. In that country the Jews would build a new society, marked by democracy, equal rights and social justice. To achieve that goal required a new kind of Jew, strong in body and spirit, able to build the land and defend it. His speech made a deep impression on me.

The lectures and discussions—about Judaism, socialism, capitalism, Darwinism, and other isms—took place in German, since that was the native tongue of all participants. The discussions were often heated and dragged on, until the leader cut them off. Once the discussions were over, singing and dancing began. The youngsters formed a circle, linked arms, and spun into one *horah* after another, while singing at the top of their lungs. I joined them and danced until I was out of breath. That's where I learned to dance *hava naghilla*. No one wanted the evening to end, but it did end when Abrasha cried out, "That's it for tonight!" Everybody left in high spirits.

107

Gradually, these meetings instilled in me a sense of Judaism without religion. It was a kind of Judaism very different from what I had learned from my grandfather. I discovered that one could be strongly attached to Judaism without being religious. I also learned that throughout history Jews had made an enormous contribution to human culture and civilization. I began to realize that I shouldn't be ashamed of being a Jew.

Bertha made friends in the organization with several bright young men and women. Among them were Selma Meerbaum-Eisinger, Yuda Wasser, and Leiser Fischmann. Selma, a sprite of a girl with dark shiny eyes, curly, unmanageable hair, and a scattering of freckles across her shapely nose, already wrote poetry and was one of Bertha's best friends. Yuda, with black intelligent eyes and a curl of black hair dangling over his forehead, tried always to be in the company of my sister. I think he was in love with her. Leiser had a good sense of humor and was attracted by Selma.

Boys and girls from different organizations would often come to our house and discuss politics, philosophy and literature. There was very little small talk. They all loved classical music, and Bertha entertained them by playing Beethoven or Chopin on the piano. When Bertha's friends came to visit, I often stayed with them and listened to their discussions. Having no friends of my own, I took pleasure in being in their company. Although I could not always follow their discussions, I sat in a corner near the sofa and listened. They were six or eight years older than I was, and didn't pay attention to me.

Sometimes it was a motley mixture of young people who gathered around Bertha in our home, and the discussions became quite lively. Among them were communist sympathizers, left-leaning Zionists, right-leaning Zionists, and middle-of-the-road "bourgeois" liberals. When they started a political discussion, they were soon at political loggerheads.

Sammy, a communist sympathizer, espoused the internationalist Marxist view.

"The victory of socialism over oppressive capitalism will bring freedom to all mankind, including the Jews." With a passionate voice he proclaimed that the Jewish masses should join the class struggle against the capitalist oppressors in order to establish an egalitarian socialist society. He dismissed Zionism as a reactionary movement, designed to distract the oppressed Jewish masses from the class struggle against capitalism. I did not understand much of what Sammy said, and did not know what class struggle was (was it like a brawl in a classroom?), but it sounded convincing to me.

That viewpoint, however, did not go down well with Baimy, the nationalist Zionist in the group. He was dedicated to the revival of a Jewish State in Palestine, and for him the Hebrew Bible was an historic legacy.

"Let others struggle for their freedom, while we struggle for our own freedom. Instead of inciting Jew against Jew in a class war that ultimately may lead to a bloody revolution, let's join forces and strive to establish a Jewish State in Palestine. Only in our own land can we be truly free." That also sounded reasonable to me.

Of course, such a statement was totally unacceptable to Sammy. He called it "reactionary, Zionist drivel."

Then Yuda jumped into the fray. He was a left-leaning Zionist, a member of Hashomer Hatzaïr.

"Why not have a mixed marriage between the two ideologies?" he asked. "Why not create a socialist Jewish State in Palestine? This way we could mesh together the positive aspects of Zionism and Marxism." After Yuda spoke, I tended to agree with him, too. But neither Sammy nor Baimy liked that idea.

Finally Harry, the middle-of-the-road "bourgeois" liberal, had his say. He scoffed at the ideas presented so far. For him, democratization of society and integration of Jews into that society was the best solution of all.

"I am first a man, then a Jew," was his catchphrase. "Emancipation, free participation in the life of a modern, democratic society that grants the Jews full human and civil rights, that is the goal Jews should strive to achieve. Ancient Jewish traditions that are in the way of being accepted into mainstream society, such as Chasidic garb, *kashrut*, traditional Sabbath, should be discarded." He claimed that these traditions have become ballast of an age long gone. When he finished speaking, he had convinced me.

Sammy and the Zionists in the group, however, attacked his ideas. Sammy claimed that true democracy could be attained only through class struggle against the domineering capitalist class. The Zionists accused Harry of advocating assimilation of the Jew, of abandoning Judaism and Jewish tradition.

Regardless of how heated the "the battle of ideas" was, nobody changed anybody's mind. Yet friendship withstood disagreement. The debate came to an abrupt end when Mother walked in with tea and a tray of cookies, while Bertha sat down at the piano. The guests promptly forgot the heated debate, and made themselves comfortable on the sofa or on one of the chairs. While they were sipping tea and munching cookies, Bertha played the "Appassionata" sonata by Beethoven or a mazurka by Chopin. The beautiful sounds that emanated from my sister's piano filled every corner of the room. They melted away any disagreement, and the atmosphere in the room became relaxed and friendly.

At the end of such a debate I was confused. To me, everybody had the right idea. I knew, however, that there's got to be a winner. After the visitors left, I asked my sister, "Who was the winner?"

"When you grow up, you will decide for yourself," was Bertha's crisp reply. I did not like having to wait until I grew up to find out who the winner of the debate was, but I had no choice. From those debates, however, I became aware that some questions have many answers, and that it is not always easy to decide which one is the best. Years later I realized that those discussions had helped me develop critical thinking and to formulate my own opinions on different subjects.

The Hashomer organization had a small, but very good library. Bertha borrowed books from the library not just for herself, but also for me. With her guidance, I gradually developed a taste for reading books with a social or moral content. Among them were novels by Erich Kaestner, fables by Eliezer Steinbarg and poems by Nachman Bialik. She kept me away from books describing meaningless violence, although I was tempted to read them. However, I read numerous adventure novels, mostly those by the French writer Jules Verne and the German writer

Karl May. Those novels gave free rein to my imagination. The adventures described by Jules Verne took me into the depths of the oceans and the high reaches of the atmosphere, while those described by Karl May took me into the Arabian Desert and into the tepees of American Indians. It was fascinating reading.

The activity of Hashomer Hatzaïr and of other Zionist organizations came to an abrupt end in June 1940, when North Bukovina was taken over by the Soviets.

It was a hot summer day. There had been no rain for several weeks; the air was heavy and oppressive. After having kicked the ball for half an hour outside the house, I was thirsty, tired, and wet with perspiration. It was already late in the afternoon when I decided to go back home. I was looking forward to having a glass of cold club soda, my preferred drink.

When I entered our apartment, my parents were sitting close to the radio and listening intently. It was a news bulletin from radio Bucharest, and I caught only the last words of the report: "The British and French governments are shocked by this turn of events. We will bring you more news as it becomes available." Since I didn't care much that the British and French governments were shocked, I walked leisurely to the kitchen, got the bottle of club soda and poured a generous amount of its bubbly content into a glass. I had barely finished my drink when I heard Father calling. I ran to him.

"Go buy the evening paper," he said in a commanding tone, while giving me a few coins. "Hurry and try to get the paper before it's sold out. Tonight the papers will sell fast."

"What happened?" I wanted to know.

"I'll tell you when you come back. Now go!"

Holding the coins tightly in my fist, I ran down the stairs. I went quickly to the tobacco store at the street corner. I saw a small crowd of people there, each holding a newspaper and reading it. It made me worry that the papers had been sold out, but I was still able to buy a copy. On the way home, I became curious. What was so interesting in the newspaper that the people read it on the street? On the first page I saw a big, black headline:" Nazi Germany and Soviet Russia Sign Non-

111

aggression Pact." This, apparently, was the captivating news. I didn't understand why there was so much interest in that announcement. In fact, I wasn't sure what a pact was. Still, judging from the reaction of the people around me, I had an uneasy feeling that this latest event would somehow affect our lives.

When I got home, Father grabbed the paper from my hand and started reading. The voice on the radio was commenting about the German-Russian non-aggression pact and its implications. The date was August 23, 1939.

My father read the news item again, and again, and again. He was stunned by the news. I remember him saying, "The Nazis and Bolsheviks signing a pact? That is incredible. It is like mixing fire with water." According to my father, what had been considered totally absurd, impossible, and unthinkable, had become reality overnight.

The news caused consternation in our city. Groups of people gathered in cafés, in parks and on sidewalks, heatedly debating the latest events. Everybody tried to figure out the consequences of this pact between the two dictators, Hitler and Stalin. Every person expressed an opinion. Even Uncle Joseph, who was usually very busy, dropped by to discuss the latest events with my parents. Father predicted that having eliminated the threat from Russia, Hitler would now occupy the port of Danzig and might also invade Poland. Uncle Joseph claimed that Russia had signed the pact to avoid war with Germany.

"It is a shrewd move by Stalin," stated my uncle. "It will avert temporarily the threat of war against Russia, and also give Stalin time to prepare his country for a possible future war. Hitler, on the other hand, has ensured that Russia will not attack Germany, while he pursues his plans in Europe."

My uncle had always shown a canny understanding of political events, and I admired him for that. He also claimed that the pact was against the interests of France and England. "Those countries had signed a pact with Hitler a year earlier at Munich, while refusing to sign a pact with Russia. Now Stalin had paid them back with the same currency," concluded Uncle Joseph.

There were important questions on everybody's mind: what will happen next? Will it be war? How will these events affect our lives? We did not have to wait long for answers.

One week after the signing of the German-Russian pact was announced, on September 1, 1939, Mother sent me to my grandparents to pick up her jacket. She had forgotten it there during our last visit. When I arrived, Aunt Anna opened the door. I could see on her face that she was quite upset.

"What happened?" I inquired.

"Haven't you heard? They have just announced on the radio that the German Army had crossed the border into Poland. There is war." That was the way I learned about the start of what was to become World War II.

The following day, special radio and newspaper bulletins reported that Nazi Germany had invaded Poland from the West and North, and had advanced rapidly deep into the country. Father and I stayed glued to the radio, listening to the frequent news bulletins. The Romanian papers tried to take a neutral stand, but described the valiant struggle of the Polish Army against the superior military forces of the invader. The newsreels at the movies showed Polish cavalry with drawn sabers and flying colors, trying desperately to hold back the advance of German tanks. Needless to say, these attempts failed. The newsreels also showed Warsaw in flames, following the relentless German bombing raids over the city.

It was the first time that I saw, on the screen, a city in flames. I was fascinated by the spectacle of exploding bombs turning whole neighborhoods into infernos, of city blocks being devoured by fire, of tall buildings collapsing and turning into rubble, and of desperate people trying to save some of their belongings from the burning structures. I was fascinated but also distressed by what I saw, realizing that the images on the screen did not originate in a movie studio, but showed real events.

Several days after war broke out in Poland, Britain and France declared war on Germany. Our newspapers reported this news with big headlines. About two-and-a half weeks after the start of the German invasion of Poland, while German tanks rumbled over Poland's countryside and Warsaw was burning, the Romanian radio station interrupted its regular broadcast to bring a special news bulletin. With an excited voice, the speaker announced that the Soviet Union had invaded Poland from the East. The Red Army was advancing along the entire border that used to separate the two countries.

At that point we all knew that Poland was doomed. Radio commentators concluded that the division of Poland was the result of a secret agreement between Germany and Russia. By the end of the month, the newspapers and radio announced that, overwhelmed by superior forces, the Polish resistance had crumbled. Poland had ceased to exist.

Toward the end of September I was awakened by an unusual noise in the middle of the night. Father was also awake. The noise sounded at first like the din caused by a large swarm of bees. Gradually, it became more powerful and turned into a roar. I went to the window and looked outside, but couldn't see anything. It was pitch dark.

"What is that noise?" I asked Father, somewhat frightened by the unfamiliar sound. Since war had broken out in neighboring Poland, we had all became jittery.

"These are airplanes flying in large numbers over the city. Probably Polish airplanes fleeing their country."

Indeed, at the end of September, military and civilian Polish planes flew over our city day and night, leaving behind what used to be Poland. One could hear the constant roar of their engines. Some of the planes landed at the city's airport, while others landed at the Romanian airports of Iassy and Bucharest.

When the Poles realized that they were losing their country, a flood of refugees crossed the border into Romania. The Romanian authorities decided to let the refugees enter the country. Old and young, rich and poor, soldiers and civilians—they all tried to escape from the homeland that was longer their home. They came by car, by horse-drawn carts, by airplane, and on foot. Czernowitz was only 20 miles from the Polish border, and the flood of refugees passed through our city. A constant flow of automobiles and carts loaded with bundles and suitcases, with little children and old women sitting on top, crossed the Dniester over the bridge connecting the two countries. Some Poles, who lived close to the border, crossed on foot.

It was the first time that I saw war refugees, that I saw one of the consequences of war. A column of refugees passed in front of our building, some on foot, some perched on horse-drawn carts. Their faces were somber and tired, their clothing disheveled and covered with dust. Each of them carried a bundle, a suitcase, or a rucksack. Some carried babies who were too tired to cry and had fallen asleep. Many looked bewildered. They stared at the faces of strangers standing on the sidewalk, who stared back at them. They all seemed exhausted. One could hear the rumbling of carts as they rolled over the cobblestones of our street, mingling with the sounds of neighing horses and the clopping of their hoofs, as the column moved slowly toward an uncertain future.

"Why are they leaving their country?" I asked my father, while watching the column pass in front of our house.

"They are fleeing the Germans and Russians who are occupying Poland. These people have no longer a country of their own. They are afraid of being persecuted by the new rulers."

"What does it mean to be persecuted?" I wanted to know.

"It means to be harassed, beaten, arrested. It means not to be allowed to live a peaceful life. It means not to be treated as a decent human being."

I remembered the bullies I had encountered in school, and understood what being persecuted meant.

Many of the Polish refugees who arrived in our city found temporary shelter in the Polish House (*Dom Polski*) that served as a social and cultural center of the city's Polish community. Others found shelter in the Catholic churches that served the Polish population. A soup kitchen was set up for the refugees.

There were many Jews among the refugees. Some of them had escaped from the German occupied territory and fled to the area occupied by the Soviets. From there, they crossed the border into Romania. The local Jewish Community Council made a strenuous effort to assist with food and housing the Jewish refugees who decided to stay in Czernowitz..

Among the refugees were young men and women in their late teens and early twenties, who were members of different Zionist youth organizations. They came from Lemberg, Lodz, Cracow, Lublin and some smaller Galitzian towns. The local Zionist organizations took the youngsters into their care. Old clothes were given to those in need, and housing was provided for them in the Jewish quarter. For the time being, these refugees had found shelter and food.

Several months after Poland was divided between Nazi Germany and the Soviet Union, it was our turn to gain a new master.

5. Our New Masters: the Soviets

Shortly after the fall of Poland, the fires of war spread to Northern Europe. In early December 1939, the Soviet Union attacked little Finland. The newsreels at the movies showed Finnish soldiers in winter camouflage, moving on skis through snow-covered forests, their supplies carried on wooden sleds drawn by reindeer. The pictures also showed Russian dead, frozen stiff.

Father compared that war with the struggle between David and Goliath. "There is no way the Finns can win that war," he said, "but they are putting up a mighty good fight."

I, too, was impressed by their resistance, and hoped that the small Finnish army would not be defeated. In March 1940, however, Goliath defeated David, and the Finns were forced to capitulate.

In the spring of 1940 other Scandinavian countries were engulfed in war. In April the Germans occupied Denmark in several hours, and the next day they landed troops in Norway. The British and French also landed troops in Norway to aid the Norwegian troops fighting the Germans. I closely followed the war bulletins on the radio, with my atlas in front of me. I heard, for the first time, of places like Narvik and Trondheim, where the allies engaged the Germans in bloody battles. I learned the names and location of cities, fjords and islands I had never heard of before.

In the end, Norway fell under the German boot. The Germans installed a puppet government in Norway headed by a man named Quisling—a name that went down in history as synonymous with traitor.

The tidal wave of Nazi conquest engulfed more and more lands of a continent in agony. On May 10, while fighting was still going on at Narvik, the newspapers and radio brought a special news report: Germany had started an offensive on the western front. We heard about the new German military doctrine, later called *Blitzkrieg* (lightning war).

Father and I stayed glued to the radio, listening with trepidation to the flow of news from the front. The announcer reported, "German aircraft bombed Rotterdam to rubble. Tens of thousands of civilians dead."

The BBC radio reports, to which we listened periodically, described the destruction of Rotterdam and the killing of such a large number of civilians as a terrible war atrocity. It was just one in a long string that were to follow. Only four days after the start of the German offensive, Holland capitulated.

The radio and newspapers brought a stream of disturbing news about German victories. Map in hand, full of excitement, I followed the progress of the war. With a red pencil I marked the cities occupied by the Germans. Liege, Louvain, Antwerp, Brussels—in rapid succession they fell into German hands, like fragile bowling pins, felled by a relentless, unstoppable iron ball.

On May 20, the radio announced that a German panzer column had reached the English Channel. The French and British forces in Belgium and Northern France had been cut off from the rest of France.

We were stunned! We did not expect that the Germans would be able to overpower the French and the British forces so easily. Father was very distressed by the news. "The commanders of the allied armies must be incredibly incompetent to suffer defeat after defeat in such rapid succession," he said in a somber voice. "The future of France, and of Europe, looks very bleak."

The mood in our home was also bleak. Father became worried and depressed. The wrinkles on his forehead had deepened. Mother was unusually quiet. Sister, too, had a somber expression on her face.

A few days later we heard about Dunkirk and the evacuation of the encircled British and French troops to Britain.

The floods of Nazism had washed over vast areas of Europe, devastating cities, lives and dreams. The European civilization was being systematically destroyed. A new age of barbarism had engulfed the continent.

In those days I grew up very fast. I lost interest in playing ball, chess or other games, and followed with increasing interest the war. Every report of a new battle, every snippet of news from the front was read and memorized. The animated discussions among adults about the international events helped me understand history in the making. I went to the movies mainly to watch the newsreels and the images of war. The heavy guns firing, the rolling tanks, the aircraft dropping bombs on some distant target, all fascinated me. For a twelve year-old boy, it was very exciting to watch all that action on the screen.

Besides the pictures from the front, however, there were also other images. The newsreels showed cities in flames, with collapsed buildings and destroyed churches. They showed streams of refugees on foot or in horse-drawn carts, trying to escape the fighting and bombing. There were images of roads strewn with burned out trucks and cars, lying next to dead people and horses. These pictures were very disturbing. I began to realize that war was a disastrous and fatal event for many innocent people.

One of the images I saw left a deep impression on me. It showed a column of Belgian refugees who had been strafed by enemy aircraft. There were bodies of dead children spread out on a country road, lying next to their lifeless mothers and fathers. Some of the women had died holding babies in their arms. Overturned children's carriages were resting near the bodies. The image conveyed the feeling of a heart-rending tragedy. I left the movies very disturbed.

When I came home I went directly to my father and told him what I had just seen.

"Father, why are they killing civilians? Is this the way wars are supposed to be fought?"

"Unfortunately, this is the way wars are being fought these days," replied my father somberly. "In the past, wars were fought between two armies facing each other along a front line. The civilian population, behind the front, was not involved in the fighting. Now, with the use of aircraft, the cities and civilians behind the front lines have also become targets of the enemies. The front is everywhere."

"But why do they kill children? What wrong have the children of Belgium done to the Germans?"

"They haven't done anything wrong. This is a very brutal and cruel war, in which many innocent people suffer and die. The Germans seem to be strong adepts of this inhumane form of warfare."

Watching the newsreels and listening to my father, I learned that war meant destruction, suffering and death, as well as injustice and inhumanity. It was an image very different from the one I had when I was a child and played "war" with other children, using wooden toy guns and cardboard sabers.

The German illustrated magazine, *Signal*, available at a nearby tobacco store, showed a different picture of the war. It showed German tanks rolling past columns of French and English prisoners of war, moving in opposite directions. Another picture showed *Stuka* dive-bombers hammering the British and French troops on the beaches of Dunkirk. One picture showed a German pilot standing next to his *Messerschmidt* and smiling. The subtitle said: "He had 'bagged' two enemy planes today." To contrast the racial superiority of the German Army with that of its enemies, the photo showed a group of healthy, blond, blue-eyed German soldiers next to that of a group of shabby-looking, black, French-colonial soldiers taken prisoner. The first picture had the title "Our soldiers," the second picture carried the title "Their soldiers." The magazine, however, didn't show what the racially superior troops had done to the city and people of Rotterdam.

On May 28, the radio announced that Belgium had capitulated. On June 14, the German Army entered Paris. The Nazi flag, with swastika, was hoisted on the Eiffel tower. The newsreel showed German troops marching down the Champs Elysees, while French onlookers were wiping their tears. Three days later France capitulated.

The news from the west caused dread and apprehension in my family. Father and Uncle Joseph, both pessimists, worried that war would engulf us, too. Aunt Tzili, more optimistic, contended that the German—Soviet non-aggression pact would protect us from war. Listening to the discussion, I concluded that we would soon be at war. That thought both excited and frightened me.

Before the war reached us, however, we were caught in the maelstrom of a totally different event.

The summer of 1940 brought drastic changes to our lives. In mid June I was at my grandparents' house, when Grandfather turned on the radio. In those days of turmoil in the world, he turned on the radio several times a day for the latest news. The announcer stated in a somber voice, "The foreign minister of the Soviet Union, Viacheslav Molotov, has delivered an ultimatum to the Romanian government. The ultimatum demands the return of Bessarabia to the Soviet Union, along with Northern Bucovina, including the city of Czernowitz." The Romanian government was given four days to comply with the Soviet request.

When Grandfather had turned off the radio, his face had turned white. There was stunning silence in the room. I realized it was bad news for us.

"What does it mean?" I asked Grandfather with trepidation.

"It means that the Russians are coming. Go home and tell your parents."

I ran home as fast as I could. At home, the radio was on. My parents had already heard the news and were too upset to talk to me. I turned to my sister.

"Sis, what is an ultimatum?"

"It is a request for unconditional compliance with certain demands, submitted by one government to another. The Russian government has submitted such demands to Romania."

Then she explained the meaning of the ultimatum.

"Bessarabia, a province in eastern Romania, used to belong to Czarist Russia until the end of World War I, when it was annexed by Romania. Now the Russians want it back. As compensation for the occupation of Bessarabia by Romania for nearly twenty years, the Soviets also demand Northern Bukovina, including our city Czernowitz."

"But our city has never belonged to Russia," I interjected. "Before the First World War it belonged to Austria."

"That is true. However, since a large part of the population of Northern Bukovina is Ukrainian, the Soviets claim that the area rightfully belongs to the Ukrainian Soviet Republic. The Romanians are given four days to withdraw from these territories."

"What would happen if the Romanian government refused to accept the Russian demands?"

"Then the Russians will use force. They will send in their army to occupy these lands. The Romanian army is not strong enough to oppose them. It's like a big bully demanding the pocket money from a little boy. He has no choice but to give it to him."

We didn't have to wait long to learn the decision of the Romanian government. Several hours later, BBC radio announced that Romania had officially agreed to comply with the Soviet demands. We were getting a new master.

The news about the impending changes left the residents of Czernowitz aghast. They felt like being stricken by a thunderbolt from the blue sky. Panic spread in the Romanian population. The Romanian Army and authorities began to evacuate the area immediately. Unable to carry all the government papers with them, the authorities burned huge piles of documents before leaving the city. An acrid smell spread over the whole region, and the ashes of burned papers floated in the air like dark snowflakes. Government buildings, houses, apartments and stores were abandoned. Before departing, the authorities emptied the city's prisons, leaving behind hundreds of criminals to roam the streets.

The Romanian middle-class and intelligentsia left in a hurry, by any means available: cars, trains, airplanes, and carriages. People with suitcases and bundles mobbed the main train station. On the platform there was total bedlam, with people pushing, shoving, cursing, elbowing each other, trying desperately to climb into a rail car. When the trains left the station, belching black smoke and puffing white steam, they were packed to the limit, with people sitting on the roofs and steps of the railroad carriages. Some even sat on top of the locomotives. All available rail cars—passenger, cattle, freight, and boxcars—were filled with people and their belongings, eager to be taken across the new Romanian border. Nobody knew when the last train would leave, and no one wanted to be left behind. Families paid exorbitant sums of money to carriage owners, to take them and their belongings to their destination.

The Jewish population received the news of an impending change of masters with mixed feelings. The Jews were painfully aware of the anti-Semitic policies of the Romanian government, of the increasing influence of Nazi Germany in the country, and of the hostility that a large segment of the population felt towards Jews. In spite of misgivings about official Soviet atheism, anti-Zionism, and expropriation policies, many Jews—especially the poor and the working class—were happy to exchange Romanian anti-Semitic persecutions for communist egalitarian rule. They welcomed the Soviets as liberators. Some of the well to do Jews, however, apprehensive about the new rulers and their regime, decided to join their Romanian neighbors and fled to Romania. Most of Ukrainians and Germans, as well as the workers and peasants of different nationalities, decided to stay.

My parents were worried. Sitting around the kitchen table, we discussed the upcoming changes. What should we do? Should we leave or should we stay? If we decide to leave, where should we go? We had all experienced Romanian anti-Semitism and my parents knew that we were not welcome in Romania. Moreover, we did not have the financial means to start life in a new, hostile environment. The idea of joining our relatives in Canada or emigrating to another country was mentioned, but promptly discarded. At that time, no country was willing to accept Jewish immigrants. Although Father had strong misgivings about the Soviet regime, in the end my parents decided to stay.

On June 28, 1940, four days after the ultimatum was announced, the Red Army entered our city.

It was a warm, sunny day. I was standing with my mother on the sidewalk near the Ringplatz, in the center of the city. The streets were packed with people awaiting the arrival of Soviet troops. Some talked with excitement to those standing next to them. Others stood in silence, apprehension showing on their faces. I waited with a mixture of keen curiosity and vague unease.

Then the Soviet troops arrived. First came a heavy tank, rumbling down the cobblestone-paved street. A five-pointed red star was painted on its turret. The hatch was closed and its gun pointed menacingly forward. Its metallic tracks clattered and left white streaks behind on the street's cobblestones. A small cloud of gray, smelly exhaust remained in its wake. As the tank approached us, I felt the ground vibrating under my feet; the earth shook. It was the first time I saw a tank up-close. Quite impressive. Observing the steel behemoth rolling down on the cobblestones just a few meters in front of you, feeling the earth trembling under your feet, I knew it meant business. It was not the same as seeing a tank in the movies.

Several people threw flowers at the tank and waved. At some distance, a second tank came rolling down. A Soviet officer was peering out through the open hatch, smiling and waving at the people on the sidewalk. A group of local hotheads, who had climbed on that tank, were waving a red flag and screaming communist slogans: "Long live the Soviet Union! Long live Comrade Stalin!"

Then came a column of tanks and artillery. The ground trembled as the heavy war machines rolled by. A military unit that marched in tight formation followed the column. It was an airborne unit that had landed at the city's airport. The soldiers were dressed in dark-brown leather, marched in lock step, and were quite impressive in their uniforms and demeanor. They all looked alike, as if carved from the same healthy, strong material. More Soviet troops arrived later, in trucks. Many had flowers strewn on their hoods—a gift from enthusiastic supporters. Some of the people cheered the arriving troops, while others were subdued and watched in silence. Red banners suddenly appeared in the crowd, on several buildings, and on top of the city's monuments. Excitement was in the air, mixed with the smell of tank and truck exhaust.

In the temporary vacuum created by the flight of the Romanian authorities, a number of shady elements, Jews among them, moved in. They were mostly the dregs of society, and proclaimed themselves the "Avant-guard of the Revolution." Convicts released by the Romanian authorities, laborers, and communist supporters were also in that crowd. In the name of "the people," they took over the City Hall, the post office, and other government offices. They began to behave like new masters, giving orders and threatening those they considered "exploiters." Some people were roughed up on the street.

The rule of these elements, however, was short lived. Soviet civil administrators, who arrived in the wake of the military, quickly replaced the self-proclaimed masters. The local communists became advisers, helpers, and informers to the new administrators.

In those early days of the Russian takeover, some well-to-do idealists genuinely thought that life would become much better. The new rulers impressed my sister and me. We met Jewish Red Army officers, who chatted with us in Yiddish. Their friendliness and seeming modesty was a pleasant surprise. It was in glaring contrast with the arrogance and haughtiness of the Romanian officers. We were pleased to learn of the presence of Soviet Jews in high administrative positions—a fact unimaginable in the Romanian administration. The visit by an array of Yiddish writers from the Soviet Union, the opening of state-sponsored Yiddish schools and theaters—all that made a deep impression on my sister and me.

Father, however, remained skeptical.

"It is too early to tell what life will be like under the new rulers. Let's wait and see what happens in the next weeks and months," he mused. He had a premonition that life would not be as rosy as it seemed at that moment.

After the new administration settled in, an intensive propaganda campaign spread throughout the city. Loudspeakers, blaring patriotic music from radio Moscow, were installed on utility poles at major street intersections. Soviet song-and-dance ensembles arrived from Kiev and performed in the open air, free of charge. Screens were set up in public squares and Soviet movies were shown, also without charge.

Never before have I had so much fun and free entertainment. On some days I went to see Russian or Ukrainian folk dance ensembles perform on newly mounted stages in parks and public squares. It was the first time I saw a professional dance ensemble performing on stage. I was deeply impressed by the acrobatic skills of the male dancers, the gracious movements of the female dancers, and the beauty of their colorful national costumes. Other days I went to see, and listen, to an orchestra playing Russian folk songs. In the evening I went to the movies. They were in Russian and I couldn't understand much; still, I enjoyed watching them, since they were free. In the first few weeks under the new rulers, I saw more shows and movies than I had seen in all my previous years.

The Soviet civilians that came to Czernowitz with the new administration described life in the Soviet Union in the rosiest colors: it was a happy, beautiful life, without poverty, oppression, or exploitation. The Soviet people lived in a society of plenty, where the State, under the wise leadership of the party and of comrade Stalin, ensured the happiness of its entire population. The new Russian and Ukrainian newspapers, such as the *Radiyanska Bukovina* that replaced the old papers, were full of praise for the Soviet regime. Life was beautiful in the land of the Soviets!

It did not take long, however, before the stark reality began to cut though the rosy fog of propaganda. While claiming that everything was readily available in the Soviet Union, the newly arrived people bought all they could find in the initially well stocked stores of our city. Shoes, clothing, appliances, linen, furniture, draperies and writing paper disappeared in the first few weeks of Soviet rule. Even toilet paper became a rarity. More and more stores began to display empty shelves, since store owners were unable to replenish the sold merchandise.

Many things that were taken for granted by the local population appeared to be a novelty to the Soviets. In the newly occupied territories, the Soviets discovered that most people were better dressed than they were, lived in more comfortable and better furnished apartments, and seemed to have a better life than they expected.

Sending a letter became a problem. There was an acute shortage of writing paper, and envelopes were nonexistent. To be able to write and send a letter, you had to be creative. You wrote the letter on one side of a torn-out page from a school notebook, while the other side of the page was left blank. You then folded the sheet into a triangle, with the blank side left outside. On that side you wrote the address. You affixed a stamp and this triangular missive was sent away. Often it took weeks before the letter reached its destination.

The new rulers brought drastic changes to our city and our life. The Soviet red flag replaced the Romanian national flag on public buildings. The "International" replaced the Romanian national anthem. The Romanian name of the city, Cernauti, was changed to Chernovitsy (the Russian name) and Chernivtsi (the Ukrainian name). The streets were given Russian and Ukrainian names. Russian became the official language, and the ruble became the new currency. The laws and the bureaucracies changed, the national holidays changed, and even the subjects taught in school changed. A plaster statue of Lenin replaced the bronze statue of the Romanian soldier on the Ringplatz. The new masters laid down their own rules regarding what could or could not be done, said, printed, and—later, during the war—even listened to on the radio. The local population had to learn quickly to adapt and cope with these numerous changes.

The composition of the city's population also changed. The new administration brought in a significant number of people from its own population, Ukrainians and Russians. These "newcomers" occupied key administrative, military, and judicial positions, and looked often with suspicion on the *mestnye,* the locals. That attitude, in turn, did not gain them much respect from the local population. The locals, displaying their usual sarcasm, began poking fun or making derogatory remarks behind the newcomers' backs.

The Russians we saw on the street were poorly dressed. The men wore ill-fitting, gray or dark suits, made of very cheap fabric. The locals did not hesitate to comment to each other about their masters' outfits. "Look at his cheap, wrinkled jacket. Looks like he slept in it," was one frequent remark. Not very flattering.

All men wore *shapki,* caps, since wearing a hat was considered a "bourgeois" custom. Some men were dressed in *rubashki,* shirts worn above the pants and held around the waist by a leather belt. Many wore tall leather boots.

The women were dressed in long, flowery dresses of cheap material that gave the impression of being the wrong size. "Look at that shapeless dress she is wearing," was a frequent ironic remark made by the locals. The women were neither pretty nor ugly—the same standard Soviet mass-production. Many of them had rough proletarian hands, with closely clipped fingernails. They tried to make themselves attractive by putting on some lipstick and by curling their hair. These clumsy attempts at "beautification," however, did not give their hard, unsmiling faces any feminine charm, and led to more derogatory comments by the local population.

The Russians, in turn, were not used to some of our clothing, and made ironic remarks of their own. When I walked on the street in short pants, I noticed that the Russians—especially the women—looked at my pants and giggled to each other. Evidently, boys did not wear shorts in the Soviet Union.

For winter, however, the Russians were better equipped than we were. Both men and women wore quilted, gray jackets, rabbit-fur gloves, and *valenki,* felt snow-boots. Men who had to work outdoors wore quilted, gray pants. On their heads men wore fur *ushanki,* caps with earflaps, while women wore round fur hats or shawls. These outfits were not elegant, but were very practical during the harsh winter.

The Russian men were heavy smokers. They smoked *makhorka,* a rough tobacco that they rolled into thick, shaggy cigarettes using pieces of newspaper. The printer's ink was supposed to contribute to the taste. It was said that the most widespread use of the newspaper *Pravda* was not to read it, but to turn it into cigarette paper.

The attitude of the newly arrived Soviets towards the *mestnye* was a mixture of superiority and hidden envy. Superiority for being our new masters to whom we had to submit without complaints. Envy for the realization that most locals had more and better material goods than they had. It was their first exposure to a capitalist society, and what they saw was very different from what they had been taught. In turn, many of the local revolutionary visionaries, who in the past had been brutally persecuted by the Romanian police, gradually cooled their ideological ardor when faced with the new reality. What the police beatings could not bring about, the Soviet regime was able to accomplish.

There were numerous fully furnished apartments abandoned by those who had fled the city. In the first weeks of occupation, the Soviet authorities sealed the vacant suites and later assigned them to Soviet officers. In our building there were two such apartments: one belonged to the landlord, and the other to a university professor. Both had fled across the border, taking only a few suitcases with them. The Soviets put the building's janitor in charge to show the vacant apartments to suitable tenants.

Shortly after the arrival of the new masters, a major came to inspect these vacant places. The janitor unlocked the doors of the abandoned suites to show them to the officer. I decided to tag along. When the major entered the professor's apartment, he stopped for a moment and looked around. An expression of surprise and amazement was on his face. It was obvious that never before had he seen such furniture, crystals, or carpets.

The officer stopped in front of a picture hanging on one of the walls between two windows. It showed Napoleon Bonaparte on horseback during his retreat from Russia, followed by French soldiers plowing and floundering through the deep snow. The officer recognized Napoleon. He turned to the doorkeeper.

"*Nash Kutuzov pobedil Napoleona!*" he said with a grin on his face. The janitor translated to me what the officer had said, "Our Kutuzov defeated Napoleon!" He was referring to Napoleon's defeat in 1812 by the Russian Army under the command of General Kutuzov. As I learned in time, it was a victory every Russian knew about. Only a year and a half later, the image of the defeated Napoleon near Moscow would hound Hitler and the German troops struggling in the snow in front of that same city.

The major continued to inspect the apartment. What attracted most of his attention was not the fine furniture or the thick carpets on the floor. It was the professor's writing desk. On top of it sat an old Remington typewriter, and next to it was a stack of writing paper. The officer approached the table and appeared fascinated. At first I was puzzled. What could he find so attractive at that table? Was it the Remington? Then I realized—it was not the typewriter that attracted him, nor was it the elegantly carved mahogany table. It was the stack of glossy writing paper. He kept touching it, feeling it between his fingers, and looking at it again and again. He picked up a sheet and held it to the light, wondering about the watermark impressed on it. It was obvious that never before had he seen such good-quality writing paper. When he left, he told the janitor that he would take the professor's apartment. Was it the fine furniture and soft carpets that attracted him? Was it the stock of fine writing paper that had caught his attention? Whatever the reason, I think the stack of glossy paper had played a role in his decision. The officer, later joined by his wife, became our new neighbor.

Once in place, the Soviet administration went immediately to work. Banks, factories, larger enterprises, and apartment buildings were nationalized, without any compensation to the owners. They became the property of "the people." New identification papers, called internal passports, were given to the locals. The Soviets issued two types of passports. One was marked with the number 39, and was given to former so-called "capitalist exploiters," such as landowners, factory owners, bankers, and large business owners. This was considered a "bad passport." The other was marked with the number 40, and was given to workers, engineers, teachers, doctors and clerks. That was considered a "good passport." The holder of a "bad passport" had difficulties finding a job, and could be evicted easily from his house or apartment. Later on, people with these passports were the first to be marked for deportation to labor camps.

Small shop and business owners, who had escaped nationalization, were hit with exorbitant taxes. Those complaining were blacklisted, and later deported.

Soon, even the basic necessities of life became scarce. People stood in line for hours to buy a pound of sugar, a few ounces of butter, or a bottle of cooking oil. Good-quality clothes and shoes became unavailable. When the need arose, my sister spent days walking from one store to another, trying to find a semi-decent pair of shoes.

The products manufactured in Russia were of the worst possible quality: fabrics sold in stores were like rags, clothing never fit, shoes were made of hard leather that caused blisters, writing paper behaved more like blotting paper. The former white bars of soap were replaced by gritty, dark-brown soap that rasped the skin like sandpaper. When toilet paper became scarce, many started using the newspaper, *Pravda*. (The use of the *Pravda* for that purpose left black printer ink on people's behinds and, subsequently, ended up on people's underwear.)

Among the first Russian words I learned were *stoyte v otchered* (stay in the queue). I found out that to obtain necessary goods—any kind of goods— one had to stay in line. Only merchandise nobody needed or wanted because of inferior quality was available without queues.

It was summer, school hadn't started yet, and I spent several hours every day in some line. I stood in one line for cooking oil, in another for apples, and yet another for toilet paper. Mother and sister stood in other lines. The lines disappeared only when the products were sold out. Getting used to queuing proved helpful later, during the war years, when the lines were much longer and the supply of goods much shorter.

The party and government bosses had special privileges. They had access to special stores stocked with gourmet food and high-quality clothes, shoes, watches, and other goods not available to the public at large. They didn't have to wait in line. That fact was widely known, and was another reason the average citizen felt resentment towards the regime.

While the lines at food stores grew longer and more stores displayed empty shelves and bare windows, people began to make critical remarks in public about the scarcity of food and goods. Jokes started to circulate about the "abundance" of goods provided by the state. But soon the people discovered that a new element, almost unknown in the past, had appeared in their midst—the informer.

People found out that a careless remark about shortages or empty stores made to a neighbor, an acquaintance, or while waiting in a food line, could lead to arrest and loss of job. Political jokes were no laughing matter under the Soviets. A funny remark about Stalin's mustache could lead to arrest and imprisonment. A "wagging tongue" often did lead to prison. The authorities had planted informers everywhere: in the workplace, on the street, in the queues at the food stores and in the coffeehouses. Where you least expected them, when you least expected them, they were there. It was said, only half in jest, that whenever three people got together, one of them was likely to be an informer.

My father lectured me in a stern voice, "Never make in public any joke or critical remark about the Soviet system, about its leaders, or about the shortage of food and goods."

I understood, and didn't have to be told twice. I learned quickly to watch my tongue.

The informers came from all walks of life. Some were idealists, who informed out of dedication to the regime. Others were opportunists, seeing informing as a way to gain favors with the authorities. Some did it for money, while others became informers as a result of coercion by the authorities. Many members of what used to be the middle-class or upper middle-class were forced into becoming informers through threats or blackmail. Friend informed on friend, neighbor on neighbor, student on student. It was difficult to carry on a free-flowing conversation when there was always the possibility that those who were listening might report you for making the wrong remark, for saying the wrong joke. Even within the same family, parents decided to avoid political discussions in the presence of their children, afraid that the youngsters, unaware of the consequences, might inform on them in school.

Since no documents or witnesses were required to prove the "anti-Soviet" attitude of the accused, it was a good time to settle old grievances or to exact revenge. Anyone who didn't like somebody or had a grudge, could inform on that person. It was no secret that the janitors of apartment buildings were on the payroll of the NKVD, the secret police. They reported regularly about the tenants' activities, remarks, and visitors. The fate of whole families was often decided by the janitor's report. He became the master of the building and of its tenants.

Of the local Jewish population, few intellectuals became party members. Most of them had middle-class background and therefore were "unfit" for party membership. But petty craftsmen and workers—tailors, cobblers, carpenters, plumbers—with ambitious dreams of power and of flawless social origin, were accepted in the party and given positions in the local administration. To prove their allegiance to the Soviet regime, many of them excelled in their zeal to carry out the assignments of the new masters—any sort of assignment. They turned in their former employers, informed on neighbors, and betrayed friends.

There is widespread belief that Jews tend to protect and help each other, regardless of circumstances. Under the Soviet regime, however, Jews in positions of power, dealing with other Jews, bent over backward to show their "objectivity" and loyalty to the system. They did not want to be accused of protectionism toward their fellow Jews. They wanted to show class solidarity, not national solidarity. As a result, many of the well to do Jews of the city were denounced to the NKVD by "loyal" Jewish party members and by Jewish informers. Under the Stalinist regime, "solidarity" among Jews turned out to be a myth.

The "locals" had to adapt quickly to the new system. Under dictatorship—a totally new experience for us—people learned to display unquestionable obedience to the new masters, while at the same time trying to maintain their integrity and decency. They realized that under the new rulers they had to keep their thoughts to themselves, and avoid remarks in public that could be perceived as "anti-Soviet." Telling the truth was dangerous. The new rulers lied to the local people by pretending that life in the Soviet society was beautiful, while the local people lied to the new rulers by pretending that they believed them. Everybody lied. People used words not to express their thoughts and feelings, but rather to hide them. At political meetings the participants made statements they knew the party wanted to hear, that contrasted with their true feelings and opinions. They energetically applauded the speeches of key party members, although they knew that they were told lies and propaganda. Hypocrisy became an essential requirement for life in Soviet society.

As an attorney, my father could not practice his profession under the Soviets. Obviously, the Soviet system of law was completely different from the one he knew and had practiced. Almost overnight he was deprived of his livelihood. Moreover, he was looked upon with suspicion by the authorities, since they associated attorneys with the capitalist class.

To earn a living for himself and for his family, Father tried selling some of our own belongings, and later those of friends and neighbors. Mother remarked, only semi-jokingly, that he was atoning for all those years he practiced law, defending crooks and other unsavory characters. Father also started trading in dry tobacco leaves. I learned that the peasants were eager to buy this foliage, because it was cheaper than the cigarettes in the store.

There was a public square in the city, the Austriaplatz, where people gathered once a week, usually on Sundays, to sell their merchandise. They sold clothes, house wares, and trinkets. Since the locals traded mostly their own belongings, the authorities tolerated this kind of business. I helped Father pack the old clothes, shoes, kitchenware, and tobacco leaves. Then we carried them to the market, and put them on newspapers spread out on the asphalt. Although he worked hard and spent many hours with his new activity buying and selling the thin, brittle tobacco leaves, Father was unable to earn enough to support the family. His knowledge of the intricacies of Roman law and his ability to recite, in Latin, long passages from Virgil's *Aeneid* did not help in convincing a peasant to buy a used pair of pants, or a laborer to purchase some old shoes. His university studies had not imbued him with any skill useful in haggling with his customers over the price of a few tobacco leaves. Father felt that he was not a good businessman; that he didn't have luck in business. Once, I heard him say, "If I would enter the funeral business, people would stop dying."

Mother had to find a job.

She started by working in a bookbinder cooperative. Then she worked in a salami factory. The pay was better, but the work harder. She had to stand on her feet the whole day on a cold cement floor, in a damp and smelly environment. The job, however, had one great advantage: occasionally she could bring home a whole salami, without having to wait in line for hours.

Mother came home often late. The party organized political meetings after work, which Mother and all other employees had to attend. At these meetings, the employees had to listen to long speeches praising the achievements of the Soviet Union, and to exhortations to work harder, in order to accomplish the assigned task. Such meetings took place once or twice a week. Although attendance was "voluntary," not attending these meetings would have had unpleasant repercussions.

In the fall I began attending school. Teaching was done in Russian or Ukrainian. The Soviets had also set up two ten-grade Yiddish schools, where all the subjects were taught in Yiddish. Parents could send their children to the school of their choice. My parents decided to send me to the Yiddish school No. 26. Since I had completed the first two years of lyceum under the Romanian rulers, in the fall of 1940 I was admitted into the seventh grade of the Soviet teaching system.

School under the Soviets was an experience very different from the one I had in the past. Physical punishment by the teacher was prohibited.

Jewish youngsters were no longer harassed, beaten or taunted as *jidani*, kikes, by their classmates. Life was quite cheerful for us schoolboys.

All schoolchildren of my age had to join the "Pioneers," the Soviet youth organization, while the older teenagers joined the "Komsomol." We had to wear our pioneer uniform in school: white shirts with a red scarf around the neck, navy-blue pants, white socks, and black shoes. I was proud of my uniform, and Mother made sure that it was clean and ironed every day. As pioneers we had to make a formal commitment, in front of the entire class, to study diligently, and to dedicate all our energy to the good of our great Soviet country.

We learned many patriotic songs in both Russian and Yiddish. Most of the Russian songs praised the beauty of the Soviet land and the freedom enjoyed by its people. One of the Yiddish songs told about the happy life in Birobidzhan, a Jewish National Autonomous Region in the Far East. It was supposed to be settled by Soviet Jews and become a communist Jewish land. The project ended in failure and was abandoned. Only a small group of Jewish farmers settled in that area. The song survived.

In school I learned that besides Russians, there were Ukrainians, Armenians, Georgians, Kazachs, Tadgiks, Turkmens, and a host of other nationalities in the Soviet Union. We were taught that Russians had made most modern inventions, both before and after the revolution: Popov invented the radio (Marconi's name was never mentioned), Michurin invented modern horticulture, and Lysenko laid the foundation of modern biology. Many theories accepted in the West, such as Einstein's relativity theory or Freud's psychoanalytical theories, were dismissed as "bourgeois decadence" (at that time I didn't know what those theories were, except that they were "decadent").

Soviet schools, however, were more than places to dispense knowledge. In addition to literature (Russian, Ukrainian, and Yiddish), math, sciences, history, geography, and other subjects, we were taught a new theology. We were told that God does not exist and that religion is just a capitalist tool used to oppress the working class. The worship of God was replaced by the worship of the idols of the new religion, of Marxism-Leninism: Marx, Engels, Lenin and Stalin. Our history teacher, a dedicated communist, preached the new gospel. She told us that the great accomplishments of the Soviet Union were due to the wise leadership of the Father of all children and of all working people, the genial Joseph Stalin. We were brought up to feel admiration for the Soviet motherland, for the Soviet regime, and for the communist party. We were taught to be selfless, and to be loyal to our great country and to its supreme leader.

School shaped us into the mold of exemplary Soviet youngsters. We were taught to see the world in black and white: rich and poor, exploiters and exploited, capitalists and the working class, warmongering imperialists and peace-loving socialist nations. We learned about the imperialist western enemies whom we may have to fight some day. We were taught to hate the "enemies of the working people," and to inform on them. There was a continuous assault on our minds, on our brains. I felt as if a funnel had been stuck into my head through which the thoughts of the great leader and of the party were poured incessantly, to drive out any heretical ideas I might have in my young mind.

One of the stories in my Russian textbook was that of Pavlik Morozov. He was a farm boy who denounced his father for hiding grain from the Soviet authorities, grain that he had grown on his own farm. The father was arrested and shot. Other farmers in the community became enraged by the boy's behavior and killed him. He became a Soviet hero. His story was told to every child in the Soviet Union and given as an example of true patriotism. The implication was that a child who sees something illegal done even by his own parents should inform the authorities. That was true patriotism! The interests of the State should be above filial affection. This kind of morality was instilled into our minds at an early age.

I don't know how many children in my class accepted the new morality, because I knew not to discuss such a subject. But the upbringing given to me by my parents made me question the morality I was exposed to in school. When I told my sister the story about Pavlik Morozov and asked what her opinion was on this subject, she replied somewhat philosophically, "The welfare of the state is important, but so is the welfare of the parents." Even she was careful what she said to me, since she did not know to what extent I had been "brainwashed." Still, the values I had been taught at home reinforced my doubts about the new morality. In school, however, I kept those doubts to myself.

In addition to the Russian and Ukrainian theater, there was a Yiddish theater in Czernowitz. Plays by Shalom Aleichem, Itzhak Peretz, and other classics of the Yiddish literature were performed in Yiddish, besides the Russian classics and Soviet propaganda plays. Many of the actors, who had performed in the Yiddish theater during the Romanian rule, performed now under the Soviets. We also had periodic visits from the Yiddish theater of Kiev that had excellent actors and gave high-quality performances. Tickets were very cheap, and I became a frequent attendant at those performances. When the theater didn't sell many tickets, children could enter free to fill some of the empty seats. Never before and never since had I seen so many plays in such a short time. The repeated exposure to good acting, dancing, and singing, gradually developed in me an interest for theater and the performing arts. That interest grew in time and I became an enthusiastic devotee of this form of art. In later years, as an adolescent, I myself performed on stage.

Bertha, who had finished the lyceum under the Romanians, applied for and was admitted to a Russian teaching institute, which prepared high school teachers in mathematics and in the sciences. The thorough knowledge she had acquired in the lyceum in these subjects proved to be very useful. It made her studies at the institute much easier. However, attending classes and taking tests in a language she neither spoke nor understood properly required a considerable effort. The Russian-German dictionary became the most frequently used book in the house.

Early in 1941, before I reached the age of thirteen, my parents started to prepare me for my Bar Mitzvah. Under the Soviets this was a tricky affair, due to the atheistic orientation of the Communist regime. Since the school adopted the official anti-religious position, I didn't tell anybody in school about this event. I tried to keep it secret. Even within my own family I received conflicting input—from my sister and from my grandfather—and was left to sort it out on my own. My sister, who was the most outspoken non-believer in our family, made some dismissive, secularist remarks about this religious custom. "The Bar Mitzvah ritual evolved from the ancient rites of initiation for young men of puberty age in primitive tribes. It is probably of pagan origin," she informed me. She also said that Christians have a similar ritual, called Confirmation.

My grandfather, however, told me a different story. "The Bar Mitzvah is an important Jewish ritual, a moral and religious milestone that marks the transition of a Jewish boy to that of a responsible adult. It grants the new adult the privilege to be called to the reading of the Torah in *shul* before the entire congregation, and to become part of a *minyan.*"

Grandfather promised to help me get ready for this event. When I asked him if there is proof of God's existence, he replied with a quote from second century Rabbi Akiva:

"As a house implies a builder, a dress a weaver, a door a carpenter, so the world proclaims God as its Creator." That view was as different from the Marxist view of God taught in school, as day is from night.

Of course, these contradictory views about my Bar Mitzvah and about God left me bewildered. Still, I decided to go ahead with this Jewish ritual, to please my parents and my grandparents. I also wanted to spite my sister. Her dismissive attitude toward that important event in my life irritated me. Another incentive to have Bar Mitzvah was the discovery that this is an occasion to receive some nice gifts.

Two months before the ceremony, Grandfather began preparing me for the big event. He practiced with me that portion of the Torah I was supposed to read before the congregation in the synagogue. The Hebrew lessons I had taken in previous years proved to be helpful, and after some practice I was able to read the Hebrew text fluently. Grandfather also taught me how to put on *tefillin,* the small leather case holding slips inscribed with scripture passages. He told me that observant Jews put on *tefillin* on their forehead and left arm every morning before reciting the Morning Prayer. For my Bar Mitzvah, Grandfather gave me the *tefillin* and a *tallit* as a gift.

At that time I lived in two different worlds. During the week, when I went to school, I was exposed to the Marxist, atheistic world view. I was taught that God is a figment of human imagination; that according to Karl Marx religion is an opiate used by the capitalist class to keep the working people oppressed, to have them resigned to their fate. On weekends, however, when I visited my grandfather, he and I read portions of the Torah that described God's deeds, and he taught me how to pray to Him.

All that was quite confusing for a thirteen-year-old boy. There was a split in my mind that I felt very disturbing. I had to straddle two very different teachings that collided with each other, contradicted each other, were incompatible with each other. I tried to separate the two opposing views the best I could. I did my homework and answered the teacher's questions in school as if God and religion didn't exist. I listened to Grandfather's readings from the Torah and his interpretation of its passages as if the atheistic world view did not exist.

Being exposed to contradictory influences also had a positive effect. From that experience I learned, in later years, to look with a critical eye at the different ideas, opinions and ideologies to which I was exposed. I did not accept every statement I read or heard, regardless of its source.

The Bar Mitzvah ceremony took place in my grandfather's *shul*, across from the apartment where he and Grandmother lived. The *shul* was a large room with the Ark, the Eternal Light and a seven-branched candelabrum at the eastern wall. There was a small platform in front of the Ark and a larger podium about fifteen feet from the Ark, closer to the center of the *shul*. In the middle of the larger podium was an elevated table, where the Torah scrolls were unrolled and read. The Ark and the elevated table were covered with red velvet. The cloth covering the Ark had gilded embroideries. The worshipers sat behind the large podium. There were rows of wooden benches, each set before wooden stands with sloping tops, on which the people placed their prayer books. The benches filled the space all the way to the rear wall of the room, the wall opposite the Ark. The women's section was on a balcony in the back of the room, overlooking the main area. In the middle of the synagogue ran a narrow isle that ended at the large podium. The walls and ceiling were painted in white. Several naked light bulbs hung from the ceiling.

Besides my immediate family, only a handful of old "regulars" of the *shul* were present. Younger people avoided being seen in a synagogue. The ceremony was brief and simple. With Father and Grandfather standing next to me on the larger podium, each wrapped in a prayer shawl,

I read in Hebrew from the Scroll of the Torah before the entire congregation. Afterwards, my father recited aloud the required ancient formula. The old rabbi, with watery eyes and a long, white beard, delivered a short speech in a halting voice and gave me his blessings.

"Now," he said, "since you have joined the community of adult men, you are responsible for your conduct." He smiled at me.

At the end of the ceremony, everybody shook my hand and congratulated me. Mother served *schnapps* in shot glasses and a slice of honey cake to each guest. She had been fortunate to find all the ingredients necessary to bake a good honey cake. After they had their shot of *schnapps* and slice of cake, the people left. Afraid of the ever-present informers, people avoided any kind of conversation at the end of the service.

After the Bar Mitzvah I found out that my world had not changed much. In spite of my "coming of age" and the rabbi's solemn statement that now I belonged to the community of men, I could not find any benefit in this change of status. I still had to do my school homework, and my parents still kept telling me what I should or should not do. I could not play ball in my mother's kitchen. I was scolded, as in the past, when I broke a light bulb trying to catch a pesky fly, or when I came home from school with messy clothes and ink-stained fingers. Moreover, I had to get up early in the morning, put on *tefillin* and say the Morning Prayer before going to school. Still, in the presence of other children, I felt cocky that I had become an "adult," and looked with an air of superiority on those who were younger.

Three months after my Bar Mitzvah, as a result of the atheistic influence at school and the lack of encouragement at home, I no longer put on *tefillin* in the morning and stopped saying the Morning Prayer. I decided, however, not to share that information with my grandfather. He would have been very disappointed.

I think that I was about thirteen years old when my hormones started to announce their presence with increasing urgency. Before that happened, I already knew that boys are different from girls: they dressed differently, the length of their hair was different, and their games were different. Girls liked to play with dolls, while boys preferred to play soldiers and kick the ball. Since boys and girls had different interests, I did not pay much attention to girls.

With the awakening of my hormones, things started to change. Although I did not quite understand the changes that were taking place in my body, I began to look at girls differently. The Soviet schools were coed and there were many girls in my class. During class breaks boys and girls usually gathered in separate groups. The girls used to giggle a lot, throw furtive glances at us, whispered at each other, and than burst into laughter. I never found out why they were laughing.

From some of the more precocious boys in my class, I learned about the bodily differences between boys and girls, about our sex organs, about sex. All that information was conveyed in a conspiratorial way, with meaningful glances and smiles that implied that they knew much more about this subject than they let me know. I found out about the shameful part of my body, and discovered what effect shameful thoughts had on my shameful part: they gave me an erection. I became aware that my shameful part was not always easy to control.

I started to pay more attention to girls. Kissing a girl on her lips suddenly seemed very appealing. The bare legs and the two bumps that the better-developed girls had on their chests attracted my curiosity. I quickly learned that a boy was not supposed to touch those areas— although nobody gave me a good reason why not to do it. I was wondering what really was the look and feel of those shapely forms that protruded under a girl's blouse and that ignited my imagination.

In the presence of girls, I became shy and felt uncomfortable. These were new feelings toward the opposite sex. These feelings were alien, but pleasant. Very pleasant. They gave a new dimension to my inner life. Still, when a girl looked into my eyes, I evaded her glance. While I had no close contact with girls and avoided their company, my fantasies about them grew ever more florid. At night, alone in my bed, in my flights of fancy I walked hand in hand with beautiful, voluptuous girls. Eventually we embraced each other, ignoring the rest of the world. I tried to imagine what it would feel like to press my body to that of a girl. In my imagination, I always showed more courage than in real life. Sometimes, I imagined myself having supernatural powers, like a modern-day

Superman, fighting some evil doer and being admired by the girls.

My parents and sister never talked to me about "the birds and the bees." (I learned this expression many years later in America). From the boys in my class I found out that for some reason that was a "dirty" subject, never to be discussed with parents, older sisters, or girls. Only in sly confidentiality with other boys was this topic to be addressed.

I could not quite understand why this subject was taboo, and decided to find out more about it from books and magazines. I discovered, however, that this self-education was no easy task. Under the Soviets, any literature that could be perceived as being pornographic was strictly prohibited. Pornography was the mark of "bourgeois decadence." No books or magazines containing explicit descriptions of erotic acts could be found in bookstores or libraries. In Soviet movies, even kissing between a man and a woman was a rare and brief scene. Officially, the Soviet Union was a very prudish society.

Eventually, I found a book in German that described in detail the physical interaction between man and woman. My sister had brought it home, and I was able to read it surreptitiously when she was not present. The book was quite worn out and obviously had been through many hands. It was a respectable sex manual, written by a Dutch physician, Theodoor van de Velde. The German title was, *Die Ideale Ehe*. The author was a moralist and claimed to have written the book to assist married couples to find more joy in their intimate life. The book had been published in numerous languages. The English version was called, *Ideal Marriage*, and—as I learned later—was extremely popular in the United States in the 1930s and 1940s. The book describes the human sexual organs, their physiology, and human sexual intercourse. He emphasized the beauty of sex and its importance of improving a marriage. Needless to say that I found the reading interesting, even more so since I knew that my parents would not have approved of it. (How come we enjoy doing things we are not supposed to do? It goes as far back as Adam and Eve, and it applies to children as much as to adults.)

I read only a few chapters of the book before my sister returned it to her friend. Naturally, I never told her that I had read parts of it. A "nice boy" was not supposed to read such "stuff." The knowledge about human sexuality, however, helped me better understand the changes in my body. Still, in the presence of girls, I remained shy and withdrawn. Only years later, in my late teens, was I able to break out of my shell and become more outgoing toward the fair sex.

At the time my hormones became active I noticed another change. As a teenager my feelings often fluctuated between overconfidence and insecurity, between self-assurance and apprehension. When overconfident I felt that I could overcome any challenge, that whatever I did was bound to succeed, that I could gain the recognition I craved. My overconfidence, however, evaporated at the smallest setback, and turned quickly into insecurity and apprehension. When insecure, I felt worthless, unattractive and inhibited, incapable of accomplishing anything useful, unable to gain the attention of any girl in my class. I became withdrawn. It was always more difficult to regain self-confidence than to lose it. Only years later did these fluctuations of my feelings gradually abate.

While we were in the process of adjusting to our new life under the Soviets, war was raging in Europe. After the fall of France, German bombers attacked British airfields, and later, Britain's major cities, causing considerable destruction and civilian casualties. The British, in turn, bombed military and economic targets in Germany, occupied France, Belgium and Holland. At the movies, the Soviet newsreels showed bombed out cities in the West, burning buildings, distraught people, a mourning mother, or a child killed in the bombing.

The Soviet authorities plastered posters all over the city, comparing the happy life in the Soviet Union with the death and destruction suffered by the people in the capitalist West. Two posters appeared on the wall of our building overnight. One, with the caption "Here," showed a happy Soviet woman with a smiling child on her shoulders, waving a little red flag. The other one, with the caption "Over There," showed a disheveled, weeping woman standing among ruins, holding a dead child in her arms, while airplanes overhead dropped bombs.

No one could imagine the tidal wave that was surging toward us with full force. Little did we know that the horrors of war would soon sweep over the Soviet Union and its people, bringing death and destruction on a much larger scale than the West had ever known.

Shortly after the occupation of North Bukovina by the Soviets, the German population of that area was granted permission by the authorities to apply for exit visas to Germany. This was obviously one of the agreements reached between Germany and the Soviet Union. The Germans, many of them farmers, were more than eager to apply for visas. They saw it as a unique opportunity to escape the Soviet rule, and at the same time join their brethren in Germany. Most of them were proud of being German, proud of the Führer, and proud of being able to move to the Reich. The suburb of Kaliczanka, that had a large number of German farmers, saw a true exodus. The farmers had been promised compensation in Germany for the property they left behind, and therefore didn't hesitate to leave.

The Germans gathered at the city's main railroad station with their crates, suitcases and bundles. They were in good spirits, eager to leave. They departed by train for their beloved Reich. Among those who left were also our neighbors, the Beniuks. Not being able to take the dog with them, Mr. Beniuk took the dog to the Tzetzina woods, shot him with his rifle, and buried him near a tree. Mrs. Beniuk was in tears when she said goodbye to my mother. Her husband was in high spirits, eager to join the German army and again wear a military uniform. They left in time, before Germany invaded the Soviet Union. Years later Mother found out from a cousin of Mrs. Beniuk that her husband had been drafted into the German army, sent to the Eastern Front, and never returned. His wife was sent to a German factory and apparently died during an Allied bombing raid.

The judicial system instituted by the Soviets was swift and harsh. There were witnesses and defense lawyers during the trial, but they played only a minor role. The trial itself was a well-choreographed performance. Each participant enacted the assigned, well-rehearsed part that served only to justify the sentence that had been decided by the court well in advance. The witness testimony always supported the accusations made by the prosecutor. The defense lawyer did not try to prove that the accused was not guilty, but usually admitted his guilt and only asked the court for mercy. There was, however, no room for mercy in the court's decisions.

People who made derogatory remarks about the Soviet system or those who complained of shortages while standing in line, were accused of being "class enemies," of spreading anti-Soviet propaganda, and were sentenced "in the name of the people" to harsh prison terms—usually up to twenty years. Needless to say that such sentences created an atmosphere of intimidation and gloom among the city's inhabitants.

Soon, the gloom that enveloped the city gave way to shock.

6. Deportations by the Soviets and the Beginning of War against Russia

An unexpected event occurred on June 13, 1941. The quiet of the night was suddenly disrupted. We awoke when we heard the rattling noise of trucks speeding through the streets. Then we heard a truck coming to a screeching halt near our building. A few minutes later we could hear, through the open window, subdued crying coming from the street. Without turning on the lights, Mother and I looked out at the dimly lit street. We saw a truck in front of the neighboring building. A man and a woman were standing next to the back of the truck. The woman was crying. They were sparsely clothed and it was obvious that they haven't had time to get fully dressed. Next to them were two NKVD men from the Soviet Ministry of Interior, wearing blue caps and khaki uniforms, with submachine guns dangling from their shoulders. All four climbed into the back of the truck, which then took off into the night.

We learned later that this scene was repeated in many parts of the city. The arrest of the "undesirable elements" had begun. In some instances, whole families were picked up, including the aged, the sick, and the children. If other people happened to be in the house with the people targeted for arrest, they were also taken, although they were not on the list.

The arrests went on for several nights. The NKVD men arrived in teams of two or three, pounded at the door, hauled off the frightened, half-dressed men and women to the waiting truck, and drove off into the dark. They disappeared as fast as they had arrived.

During the first night, the crying and wailing of those arrested alerted the neighbors. The authorities did not like that. Nothing should disturb the atmosphere of happiness and contentment they were trying to cultivate. They found a solution easily. During the following nights, music blared over the street loudspeakers through most of the night. This way, no neighbor could hear the crying of those arrested.

We learned quickly how to recognize, in advance, a night of arrests. Around ten o'clock in the evening the conversation in our house stopped. We became tense and nervous. We sat around the kitchen table, watching the clock, while listening to the music coming from the street. When the street loudspeakers continued to blare music past ten o'clock, we knew that arrests would take place during the night.

I was bewildered and surprised by the nightly arrests. I couldn't understand why people were pulled out from their beds in the middle of the night, pushed into the back of a truck and driven away to an unknown destination. I asked Father for an explanation, "Father, why are these people being arrested?"

"I am not sure why, but I assume they are considered 'enemies of the people'."

"What have they done to deserve that label?"

"I don't think they have done anything. They probably were wealthy people under the previous regime, or had been members of some political party or group. Under the present regime, that is sufficient to be considered an 'enemy of the people'."

"Could we also be arrested?"

"In the past I have not been rich, nor have I been politically active. But under this regime one never knows. A bad report by the doorman of our building, a slanderous accusation by a neighbor, a careless remark while standing in line is sufficient to turn us into 'undesirable elements.' Anybody could be arrested."

"But why do they pick up the people at night?"

"Arrests carried out in full daylight would shake the people's trust and confidence in the regime. Seeing armed NKVD men dragging people from their homes, loading them on trucks, and taking them away would create a lot of commotion in the city. It would destroy the image of a peaceful and happy society the authorities are trying to portray. At night, when the city is asleep, the arrests are not noticed. The following days, only a few friends or neighbors would observe that some people had disappeared. It wouldn't create much of a commotion. On the surface, life in the city would remain the same."

How unpredictable life had become! One day our neighbors were here, living a normal, peaceful life, and going about their business. The next day they were gone. Vanished. They left behind empty, silent apartments, a testimony of shattered lives. In the rush of their forced departure, many families left the doors and windows unlocked. Sometimes, one could hear though an open window the whining of a dog or mewing of a cat left behind.

I became aware of the glaring contrast between the rosy picture of Soviet life portrayed in the newspapers, books, on the radio, and in school, and the stark reality of personal experience. In school we had been taught that communism brings justice, freedom and happiness to the world. Well, that was not the case with the world I saw. Father was right when he said that political and social systems, as well as people, should be judged by their deeds, not their words. I started to loathe the unrelenting barrage of propaganda. I realized, again, that we lived under a system where hypocrisy was king. Under the veneer of tranquility and happiness pulsated a life filled with anxiety and uncertainty. We didn't know what the next day—or the next night—had in store for us. It was a very unsettling feeling.

At night, I couldn't sleep. I was listening intently to the noises from the street. Were any trucks driving in our neighborhood? What if a truck with screeching breaks stops in front of our house and NKVD men with their submachine guns burst into our apartment? Just the thought of it made me shudder and kept me wide-awake. Only shortly before sunrise did I fall asleep.

The NKVD divided those arrested into two categories. The first category was that of "convicts," and consisted of those who had committed "serious crimes" against the working class. These were bankers, big landowners, owners of large businesses, former politicians, leaders of Zionist organizations, and all those considered "exploiters" and "enemies of the working people." Most of those people had No. 39 passports and had been blacklisted from the beginning of the occupation. People who had made derogatory remarks about the Soviet system while standing in long lines to buy groceries and had been turned in by informers, were also in that category.

The second category was made up of "volunteer settlers," consisting of small business owners and land owners, small shopkeepers with a few employees, minor clerks in the Romanian administration, families of those in the first category, and, in general, those who were considered "untrustworthy elements" by the Soviet authorities.

Those arrested were taken to the railroad station and loaded into cattle cars. The "enemies of the people" from neighboring villages were also brought to the railroad station and loaded into the waiting trains. Neighbors and friends of those arrested came to the station with small packages of food and clothing, to help those that were being deported.

Mother and I also went to the station with a small package. There were several long trains packed with people and guarded by armed NKVD men. The locomotives, like huge iron monsters, hissed and spewed black smoke impatiently, eager to take their human cargo to faraway lands. The people on the trains tried to communicate, from a distance, with those on the loading platform. There was a cacophony of voices, mingled with the smell of smoke from the locomotives. Mother had learned about the arrest of a couple who used to own a clothing store. Over the years she had befriended those people and now wanted to help them. We walked along the trains until we saw the couple. Mother slipped one of the guards a few rubles to look the other way, and then sneaked the package to her distressed friends through the open door of the cattle car. The woman had tears running down her cheeks and didn't know how to thank my mother. When the train finally left, some of those locked in like cattle were crying.

During the first year of Russian takeover, about four thousand people were deported from Northern Bukovina. Many of those deported were Jews, since Jews were often involved in occupations that, from the Soviet point of view, made them "enemies of the people." Leaders of the Jewish community, leaders of Zionist organizations, and members of the Jewish intellectual elite were also deported. Among them were Abrasha Gimpelmann, head of the Zionist youth organization "Hashomer Hatzaïr," and several other members of that organization.

Later we learned that those accused of "serious crimes" against the working class were separated from their families and sent to labor camps in the frigid north, mostly to the Komi Autonomous Soviet Republic. There they found company. A year earlier, "bourgeois" elements and "enemies of the people" from Soviet-occupied Poland and the Baltic states had been deported to the same region. The camps were in the middle of the dense taiga forest near the Arctic Circle, where temperatures would drop to -50 degrees C. Completely isolated, the camps were often accessible only on horseback or on foot. That was the region where the "enemies of the people" were sent to build socialism.

They did back-breaking work in sawmills and coal mines, cut spruce and birch trees deep in the frozen taiga, tied logs into rafts and sent them down the Pechora River during the brief summer months. Not being used to hard labor and to the harsh, inhospitable climate, many of the deportees succumbed within several months of arrival. They joined the ranks of millions that had been sacrificed on the altar of socialism, for the greater glory of the Marxist God, Joseph Stalin.

The "volunteer settlers" had to sign a document, stating that they agreed, voluntarily, to resettle. If some nosy, western journalist had raised the question of why thousands of people had disappeared overnight, a government official would have shown him written proof that all these people had volunteered to resettle. Case closed. The naïve journalist—and most western journalists were naïve in those days—would have left, convinced that the volunteers were driven by pure patriotism.

The harsh reality, of course, was quite different. The deportees were deprived of their civil rights and were sent to Siberia or Central Asia, where they were allowed to live only in rural areas. Uprooted from their homes, torn away from their families, they were suddenly plunged into a world of hostile strangers, a world totally different from the one they had lived in most of their lives. They couldn't speak the language—Russian—and were surrounded by a culture and customs that were alien to them. In order to survive they struggled to adjust. They were allowed to do menial work in factories, cooperatives and *kolhozes*, but had no access to any well-paying jobs. During the war they suffered hardships and deprivations that were the lot of most Russian people during those terrible years. After the war, those who survived the deportations returned to Czernowitz, and told about their ordeal.

While the nightly arrests were still taking place, who could have predicted that much worse was in store for the Jewish population of Czernowitz?

On the morning of June 22, 1941, the whole family got up early. It was a beautiful, warm day, and we got ready for our Sunday activities. Mother went to the market to buy some food, while Father got ready for the flea market. Since school had ended earlier in the month and vacation had already started, I helped Father pack his "merchandise" of used household wares into an old suitcase. I had just wrapped an old teapot into a towel and placed it into the suitcase among some used clothes, when Mother returned, much sooner than we expected. Out of breath and very agitated, it was obvious she had been running. Before we could ask her what happened, she blurted, "War has broken out!"

"What?" my father and I exclaimed almost in unison.

Trying to catch her breath Mother continued, "They have just announced it over the public loudspeakers in the market. The Germans have invaded the Soviet Union."

We were stunned. At that moment we all knew that our lives would take a drastic turn for the worse.

Before we could recover from this news, we heard explosions in the distance, coming from the direction of the airport. I ran to the window and leaned out to get a better view. A large, dark-gray plume of smoke billowed into the sky in the distance. It was the first flight by German bombers over our city. The deadly tentacles of war had reached us.

We were not the only ones German airplanes visited that morning. Later we found out from radio reports that without any declaration of war, German bombers had attacked airports and railroad stations across all the western Soviet Union. Soviet planes were caught on the ground and went up in flames. Railroad stations were turned to rubble before the people realized what was happening. Soviet troops, caught in their barracks, were blasted to pieces. At the same time, large German tank and infantry units crossed the border. From the Baltic to the Black Sea, a hurricane of fire and steel swept over the Soviet land with devastating fury.

My parents, who had experienced World War I, knew that war leads to immediate shortages of food and basic life necessities. Mother and I rushed to the market, each of us armed with two large shopping bags.

In the city there was panic. Food stores were mobbed. In the open-air market, where peasants sold their produce, anything edible was snapped up in no time. In addition to food, people bought whatever they could find—fuel, clothes, shoes, toilet paper, matches, candles, flashlights. Everywhere there was pandemonium.

The days that followed saw the same chaos. The air-raid sirens kept wailing day and night, making people scurry repeatedly into air-raid shelters, usually located in cellars. Signs were posted on the streets, pointing to the nearest underground air-raid shelter. Sandbags were stacked in front of public buildings. The German bombers returned over the city. The airport and rail station were attacked again. Black columns of smoke rose from the airport. The acrid smell of burning buildings spread over the city. Antiaircraft guns placed on top of tall buildings, in open squares inside the city, and in surrounding fields barked furiously at the attacking aircraft. Small puffs of black smoke marked exploding projectiles in the sky. Sometimes Soviet airplanes also appeared and engaged the enemy. One German plane was shot down and crashed into a house in our vicinity, killing its inhabitants and the pilot. The building caught fire, and the smell of the burning structure, mingled with the odor of burning aircraft fuel, spread over the neighborhood. But rarely did I see Soviet aircraft in the sky. Many of them had been destroyed during the first day of attack, and the remaining ones were used on other fronts.

During the first week of war we had air raid alarms every day and night. Often there were several alarms during the same day or night. When the wailing of the sirens started, the *militiants* (Soviet police) on the street, whistles in their mouths, directed the running and frightened people to the closest shelter. Every day and night my parents, sister, and I ran down the two flights of stairs in our building, into the cellar. The room had no ventilation, and the air was stale and moldy. The only light came from two candles. Along with the other tenants, we huddled in the wet, cold room, wrapped in blankets or coats, and listened with trepidation to the barking of the antiaircraft guns and the occasional explosion. When the prolonged sound of sirens announced the end of the alarm, I could hear a collective sigh of relief.

I shared the excitement generated by the air raid alarms, and was fascinated by the booming of the antiaircraft guns. It was a totally new experience for me, a thirteen-year-old boy. The people around me, had a different reaction. The constant alarms deprived them of their sleep, frayed their nerves, and created feelings of tension and exhaustion.

The major streets of the city were clogged with military vehicles moving toward the front. Grim-faced Soviet soldiers, wearing khaki uniforms and helmets, sat in compact rows on open-air trucks, holding their rifles tightly between their knees. The trucks were covered with leafy tree branches for camouflage. The heavy smell of exhaust filled the air. At intersections, military women in tidy uniforms and tall, black boots directed—with robotic motions—the traffic. One could hear the rattle of vehicles day and night as they rushed over the cobblestoned streets to their destinations. The military trucks were moving south, towards the Romanian border. Allied with Germany, Romania had joined the Nazis and declared war on the Soviet Union.

The Soviet authorities issued a series of directives, related to the state of war. Total blackout was ordered, fuel was rationed, and a night curfew was declared. Spreading rumors was punished with long prison terms. To prevent the population from listening to foreign radio broadcasts, an order was issued to turn over all radios to the authorities. Most people complied. To avoid trouble, my father turned in our radio.

Some people, taking great risks, defied the order and kept their radios. Since radio Moscow broadcasted mostly patriotic music and unreliable news bulletins, those who kept their radios listened secretly to the BBC war reports from London. After the first few days of confusion, it became clear that the Germans had overwhelmed the bewildered Soviet troops, had broken through the Soviet border defenses in what used to be Poland, and were advancing rapidly eastward.

The outbreak of war was an exciting time for me. The German airplanes flying over the city, the burning building of the main railroad station, the military convoys racing through the streets raising clouds of dust, the military marches blaring from the public loudspeakers—all that was exhilarating for me. I helped Mother paste strips of paper on the windowpanes, filled every bucket in the house with water, and assisted the doorkeeper of the building to fill pails with sand, to have them handy in case of fire. I went to the railroad station to see the bustling activity on the platform, the bomb-damaged train station, and the movement of trains packed with soldiers and military equipment. I listened avidly to the public loudspeakers for the latest news, and noted the changes of the front on my map. I was deeply involved in these activities and ignored everything else.

One week after the start of the war, I noticed that the flow of Soviet military convoys had changed direction. The convoys were not moving toward the front anymore. They were moving eastward, away from the front. At the same time, Russian families and Soviet civil administrators were leaving town in great hurry. Most of them left in trucks provided by the government or the military. Each person carried only a small bundle or suitcase, not to take up too much space in the crowded vehicle. Others left by train in the few railcars set aside for the civilian population.

The Soviet retreat had begun.

7. The Fascist Takeover

In 1940, after the surrender of Northern Bukovina and Bessarabia to the Soviet Union, the political atmosphere in Romania remained tense. In early July, a new nationalist government was formed under the leadership of Ion Gigurtu. At the same time, Hungary and Bulgaria intensified their demands for territorial concessions from Romania. Hungary claimed Transylvania, a region in the northwest of Romania with a significant Hungarian minority. Bulgaria demanded Dobrogea, a region located between the Danube and the Black Sea. In preparation for its war against the Soviet Union, Nazi Germany insisted that its allies settle their differences. Under German pressure, Romania ceded the northern part of Transylvania to Hungary, and Southern Dobrogea to Bulgaria, in August 1940.

The Romanian population was outraged. Most Romanians felt bitter and deeply humiliated by the loss of nearly a third of their country in the span of several weeks. Protest demonstrations took place in Bucharest and other major cities, demanding the abdication of the King. They held Carol II responsible for the disasters that had befallen their country. Under intense pressure, the King invited General Ion Antonescu to form a new government, and invested him with full powers. But the demonstrations against the King continued. To put an end to popular unrest, Antonescu asked the monarch to abdicate. On September 6, 1940, Carol II abdicated in favor of his son, Michael. He left the country with his mistress, Mme. Lupescu, and with nine railway cars filled with valuable possessions. Thus, the dethroned King made sure that he would have a comfortable and

"Old Czernowitz"

Israelite Temple before it was
burned down by the
Germans in 1941

Jewish Community
Building

Main Railway Station

Metropolitan Residence until 1940; Now
Chernivtsi National University

National Theater

pleasant life wherever he settled. After moving from one country to another, Carol II and his mistress eventually settled in Portugal.

A week after King Carol's abdication, General Ion Antonescu declared himself *Conducator* (Leader) of the State. He named Horia Sima, the leader of the Legionary movement, Vice-President of the Council of Ministers. Except for the Legionary movement, all political parties were dissolved. The Legionary government had now absolute power.

The Legionaries unleashed a wave of terror. Leading Romanian politicians, such as Professor Nicolae Iorga and Virgil Madgearu, were murdered. The Jews, a defenseless and despised minority, were ideally suited as scapegoat for the mass discontent. Embedded in the minds of the masses for generations and aroused by green-shirted agitators spewing anti-Semitic venom, Jew-hatred exploded with a vengeance. Pogroms were perpetrated against the Jews all over the country. Jewish property was plundered or put to the torch. In Bucharest, Jews were dragged into the city's slaughterhouse and killed. Afterwards, their bodies were hanged on hooks like slaughtered cattle, and pieces of paper with the inscription "kosher meat" were attached to each corpse. A group of about 100 Jews was marched into the Jilava forest, ordered to undress, then shot.

The terror perpetrated by the Legionaries led to friction between Ion Antonescu and Horia Sima that resulted finally in an open break. In January 1941, the Legionaries rebelled against Ion Antonescu. After three days of fighting, Antonescu, who had the support of the army, crushed the rebellion and became the sole ruler of the country. He restored order. When Nazi Germany invaded the Soviet Union in June 1941, General Antonescu ordered the Romanian troops to join the war against the Soviets, to liberate the territories lost the previous year. He also proclaimed himself Marshall.

When the Soviets began their retreat, the Jewish population of Czernowitz faced a dilemma: should they join the retreating Red Army or stay put and await the Romanian-German reoccupation of the city? The question was also raised in our family, but the discussion soon became irrelevant. The military situation changed so rapidly that fleeing the city became almost impossible. Only a few people, mostly party members, joined the Red Army units and fled eastward. From our family, Aunt Ruchel's youngest brother, Ebert, joined the fleeing Soviets. Months later we learned that the Germans had captured and killed most of those people. We never heard from Ebert again.

In the wee hours of July 5, the still night air was shattered by the deep thump of a powerful explosion. The shock wave generated by the blast shattered the windows of our apartment, spreading glass shards all over the parquet floor. We jumped out of our beds, dressed quickly and ran outdoors to see what was going on. What we saw looked like a scene from Dante's inferno.

The partially demolished main post office stood about two hundred yards away. The building also housed telephone and telegraph equipment, which had been blown up by the retreating Soviet troops. Another structure across the street, used by the Soviet authorities to store thousands of seized radios, was engulfed in flames. Obviously, the Soviets had no intention of letting those radios fall into enemy hands. Further down the street, two well-stocked food stores had also been torched. They used to serve exclusively the party and government elite. Flames were leaping from the windows on both sides of the street, and the fires were spreading. Black billows of smoke engulfed the entire area. Fires had also been set on neighboring streets. After blowing up and torching whatever they thought might be of value to the enemy, the Red Army abandoned the city, leaving its center in flames.

People who lived in or near the burning buildings panicked. Unable to control the devouring flames, they tried to salvage as many of their belongings as possible. Running, stumbling, perspiring, driven by despair, they carried clothing, pillows, furniture, pots and pans, books—whatever possessions they could grab. They placed them at a safe distance on the sidewalk or on the street; then rushed back to salvage a few more objects.

Looking at the burning buildings, at the chaotic behavior of the people desperately trying to salvage their belongings, I instinctively realized that the life of yesterday was slipping away, sliding into a past from which there was no return.

Father realized that the spreading fires would soon reach our apartment. My parents had already packed some of our belongings shortly after the Soviets started the deportations. They wanted to be prepared in case we were on the NKVD list. We hurriedly packed more of our portable possessions.

My mother's sister, Aunt Tzili, lived two blocks from our street, on Hormuzakigasse. She had a three-room apartment on the third floor of a building where most tenants were middle-class Jewish families. My parents and Aunt Tzili decided that we should move to my aunt's apartment. Mother was able to find a porter with a two-wheel pushcart. We loaded the cart with suitcases filled with clothing and linen, cardboard boxes filled with food staples, bundles of pillows, and blankets. Together with the porter, we all pushed the overloaded cart into the middle of the street, through black clouds of smoke, past the burning and collapsing buildings, until we reached Aunt Tzili's place. Bertha's friend, Selma Meerbaum-Eisinger, joined us and helped with the move. Aunt Tzili gave us one room in her apartment, where we deposited our belongings. Then we went back to salvage more of our possessions.

In the meantime, with the Red Army and the Soviet authorities gone, mobs took over the streets. They broke into stores and looted them, they ransacked the former quarters of the Soviet administration, they ripped communist symbols off the building walls, tore up pictures of Stalin and other Soviet leaders, and threw them into the street. Some of the abandoned apartments were plundered. The streets were littered with debris, broken glass, and household items. The latter had been lost or discarded either by the overloaded looters, or by those trying to flee the flames. Many in the mob, who a year earlier had greeted the arriving Soviet authorities with red flags, were now donning armbands with swastikas. It was amazing how quickly some people could change their ideological orientation with changing circumstances ...

On July 5, around noon, the first Romanian military patrols appeared in the city. They belonged to the Romanian Third Army and moved cautiously among the burning buildings. Local civilians, dressed in Romanian national costumes and wearing armbands with swastikas, accompanied them. These civilians were guiding the patrols through the blazing, smoke-filled center of the city. Soon, military trucks filled with German troops in gray and green uniforms came rumbling down the debris-strewn streets, raising clouds of dust. Our new masters had arrived.

When we returned to our apartment, the fire from the adjoining buildings was already dangerously close. Seeing that our apartment could soon be engulfed in flames, my father decided to salvage the most precious object we had in our home: my sister's grand piano. Using the porter's heavy ropes, he and the porter carried the piano from the second floor to the sidewalk, loaded it on the pushcart, and together we pushed the heavy load down the street. We intended to take it to Aunt Tzili's apartment building, and leave it in the lobby until we could find a place for it.

As we pushed the heavy cart, I looked at the buildings ablaze on both sides of our street. The bright glare of the flames was dazzling, while the biting smoke stabbed at my eyes. I was coughing and choking. The fires roared amidst crashing beams and collapsing walls. We were forced to walk in the middle of the street to avoid the flames and thick smoke. Sweat streamed down our foreheads, from both the heat and the strenuous physical effort. Father, Mother, the porter and I pushed the cart with the piano, while Bertha carried a stack of musical scores. Selma, always willing to help, carried the piano's music stand under her arm.

Through the smoke we noticed a patrol of four Romanian soldiers approaching from the opposite direction. Two civilians wearing armbands with swastikas accompanied the patrol.

Having a premonition, my father shouted, "Get out of their way!"

He tried to push the cart closer to the sidewalk, but the heat and smoke made it impossible to move any further. The next moment we were face-to-face with the patrol. One of the civilians must have recognized that we were Jews. There was hatred in his eyes, vicious hatred that conveyed the message, "I want you dead." With the slur *jidani bolsevici* (Bolshevik kikes) on his lips, he pushed the piano off the cart and into my father's chest. The heavy piano threw him to the ground. It then crashed on the cobblestones, trapping Father's legs. I could see, on his contorted face, that he was in terrible pain. The other civilian that accompanied the patrol did not stay idle. He grabbed the piano's music stand from Selma's hand

and smashed it against her head. The wooden stand broke under the force of the blow. Selma staggered, while blood streamed from a large gash on her forehead. It ran down her face and formed deep-red blots on her white blouse. Still cursing, the patrol and its companions moved on.

While Mother and the porter moved the cracked piano, then helped my father to his feet, Bertha tried to console a distraught Selma. She wiped the blood from her face with a handkerchief, and used soothing words to calm her. My father felt intense pain due to a broken leg and was unable to walk. He had to be carried on the pushcart to Aunt Tzili. When we reached my aunt's apartment, Tzili called a Jewish doctor who lived in the same building. He attached a splint to my father's broken leg and bandaged Selma's head wound.

This was our first encounter with the new masters. We had come face to face with unrestrained evil and brutality. People filled with rage and hatred were bent on inflicting pain and destruction. I became aware that we lived in a very wicked world.

Only later did we realize that, in spite of our misfortune, we had been very lucky. We were alive.

Before the war, some Jews had been forced by the anti-Semitic regimes to cast their lot with the Soviets. Now, all Jews were perceived by the non-Jewish population and by the Romanian military as supporters and collaborators of the Bolsheviks. The day of the Great Revenge had arrived. In the city's suburbs of Billa and Klokuczka, Romanian soldiers, led by local informants, entered the homes of Jewish families, robbed them of their valuables, raped the younger women, and then shot the inhabitants. Among the victims was a friend of my father, Dr. Lerner, who was in his apartment when he was shot dead. We learned the news from a young peasant woman that used to bring milk to our house.

Shocking news reached us from the surrounding towns and villages. People who were able to flee to Czernowitz reported the rampage and murder of Jews perpetrated by the new occupiers. In the first three days of occupation, mass executions of Jews took place in Siret, Storojinets, Ropcea, Czudin, Jadova, Novoselitsa, Banila, and many other towns and villages of Northern Bukovina. The murders were carried out by rampaging Romanian soldiers, with the assistance of the local population, who were mostly Romanians and Ukrainians. In the first days of occupation, it became clear that the Romanian troops and civilians had a free hand to vent, unrestrained, their hatred of Jews.

Some of the soldiers used murder not only to express their hatred, but also as a form of entertainment. They came up with more creative, more original methods of murder than simple shooting. One such innovation was the "enema" treat. A survivor from the village of Banila recounted how a group of soldiers forced his neighbor, a freshly married Jewish man, to undress and kneel, leaning on his elbows in the middle of the road. While two soldiers held the man down, a third one pushed the end of a fire truck hose into the rectum of the screaming victim. While the crying wife of the young man watched, a soldier turned on the water. The immense water pressure propelled the hapless young man several yards down the road and ruptured his internal organs. Within minutes he was dead. The soldiers laughed, they were amused. Some amusement!

After the first three days, the commander of the Romanian Third Army, General Peter Dumitrescu, issued a series of decrees. These *"Ordonantze"* (military decrees) were posted on the walls of buildings throughout the city. The decrees ordered the population to obey the new rules under penalty of death. All weapons, including hunting rifles, had to be turned over to the authorities within 24 hours. Looters were to be shot on the spot. Total blackout was ordered. A curfew was imposed on the Jewish population of the city. "Any Jew caught on the street between 6 p.m. and 8 a.m. will be shot," read the order. After these decrees were issued by the military command, the rampage by the soldiers came to an end. The ordeal of the Jewish population, however, was far from over.

In the first days of occupation, along with German and Romanian troops, the SS arrived in the city. They set up headquarters at *Zum Schwarzen Adler* (The Black Eagle), the hotel I had admired in my early childhood. Their main task: dealing with the city's Jewish population. With German efficiency they went promptly to work.

One of their first actions was to arrest Chief-Rabbi Dr. Abraham Mark, Main Cantor Gurmann, and Temple-chorus Conductor Towstein. The SS picked them up at their homes. I happened to stand at the entrance of our house when the three arrested men walked by, guarded by two armed Germans in uniform. They walked in a single line, one behind the other, with one German in front and the other in the rear. They were downcast, but walked with dignity. The deep sadness in their eyes showed that they suspected what the SS had in store for them. Several other leading personalities of the Jewish community were also arrested. They were taken to the SS headquarters at "The Black Eagle." The hotel staff related later that Dr. Mark was kept in an elevator shaft for two days, without food or water. In addition to physical deprivation, this was also psychological torture, since there was the constant threat of being crushed by the moving elevator.

As in many other areas that fell under control of the German Army and its allies, among the first steps taken by the SS was to eliminate the spiritual and intellectual leaders of the Jewish community. Deprived of such leadership, the Jewish community was left demoralized and less likely to organize any resistance to future repressive measures.

Shortly after the first Romanian and German troops arrived in the city, I walked with my mother to our apartment to pick up more of our belongings. Mother did not look Jewish and did not fear to be molested on the street. She had always been a tower of strength.

As we passed the Main Temple, we saw that a German military vehicle had stopped in front of it. A German officer got out, planted his booted feet in front of the main entrance, and, with hands firmly set on his hips, inspected the façade of the temple. After a few minutes he got back into the vehicle and drove off.

People who lived across the street related that several hours later, a German military truck loaded with drums stopped in front of the temple. A military command car accompanied the truck. Several Germans jumped out of the command car, approached the main entrance to the temple, broke down the door, and entered. A short while later they emerged, carrying the silver ornaments from the Torah scrolls they had found in the sanctuary. I had seen those ornaments during the High Holiday services: they were centuries-old, artistically crafted Torah crowns, exquisite silver breast plates, and embossed headpieces with silver bells. The Torah crowns were studded with colorful, semiprecious stones, while the silver breastplates were embellished with lions, pillars and intricate floral wreaths. The Germans threw the silver decorations into the trunk of the command car, then went to the truck. They unloaded the drums from the truck, and rolled them inside the temple. It turned out that the drums were filled with gasoline. They poured the gasoline all over the temple floor, set it on fire, then emerged quickly, and drove off.

Soon black smoke billowed through the windows of the temple, and flames engulfed its dome. Since the temple was on a hilltop, this fiery spectacle could be seen from every corner of the city. It burned late into the night, like a huge torch on top of a hill. The flames lighted the streets and buildings nearby brighter than daylight, casting trembling, twisting shadows. The surging mass of smoke enveloped the neighborhood, burning people's eyes and impeding their breathing.

While lying on the floor in Aunt Tzili's apartment, unable to sleep, I watched the glow of the fire flickering on the wall facing the window. It was a frightening sight. Why have they torched our beautiful temple? The people who had worshiped in it belonged to the city's elite, and had always been great admirers of German culture and civilization. I remembered from my early childhood how effusive my father used to speak about the German *Kulturvolk* (people of culture). What an irony! Now I was facing a different display of German civilization, of German *Kultur* (culture). I was baffled. I felt that I lived in a world of confusion, a world in which everything I had been taught was crumbling.

Next morning, only the blackened walls and the metal girders of the temple dome remained standing, like remnants of a dreadful nightmare. We found out later that it was the SS who had put the temple to the torch.

The Jewish community learned from a Romanian officer that the SS men were under the command of *Hauptsturmführer* (Captain) Finger. While the temple was burning, the *Hauptsturmführer* and his men were busy at work in other parts of town. We learned what happened from a Romanian woman who used to bring us milk. The SS cordoned off several streets inhabited mostly by Jewish families. Then they carried out house-to-house sweeps, rounding up all Jewish men. Those arrested were taken to a large building, called "House of Culture." Under the Soviets, concerts and artistic performances used to take place in that building. Now, it had become a place where Nazi-Germany's *Kultur* was put on display.

Later in the day, Chief-Rabbi Dr. Mark and his companions were taken from SS headquarters to the House of Culture. After verifying that all those arrested were Jews, they forced them into a column and marched them outside the city, to the suburb of Bila. There, in an open field, those arrested were given shovels, and ordered to dig a large ditch. When the ditch was completed, they were lined up and systematically murdered with gunshots to the head. Another group of Jews, rounded up from their homes and forced into a work detachment, was brought in to cover the mass grave. The members of that work detachment brought back the news of the massacre.

The SS had not yet finished their work. The following day they cordoned off another street, went from house to house, arrested all Jewish men, and took them to the House of Culture. They lined them up along the walls of the large dance hall, and ordered them to count to ten. Each tenth man had to step forward and was taken out of the building. They were herded into a column, marched to a field near the Tsetsina woods, and shot. A Jewish work detachment buried them. The remaining people in the House of Culture were declared "not guilty" (not guilty of what?) and were released by the SS.

It was a trick designed to amuse the killers. A sadistic trick. When the terrified people walked out of the building, they walked into a trap. Armed patrols were on the streets. The "freed" Jews were released from the House of Culture, late in the afternoon, past 6 p.m., the hour after which any Jew found outdoors could be shot. As these unfortunate people stepped out, shooting started. The Romanian soldiers were having fun shooting at defenseless people. Trying desperately to escape the snipers, fleeing, stumbling, dodging bullets, slipping, falling, rising again, running on the blood-splattered pavement, jumping over those fallen and bleeding, their faces distorted by terror, the horrified victims were driven relentlessly by that primordial instinct—survival. The bullets cut down many of those who were fleeing. It was a joint display of German-Romanian civilization!

Hidden behind a window curtain in Aunt Tzili's apartment, I watched transfixed with horror the bloody spectacle of men running and falling. Terror and rage swept through my whole body. I realized I was trembling.

The screams of those hit intermingled with the sound of firing rifles. Still, many of the terrified people were able to escape into adjacent buildings. Many of those hit by bullets were only wounded and survived. One of the injured, bleeding profusely from a leg wound, crawled into Aunt Tzili's building. He left a trail of blood behind.

When the shooting stopped, an eerie silence settled over the bloody scene. I could hear only the occasional moaning of the wounded. Under the watchful eye of the Romanian soldiers, a work detachment of Jewish men, who were rounded up at their homes, was brought in. They loaded the blood-covered bodies of the dead into trucks and took them to the Jewish cemetery. Those still alive were taken to the Jewish hospital. Afterwards the work detachments were ordered to clean up the blood-splattered pavement with buckets of water and brooms. An hour later the scene looked normal, as if nothing unusual had happened.

The bloody events I witnessed left me bewildered, scared and horrified. I realized that the wave of murderous barbarism that was sweeping over Europe had now engulfed our city. The world in which I had grown up was being turned upside down. Not only were flames and explosions destroying the physical world around me, but the moral world had also collapsed. What I had witnessed was a violent attack not only on innocent people, but also on the values that I had been taught. They were values I had learned to cherish, values that my parents had instilled in me since early childhood. They had become part of my character and personality. Now I saw goodness, compassion, decency, and respect for other people being replaced by evil, cruelty, brutality, and murder. I couldn't understand what was happening, and I was frightened.

I had to find an explanation. I turned to my father who was standing next to me watching the street. "Father, what is happening? Why are they tormenting and shooting these people? What horrible crime have they committed to deserve such punishment?"

"They haven't committed any crime. Those who torment and shoot them are committing a crime. They prove themselves worthy descendants of Vlad the Impaler. Indeed, they have inherited his mettle." From his voice I realized that Father was very angry. (Vlad the Impaler, who served as a model to modern Dracula, was a 15th century Wallachian prince who became infamous for his unbelievable cruelty. Wallachia was a principality that became later part of Romania.)

"But why are they doing this?"

"Because they are driven by a murderous ideology."

I didn't know what a murderous ideology was, but I suspected it was something very evil. I realized that life had become very precarious and dangerous.

From a Romanian officer who was on friendly terms with a member of the Jewish Council, we learned that the SS chief was not happy with the way the whole operation was carried out. *Hauptsturmführer* Finger had a not-so-friendly discussion with the Romanian commander of the military units that patrolled the area around the House of Culture. The Captain expected the Romanian military to arrest the Jews released by the Germans during the curfew, take them to the Tsetsina woods, and have them shot. He did not expect to see a bloody mess in the heart of the city. It went against his Germanic sense of order and cleanliness. He wanted it to be a neat, methodic operation, removed from the view of the non-Jewish population, without corpses spread on the pavement. The *Hauptsturmführer* was also unhappy that many of the people released by the Germans were able to escape. He was upset that the Romanians did not carry out mass murder with the same efficiency and thoroughness as his own men.

During the days following the bloody event, I remained obsessed by the images of the horror I had seen. I was distressed and restless. I went to see my sister.

"Sis, why is there so much injustice, so much pain and suffering in the world?" I wanted to know. I was hoping she had an answer that would calm me down.

My sister looked at me thoughtfully with her green, bright eyes, trying to find an answer. She knew what made me ask that question. "Simple questions do not always have simple answers. People have asked this question since ancient times. It is the central theme of Greek tragedies.

Prophets and philosophers, God-fearing man and non-believers have struggled with it. They arrived at different answers, but non to everybody's satisfaction."

"Father said that the ancient Greeks had many learned and wise men. How did they explain man's suffering?"

"They believed that man learns from suffering, that from suffering comes wisdom."

"Do people still believe that?"

"Some do. More recent thinkers claim that suffering steels man's character. Others have concluded that man's fate is to suffer."

I gave some thought to these explanations. I could not see how much wisdom people acquire or how much their character is strengthened when they are shot dead.

"Is there a religious explanation for man's suffering?"

"The Hebrew Bible claims that God makes man suffer in order to test his faith. Such was the case with Job, a good man, a just man, who lost everything—his family, his health, his wealth—and still didn't give up faith in God. Some theologians claim that people suffer because they have sinned. The Christian religion claims that man is bound to suffer due to the original sin committed by Adam when he ate from the forbidden tree of knowledge."

I was baffled. I couldn't understand why good, innocent people, including children, would have to suffer at the hand of killers in order to prove their faith in God. Then I thought of the images of war shown by the newsreels, of airplanes bombing columns of civilian refugees and blowing toddlers and their mothers to pieces. What sins have those poor toddlers committed to deserve such a fate? Nor could I understand why innocent people could be cursed by God to suffer because Adam, who had lived a very long time ago, had bitten into a forbidden apple.

"Grandfather says that there is an almighty, merciful God in heaven that rewards the just and punishes the wicked. But the evildoers are laughing, while good people suffer and die in pain and agony. Many innocent people have been murdered in our city in the last few days. Countless innocent children have been killed and are being killed in wartime. Every year, thousands of good, God-fearing people have their lives devastated by hurricanes, floods, and earthquakes. How is the suffering of innocents compatible with divine justice? Does it mean that God is unable to protect them, that He is not omnipotent? Or, if He is able but not willing to do it, how can we call him a merciful God, a God of justice?"

I was expecting a good explanation from my sister. After all, she had read many books, and was much more knowledgeable than I was.

"There are some who say that man cannot always understand God's ways," replied my sister thoughtfully. "The medieval philosopher, Maimonides, who struggled with the same question, claimed that God is incomprehensible and inaccessible to the human mind."

I was disappointed by my sister's response. I had expected a better reply.

"Isn't this a way to weasel out from an answer?"

Sister smiled. She was not what one might call a deeply religious person. "Well, it is a reply for a question to which people have no answer. Maybe there will never be a satisfying answer. The same way as the brain of a dog is not "wired" to solve mathematical equations, our brain may not be "wired" to comprehend all the mysteries of nature and divinity. Nevertheless, some people believe that God will reward them in heaven for their good behavior on earth. Others, however, have turned away from God and religion."

I realized that three thousand years of human thought had not found a satisfactory answer to the innocent question that started this conversation. Following our "philosophical" discussion, I also became aware that man's ability to explain all aspects of its existence is very limited. If God, I told myself, would decide to come down on earth and meet me, I would have a long list of questions to ask Him. And He would have a lot of explaining to do.

One thing was clear to me: God is far away, in heaven, while the evildoers are next door. They are eager to inflict pain and kill. Considering what goes on in the world, I thought, maybe God is too busy to pay attention to each individual's needs. I concluded that we would have to protect ourselves from evildoers the best we can, and not to rely on divine assistance. Of course, if God can find time to help us, I will always welcome His help.

I decided not to share my unorthodox thoughts with anybody. Surely not with my grandfather, who would have said that such thoughts are those of an *apikores,* an heretic and non-believer.

In the first week of July, terror and chaos reigned in the city. Fear, hatred, and pain prevailed, while dignity and decency had become non-existent. The orgy of retribution went on unabated. Jewish patients were kicked out from the main hospital and from the city's mental institution. Jewish children were driven from the city's orphanage. In many parts of the city, bodies of murdered Jews were lying in the street or in looted apartments, since Jews did not venture into the open to bury the dead. During those hot summer days, the sickly stench of decaying bodies was pervasive in many parts of the city. Even those who died of natural causes were kept at home. Only after General Dumitrescu issued the military decrees and some order was restored, were the Jews finally able to bury their dead.

While the anti-Jewish terror reigned in the city and in the suburbs, German troops marched through the city's main streets. Dressed in green uniforms and wearing hobnailed boots, they marched in tight formation, exuding the self-confidence of the conqueror. The thud of their boots hitting the cobblestones reverberated through the streets. Other troops sped through the city in camouflage-painted automobiles and trucks, leaving behind clouds of dust and the nauseating smell of engine exhaust. From Aunt Tzili's window, I watched them with a mixture of curiosity and anxiety. I knew they were not my friends.

As the German and Romanian troops advanced deeper into the Soviet Union and the front moved eastward, some military units left our city and moved with the front. The SS also left the city, since they had a lot of work to do in the newly conquered territories. In the latter part of July, the Romanian civil administration was established.

In mid July, several Jewish refugees arrived from the neighboring province of Bessarabia, and told us about the bloodbath perpetrated by Romanian troops in that province. In the first weeks of occupation, thousands of Jewish men, women and children were murdered in

Kishinev, Balti, Hotin, Edinet, Marculesti and numerous other towns and villages of Bessarabia. A military brothel was set up in Soroca, where young Jewish women and girls were forced to "work." A ghetto was later established in Kishinev for the Jews who survived the massacre. From the ghetto they were eventually deported to Transnistria.

We also learned about the terrible pogrom perpetrated by the Romanian troops in the city of Jassy in Northern Romania. At the end of June several thousand Jews were arrested in that city and herded by soldiers and gendarmes into the courtyard of Police Headquarters. First they were brutally beaten with rifle butts, then the soldiers started firing into the dense mass of defenseless, horrified people. When the shooting stopped, corpses were lying all over the courtyard. About two thousand four hundred Jews who survived the massacre were driven to the railroad station and loaded into a train of thirty-three freight cars. The army had requested enclosed freight cars and not cattle cars, since such freight cars were almost airtight. Squeezed in like sardines, without water, barely able to breathe, the Death Train, as it was called later, left Jassy for an unknown destination. Romanian soldiers accompanied the train.

During the torrid days and nights the train moved at a snail's pace from one station to another. People became delirious. Then they started to die. They were dying of thirst, from lack of air, of the wounds inflicted during the beatings. The train would stop at a railroad station and unload the corpses. Those still alive, with their throats parched and close to suffocation, were gasping for air. The soldiers answered their desperate cries for water with mockeries and obscenities. The doors were shut and the train continued its winding route. At the next station that scene would be repeated. At the end of the trip, when the few survivors were released from the hellish confinement, their state of mind bordered on madness.

When I heard the horrific story of the Death Train, as told by one of the survivors of the hellish train ride, I was stunned. I realized that our ruler's capacity for cruelty and evil was endless. Without the restrains of the law, hatred and prejudice had turned these men into bloodthirsty beasts. I also realized how helpless we were in the face of hate filled, armed soldiers. Again and again I asked myself, "Why does this happen? Why does man show so much cruelty toward his fellow man? Why does God allow such horrible things to happen?" I didn't know the answers and I was scared.

On July 20, 1941, the newly appointed governor of Bukovina, Colonel Alexandru Roseanu, arrived in Czernowitz. He restored a semblance of order. The streets in the center of the city were swept clean, some of the debris from the burned out buildings was removed from the sidewalks, and some shops were opened. The governor also ordered the creation of a Jewish Council to represent the city's Jewish community. The Council, headed by Dr. Neuberger, set up its offices in the building of the Jewish hospital, on Stephaniegasse. The Romanian authorities used it to convey its orders to the Jewish community. One of its major tasks was to select and supply Jewish labor for the work detachments. Later, it assisted the authorities in the selection of people for deportation. The Council also supervised the Jewish hospital and orphanage.

Among the first orders given by Roseanu to the Jewish Council was to organize Jewish work detachments to be used by the Romanian and German authorities. Several thousand Jewish men were forced into these units. Jews with some military experience led the detachments. There was plenty of work to be done. The Jewish work detachments were used to clean the streets, repair the railroad stations, collect and bury unclaimed corpses, and to demolish the burned out buildings left behind by the retreating Red Army.

The work detachments under German command helped rebuild the two bridges over the Prut that had been blown up by the Soviets. Some of the men worked with shovels, and some carried heavy wooden beams on their shoulders; others were lifting the beams with ropes and pulleys, while still others were fastening the beams with iron clamps. The members of these detachments, while carrying out the work, were often brutally beaten whenever their guards thought they did not work fast enough. The German engineering unit, "Todt," that rebuilt the bridges, excelled in brutalities towards the Jewish laborers, by using iron rods to beat and prod them to work faster. Many of those beaten, unable to walk anymore, had to be carried by their companions to the Jewish hospital. Jewish men who worked at the bridge under German command called that place "the bridge of sighs."

At the end of July, Governor Roseanu issued an order, requiring all

Jews to wear the yellow Star of David. The star was of specified size, and had to be worn on the left side of the chest. Any Jew caught outside his home without the star was promptly arrested. By being forced to wear the yellow star, Jews could be easily recognized, avoided, and mocked in public. Whenever they appeared on the street, they were taunted, harassed, insulted and often assaulted. On occasion, Jewish men were grabbed on the street and forced to sweep the streets. Jewish women and girls were picked up and forced to do house cleaning for Romanian families, for free. Young hoodlums made it a sport to pelt with rocks and spit on adults wearing the yellow star. They beat up Jewish children, who were also forced to wear the star. The policemen found a new source of income: they arrested Jewish men and women on the street, claiming that they were trying to hide the yellow star with a briefcase, a handbag, or a book. After being paid a handsome *baksheesh* (bribe), those arrested were released.

When Mother learned about the order given by the authorities requiring all Jews over the age of six to wear the Star of David, she decided to make the yellow stars for the whole family. I was eager to help. I cut pieces of shoebox cardboard into triangles of required size, while Mother wrapped them in pieces of yellow fabric. She then sewed them together in pairs in the form of Stars of David, and attached them with a safety pin to our clothing. I felt good doing this work. I didn't think that the yellow star was a badge of shame, and was proud of wearing it.

Some enterprising Jews made artistically designed Stars of David from thin sheets of plywood, painted them yellow and sold them for a small profit. Many Jews—especially women—bought these artistically designed yellow stars and started to wear them with a certain pride. My sister bought such a yellow star and wore it proudly on her chest. She turned the badge of shame into a badge of honor. The authorities, however, had no intention to let the Jews use the yellow star as an embellishment, and ordered that only plain yellow stars made of cardboard and fabric should be worn. The artistically designed Star of David had a short life under our new rulers.

Jews were allowed to shop only at specified hours. Shopping in stores was allowed only between 12 noon and 1p.m. In the market, where the peasants sold their produce, Jews could purchase food only between 10 and 12 in the morning, after the non-Jewish population had finished its shopping. When the Jewish housewives arrived at the market, they would find only leftovers, if any food at all.

While vegetables and fruits sold by the peasants in the open market were not rationed, other foods and fuel were strictly rationed. Even with ration cards, people had to stand in long lines to get the basic necessities, such as bread, sugar, cooking oil, and fuel. The rations allocated to Jews were smaller and more expensive than those allocated to non-Jews. Separate food lines were set up for Jews. They were served only after the people in other lines had been served. Mother, Bertha and I spent many hours standing in line daily for a loaf of bread or a pound of sugar. There were separate lines for each item, so that each of us stood in a different line. Even then we never knew if we would get what we wanted. Often the stores ran out of food before we could get our share.

Some people tried to avoid standing in line by cutting in front of others. This happened especially when people knew that there was not enough food for all those standing in the queue. It resulted in a lot of pushing, shoving, shouting and name-calling. Other people resorted to different ruses. I remember standing in a bread line when a young woman with a big belly walked directly to the store entrance and tried to enter, claiming to be pregnant. Another woman, who was standing next to her, touched that woman's belly and cried out: "It's a pillow, not a baby!" The woman with the big belly left quickly, accompanied by a chorus of expletives. It is amazing how imaginative some people can be when they want to do something illegal or dishonest...

Taking the racial laws of Nürenberg as a model, the Antonescu government passed legislation designed to deprive the Jewish population of its civil rights. In the territories occupied in 1940 by the Soviets, additional anti-Jewish decrees were issued. In Bukovina, they were issued by Governor Roseanu and by his successor, General Corneliu Calotescu. Former Jewish properties, such as factories, apartment buildings, and stores that previously had been nationalized by the Soviets, were nationalized or "Romanianized" by the new masters. In those enterprises where skilled Romanian managers and workers were not available, the former Jewish owners and Jewish workers were allowed to work, provided they trained the assigned Romanian replacements. Once the training was completed, the Jews were dismissed, and many ended up on the deportation lists.

The stationery and office supply store that used to belong to my uncle and Grandfather was also "Romanianized." It became the property of a Mr. Nistor. Since he had no experience in this field and had no idea how to manage the enterprise, he kept my uncle and Grandfather to run the business. Mr. Nistor just showed up in the store by the end of the day, collected the receipts, chatted for a few minutes with my uncle, and left. Since he was completely dependent on my uncle and Grandfather, he treated them fairly well and gave them a decent compensation.

Jewish lawyers and journalists were not allowed to practice their professions. Jewish newspapers could not be published. Jewish teachers could not teach, and Jewish children could not attend public schools. Gatherings for religious services, even on holidays, were prohibited. Jews could be evicted from their rented, or from their own, apartments, with no right of appeal. All these harsh measures were only the beginning of things to come.

In an attempt to escape persecution, several hundred Jews, mostly intellectuals, converted to Christianity. The baptized Jews did not have to wear the yellow star, did not have to comply with the curfew imposed on Jews, and were not exposed to assaults and mockery in the streets. However, the authorities were skeptical about the sincerity of those converted. They had doubts about all those converts who suddenly discovered the new religion, saw the light, and accepted the teachings of the church. Many Romanians knew that about four hundred and fifty years earlier, under duress, many Spanish Jews had converted officially to Catholicism, but continued to practice their old traditions in secret.

The authorities decided to take legal action against many of the new converts. Only with substantial bribes to the prosecutors and judges who handled those cases were those accused able to avoid harsh penalties. In several instances, the conversions were annulled.

If the situation of the Jewish community in Czernowitz was bad, the news received from the Jews in the smaller towns and villages of Northern Bukovina was much worse. After the executions in the first few days of occupation, the Jews left alive were forced out of their homes and taken to holding camps in Lujeni and Vizhnitsa. Later they were marched to the larger concentration camps of Edinets and Secureni, in Bessarabia. It was a long march, which lasted several days. Moving slow mile after slow mile over the endless fields of Northern Bessarabia, dragging their bundles and suitcases that became heavier by the hour, they advanced slowly towards their destination. Under constant prodding by the gendarmes, deprived of food and water while marching in the searing sun with no rest, some of the older people and children collapsed. Those who died were dumped in ditches along the road and covered with dirt. We found out about these events from people who, under cover of darkness, were able to escape and fled to Czernowitz.

Occasionally, there were Romanians in positions of authority, who showed compassion towards the victims of persecution. In mid-July, a small group of Jews came to Czernowitz from the town of Storojinets. They were the survivors of some of the worst atrocities committed in Northern Bukovina during the first days of occupation. When the survivors arrived in Czernowitz, they were arrested and kept in a cellar at Police Headquarters. SS commander Finger learned about the arrest and requested that those arrested be turned over to him. Police Chief Alexandru Grossar, well aware that turning over these Jews to the SS meant certain death for them, refused. After three days, he ordered that those arrested be released. Thus the lives of a small group of Jews were saved, although only temporarily. Shortly thereafter, the police chief was dismissed.

During the first week of occupation, we stayed indoors at Aunt Tzili's apartment. After the encounter with the military patrol, we were afraid to go outside. Only twice did Mother venture outdoors to buy some food. My father's legs were still hurting, and he could barely walk supported by a cane. He spent most of the time lying down and brooding. He saw the world around him collapsing, and felt helpless. Mother was busy in the kitchen or talking to neighbors to find out what was going on outside. She always appeared calm, regardless how distressing the news was. My sister and I were restless, but did not dare to leave the house. Only once did I go outdoors with my mother. That was when we saw Chief Rabbi Dr. Mark taken away by the Germans. At night, we all bedded down in one room. We tried to sleep on the hard floor, and derived some comfort from our togetherness.

On the fourth day of our stay at Aunt Tzili's, we ran out of food. Mother decided to go into town to buy some in the open market and to check out our apartment on Postgasse. She came back with the news that the building with our apartment had been only partially destroyed by fire, but our apartment had been spared. Although the apartment had been broken into and looted, the furniture was still there. After a brief discussion, my parents decided that we should move back to our home.

With burned out buildings on both sides of the road, our street was barely recognizable. Some of the fire-blackened walls had collapsed, while those still standing had ghostly, rectangular openings where there used to be windows. Roofs and upper floors had collapsed into piles of rubble. Among the blackened ruins, only the undamaged chimneys were standing, reaching out toward the sky like lonely ghosts. The Post Office building, blown up by the Soviets, and the stock market building, where the seized radios had been stored, were empty, burned out shells. Further up the street, "Hotel Gottlieb" had burned to the ground. Bent pipes and twisted iron rods were sticking out among piles of bricks and mortar. Battered bathtubs, metal bed frames, and smashed tile stoves could be seen in the rubble. The acrid smell of burned-out buildings filled the air. Some of the former inhabitants were picking through the rubble, looking for some of their belongings.

Our apartment offered a desolate picture. The entrance door was broken and partially open. Looters had strewn clothing, papers, pictures, and broken dishes over the floor of the apartment. Half-empty drawers, ripped out from the linen chest, were lying on the floor of the bedroom. Glass shards from the windows, broken by the blast set off by the retreating Red Army, were scattered all over the floor. The chandelier in the living room had been ripped out from the ceiling. The bathroom had been vandalized; its fixtures were missing, and there was neither water nor electricity.

Mother wasted no time and started the cleanup. Bertha and I also gave a helping hand. Father was too weak to help. We arranged the furniture, removed the trash, and swept the floors. Because we had no running water, we had to carry water in buckets from a neighboring street, up to the second floor to our apartment. Once the broken glass and dishes were removed, Mother got down on her knees to scrub the floors, to make them clean and shiny again. After a full day's work, the apartment looked inhabitable. When night fell, we were happy to be again in our beds.

Since it was summer, the broken windows didn't bother us too much. We grew accustomed to the pervasive acrid smell that came from the burned-out buildings. Having no electricity, we went to bed early in the evening. Later on, Mother found a kerosene lamp and bought some kerosene on the black market. We brought water in buckets from outside. Otherwise, we had running water in our apartment only when it rained; then the water came in through the broken windows, ran down the walls, and made puddles on the floor.

When I looked at our vandalized apartment, at the burned-out buildings nearby, at my helpless father, at my mother on her knees scrubbing the floor—I realized that our lives had been shattered, and that the world around us was unraveling.

This was only the beginning. Worse was in store for us.

8. The Ghetto and the Deportations of 1941

In early October 1941, the Antonescu government appointed Brigadier-General Corneliu Calotescu Governor of Bukovina. He succeeded Alexandru Roseanu, who had died unexpectedly. Calotescu set up a military cabinet, which consisted mostly of close friends. Although the activity of the cabinet was kept secret, rumors began to circulate about the impending establishment of a ghetto and of the deportation of "undesirable elements." The authorities denied any such intentions. However, when a battalion of gendarmes was brought into the city, the people became restless. The Jewish community felt that some action was imminent. A Jewish printer, who worked for the government, notified the Jewish Council that forms were being printed regarding the takeover of Jewish apartments and other property.

The blow fell on a gray, chilly autumn day brake. In the wee hours of the morning of Oct 11, 1941, the leaders of the Jewish Council were summoned to the military commander of the city, General Vasile Ionescu. The Council leaders were told that by order of the Govenor, all Jews had to move into a specified section of the city by 6 p.m. They could take with them only the bare necessities. "Any Jew found outside the designated area after 6 p.m. will be shot," said the general. When the members of the Jewish delegation asked for a written order, they were rebuffed. "An oral order is sufficient," replied the general brusquely. Obviously, the Governor was a cautious man. He had no intention of giving a document to the Jews that would link him to their persecution. General Ionescu handed the delegation a map of the city, on which the section assigned to the Jewish ghetto was outlined with a pencil.

The Jewish leaders hurried back to their community. The news spread like wild fire. Neighbor informed neighbor, friend informed friend, relatives informed each other. Leaflets were typed at the Jewish Community Center and distributed by hand or posted on buildings. Many families, expecting to be moved, had already packed suitcases and boxes with essential clothing and food. Some people had their suitcases packed since the Soviets began the deportations.

The Jewish population moved quickly. The threat of being shot after 6 p.m. if caught outside the ghetto played no small role in the speed at which people packed and moved their belongings. Suitcases, baskets, pillow covers, and cardboard boxes were filled hastily with clothes, linens, shoes, dishes, pots, and food. They were loaded on baby carriages, wheelbarrows, or on two- or four-wheel carts, and carried to the ghetto area.

The area designated as ghetto was a poor section of town, which included the Jewish quarter, and was already inhabited by about 10,000 Jews. In the time span of ten hours, another 40,000 moved into that space. Those who had family or friends in the ghetto moved in with them. Many of those who already lived there shared their quarters with strangers. Some of the people, unable to find other accommodations, spent the first night on the street.

Mother brought home the news about the creation of a ghetto. In the morning of October 11, she went to market to buy some food. She came back sooner than expected, very agitated. On the way to market she heard that we had to move to the ghetto area on the same day. Since the creation of a ghetto had been rumored for several weeks, the news came as no shock. But none of us expected that we would be given only a few hours' notice.

We started packing with feverish haste. Mother told each of us what and how to pack, while Father, my sister and I followed her directives. After all, we already had experience with moving on short notice. Some of our belongings remained packed from the day we moved to escape the fire. After returning to the apartment, my parents had decided to unpack only what was absolutely necessary, since they suspected that soon we would be forced to move again. For that reason, on the morning of October 11, some of our suitcases and boxes were already filled and ready. While we were packing our remaining belongings, my parents debated where to move.

From a neighbor, we learned what area had been designated as the ghetto. Fortunately, the apartment of Aunt Tzili was inside the ghetto. Mother ran over to see Aunt Tzili, to ask her if we could move again into her apartment. She immediately agreed. Soon all of us were carrying, dragging, or pushing suitcases, boxes, and bundles from our apartment, down two flights of stairs, on the sidewalk along several streets,past burned-out buildings and up three flights of stairs to Aunt Tzili's apartment. Then we rushed back to our apartment and repeated the process.

I was perspiring profusely, sweat running down my forehead into my eyes. My palms were wet, my shirt was drenched, and I felt clammy all over my body. I was tired and my dry throat was burning from thirst, but I did not stop. I had to hurry. On the street I kept bumping into other people carrying suitcases and boxes, everybody in a hurry to reach his or her destination before 6 p.m. Some were lucky to find enterprising peasants with horse and wagon. For a substantial amount of money the peasants would move the belongings into the ghetto area. We did not have such luck. While we were packing, Bertha's friend Selma arrived. Since she did live in the ghetto area and did not have to move, she came to help us. It proved again how valid the saying was that in need you find your true friends.

By 6 p.m.—the deadline set by the authorities to complete the move into the ghetto—we were able to bring all our suitcases and boxes into my aunt's apartment. By nightfall, completely exhausted, we finally sat down on our suitcases to rest. My grandparents and Aunt Anna, who lived outside the ghetto area, also moved to Aunt Tzili's apartment, where we all shared the same space. It was very crowded, with the luggage piled in the middle of the room. Mother arranged bedding for us on the floor in one corner of the room, while the grandparents slept in the opposite corner. Aunt Anna slept in the third corner. It was not a comfortable way to sleep, since we had no mattresses and the parquet floor was hard. We had, however, a roof over our heads, and we didn't feel the autumn chill. Outside the apartment, the stairway was packed with people and luggage. Having no friends or relatives in the ghetto area with whom they could move in, these people had to spend the night on the cold stairways and hallways of buildings. Only later did the Jewish Council help them find a place to live.

By nightfall, the military had put up a ten-foot high wooden fence topped with barbed wire at the entrances into the ghetto. There were two entrances, both guarded by gendarmes. The whole Jewish population was thus sealed off in a small section of the city, looking at an uncertain future. I thought of the circus animals that are locked in cages, and I felt like one of them.

In the following days, feeling that the time was right to take advantage of those in despair, Romanian civilians descended in droves into the ghetto. They came like vultures ready for a feast. They came en mass. They hovered, they swooped, and they swarmed. They picked and scavenged and devoured everything they could get their hands on. They "bought" valuables and household goods for ridiculously low prices. Often they walked away with the acquired objects without bothering to pay even those minimal prices. They helped themselves to people's possessions, stole whatever they liked, grabbed whatever they could. They walked away with the goods, knowing well that the Jews were too intimidated to complain. After all, to whom could we complain?

Those "buyers" came also to our room. A young Romanian woman in a chic, flowery dress bought some silver cutlery from my grandparents for a ridiculous price. She then noticed a folded Damask tablecloth, on which Mother had earlier served lunch to our family. The woman grabbed the tablecloth, stuffed it into the large shopping bag she was carrying, and without saying a word walked out the door. She stole with no shame. It didn't bother her that everybody in the room had seen what she had done. Stealing from Jews had become legal.

I discovered that in the absence of law or fear of punishment, even well-mannered, well-dressed middle-class people could turn into rapacious predators. They discard the laws of civilized behavior and replace them with wanton, unscrupulous greed. They steal, they rob and they trample the dignity of defenseless people, who until yesterday had been their neighbors. I was troubled and depressed to see such crude lawlessness perpetrated against my family. Anger, mingled with a feeling of utter helplessness, welled up in my soul against such wanton behavior.

There was also another kind of vulture. To exploit the atmosphere of uncertainty and anguish among the Jews, certain shady characters appeared in the ghetto and claimed to have access to the governor and to his cabinet. They asserted they could protect a whole family from deportation, for a price of course. The price consisted of jewelry, oil paintings, Persian rugs, or other valuables. Once the valuables had been collected, these individuals simply disappeared, never to be heard from again. Others denied receiving any valuables. Taking shameless advantage of the despair of their victims, these unscrupulous individuals enriched themselves by deceit and fraud.

Conditions in the ghetto soon became appalling. In many instances, ten or twelve people were crammed in one room. In most buildings, the hallways and cellars were also jammed with people. There was insufficient water, since two of the three pumping stations in the city had been damaged by the retreating Soviets. Even elementary hygiene was difficult to maintain. The pungent odor of sweat, intermingled with that of urine, pervaded every building and street. At night, the stuffy, smelly air, the coughing and snoring of neighbors, as well as the hard floors, made sleeping in the crowded rooms very difficult.

My parents, my sister, and I, bedded in a corner on the floor of Aunt Tzili's apartment, could hardly sleep. The blanket on which I slept was thin, and the hardness of the wooden floor made my bones ache. Restless, I kept turning from one side to the other, trying to find a position in which I would feel somewhat comfortable. It was in vain. My whole body ached, and I couldn't sleep. From the movements next to me I realized that my family couldn't sleep either. The heavy air in the room and the snoring next door didn't help. Lying on the floor gradually turned into torment. Only toward the morning, tired and aching, was I able to fall asleep for a few hours.

The living in cramped quarters, the shortage of water and absence of

186

soap brought a new plague: lice. They were everywhere: in the hair, in the clothes, in the underwear. Lice did not discriminate. This scourge afflicted old and young, men and women, rich and poor. Mother had my head shaved, so lice wouldn't be able to hide in my hair. I was not happy that my shaved head looked like a bowling ball, but I saw the advantage of not having the little creatures crawling on it. Still, fighting them was a losing battle. And they spread disease in our midst. Typhus broke out in the ghetto and took its toll, mostly among the old and the very young. The *Chevrah Kadishah*, which handled Jewish burials, was very busy.

In this oppressive environment there was a constant flow of rumors. Rumors were heard, repeated, invented, and dissipated. The most persistent rumors claimed that deportations were imminent. On October 11, the first day of the imposed ghetto, a cattle train packed with Jews from Suceava stopped for several hours at the main rail station. The train was on its way to Transnistria, Romania's penal colony across Dniester. In the following days, other trains filled with Jews from Campulung, Gura Humorului, Vatra Dornei, and other towns of Southern Bukovina—an area that had not been under Soviet occupation—passed through Czernowitz on their way to Transnistria. The Jews in the ghetto knew that it was only a matter of days before it was their turn.

The deportations started on October 14. In the morning hours, gendarmes cordoned off a section of the ghetto where about 5,000 Jews lived. The people were herded from their homes, formed into a convoy, and then marched towards the main rail station. My mother and I watched the column from a distance.

Rabbi Friedmann from Bojan led one group, surrounded by his family and followers. He wore his best outfit, carried a Torah scroll in his arms, and walked with calm and dignity in the middle of the street. Men, women and children, each carrying a suitcase, a bundle, or a knapsack, were walking slowly behind the rabbi. Their faces showed sorrow and resignation, but none cried. They walked in silence. Only the scraping of their boots on the cobblestones could be heard. Toddlers were strapped on the backs of their mothers, in rucksacks with two holes cut in the bottom, from which their tiny, tender legs were dangling. Many of the marchers were wearing two or three layers of clothing; it was easier to carry them that way. Younger members of the family propped up some of the older people. I can still see Mr. Steinberg's mother, in her 80s, all bent over with age and arthritis. She wore a heavy winter coat, sagging stockings and a dark scarf over her white hair. Resting on her son's arm, she moved haltingly over the street's pavement. I felt a twinge in my heart for the old woman, dragged from her home and taken to an unknown destination.

Then I saw my cousin Eddie and his father, David; they moved slowly with the rest of the people, staring straight ahead. Each had a knapsack on his back and a suitcase in his hand. They appeared resigned to their fate. Gendarmes with bayonet-tipped rifles accompanied the slow moving column. From time to time one could hear them yelling, "Faster, move faster!" I was struck by the contrast between the brutish and rough demeanor of the gendarmes, and the resigned, sad expression on the faces of their victims.

Christian onlookers stood in silence on the sidewalks, watching the column of doomed pass by. I was wondering what went through their minds when they saw neighbors and acquaintances hauled from their homes and shipped to a harsh, distant land. Did they feel outrage for the injustice perpetrated in front of their eyes? Did they feel compassion for the innocents trotting wearily on the street's cobblestones? Or were they indifferent? I looked at their faces. Some had an expression of curiosity, while others showed cold indifference. I didn't see any face that expressed outrage or compassion.

At the railroad station, long trains of empty cattle cars were waiting, surrounded by gendarmes. Using their rifle butts, shouting orders and cursing, they herded the frightened, demoralized people into the cattle cars. Forty to fifty people and their luggage were squeezed into each car. Once the cars were full, the gendarmes locked the doors, and the train left the station. Then they started filling the next waiting train. Man's organized inhumanity to man worked like clockwork. One after another, the trains packed with distraught men, women, and children, together with their bundles, suitcases and rucksacks, left the railroad station and started on the road to the unknown.

That night I couldn't sleep. In the darkness, the images of the day came back to life. With my inward eye I saw again the convoy of men, women and children moving slowly over the pavement, each with a bundle or suitcase in hand. The snarl of the gendarmes still reverberated in my ear. I saw the sad, resigned faces of my uncle and cousin. They had both been good to me. When I was a little boy, Uncle David had always had a smile and a piece of candy ready for me. Cousin Eddie, although nearly ten years older than I was, never refused to play a game of chess with me—and let me win.

But the image that persistently came back to my mind was that of the toddlers strapped to their mother's back, and of the small boys and girls with tiny rucksacks, walking bravely next to their parents. The children didn't understand what was happening, and were frightened by the gendarmes and their rifles. I didn't know any of the children, nor their parents. Still, I was drawn to them; I felt their anguish, their despair. I kept asking myself again and again: why should these children suffer? What wrong have they done to be sent away to a strange, hostile place, where there will be neither kindness nor compassion? Why was so much injustice, so much suffering in the world that surrounded me? I didn't know the answer. I suddenly realized that tears were running down my cheeks. I wiped them off quickly. A boy was not supposed to cry.

The deportations went on for two days, October 14 and 15. Then, unexpectedly, they came to a halt. This was the result of the action of a single man. His name: Traian Popovici.

When the Romanians occupied Northern Bukovina in the summer of 1941 and Alexandru Roseanu was named Governor, he appointed Traian Popovici as Mayor of Czernowitz. Popovici was an attorney, who had spent most of his life in the city. Over the years he had established friendly relations with members of the different ethnic groups that made up the city's population. Although a nationalist, he had learned to respect the culture and customs of others. He was a man of strong character and integrity. In spite of the wave of anti-Semitism that swept Romania in the years preceding the war, he maintained friendly relations with many Jews, mostly intellectuals. He was familiar with, and respected, the role played by the Jewish community in making the city a major cultural and economic center. He was friendly with my father, whom he met during their professional activity in the courtroom before the war.

During the summer of 1941, Mayor Popovici watched with dismay the brutal behavior of his compatriots towards the Jews. He knew about the beatings, the shootings, and the suspension of basic human rights. He was upset when he saw Jewish intellectuals, many of whom he knew, being forced to do demeaning hard labor. He was appalled by the arbitrary arrests and shameless extortion practiced by his Romanian compatriots, by the eviction of the sick from hospitals and mental institutions, by the ejection of teachers and pupils from public schools, and by the "Romanianization" of Jewish property. As a Romanian, he felt that such behavior by the authorities and by a large number of Romanians was demeaning for his country. As a man of decency and integrity, he felt revulsion and disgust for the injustices perpetrated against a frightened and helpless population.

In the first few months, his attempts to intervene in behalf of the Jewish population were overridden by the Governor. He came under attack from anti-Semitic politicians, from nationalistic intellectuals, and from the local Romanian newspaper, *Bucovina*. He received anonymous death threats. In contrast, the Jewish community saw in Traian Popovici the only person in position of authority willing to help them. Jewish leaders often went to his office to make him aware of the plight of their people and asked for his help.

During a meeting in the Governor's office on October 10, Popovici was told of the planned deportation of the Jews from the ghetto. The plan envisioned the deportation of the entire Jewish population of about 50,000. The apartments of those deported were to be sealed and taken over by the state, together with their contents. The Governor then asked the Mayor to take the necessary measures to facilitate the implementation of his decision.

We learned later what happened next. The Mayor reacted strongly against the plan. He pointed out to the Governor that the deportation would have disastrous consequences for the local economy and for that of Bukovina, since it was impossible to replace the Jewish professionals and tradesmen overnight. Furthermore, sending so many thousands of people, shortly before winter, into war-ravaged Transnistria, where access to food and fuel was extremely limited, meant sending many of those people to their death.

In these times of violence, the Mayor dared to speak of justice; in these times of hatred, he dared to speak of fairness; in these times of madness, he dared to speak of decency. He showed no fear, no cowardice. He stood up against the man willing to perpetrate mass murder. He shone like a beacon of light in the darkness of night.

At first, the Governor remained unmoved. He professed that Marshall Antonescu himself had given the deportation orders and that these orders had to be carried out. Overnight, however, the Governor changed his mind. He realized that the deportations would indeed cause serious damage to the economy, and that at some point he may be held responsible for that situation. He had to change his plans. During the afternoon of the second day of deportation, on October 15, the Governor summoned the Mayor to his office. In order to prevent damage to the local economy, he told the Mayor that Jews with skills useful to the state would be exempt from deportation. Lists of those people had to be compiled and submitted to the Governor for approval. In the meantime, the deportations were to stop. Obviously, the strong stand taken by the Mayor in previous meetings with the Governor has had some effect.

In the evening, the Mayor went to the Jewish hospital to inform the Jewish Council of the Governor's decision. Hearing that for the time being the deportations had been stopped, the members of the council were elated. Although they knew that the reprieve was only temporary, they enjoyed the moment to the fullest. Many expressed their gratitude to the Mayor in a highly emotional way, with tears in their eyes. Everybody knew that Traian Popovici was the driving force behind the Governor's decision. Then the Mayor turned over to the Jewish Council the task of compiling the lists. Once completed, the lists had to be submitted to the authorities for verification and approval.

The same evening, the news spread like wildfire in the Jewish community. There was general rejoicing. Everybody savored the good news of the moment. The following morning, long lines formed in front of the school building on Landhausgasse, where the Jewish Council members started to compile the lists. Doctors, lawyers, engineers, businessmen, and tradesmen lined up to apply for residence permits (*autorizație*) to remain in the city. There was a lot of pushing, pleading, and crying by people cramming into the classroom where the Council members were working on the lists. Some Jews, who had key positions in "Romanianized" enterprises, asked for and were given letters by the new Romanian owners, stating that they were indispensable for the proper functioning of those enterprises. Other Jews, who did not have key positions in those enterprises, received the coveted letters in exchange for substantial bribes. Many Jewish employees in the "Romanianized" textile factories of the city received such letters. The Romanian owners were interested in keeping the Jews working in their enterprises, since in most cases, they themselves had no idea how to run the businesses. Those Jews who were able to present such letters to the Jewish Council were put on the list.

The council members did not always decide objectively who should be on their lists. As could be expected, relatives and friends of the council members ended up on these documents. The initial lists were repeatedly modified, and finally sent to the Mayor's office. His staff had to verify the validity of the claims made by the applicants, based on documents or witness testimony. Once verified, the lists were sent to the Governor for his signature and for the issuing of the residence permits. Nearly 15,000 people received permits from the Governor.

When the Governor refused to issue any more permits, Mayor Popovici started issuing permits over his own signature. In addition to permits for professionals and people with useful skills, he also granted permits to families with small children, to people in the old age home, to children in the orphanage, to hospital and mental patients, as well as to people he knew personally as decent citizens. Popovici knew that the Governor could easily annul the permits issued by the Mayor. However, by using his signature and his position, the Mayor was trying to delay the deportations. At a time of callous hatred and cruelty, when justice was as rare as a snowstorm in August, the mayor stood out as a man of decency and fairness.

The gamble paid off. While the Mayor was issuing permits, an order arrived from Bucharest to temporarily stop all deportations. It seemed that Marshall Antonescu made the decision after receiving information about the disastrous effect that these deportations would have on the local economy. An urgent plea by Dr. Fildermann, the head of the Council of Jewish Communities of Romania, may also have had some effect. However, everybody knew that the halt was only temporary, and that the deportations could resume at any time.

People with permits signed by Calotescu or Popovici were allowed to leave the ghetto and return to their apartments in the city. In their absence, the authorities had sealed the apartments. However, most of the homes had been broken into and burglarized. In some instances, Romanian officers or civil servants had moved into the vacant apartments. They were not willing to give up those comfortable living quarters, and threatened with deportation those who were too persistent. In most cases, this form of blackmail proved effective.

Following the initial deportations and the subsequent move of some people out of the ghetto, the fenced-in area became smaller. At the same time, the authorities started a new revision of documents, in order to establish again who may and who may not remain in the city. This time military personnel carried out the revision. Those considered acceptable by the authorities received new identity cards. The new ID card had the word "EVREU" (Jew) printed in large letters across it. Those who were not able to present all the required documents, or had no permit signed by Calotescu or Popovici, were marked for deportation. A few were able to obtain the new ID cards through bribes or connections. The rest were deported. The last transports left in November 1941.

The assets left behind by those deported were seized by the state and turned over to an organization called *Patronaj*. This was a semi-private, social organization, which was supposed to use the confiscated assets to help Romanian war invalids and hospitals. In reality, most of these assets ended up in the hands of key leaders of the organization and their friends. During the auctioning of confiscated goods, family members of the *Patronaj* bosses and the wives of leading politicians, high-level civil servants and high-ranking officers acquired most of these goods at ridiculously low prices. They filled their homes with exquisite furniture, fine draperies, Persian rugs, oil paintings, crystal, and other valuables, most of them acquired at *Patronaj* auctions. Some of the items were also acquired in the ghetto directly from well to do Jews, at similar ridiculous prices.

Shortly after the first transport left, authorities decided to shrink the ghetto. The surrounding fences were moved, forcing the ghetto inhabitants into a smaller area. The street where we lived in Aunt Tzili's apartment became off limits to Jews. We were given 24 hours to move.

This time, we had no relatives or friends to move in with. While we were packing our belongings, not sure where we would move, Selma arrived. She suggested that we temporarily place our belongings on the patio of her grandmother's apartment in the Judengasse, where she lived. Afterwards we could start searching for a dwelling. Since we had no better choice, my parents accepted the offer.

We spent the night outdoors on the patio of Selma's grandmother. These were cold October nights and we did not get much sleep. In the morning we had to shake the frost from our covers. I felt stiff and my body was aching. Later on, my parents went in search of a dwelling. After a long day of frustrating search, they returned exhausted and depressed. They had been unable to find a place where we could move. Every room and hallway in the shrunken ghetto was packed with people. Seeing the despair of my parents, Selma's grandmother decided to share her two-room apartment with us. Selma and her grandmother shared one room, while the four of us shared the other room. We were happy to have again a roof over our heads, and a stove to cook a hot meal.

We had barely settled in our new home, when we heard the news about "residence permits." To avoid deportation, we had to get such a permit from the authorities.

The following day, early in the morning, Father went to the office set up by the Jewish Council in the school building on Landhausgasse. In his pocket he carried documents proving his professional status. There were rumors that professional people and those with useful skills had a better chance to receive a permit.

Father had to stay in a long line of exhausted, unruly people. Their nerves frayed, they were pushing and shoving, trying to get inside the office. Once inside, they had to convince a harried commission to put their names on the list that had to be sent to the Mayor's office. Everybody knew that only a limited number of permits would be issued. Many believed that the sooner their name appeared on the list, the better would be their chances of receiving a residence permit. Therefore, the pushing and shoving. Some people tried to gain access to the commission using other means, such as bribes and connections.

After standing in line almost the whole day, his feet hurting, Father came home in the evening totally exhausted. He had been able to reach the commission and give them the required documents. But he was not sure if they would put him on the list. After all, a Jewish attorney, who was not allowed to practice his profession, was not an essential element for the Romanian economy or society.

The names of those to whom permits had been granted were posted daily on the walls of the school building. Day after day my parents checked the lists, but our names were not there. The chances of avoiding deportation were decreasing every day. Gloom turned gradually into despair. Something had to be done. But what?

After another disappointing day, my parents decided that Father should try to contact the Mayor in person. This way there was a chance, albeit a slim one, that we may get a residence permit. Father was hoping that their acquaintance, from the days when they both practiced law, might prove helpful.

The following morning Father went to Traian Popovici's office. People with petitions crowded the mayor's anti-chamber. After several hours of waiting, Father was able to see the Mayor. He recognized his former colleague, shook hands with him, and treated him cordially. Popovici filled out a permit on the spot for my father and his family. To ensure that we received a permit signed by the Governor, the Mayor gave him a letter of recommendation to General Calotescu. The letter described Father as an honest, loyal citizen, who belonged to the city's intelligentsia elite, and asked respectfully that the Governor grant a residence permit to him and his family.

The next day, when Father went to the Governor's office, he heard on the street that the General had decided not to sign any more resident permits. Still, my father was determined to try. At first, the military guard in front of the Governor's building refused to let him through. Only after showing the guard the Mayor's letter and slipping a *baksheesh* into his hand, did the guard let him enter the building. Once inside, Father was sent to the office of the General's adjutant. The officer took the letter, read it, and then told my father to wait outside in the hallway.

After about two hours of waiting, the adjutant opened the door and called out, "Jew Scherzer." Father rushed to the adjutant, who handed him a piece of paper. Then, without a word, he slammed the door in my father's face. With trepidation, Father looked at the paper. It was a residence permit with the Governor's signature! The Mayor's letter had proven invaluable.

Father came home elated. He entered the kitchen waving the document, his eyes shining, and his face red with excitement.

"I have the permit!" he cried out.

Hearing that, Mother's face lightened up. "Thank God!" she exclaimed. She rushed toward my father, grabbed the paper from his hand, and started reading it.

When I heard the news, I jumped with joy. Then I ran to the neighboring room where my sister was.

"Sis, Father got a permit. We are going to stay here!"

First she looked at me incredulous, then her face brightened. She rushed to the kitchen and read the miraculous piece of paper. She gave a deep sigh of relieve. "For the time being we are safe," she concluded with a smile.

The star of hope shone over us again. After the long days of nerve-racking waiting, of uncertainty and anguish, we finally had the piece of paper we all craved for: the paper that would allow us to remain in our city, at least temporarily. In these uncertain times, when nobody could predict what the future had in store, we learned to enjoy the good news of the moment. We will worry about the future later. It had been a long time since we have had any good news, since I had seen my parents in such a good mood.

The permit granted to us by the Governor was one of the last he signed. In the days that followed, the permits that were issued had only the Mayor's signature.

While Father was struggling to obtain a residence permit, other members of our family were also striving to get such permits. My grandparents were lucky. Before the war, they happened to live almost next door to Traian Popovici on Karolinengasse, and were well acquainted with him. Over the years they talked often to each other, and the Mayor always showed respect for Grandfather's wisdom and dignified behavior. This familiarity helped my grandparents to be among the first to receive residence permits signed not only by the Mayor, but also by the Governor. Uncle Joseph, his wife Ruchel, and child Elli, who were known to the Mayor, also received such permits. The written statement given by Mr. Nistor to my uncle, stressing his importance to the business, was helpful. Since the Mayor sent a note to the Governor, vouching for the loyalty of his neighbors, the Governor signed their permits. Aunt Anna and Tzili, as well as Aunt Jetty with husband Bernhard and eight-year-old daughter Gusta, who lived in another part of town, got permits signed only by the Mayor.

Residence permits signed by the Governor or Mayor protected the holders of those permits from deportation. A few months later, however, the difference between the two types of permits was to play a fateful role in the lives of thousands of people.

The news from the Russian Front was not good. Since their assault on the Soviet Union in June 1941, the German armies and those of their allies had advanced deep into Russia. Moving fast and with overwhelming force, German tank and infantry units advanced rapidly into Soviet territory, crushing any resistance in their way. The Red Army units that tried to resist were thrashed by massive tank forces, ripped apart with machine-gun fire, blown to pieces by bombs dropped from German *Stuka* bombers. By using the *Blitzkrieg* tactic, the Germans inflicted horrendous losses on the Soviets, both in men and territory. In a series of pincer battles, such as those in the region Bialistok-Minsk, Smolensk, Viasma, and Kiev, the Germans encircled and destroyed numerous Soviet armies. The newspapers reported gleefully the capture of over a million prisoners. It appeared that the German juggernaut was unstoppable. By the end of November, the German armies were closing in on Moscow.

My father and I read the news in *Timpul*, one of the Romanian national newspapers. We also studied the maps. As the German army advanced deeper into Russia and the papers announced one victory after another, my father's mood darkened. He looked grim as he studied the war maps that showed the German advances. He became increasingly depressed and irritable. When the big German victory in the Kiev region was announced, I watched my father pacing nervously back and forth in the kitchen, hands clasped behind his back, head bowed, with a deep furrow between his brows. I heard him say to Mother: "If Hitler wins this war, we are doomed." Mother didn't reply. She had lately become very quiet—a sign that she was also worried.

I followed closely each of the battles fought on the Eastern Front. On my map of Russia, spread out on the kitchen table, I tracked the advance of Hitler's armies, marked each of the cities conquered by them, and located each of the sectors where the two implacable enemies fought each other fiercely. I also learned the names of the tanks and aircraft involved in those gigantic battles; and read daily the announcements of the O.K.W. (the German Supreme Command) reported by the papers. The headlines screamed:

"German panzer units breach enemy lines. Three Russian armies encircled."

"Bolsheviks retreat in disarray. Hundred of thousands captured."

"Kiev in our hands. Six-hundred-thousand taken prisoner."

I followed the news with mixed feelings. It was exciting to read about the enormous battles fought along a three-thousand-mile front, about the clashes between millions of armed men and their machines. But I was also aware that every victory of Hitler's armies would encourage the Romanian government to intensify its persecution of Jews, and bring us closer to doom.

In store windows, maps of the Eastern Front were on display, with little blue flags showing the daily progress on the front. The German illustrated magazine, *Signal,* was full of pictures from the front. They showed advancing German armor passing destroyed Soviet tanks, German infantry advancing through burning villages, and endless columns of bedraggled Russian prisoners of war passing motorized German columns, moving in the opposite direction. They also showed pictures of cheerful Ukrainian peasant girls receiving smiling German soldiers with bread and salt, the traditional sign of welcome.

What the pictures in *Signal* did not show was how the Nazis treated the Soviet prisoners of war and the population in the conquered territories. In German-occupied lands, tyranny and terror went hand in hand. People, who were able to listen to BBC radio, told about reports of atrocities committed by the Germans in occupied Russia: executions, use of the Russian population as slave laborers, and mass-killings of prisoners of war.

The worst reports, however, were those about savageries committed by the Nazis against the Jews. Jewish refugees from German-occupied Poland, who managed to escape and cross the border into Romania, brought tales of atrocities and large-scale mass-murder. Not everybody in Czernowitz believed those reports. Many Jewish intellectuals in the Bukovina, educated in Austria and strongly attached to German culture, could not believe that the German *Kulturvolk*, as they used to call themselves with pride, was able to commit such atrocities against innocent and defenseless men, women, and children. Even my father said, "These reports are the product of an overheated imagination."

Only years later, after the defeat of Nazi Germany, did we learn the full extent of the crimes perpetrated by the Nazis against the Jewish people. Reality turned out to be much worse than the rumors we had heard during the war.

On December 16, 1941, a steamer named *Struma* left the Romanian port of Constanta on the Black Sea with 769 people on board. The steamer was old and not sea worthy, but embarked on a dangerous journey. This sea voyage was a desperate attempt by several hundred Romanian Jews to escape from fascist terror. They were trying to reach Turkey, a neutral country, and from there to travel to Palestine. Except for the crew, all people on board were Jews, 70 children among them. They had secured a place on the ship after paying huge bribes to the Romanian authorities and a substantial amount of money to the ship's captain, in the hope of escaping to freedom. Among the passengers was our former landlord, Dr. Simche, and his family. They had left Czernowitz in June 1940, shortly before the Soviets arrived, and had settled in Bucharest.

When the vessel reached Istanbul (Constantinople), the Turkish authorities refused to let it pass through the Bosporus on the way to Palestine. The British government had informed them that the quota for Jewish immigration to Palestine had been filled, and that no further entry visas would be issued to Jewish refugees. The Turks did not allow the passengers to disembark, and the ship drifted off shore for several weeks. As time went by, the living conditions on the vessel became unbearable, and the ship itself, already in bad shape upon arrival in Turkish waters, continued to deteriorate. On February 24, 1942, the Turkish authorities had the *Struma* towed into the open sea, and left it there. Shortly afterwards the ship sank, apparently torpedoed by a Soviet submarine that mistook it for an enemy vessel. The ink-black waters of the sea swallowed the ship without leaving a trace. Only one passenger survived. Dr. Simche and his family perished along with the rest of the passengers. This was the tragic end of a desperate attempt by a group of Romanian Jews to escape to freedom. After the war, a monument was raised in the Jewish cemetery of Bucharest, in memory of those who perished with the *Struma*

For the Jews on the Struma the tragedy had come to an end. For the Jews of Czernowitz, however, the tragedy was still in progress.

9. Transnistria—the Penal Colony

The Jews deported from Czernowitz, as well as those from the rest of Bukovina, were all sent to Transnistria. That territory is located east of Romania, between the rivers Dniester and Bug. The Romanians named that region Transnistria, which means "On the other side of the Dniester" (Trans-Nistru). In the south it borders the Black Sea, while in the north its boundary runs west of Moghilev, not far from the prewar border between the Soviet Union and Poland. Before the war, under Soviet rule, the western part of that region was the Moldavian Soviet Republic, with the capital at Tiraspol. The eastern and southern part of that territory belonged to the Ukrainian Soviet Republic.

Before 1941, the population of Transnistria consisted of a mixture of different nationalities: Moldovans (related to Romanians), Ukrainians, Russians, and Germans. There were also tens of thousands of Jews in the area. By August 1941, most of Transnistria had been occupied by German and Romanian troops, except for the port of Odessa and its surroundings. After bloody fighting, Odessa eventually fell to Romanian troops in October 1941. Following the agreement between the German and Romanian governments ("The Tighina Convention"), Transnistria came under Romanian administration.

Most of the cities and towns of Transnistria were either destroyed or heavily damaged during the first few weeks of war. Artillery fire and aerial bombing by the Axis forces, followed by explosions and fires set by the retreating Red Army, caused widespread devastation. The villages in the rural areas, however, as well as the *kolhozes* and *sovhozes* (collective and state farms), suffered less damage.

201

The heaviest fighting took place in and around Odessa, a major port on the Black Sea, which had a significant Jewish population. Although encircled and cut off from any supplies, the city resisted fierce attacks, mostly by Romanian troops, until the middle of October. When the city finally fell, the Romanians, who had suffered heavy losses, took their revenge. Besides shooting many prisoners of war and communists, many thousands of Jews were rounded up and executed by shooting and hanging. The atrocities committed by the Romanian army against the Jewish population of Odessa became especially savage after partisans blew up the army's headquarters.

Marshall Antonescu named Gheorghe Alexianu Governor of Transnistria. He took up residence first in Tiraspol, and later in Odessa. The Romanian government decided to use Transnistria as a penal colony for "undesirable" elements. Deprived of food, fuel, medicine, and other basic necessities of life, in an area known for its harsh winter, the government expected that these people would die quickly of "natural causes." This was the area where those deported from Bukovina and Bessarabia were shipped. From letters, smuggled by couriers from Transnistria to families and friends left behind in Czernowitz, we learned about the fate and travails of those deported. Later, after liberation, the returning survivors told us in more detail about their suffering. (Note: The persecution of Jews by the Romanian authorities in Transnistria was revealed in full after the war, during the trial of members of the Antonescu government in Bucharest, in 1946. The suffering of the Jews under Romanian fascism was chronicled immediately after the war by Matatias Carp in *The Black Book*, in 1946. See also Bibliographical Note at the end of this narrative.)

The trains that left Czernowitz with their human cargo under military escort in the fall of 1941 reached a small village on the Dniester called Atachi. This was one of the crossing points into Transnistria. Across from Atachi, on the eastern shore of the Dniester, was the town of Moghilev. Other trains took their human cargo to the holding camp Marculesti in Bessarabia. The trains arriving in Atachi from Czernowitz disgorged their human cargo and their baggage in the small railroad station. On the ground, the people found themselves surrounded by gendarmes. After traveling in cramped cattle cars, many could barely stand on their feet.

Using their rifle butts, the gendarmes pushed the new arrivals to the "custom office," where unscrupulous inspectors searched the new arrivals for "illegal" objects. It was just another way to rob the defenseless victims of anything valuable. Even their documents were taken and destroyed. They had become non-persons. After having passed the custom control, the newly arrived had to wait until the next day to cross the Dniester. Some spent the night on the shore of the river or in a field nearby. Others found shelter in empty barns or in vacant, Jewish houses, whose owners had been killed during the first weeks of the war. On the doorposts of some of those abandoned homes one could still see a *mezuzah*, the small case containing a roll of parchment inscribed with biblical text.

During the night gendarmes with flashlights walked around the huddled, exhausted mass of people lying or sitting in the cold field, trying to rest on their bundles. When they saw a man who tried to protect himself against the night chill with what appeared to be a good-quality woolen blanket, they grabbed it and walked away with it. But the gendarmes were looking mostly for young women. Those they found were ordered to come with them, supposedly to be searched for concealed jewelry. The vehement protests of parents and family were to no avail. They took them to an empty barn, and soon one could hear the screaming of the women being raped. After awhile the women returned, their clothes disheveled, their hair unkempt, and they were crying. Some of the raped girls were in their early teens. They were still children.

The crowd of hapless people, driven from their homes, shipped like animals in cattle cars, robbed of their valuables, and deprived of the most elementary human rights and dignity, were now at the mercy of gendarmes. These brutish, cruel men in uniform, many of them illiterate, who under normal conditions had been powerless and insignificant, suddenly had absolute power to torment with sadistic pleasure defenseless victims, to inflict physical and psychological harm even on children.

The next day the Dniester was crossed in primitive barges, which could accommodate no more than twenty people each. Only a few barges were available. To speed up the crossing, the gendarmes came up with an effective solution: they pushed some of their victims over board, most of them old people. Many were unable to swim and splashed the water in despair, while trying to hold on to the rim of the barges. They had no chance. The gendarmes hit them on their heads with rifle butts, until they drowned. Their corpses floated gently down the river among the slowly moving barges.

It took several days to ferry all those deported to the eastern shore. Many of the new arrivals were settled in the Moghilev ghetto. Other transports from Czernowitz were sent to Balta and Tulchin counties, east of Moghilev, near the river Bug.

The area assigned to the Jews in Moghilev had been devastated by war. Many of the houses had been destroyed. Other houses, while still standing, had no doors or windows and had been abandoned. Few of them had stoves. On the threshold of winter, the newcomers had to settle wherever they could find shelter.

Once installed in the Moghilev ghetto, the struggle for food began. The Romanian authorities prohibited the sending of food, clothing, or money to the Jews of Transnistria. The local peasants would sell their produce at exorbitant prices, and often would trade it only for valuable items, such as clothes. Most of the newly arrived resorted to barter. They exchanged a pair of pants, a sweater, a blouse, or a piece of soap for a loaf of bread, a pound of cornmeal, or a bag of potatoes. Malnutrition spread in the ghetto. The lack of food, medicine, hygiene and adequate housing soon led to a typhus epidemic. Of the nearly 7,000 people affected, less than half recovered. One could see daily horse-drawn carts passing through the streets of the ghetto, loaded with the stiff bodies of men, women, and children, the carts moving slowly towards the cemetery.

Then it started to snow. The pure white snow fell gently over the village and enveloped it, hiding the pain and evil under a blanket of innocence. But the misery persisted. The typhus epidemic was exacerbated by an extremely harsh winter, one of the harshest of the century. Icy winds blew incessantly from the Ukrainian steppe, bringing blizzards and bitter cold. At night, old and young, parents and children, huddled together, trying to keep warm, trying to sleep, trying to ignore the complaints of their empty stomachs and freezing bodies. Living in dilapidated houses, deprived of adequate heating and clothing, on the brink of starvation, the old and the weak could not resist. Typhus, hunger, and bitter cold decimated them. Many of those who had brought winter clothes had traded them for food in the first month in the ghetto. Getting food was a priority for the starving. Now they were freezing.

In spite of the hardships, the Jews of Moghilev decided not to give in. In order to survive, they began to organize their lives. They set up orphanages for nearly 1,500 children. Jewish craftsmen—tailors, cobblers, tinsmiths, cabinetmakers—got together to produce goods or provide services that could be bartered for food with the local peasants. With the assistance of Jewish teachers, "schools" were improvised for the ghetto children. Although the Jewish doctors lacked medicine, they set up a medical assistance center. Some improvised. Necessity forced them to invent new remedies. One of the doctors advised women who suffered from a lack of iron to stick a nail into a green apple, let it sit there for several days, and then eat the apple that contained dissolved iron. Many women followed this advice.

A Jewish engineer, by the name of Jägendorf, was granted permission by the authorities to repair an abandoned foundry and hire a number of Jews to work there. In the spring of 1942 some of the deportees began planting vegetables on barren plots, to supplement their meager diet. With considerable effort, ingenuity and initiative, under harsh living conditions, the Jewish community of Moghilev did its utmost to make life bearable. Periodically, the Jews of Moghilev paid bribes to the Romanian civilian and military authorities, to avoid further deportation to small villages near the Bug, where life was much harder and more dangerous.

If life was difficult for the Jews of Moghilev, it was much more difficult for those sent to Bershad, a small Ukrainian village in Balta County in northern Transnistria. Since no railroad line passed near Bershad, they arrived there on foot. After crossing the Dniester, they were marched for days over rain-soaked, muddy fields, buffeted by cold winds and drenching rain, under constant prodding by the guarding gendarmes. Many of the weak and sick perished during the long march, and their emaciated bodies were left lying in ditches next to the road. Once arrived in the village, the exhausted, freezing and hungry men, women and children found shelter in abandoned, dilapidated houses. Many of those houses had belonged to Jews killed at the beginning of the war by the German and Romanian troops, or had been abandoned by those fleeing the advancing enemy armies. The houses had been looted, and many had no doors or windows. Rain was leaking through the damaged roofs. Cold winds and rain lashed the exhausted bodies huddled together under the leaking roofs, trying to stay dry and warm. Only later were they able to do some minimal repairs on those houses to keep out rain and wind.

There were about 20,000 deportees in Bershad that came in a series of transports from the ghettoes of Bessarabia, Czernowitz, and Southern Bukovina. There were also about 4,000 local Jews that had survived the massacres of the first weeks of war. Starvation was pervasive and weakened body and mind. People thought only of survival from day to day: to feel some warmth, to have something to put in their stomachs, to have a roof over their heads. Young women and girls prostituted themselves for a loaf of bread or a bag of cornmeal.

During the winter months of 1941/1942, a typhus epidemic, hunger and the bitter cold took a heavy toll on the Jewish community of Bershad. At that time there were no sanitary facilities, and soap was only a vague memory. It did not take long before everybody was infested with lice, and typhus began to spread through the village. Thousands died during this extremely harsh winter, when the sap in the trees froze and their trunks burst. Old men and children died on the street while begging for food, stricken by typhus, cold or hunger. The corpses were collected from streets and houses, loaded on sleds, and taken to the cemetery. There, the stiff, frozen bodies were left in a pile until spring arrived, when the soil became soft enough to dig a mass grave and bury them.

Periodically, the Romanian gendarmes selected a group of Jewish men and turned them over to the German organization Todt to work on road and bridge construction. Weakened by hunger and submitted to a brutal slave labor regime, few of these men returned.

The Jews of the Bershad ghetto were also accused of supporting the Soviet partisans that roamed in that area. Whenever the partisans blew up a military train or ambushed a military convoy, dozens of Jews from the ghetto were arrested, accused of helping the enemy and executed.

Persecuted by their oppressors, tormented by hunger and ravaged by disease, the Jews of this ghetto decided not to give up. In spite of the brutal living conditions, they began to organize themselves to make life more bearable. A Jewish Committee was set up to maintain contact with the authorities. The Committee pleaded with the Romanian rulers of the region, both civilian and military, to improve the living conditions in the ghetto, and funneled the necessary bribes to obtain some concessions. It collected periodically bribe money from the community and delivered it to the masters. With the assistance of the Committee, a school was established for the children of the ghetto. The deportees even organized some cultural activities, such as occasional literary evenings. These activities helped them forget, temporarily, their desperate situation and lifted their spirits. Their oppressors were able to batter them physically, but could not break their spirit.

Among the Jews forced into ghettoes and camps in Transnistria, those in the southern counties experienced the savagery of the Romanian fascists to the fullest. In Golta County, where Romanian Colonel Modest Isopescu was prefect (chief administrator), there were three camps. The one at Bogdanovka was the largest. Most of the Jews in the camp were survivors from the massacres at Odessa and the southern counties of Transnistria. They all were Ukrainian Jews.

From the beginning of their internment, these Jews were submitted to a savage regime of plunder, hunger and misery. A loaf of bread could be obtained at the camp bakery only in exchange for a gold object. Those without valuable objects that could be exchanged for food starved. Death became a daily visitor. Without soap, without hot water, without proper clothing in the merciless cold, invaded by lice, infected with typhus, weakened by starvation, the people in the camps died in droves.

Death from starvation or disease, however, was a process too slow for the colonel. He was an impatient man. In December 1941, Colonel Isopescu gave the liquidation order. The old and sick were locked in barns and through openings in the walls were machine-gunned. When the killing was completed, the barns were doused with gasoline and set on fire. The remaining Jews were marched in groups to a precipice near the

River Bug, forced to undress in the freezing weather, and shot. The shooting continued day after day (except for Christmas), and by the end of December all the Jews of the Bogdanovka camp had been massacred. The corpses of those murdered were burned by a work-detachment of 200 Jewish survivors selected by the Romanian gendarmes. Once the burning was completed, about 150 of the members of the work-detachment were also shot.

The massacre at the Bogdanovka camp was one of the worst atrocities perpetrated by the Romanian fascists during the war. Similar massacres were carried out at the Dumanovka and Akmecetka camps that were also under Colonel Isopescu's administration. After the war, Isopescu was tried in Bucharest as a war criminal and sentenced to death. The sentence, however, was later commuted to life imprisonment.

The Romanian authorities prohibited any exchange of letters between Transnistria and Romania. Still, the Jewish community of Czernowitz was able to establish a connection with the Moghilev ghetto through messengers. They were Romanian officers or gendarmes, who traveled between Moghilev and Czernowitz. Connections were also established later with the ghetto of Bershad. For a generous compensation, the messengers carried letters and sometimes money. In the latter case, the messenger took as compensation half the money they carried. In more than a few instances, the messengers disappeared with all the money. After all, to whom could the losers complain?

The letters sent from Moghilev and from other Transnistria ghettos reflected the despair of those deported. They begged their friends and relatives in Czernowitz to send them food, clothing and money. Suffering itself from severe shortages, the Jewish community of Czernowitz did its utmost to help those in greater need through the messenger network. Though sending money or packages to Transnistria involved the risk of court martial for both sender and recipient, some assistance still went through. The head of the Jewish Council in Czernowitz, Dr. Ludwig Dische, was active in organizing the shipment of packages to the ghettoes of Transnistria. He also informed the leadership of the Jewish Federation in Bucharest about the desperate situation in Transnistria. He asked them to organize assistance for those deported, and to intervene with the government on their behalf.

Gradually, the Federation set up its own clandestine messenger network to help those freezing and starving in Transnistria's ghettoes. The Romanian government, however, ignored the Jewish Federation's pleas. Only after the German defeat at Stalingrad in early 1943 did the Romanian government gradually change its policy toward those it deported.

My father's relatives from Suceava were deported with the rest of that city's Jewish population in October 1941. Most of those banished were sent to Shargorod and Murafa, in northern Transnistria. My father's cousin, Dr. Emanuel Scherzer, a veterinarian, was in a transport sent to Djurin, a village northeast of Moghilev. We were unable to make contact with any of our Suceava relatives during the war. Later we learned that Dr. Emanuel Scherzer, who was frail and had poor vision, died in the ghetto of Djurin. None of my father's relatives survived in Transnistria.

In the ghetto of Czernowitz, the weeks of autumn passed slowly. The leaves turned yellow and fell from the trees, swirling back and forth at the whim of the capricious wind. By November the trees were almost bare. Solitary leaves clung to the branches as tenacious reminders of life. It rained and the leaves lay rotten in the gutters. The chilly, rainy fall gave way gradually to freezing winter. By December, an ice-cold wind started to blow over the city. It whistled through the branches of bare trees and drove off the last of the dead leaves. The sun was low and weak, casting long shadows across our street. At night, the sky was clear and dark, bejeweled with cold and distant stars.

Soon, however, heavy clouds gathered overhead and it started to snow. It snowed during the day, it snowed during the night, and next morning it snowed again. A heavy white blanked wrapped our city, and gave it a peaceful, idyllic appearance. When it stopped snowing, the icy winds returned with a vengeance. The temperature dropped precipitously, clasping the city and its inhabitants in an icy grip. Beneath the apparent tranquillity, there was a stark reality of suffering and misery.

In December 1941, when the deportation from Czernowitz of those Jews without residence permits had been completed, the walls of the ghetto came down. Those who had escaped the deportation tried to return to their previous apartments. Some of the better apartments, together with their furniture and household goods, had been taken over by Romanian functionaries and officers, and were no longer accessible to their initial Jewish owners. Jewish apartments in mostly run down houses had been left unoccupied, and the owners could return to those homes.

When we returned from the ghetto to our apartment on the Postgasse, we found it broken in and looted. It was the second time that we returned to a looted apartment. Almost everything we had left behind was missing or broken. The large, wood-framed mirror in my parents' bedroom, that had survived the first looting, lay shattered on the parquet floor. While the drapes had been stolen from the living room and bedroom during the first looting, this time the drape rods had been ripped out from the walls. Only the larger pieces of furniture—bed frames, sofa, dinner table, and cupboard—that were too heavy to be moved by thieves, were still there. We also learned that the partially burned out building in which our apartment was located had been condemned by the city administration. The building had no water, no electricity and the sewage pipes were broken. We had to find another place.

My parents found a small apartment on Morariugasse in the Jewish section of town. A family that had been deported had previously occupied this apartment. It consisted of two small bedrooms plus kitchen and toilet, and was located on the second floor of a two-story apartment building. The other people who lived in the building were also Jews, except for the doorkeeper who was Ukrainian. Mother hired a peasant with horse and cart, who moved whatever was left of our belongings to the new dwelling.

My grandparents returned from the ghetto to their two-bedroom apartment on Karolinengasse, not far from the burned-out Temple. When Uncle Joseph with wife Ruchel and son Elli went back to their apartment, they found it occupied by a Romanian family. Unable to find another place, they moved in with my grandparents. Aunt Anna and Tzili also lived in the same apartment. The Grandparents and Uncle Joseph's family occupied the two bedrooms, while my aunts slept in the kitchen on cots that were removed during the day. It was a crowded place, but they had a roof over their heads. Aunt Jetty with husband Bernhard and daughter Gusta moved back to their apartment on Wolangasse on the third floor of the building they once owned.

During the harsh, merciless winter of 1941-1942, there was a severe firewood shortage. Firewood was rationed, and the allocation to Jews was very meager. The available firewood was green and wet. When burning, it generated more smoke than heat. Due to the lack of firewood, our home turned into an icebox. The windows were covered with large, white ice flowers, while outside the wind howled and gusted tirelessly. We spent most of the day in the kitchen bundled up in heavy coats, wearing boots and fur caps, trying to ignore the cold.

With nothing else to do, I often stood next to the ice-covered window breathing on it to form a little melted circle. Through this spy hole I looked out at the white-covered street and the rare pedestrian, struggling to advance in the deep snow. Occasionally a horse-drawn sleigh passed, its bells echoing through the cold, thin air. I watched the snowflakes descending from the gray sky, floating gently through the transparent atmosphere and settling softly on the ground in a white, immaculate layer. Although shivering and freezing, I was still able to admire the beauty of nature.

The happiest time of the day was when Mother lit a fire in the stove to cook a meal. It consisted of watery soup and some potatoes. The snapping and crackling of wood inside the stove sounded like magic to me. The dancing flame promised warmth and comfort. We all crowded around the iron stove, hands and feet almost touching the hot metal, trying to catch as much of the heat as we could. Sitting close to the hot stove, I was seized by a wonderful feeling of well being. The warmth penetrated through my skin and made me weak and languid. An inexpressible delight filled momentarily my whole body. I wanted to drink in the warmth emanating from the stove and dose. The hot meal also gave my freezing body a respite from the cold. It was a wonderful sensation to feel the hot soup in my stomach, warming body and soul. As soon as the fire was out, however, and the last spoon of hot soup had been swallowed, the merciless cold took over again.

In the evening, Mother would light a fire in the bedroom stove to drive out some of the cold before going to bed. Although the tile stove in the bedroom kept the heat longer than the iron stove in the kitchen, shortly after the fire went out the room turned again into an icebox. Trying to sleep in a cold, drafty room, while the wind was howling in the chimney, was not easy. Although dressed in cap, wool sweater and long underwear, burrowed under the bulky goose-down comforter while keeping a passage open to breathe, I was still shivering throughout the night. When Father once left a glass of water on the night table overnight, next morning we found ice in it. When the cold became unbearable, Mother would light a fire in the stove, heat several bricks that she kept near the stove, wrap the hot bricks in towels, and give each of us one of the bricks to keep in bed at our feet. That gave us some temporary relief.

During these freezing nights the water pipes burst and the sewer line froze. We had to bring water, in buckets, from a neighboring building, where water was still running. Mother kept the buckets with water close to the kitchen stove to prevent it from freezing during the day. At night the water would be covered with a layer of ice that would melt in the morning only after Mother lit a fire in the stove. We couldn't use the toilet anymore and had to use a bucket instead. Its contents had to be promptly discarded outdoors before it froze solid.

Father had frequent coughing spasms. The freezing cold, combined with his smoking, had made his cough worse. When he had a seizure, his face turned crimson, and his whole body was shaken by convulsion. Holding on with one hand to the wall or to the table, he pressed his other hand to his chest, as if trying to stop the cough. The seizure exhausted him, and more and more often he did have to rest after the spell subsided.

Since cigarettes were rationed, Father always ran out of them before he could buy a new pack. Without a smoke, he became short tempered. His feet were hurting in the cold. They had never healed completely, and he always walked with a cane. Without income, without an occupation, without hope, tormented by a nagging cough and short of cigarettes, my father was, most of the time, irascible and in a bad mood. I often felt the consequences of that mood. Whenever I did not do what I was told to do, such as not to play ball in the house or bring firewood from the cellar, I was promptly scolded. I learned quickly to avoid my father when he was irritated. There were also occasional arguments between my parents, but usually Mother kept her cool.

Buying food during the harsh winter months was no easy task. Getting a loaf of bread in return for a ration coupon required standing in line outdoors in the bitter cold, sometimes during a snowstorm. Even bundled up and stomping the snow constantly in an attempt to keep warm, the cold still penetrated to the bone. My nose and cheeks were freezing, the fingers went numb, and the skin chilled all over my body. While standing in line for hours when it snowed, the heavy snow settled on my shoulders, wrapping me gradually in a white shroud. My moist breath turned quickly into a puff of frozen steam that powdered my eyebrows and lashes winter-white. Periodically, I had to shake off the snow, not to be turned into a snowman.

Mother, Bertha, and I usually took turns standing in the same line. While one of us was in line, the others could warm up indoors. When we finally came home with the loaf of bread or a small bag of potatoes, we were frozen and exhausted, but pleased that we would not starve the next few days.

Early in January, Mother went to visit my grandparents and Uncle Joseph, who lived together at that time. When Mother came home a few hours later, her eyes were swollen and red. We saw that she had cried. Never before had I seen Mother cry. Alarmed, we asked her what had happened.

"Uncle Joseph," she said with a deep sigh.

"What about Uncle Joseph?" Father wanted to know.

"He has been brutally beaten. He is in very bad shape," she explained with a voice choked with pain. "The previous day, while walking home from the store, Uncle Joseph encountered a group of Romanian soldiers. They grabbed him and took him to their quarters. There, they took turns pummeling and kicking him, spitting in his face, and beating him with their belts. For them, it was a form of entertainment. The soldiers held him for several hours, and after removing his winter coat, fur hat and gloves, they kicked him out into the snow. He was barely able to walk home. When he arrived, his face was swollen from the beatings, his blood-shot eyes were surrounded by black marks, and his body was full of bruises. These soldiers are animals, not people," concluded my mother, while wiping her eyes.

When Mother saw him he was in bed, his body and face covered with cold compresses and bandages. It took Uncle Joseph several weeks to recover.

By the end of March 1942, spring finally arrived. The ice flowers on the windows disappeared, the dirty snow on the streets and sidewalks melted away, and the mild sunshine brought out the first buds on trees that had been bare. Bushes and trees came alive with birdsong. Chirping warblers heralded the arrival of spring. The dreadful winter was behind us.

Although it was a cold spring, with rain and strong winds, the milder weather made life somewhat easier. Standing two or three hours in line for bread or sugar was now easier to bear than during the freezing winter months. The Jewish work detachments still had to do hard labor and face the gendarmes' brutality, but at least they were not freezing while working outdoors. Washing with mildly cold water was less unpleasant than washing with ice cold water. It is surprising how a very bad experience makes a merely unpleasant experience much easier to bear.

The arrival of spring made it possible for my parents to start earning some money. Every Sunday there was a flea market on Austriaplatz. The market had been started under Soviet rule and continued its existence under the Romanians. On weekdays the square was used as a food market, where peasants from the city's surroundings sold leftover produce after selling the required quota to the government. But on Sundays, the city's inhabitants came to the square, either to sell or to buy used household items. Father already had some experience in this kind of business from the time of the Soviet occupation. This time, Mother helped out. I also helped by packing and carrying the "merchandise" to the market.

In the wee hours of every Sunday my parents carried heavy bundles of a variety of household goods to the market, spread them out on a blanket on the ground, and waited for buyers. The merchandise offered by my parents consisted of used dishes, cutlery, a variety of pots and pans, old clothing, linen, tablecloths, worn-out shoes, and all kinds of bric-a-brac. The buyers were Romanian housewives, Ukrainian peasants, Polish craftsmen, and Russian laborers. When a buyer showed some interest in any of the merchandise, the haggling began. Mother turned out to be much better at this business than Father was. My parents sold our own household goods as well as those of our neighbors and acquaintances. For the sale of goods that did not belong to us, my parents received a "commission" from the owners. Although the earnings from these sales were meager, they allowed my parents to pay for the basic necessities, such as rent and rationed food, and to buy some additional food in the market.

The arrival of spring brought a new activity for kids: school. Well, we called it school, although it was quite different from a normal school. In fact, Jewish children were not allowed to attend school, and Jewish teachers had been ejected from schools and from the university. Under those circumstances, Jewish parents decided to bring together the unemployed Jewish teachers with the Jewish children and improvise a school. Assisted by the Jewish Council, Jewish teachers started giving private lessons to Jewish children in the teacher or student's home. Some of the teachers were former university professors, who had been prohibited from teaching at the Czernowitz University. The parents paid the teachers only a nominal fee, since most of the Jewish families had no income.

We studied the same curriculum as in public schools: Romanian literature, French, Latin, physics, chemistry, math, history, and geography. It was not an easy way to study. There were no textbooks, and most of the studying was done from handwritten notes. We were often hungry, and it required an extra effort to concentrate on the lesson rather than on the stomach. I still remember how, during the lessons, while the teacher described the conquest of Gaul by Julius Cesar or discussed the Pythagorean Theorem, I kept thinking of fresh, crispy rolls with butter and jam. Those thoughts made my mouth water and distracted me. The teaching was often interrupted by curfews, and later by deportations.

The Romanian authorities found out of the existence of this schooling system and had to be bribed periodically to turn a blind eye. This was the silver lining of living in a corrupt society: with bribes, one could ameliorate the harshness of persecution.

At home, I got additional tutoring from my sister. During the day she worked at a Jewish food distribution center, that provided food to the Jewish hospital and orphanage. In the evening, after work, Bertha spent about an hour with me, helping with math problems, French lessons, or literary essays. She also guided me to reading good literature that she borrowed from her friends. Much later, after the war, the guidance and tutoring provided by my sister, together with the knowledge acquired during the private lessons with different Jewish teachers, made it possible for me to pass exams and to skip two years of formal high school.

My sister was also involved in other activities. She and some of her friends joined the Zionist youth organization Bethar. Since the organization had a right-wing orientation, its members expected little interference from the authorities. Some of the key members of Bethar were Polish refugees. Among these refugees were three close friends: Shmuel, Itzhak, and Mordche. They came originally from the Lodz area. In 1939, when Germany and the Soviet Union invaded Poland, they fled to the Soviet-occupied area, while their families remained in Lodz under German occupation.

After the Soviet occupation of Northern Bukovina, the three friends came to Czernowitz. Assisted by the local Bethar organization, they moved into a small room not far from our apartment. They supported themselves by trading, both under the Soviets and later under the Romanians. The three also took an active role in organizing the Bethar under the new conditions created by the war and the Antonescu regime. Meetings took place regularly in the private home of one of the members. They kept changing the meeting place, to avoid drawing the attention of the authorities or informers.

At one of these meetings, Bertha met the three Polish friends. There were often heated debates among them on matters of ideology. Bertha expressed her left-leaning Zionist opinions, acquired in earlier years at Hashomer Hatzaïr, while the three Poles countered with their right-wing Zionist ideas. Bertha argued that the foundation of a Jewish homeland in Palestine could be laid only by building *kibbutzim* (collective farms), and by turning the desert into farmland. The Poles insisted that the only way to establish a Jewish State was by armed struggle against the British colonial power and against Arab gangs. None of them changed their minds. Still, in spite of frequent differences of opinion, Bertha and Shmuel became close friends.

Shmuel, who eventually married my sister, told me more about his past many years later. He was born and grew up in the Polish village of Aleksandrow, near Lodz. Shmuel's father, an Orthodox Jew, was a grain dealer. He bought grain from the peasants, took it to a mill to have it ground into flour, and sold it to the city's bakers. He had two daughters and three sons, of whom Shmuel was the oldest. Their village had a mixed population of Poles, Germans and Jews. When the Germans invaded Poland, Shmuel and several friends tried to flee to Warsaw, but were soon overtaken by the German troops. He and his friends were detained and locked up in an empty school building.

In that group was also a young, attractive woman who spoke German. After a few days of detention, using her charm, she convinced the guard to let the whole group go free, since they were not members of the Polish Army and had not committed any infraction. Once freed, the group disbanded. Barely released from detention, on his way back home, Shmuel was stopped at a German military roadblock and asked for his identification. The papers showed that his last name was Schmidt, a German name. The fact that he was blond and blue-eyed also helped. The German concluded that he was a *Volks-German* (ethnic German) and let him go.

After the Soviets occupied the eastern part of Poland, the Germans tried to convince the Jews living close to the new border to cross over to the Russian side. In many instances, they just dumped groups of Jews over the border. The Russians, however, refused to accept them. Still, fearing the vicious Nazi anti-Semitism, hundred of thousands of Jews in German-occupied Poland wanted to cross the border into the Soviet-occupied area.

Officially, the Soviet troops guarding the new border had orders not to let in any refugees from the German side. Trying to help the refugees, some Soviet-Jewish officers hinted that if they marched to the border waving a red flag and singing the "International" (the international Communist anthem), the refugees would be accepted by the Soviets. The refugees took the hint and thus were able to cross over in large numbers into the Soviet occupied area. Shmuel was one of them. A large number of those who crossed the border were later deported by the Soviets to the Ural region and Siberia. It is a bitter irony that many of the deported Jews were thus saved from the slaughter by the Nazis after Germany invaded the Soviet Union.

Once in the Soviet-occupied area, Shmuel began to make plans to cross the border into Romania. He did not want to live under the Soviets. He was a dedicated Zionist and was hoping to travel from Romania to Palestine. When he arrived at the border town of Kolomyya, he inquired about the possibility of crossing the border. He found a guide who promised to take him across the border during the night. When darkness fell and the two started to walk on a narrow path through a forested area, they came face to face with a Soviet military patrol. It turned out that the "guide" was a Soviet agent who led Shmuel directly into the hands of the border guards.

Shmuel was promptly arrested and taken to the commanding officer for interrogation. He tried to explain to his interrogator that he was unemployed and was looking for work. That he had not been able to find any work in Kolomyya, and that he was trying to cross the border and look for work in Romania. The interrogator was apparently convinced and set him free, but warned him not to try again to cross the border. Shmuel was able to come to Czernowitz only after the Soviets occupied Northern Bukovina in the summer of 1940.

There was more to Bertha's membership in Bethar than met the eye. She and some of her friends from Hashomer Hatzaïr had joined the organization as a cover for antifascist activities. The group met periodically at one of the member's home, supposedly to discuss different Zionist topics. In fact, during these meetings, the group planned and organized a variety of antifascist activities. One of these activities consisted in mimeographing and distributing a collection of news, picked up secretly by one of the group members from radio London and Moscow. The mimeographed leaflets contained reports about the losses or defeats the Nazis had suffered on different fronts—news that was never reported in the official Romanian media. The leaflets reported the latest political activities in the allied countries, about partisan activity behind the Nazi front, and described the barbaric behavior of the Nazis in the occupied areas. The printed material also contained news from the ghettoes and camps of Transnistria. It was designed to inform and to maintain hope in the oppressed and gloomy Jewish community of our city. The mimeographing and distribution of these leaflets was a highly dangerous activity, and none of the other Bethar members knew about it.

In the spring of 1942, I had my first encounter with the Romanian police. I was on my way to the home of one of the Jewish teachers, where I was supposed to take a math lesson with other boys. It was a cold day and I was wearing my winter coat and cap. Walking to the teacher's home, I heard someone yelling, "Hey, you!" I turned around and saw a policeman standing near a lamppost. He was a tall, bony individual with penetrating eyes, sharp features and a black mustache. In his dark-brown police uniform embellished with gilded brass buttons, a thick leather belt around the waist and revolver holster on the side, he looked strong and intimidating.

When he caught my eye, he ordered me to approach him. His face was gray and hard like rain-beaten stone. I felt an inward shudder. A chill ran down my spine. At home I had often heard my parents talking of the brutality and corruption of Romanian policemen, of their harassment of Jewish pedestrians, and of the extortion of money from innocent people. What could he want from me? I was tempted to run away as fast as my feet could carry me. But something told me it was not a good idea. I approached him with trepidation.

"Are you a Jew?" he snarled in a harsh, raspy voice.

"Yes," I replied in a shaky voice.

His steel-gray eyes pierced through the very core of my soul; eyes that spewed hatred, eyes that intimidated and frightened.

"Where is your yellow star?" he yelled, still staring at me. I looked at the lapel of my coat, and realized with horror that I was not wearing the star. In the morning, I had been in a hurry not to be late for my math lesson and forgot to transfer the yellow star from my jacket to the winter coat. My palms grew clammy, my mouth got dry, my belly churned.

Simmering with rage, the policeman looked down at me. His brows were knit together in one dark, threatening line across his forehead. "You little kike, you think you can walk all over town without the yellow star, don't you?" he barked at me.

"I forgot to put it on my lapel," I replied with trembling voice, as if this would be a good excuse for my infraction. Fear twisted a knot in my stomach.

"You forgot? First you come from Poland illegally, and now you walk around without the yellow star!" he snarled, his eyes sparking with anger.

If he wanted to frighten me, he surely succeeded. I knew that any Jew that came from Poland to Romania illegally was sent back to Poland, where his fate at the hands of the Nazis was well known. I started to tremble like a leaf in the wind. I could barely stand on my feet. A wave of fear went through my whole body.

"I did not say that I came from Poland," I replied meekly.

"Liar, you did say that you came from Poland!"

He then grabbed me by my lapel with his left hand and lashed out with his right, landing a bone-jarring blow in my face. I lost my balance, and my head crashed into the nearby metal lamppost. Sparks flashed in front of my eyes. I felt a sharp pain in my face and blood started to run from my nose and mouth. I realized that by hitting the lamppost with my face I had broken my front teeth. Terrified, hurting and bleeding, I started to cry.

At that moment, like a saving angel, Uncle Joseph appeared. A neighbor had seen what had happened and alerted my uncle, who came running. He arrived just before the policeman would take me away. Uncle Joseph talked quietly to him, then slipped a substantial *baksheesh* into his palm. The bribe disappeared quickly into the policeman's pocket.

"Don't you ever walk around without the yellow star," he hissed in a gruff voice, shaking his finger at me. He then turned and slowly walked away. My uncle had saved me with a *baksheesh*. Corruption had shown again its benefits. However, my uncle arrived too late to save my teeth. Only many years later was I able to fix my broken front teeth.

In spite of constant harassment and persecutions, the Jews of Czernowitz were still able to poke fun at themselves and at their enemies. When two Jews got together, they usually talked about the situation on the front, about the latest anti-Jewish edicts issued by the government, or about the abuses perpetrated by some local policeman. These conversations were very depressing and left them with a feeling of gloom and doom. To console one another, they started telling jokes. Humor had often been a weapon used by Jews in times of despair, to fight off depression and keep their spirits high. We called it "gallows humor." Hitler, of course, was the butt of many jokes during the war. The best anti-Hitler humor those days was a parody on "Die Bürgschaft" (The Bail), a ballad by the famous nineteenth century German poet Friedrich Schiller. In the parody, in which Hitler is substituted for the ancient Greek tyrant Dionis, poetic talent and biting humor are combined to mock the "Führer" and his Nazi regime (see Attachment).

While the Jewish community did its utmost to adapt to a difficult life, more dramatic events were in store for the Jews of our city.

10. The Deportations of 1942

In the spring of 1942, the Governor dismissed Mayor Traian Popovici. A man of honesty and decency had no place in the fascist administration. In May, rumors started to circulate that new deportations were imminent. The word spread that the authorities were putting together lists of those who had resident permits signed only by the Mayor ("Popovici permits"), but not by the Governor.

In June the rumors turned into reality. Governor Calotescu issued a secret order that all Jews with "Popovici permits" be deported. Major Marinescu, from the governor's council, was put in charge of this operation. Following the German and Soviet example, he ordered that the round-ups take place after dark.

During the night of June 7 to 8, gendarmes carrying bayonet-tipped rifles cordoned off the city. Armed military units patrolled the deserted streets. In contrast to previous nights, the streets were well lit, to make any escape from the buildings more difficult. Police and military, with lists in hand, went to specified addresses to pick up the residents. Those arrested were allowed to take only what they could carry. Their apartments were searched, anything valuable was removed, and then the dwellings were sealed. The residents seized were taken by truck to the Maccabee sport arena outside the city.

All night truckloads of people were brought to the arena. In the early morning hours of June 8, the authorities ordered those arrested to exchange their Romanian currency (*lei*) into the German currency used in Transnistria (*Reichskredit-Kassenscheine* or RKKS). The gendarmes checked the documents of those arrested and did body searches for hidden valuables. The people were then formed into a convoy and marched to the railroad station. Long trains of empty cattle cars were waiting. The scene was an eerie reminder of the events of October 1941. About 50 people and their belongings were squeezed into each cattle car. Once the cars were full, the doors were closed, locked and sealed. Screeching and puffing, the trains slowly left the station, with their sorry load of distraught people.

The same operation was repeated on June 14 and again on June 28. Police and gendarmes carried out those arrests at night, with assistance from the military. Those arrested were taken by truck to the sports arena and then marched to the railroad station. All those arrested had "Popovici permits." During the roundup of June 28, the authorities discovered that they had not arrested sufficient people to fill the trains. Major Marinescu ordered that the section of the city between the suburb of Rosch and Piteegasse be cordoned off, and the Jews living in that area be arrested and taken to the train station, regardless of the kind of residence permit they possessed. The trains had to be filled to capacity.

The nights of June 1942, when 4,000 and 5,000 people were rounded up and deported, saw many tragic events. A large number of those arrested were old people, who had been protected so far by "Popovici permits." They were barely able to walk, and were unable to carry their bags. Several old women were wearing nightgowns, since they were taken from their beds and not given sifficient time to get dressed. Some of them collapsed on the way to the railroad station, and had to be carried or supported by younger people in the convoy.

During the roundup on June 8, police and gendarmes entered the Jewish mental hospital and forced some 70 mental patients into the street. It was already daylight when the mentally ill were marched to the stadium. From the window of our apartment, I could see the column slowly moving over the pavement. Most of these patients were not aware of what was happening. Some were laughing constantly, others behaved like sleepwalkers, while still others had seizures and had to be restrained. The guards beat without mercy those who did not obey the orders or displayed erratic behavior. To see these human wretches being marched under police escort to the railroad station was a macabre sight. The stark contrast between the blissful serenity, the laughter of some of the madmen, and the cruel brutality of their guards made me shudder. Non-Jewish passers-by who saw the eerie convoy of mentally ill, stopped and crossed themselves. It seemed like a picture from a horror movie.

When the police could not find those on the list, they arrested other people living at that address or in that building. The cattle cars had to be filled. Such a tragic situation occurred in my family.

After the struggle to obtain residence permits in the fall of 1941, members of our family ended up with different permits. My parents, grandparents and Uncle Joseph's family had residence permits signed by the Governor ("Calotescu permits"), while Aunts Anna, Tzili and Jetty with her family had permits signed only by the Mayor.

When rumors started to circulate that those with "Popovici permits" would be targeted for deportation, my aunts started to prepare themselves for the journey. They purchased warm cloths and heavy boots, since these were essential to survive the harsh winter in Transnistria. They also prepared food for several days of travel. Aunt Jetty bought a warm winter coat for my cousin Gusta, as well as children's boots. They packed their suitcases and waited.

The police came to pick them up during the third roundup, on June 28. Bernhard, Jetty and Gusta were the first to be picked up by police. As related later to my mother by neighbors, little Gusta was crying bitterly when she and her parents were forced out of their apartment. When they stopped for a moment outside the building, the Ukrainian janitor was waiting. Christian neighbors were also outside, watching in silence. The janitor spit in Aunt Jetty's face, cursed her and grabbed the blanket she was holding on her arm. The blanket was to protect Gusta during the cold nights they expected to spend in open fields. Accompanied by the doorkeeper's cursing, Jetty, Bernhard and weeping Gusta were forced to climb into the waiting truck and were taken to the Maccabee sports arena.

When I heard about the vicious behavior of the hate-filled janitor, I remembered when Aunt Jetty had hired her several years earlier. My aunt had advertised for an apartment building janitor in the local newspaper,

and a young peasant woman had applied for the job. She had moved to
the city recently, but could not find work. She begged Aunt Jetty to hire
her. My aunt took her out of pity rather than out of conviction that she
was suitable for the job. She gave her a small apartment in the building and
a monthly salary. The young woman was elated when she was hired. Soon,
however, Aunt Jetty found out that she had made a mistake. The woman
turned out to be lazy and unreliable.

When the building was nationalized by the Soviets and later taken over
by the Romanian authorities, the janitor's attitude towards my uncle and
aunt changed drastically. Her initial humble, submissive attitude changed
to one of arrogance and insolence. She behaved as if she were the mistress
of the building. Now that Uncle Bernhard, Aunt Jetty, and little Gusta
were totally helpless, all the venom and hatred came out from that
woman's dark soul: she cursed and spit in the face of her benefactors. I
remembered a Latin proverb that my father often used in those days:
"Homo homini lupus" (People behave like wolves to each other). Jew-
hatred, fanned by the fascist regime, had poisoned the souls of many
people, and turned some of them into vicious animals. The janitor had
become such a creature.

In the early morning hours of June 29, policemen knocked at my
grandparents' door. They had come to pick up Aunts Anna and Tzili.
Anna was home and they took her to the waiting truck. Tzili, however,
was not home. Since rumors started circulating in mid May about the
possible deportation of those with "Popovici permits," Aunt Tzili stayed
with us. She felt it was safer to be with us, since we had a "Calotescu
permit." But she had not considered the cruelty of the Romanian police.

After searching my grandparents' apartment and not finding Aunt
Tzili, one of the policemen turned to Uncle Joseph and said to him in a
threatening voice: "If you don't tell us where your sister is, I will take you,
your wife, and your child instead."

Pleading and offers of pecuniary compensation (bribes) left him
unmoved. Joseph and Ruchel knew that, if deported, their one-year-old
baby had no chance to survive. In despair, Uncle Joseph came with one
of the policemen to our apartment. When Tzili saw her brother with the

policeman, she burst into tears. She knew what it meant. The policeman, a tall, bony man with cold eyes and a small, black mustache, asked in a harsh voice, "Who is Cecilia Neumann?"

Barely audible, Tzili replied, "It's me."

After verifying her documents, the policeman barked at her, "Let's go!"

We were all crying. In her mid twenties, Aunt Tzili was the youngest of my aunts, and the most loved one. We embraced her and she left in tears, with the policeman behind her. Uncle Joseph followed them into the hallway and slipped the policeman 100 lei not to inform his superiors that Tzili was hiding in our place. Otherwise, we may have had to join her.

We never saw Aunt Tzili again.

The summer of 1942 was a summer of anguish and tears. Many of our friends and neighbors were deported in June of that year. Several members of the Weissglass family—relatives of my grandfather—were among them. Bertha's friend, Selma Meerbaum-Eisinger, together with her mother and stepfather, were also deported. They were in the last transport of June 28, on the same train with my family. Of the three June transports, the people in the last one were to have the most tragic fate.

Some of the survivors described later the fate of the three June transports. All trains took their live cargo to Atachi—the same crossing point into Transnistria that had been used for deportees the previous year. Waiting gendarmes, using their rifle butts and cursing, cleared the trains in several minutes. Many of the sick and old, pushed and kicked out of the cattle cars, left their baggage on the train. The people were herded on the shore of the Dniester, where they spent the night under the open sky. The following day they crossed the river in barges, each packed to capacity. In the process, some of the baggage was stolen or lost.

Once they arrived on the eastern shore of the river, they were forced to submit to a thorough search by gendarmes. Anything of value— wedding rings, bracelets, watches, gold earrings—was seized. After spending another night under the open sky, the people were sent to several camps. Most of those from the first and second transport were sent to Cariera de Piatra. Others ended up in Moghilev and Tulcin, where they found many of the Jews who had been deported from Czernowitz in the fall of 1941. The existing Jewish communities in those locations helped the new arrivals to adapt to their new life, finding shelter for them, and later, work.

After crossing the Dniester at Atachi, the Jews of the third transport were taken first to *Cariera de Piatra* ("The Quarry"), a transit camp near the river Bug. Once there, they were kept in an open field, in the rain, not far from several decrepit, empty barracks. Only after pleading and bribing the guards were they allowed to take shelter in the barracks. These were large, barn-type structures, with trashy dirt floors and missing doors.

After spending a week in the barracks, with barely anything to eat, they were taken to Chetvertinovka, another transit camp on the Bug. There they were quartered in the barns of several former *kolhozes* (collective farms). Three to four hundred people had to live in a barn, which previously served as a shelter for cattle and pigs. Appalled by what they saw, some of the people considered escaping to other ghettos or camps, where living conditions were more humane. A few escaped to Tulcin, Obodovka, and Bershad, but most remained in Chetvertinovka.

To eke out a living, they sold, to the local peasants, some of the belongings they still had. A few people started working on the farms in the neighborhood, in return for a loaf of bread or some potatoes. This lasted about two months. In August 1942, the German military command requested several thousand Jews from the Romanian authorities, who were to work on construction and other projects. The work was to be performed east of the Bug, in an area under German administration. The Romanian authorities complied with the request.

As a result of the agreement between the Romanian and German authorities, most of the Jews of Chetvertinovka were taken across the Bug near the village of Ladyzhin. There they underwent a thorough search by SS men, who claimed they were looking for weapons. They did not find any weapons, but money, clothing, and linen in good condition were seized. To allay any fear and to assure that the people would comply peacefully with his orders, the German commander, SS-*Hauptsturmführer* Mass, made rosy promises. He told the frightened mass of people that they would be loaded on trucks, taken to a central labor camp, and would then be dispersed to several smaller camps. Each person would be assigned a job suitable to his or her skills. They would also receive food three times daily, and would have individual beds at night.

In despair, people were grasping at straws. They wanted to believe these promises and became more relaxed. The outlook was not too bleak. After all, the Germans were a civilized people, a people of culture and could be trusted, couldn't they? Soon, the empty trucks arrived to take the people to their destination. In the belief that they were going to the same central labor camp, members of the same family jumped on different trucks, wherever they found room. Only the following day did they find out that they had been taken to different camps. Parents were separated from their children, husbands from their wives. They would not see each other again.

From Ladyzhin, the people were sent to camps in Ivangorod, Mikhailovka, Teplik, Oradovka, and others. In these camps, the people were assigned to the German construction organization Todt. Every morning the men lined up and were marched to the work place, usually several miles from the camp. After arriving at their destination, they had to do hard labor 12 hours daily, digging ditches, constructing roads, erecting bridges, and building fortifications. The women were assigned to tailor shops, to make new German uniforms or repair old ones. They slept in barracks in crowded bunk beds. The food was often spoiled and far from sufficient for the hard physical labor required. Deprived of food and overworked, an increasing number of people fell sick. The emaciated bodies fell easy prey to disease. Typhus spread in the camps and took its toll in death among young and old.

Two months after arriving in the camps, on Yom Kippur day 1942, the first *Aktion* (purge) took place. The Germans had a knack for carrying out major operations, such as deportations or mass-executions, on Jewish holidays. On Yom Kippur morning, the able-bodied men and women were marched off to work, while the old, the sick, and children stayed behind. In the evening, when the people returned from work, the camp was empty. The SS men had taken outside those left behind in the morning, and shot them. They were buried in shallow mass graves. Almost everybody who returned had lost one or several family members.

With threats of further executions, the SS men suppressed the wailing and crying that pervaded the camp.

As time went by, more and more people became unable to work due to illness and lack of food. Additional *Aktionen* took place at several months' intervals. As in the Yom Kippur purge, after the able-bodied men and women were marched off to work, those weak and sick were taken outside the camp and killed. The camp population was shrinking rapidly. It became clear to those still alive that everybody would soon die from disease, emaciation, or at the hand of the SS executioners.

Some people tried to escape by fleeing across the Bug. Those caught were brutally beaten and then killed. A few escaped and were able, later, to bear witness to the atrocities committed by the Germans in those camps.

We were unable to establish to what camp Aunts Anna, Tzili and Jetty, as well as Uncle Bernhard and Cousin Gusta were taken. We only knew that they were in the third transport of June 1942, and that most people from that transport ended up across the Bug, under German rule. Only after liberation by the Red Army did we learn their fate.

In the summer of 1942, my parents decided that it was time for me to start working and earn some money. Such work would help the family and keep me busy. I ended up working in a lumberyard. There was plenty of menial labor for me. I carried studs from one place to another, pushed carts loaded with wooden boards, and helped grown-ups with their work at the yard. The work was physically demanding, since I wasn't used to carry heavy loads. Needless to say, the earnings amounted to a pittance.

Physical and mental abuse from adults and from work mates was a daily occurrence. While other people were addressed by their name, I was addressed with the word "*jidan*" or "*pui de jidan*." There were a few older boys working there, mostly Ukrainians, who made a sport to hurt and harass me: they hit me "by accident" with wooden boards, they dropped wooden logs on my feet "by accident," always laughing afterwards. More than once, I cried because of pain and humiliation.

Still, I didn't complain openly. I accepted any task given. I swept the sawdust, scrubbed the cement floor, pushed the wheelbarrow that held scraps of wood, hauled the trash, and stooped low to pick up the heavy beams for the *Meister*, the master. Never said "no" to the grownups who ordered me around. I did whatever I was told to do, and swallowed the insults. I did it because I knew that life for little Gusta, for my aunts, and for the many others shipped to that grim and hostile land called Transnistria, was much worse than my own. I also knew not to complain about the job, regardless of how miserable it made me and how ridiculous the pay. I had to earn some money, albeit very little, to help my struggling family. The money I earned would help pay for a loaf of bread, a pound of sugar, or a bottle of cooking oil.

There were also decent people among the older workers. Once, while I was carrying a heavy load of wooden logs, one of the boys pushed his elbow into my ribs. I dropped the logs on my feet and started crying in pain. An older, white-haired worker, who had seen what happened, approached the boy that hit me, slapped him hard in the face, and said something to him in a harsh tone. I didn't hear what he said, but I know that after the incident that boy didn't harass me anymore. He even started calling me by my real name. I discovered that bullies turn into sissies when the tables are turned on them. What a change!

After work, at home, I had to do some studying with my sister. Often I was tired and did not feel like solving math problems or conjugating French verbs. But my sister would not have it otherwise, and trying to contradict her would have been useless anyway. Once she had her mind made up, no mortal could have changed it.

After working for two months in the lumberyard, a change occurred in my activities. In early September, Mother met Moishe Weissglass in the market. He was a cousin of my grandfather, and a locksmith. His small shop was in the basement of an old building in the Jewish quarter. Mother told him about my work in the lumberyard and about the harassment I endured. Mr. Weissglass said that he needed some help in his shop, and asked my mother if she would let me be his apprentice. He promised to teach me the skill of a locksmith, and also to pay me a small salary. Mother was pleased with the offer and accepted. She felt that it would be better for me to work with a relative and learn a new skill, rather than do strenuous physical work in the lumberyard in a hostile environment. Three days later, I left the lumberyard and became a locksmith apprentice.

Mr. Weissglass was a good-natured, friendly, elderly man with blue, watery eyes, a short, white goatee, and an endless supply of jokes. He always seemed content, regardless of circumstances. In his poorly lit locksmith shop he had a worn-out workbench with a vice mounted at its end. Next to it stood a wooden, ancient cabinet with numerous drawers that contained a variety of tools: hammers, pliers, wrenches, files of different shapes, a hand drill, a soldering iron, solder, a variety of screwdrivers, a hacksaw, and different hacksaw blades. In the bottom drawer there were various old locks and lock components, such as latches, bolts, knobs and handles. In a corner of the room there was a bundle of iron rods and bars used for making keys. A single electric bulb hung from the ceiling, and the floor was covered with wooden planks. There were two small dirty windows close to the ceiling, at the level of the sidewalk, which allowed only a few anemic rays of light to enter the room. The air in the shop was musty and stale.

During the first week, Mr. Weissglass taught me how to use each tool. Predictably, I ended up with nasty cuts on my fingers. Still, I learned how to mount a blade on a hacksaw, how to cut an iron rod without cutting off my fingers, and how to use a hammer without slamming it on my fingernails. He taught me how to operate a hand drill without perforating some part of my body, and how to handle a soldering iron without burning my clothes or myself. Mr. Weissglass was a very patient man, and kept a close eye on me. Whenever I botched the job assigned, he corrected me, often with a smile. He treated me like a grandson. He always kept his cool, regardless how often I made a mistake, cut a deep groove in the workbench with the hacksaw, or cut my finger. When I hurt myself, he always had a soothing word for me. Although by the end of the first week I had bandages on my left thumb and forefinger, I also knew how to handle most of the tools.

In the following days, I learned how to make a door key. In those days, keys were about four inches long and quite heavy. They had a ring-shaped handle at one end and a dented part at the other. I learned how to cut the iron rod into four-inch-long pieces, how to solder the ring-shaped handle to the iron rod, how to attach a small, flat square of metal at the other end, and how to cut the necessary notches into the metal square with hacksaw and file. The first keys I made looked nice, but were not able to lock any doors. When I finally made the first key that was able to open and lock a door, I felt very proud. It gave me a deep satisfaction to have completed my assignment, to have made something useful with my own hands. I started to like my work in the shop, and was on the way to becoming a good locksmith.

My parents, however, had other plans for me. In early fall, when the improvised school for Jewish children started again, my parents decided that I should go back to school. My education was very important to them. "A good education opens the door to a better future," my father used to say.

After having worked for several weeks as a locksmith, I said good-bye to Mr. Weissglass. I returned to school to study algebra, physics, and French, to prepare myself for that "better future."

Toward the end of 1942 the news from the Eastern Front was not as bleak as earlier in the year. True, the Germans had reached the Volga near Stalingrad; German panzer columns had reached the foothills of the Caucasus Mountains and had occupied part of the Grozny oilfields. Bloody fighting in and around Stalingrad continued, however, in spite of German claims that the ruined city had "almost" been captured. In November 1942, the Soviets started a powerful counter-offensive. The German and Romanian news agencies reported "strong enemy attacks," "huge enemy losses," and "heavy defensive battles" in the Middle Don region. The triumphant tone of previous military reports gave way to a more restrained, almost somber tone. It became clear that an enormous battle was in progress, and that Hitler's armies were on the defensive.

In December the newspapers started to use the terms "mobile defense" and "elastic defense" when describing the fighting on the Middle Don and in the Caucasus. From people who listened to BBC radio, we found out that "mobile" or "elastic defense" were euphemisms used by the German High Command to report the retreat of German forces. From the same radio broadcasts we learned that the Red Army had broken through enemy lines and trapped the German Sixth Army and several Romanian divisions in and around Stalingrad. German attempts to free the encircled forces failed. After several weeks of bloody, savage fighting in the Stalingrad region, the remnants of the German Sixth Army surrendered to the Red Army at the end of January 1943. The Romanians also suffered heavy losses. The Romanian Third Army, that eighteen months earlier had massacred defenseless Jews in the towns and villages of Northern Bukovina, paid a heavy price in blood on the killing fields of Stalingrad.

Finally, we had good news from the front! The German army had been beaten at Stalingrad! The army of the "master race" was not invincible, after all, as many had been inclined to believe. The Romanian fascists had also been taught a lesson. Our spirits soared.

I became very excited by the latest developments. I wanted to know every detail of the gigantic battle that took place around Stalingrad. When Father or Mother came home after spending time in town, my first question was, "What's new on the front? What is the latest BBC radio report?" When I read the newspapers and saw repeated reports of "very heavy fighting" and of "bloody battles," I knew that the Germans were not winning. I became elated when I heard my father commenting that, in spite of its past victories, Germany could still be defeated. What until now was a mere wish, a dream, came closer to reality. My enthusiasm, however, was somewhat tempered by a nagging question that kept popping up in my mind: when the fascists realize that they are losing the war, will they not take revenge on the Jews still living among them? But I quickly suppressed that thought and enjoyed the Russian victory at Stalingrad.

While the Romanians turned somber and morose, Jews who met on the street talked with excitement about the Russian victory. For the Jews living under the boot of the oppressor, it was the first ray of hope after long years of darkness.

The defeat at Stalingrad also brought changes in the attitude of the Romanian authorities. They began to realize that winning the war against the Soviet Union was far from certain. To protect themselves, the government decided to moderate its policies toward the Jews. Further deportations of Jews were suspended. Anti-Jewish legislation was not as strictly enforced as in the past. For the Jews of Czernowitz, it became easier to buy food and fuel. It also became easier to send packages and money to the deportees in Transnistria. Early in 1943, the boot of the oppressor on the neck of the Jewish community was not as heavy anymore.

Our troubles, however, were far from over.

11. The Soviets Return

While the year 1943 started out on an optimistic note, in the spring of that year a shocking event happened in our family: Bertha was arrested. It occurred during a meeting of the Bethar organization in the private home of one of its members. The meeting was attended by Bertha and by about a dozen other young people, and was led by Shmuel. His friends, Itzhak and Mordche, were also present. The Ukrainian neighbors had noticed the gathering of a large number of Jews and informed police that a communist meeting took place in the building. Police cordoned off the building, broke down the locked door and arrested the whole group. We found out about Bertha's arrest from a neighbor who had witnessed the event. My parents rushed to the police station to inquire about my sister, and were told that Bertha and the rest of the group had been arrested for communist activity.

It was a heavy blow for the whole family. Long prison terms or deportation of those arrested was a real possibility. For Shmuel, Itzhak and Mordche, who were illegally in the country, there was also the threat of being sent back to Poland. That would have meant certain death for them.

The families of the arrested teenagers, including my parents, appealed to the leadership of the Bethar and to the Jewish Council for help. Since Bethar was a right-wing Zionist organization, its leaders had connections at the Mayor's office and at Police Headquarters. The Jewish Council also had connections at the Mayor's office. They intervened on behalf of those arrested. After several days of detention and interrogation, and after a substantial amount of money changed hands, the girls in the group, including Bertha, were released. No proof of subversive activity was found. The leaders of the group, Shmuel, Itzhak and Mordche, as well as the other arrested men, had to spend several weeks in jail and, after another substantial bribe, were finally released. Again, the notorious corruption of the Romanian authorities showed its silver lining.

Throughout 1943 the news from the front was very encouraging. After the battle of Stalingrad, the Red Army expanded its offensive along the entire front. In the process, it liberated large areas of the country from German occupation. Naturally, the announcements made by the German High Command (OKW) and reported by the Romanian newspapers never admitted the success of Soviet forces. The special bulletins, however, as those issued in the previous years announcing victory after victory on the Eastern Front, had disappeared from the newspapers. Instead, the reports stated that German troops were in the process of "straightening out" the front line, or of "detaching themselves from the enemy," euphemisms used to cover up withdrawal and defeat. The triumphant confidence of the previous reports had disappeared. We knew from BBC radio reports that the Germans had suffered a series of defeats and were on the defensive along the entire front.

In the summer of 1943 we heard that the largest tank battle of the war was taking place in the Kursk region. I followed the war from newspaper reports and saw pictures of the battle in the German illustrated magazine, *Signal.* At night, the pictures of the battle shown in the magazine flashed before my inner eye: tanks firing at tanks, antitank guns firing at enemy vehicles, corpses of soldiers hanging out of the turrets of burned-out tanks. Those were exciting scenes for a fifteen-year-old boy. When I finally fell asleep, I had refought in my mind the whole battle.

A few days later, to my delight, I learned that the Germans had lost the Battle of Kursk along with thousands of tanks. From then on they were unable to mount any major offensive on the Eastern Front and were in general retreat.

Towards the end of 1943 and early in 1944, the front moved closer to Transnistria. Partisan activity in the area increased. The Romanian troops were not eager to capture the partisans, since they realized that the war was lost. More and more often the partisans came boldly into villages, demanding food from the peasants, not afraid of being arrested. At night they frequently ambushed Romanian patrols, but did not shoot them. They only asked the soldiers if their officer treated them well. If the answer was "no," they shot the officer. But in most instances, they just disarmed the ambushed patrol and disappeared in the darkness with their weapons.

With the German troops across the Bug, the situation was different. German trains loaded with war material were derailed or blown up. Nazi officers and soldiers perished in railway "accidents." Those Nazis who survived the train disasters and tried to walk or crawl away from the wrecked train were shot dead at close range by the partisans. German trucks packed with Nazi soldiers were attacked with grenades and raked with machine gun fire. Isolated German soldiers were stabbed or shot dead from behind a house or a tree.

The Germans responded in kind. Any partisan captured by the Germans was tortured, then hanged or shot. Some partisans were hanged in the village square, as a deterrent to the rest of the population. The partisans, in turn, did not take any German prisoners. They killed them. The rule of engagement between the two sides was simple: kill or be killed. There was no mercy shown on either side.

As the front moved closer, the possibility that German troops might occupy Transnistria became very real. Should that occur, the Jewish population could face total annihilation. The Jewish leadership in Bucharest began intense negotiations with the government to have the deportees returned, starting with the orphaned children. Considering the situation on the front, this time the Romanian government was much more willing to listen to the pleas of the Jewish leaders. While the negotiations went on, more packages of food and clothing, as well as money, was sent by the Jewish community of Bucharest to the ghettoes and camps of Transnistria. No food or clothing, however, could reach those who were still alive in the camps east of the Bug, under German administration. Those deportees were doomed to total annihilation.

In 1943, tragedy struck Uncle Joseph's family. In the spring of that year, his four-year old boy, Elli, complained about pain in his belly. The pain got worse by the hour, and the child's fever rose. Uncle Joseph called a well-known pediatrician. The doctor examined the child and concluded that the pain was due to a cramp in the child's leg. He recommended physical exercises and had the child crawl on the floor repeatedly. Still, the child kept crying and the fever kept rising.

While Elli was in pain, I spent some time with him. I felt pity for the little boy and wanted to help. The doctor had recommended wrapping the child in cold, wet bed sheets to control the fever. I dipped the sheets in cold water, wrung them to drive off most of the water, and gave them to Aunt Ruchel. She wrapped the crying child in the wet bed sheets, then sat down next to Elli and caressed his head. While she watched him squirming in pain, tears were running down her cheeks. I also felt like crying. Every fifteen minutes we wrapped the child in a fresh, wet sheet. But neither the fever nor the pain subsided.

While we were trying to sooth the child's suffering, there was a knock at the door. My uncle opened it. A young medical student, who lived in the same building, had heard Elli cry and came to inquire. Uncle Joseph told him what the doctor had diagnosed.

"Mr. Neumann, may I look at Elli?" inquired the student. "I'm no doctor yet, but I would like to examine the child."

"Of course," replied my uncle. " I would be glad to have a second opinion."

The student examined the child for about ten minutes. He then turned to my uncle. His face was worried.

"Mr. Neumann, in my opinion, the pain is not caused by a cramp in the leg, but by an infected appendix. Take Elli immediately to the hospital and have his appendix removed. And don't force the child to crawl on the floor anymore."

Uncle Joseph went right away with the child to the hospital. The examining doctor agreed with the student's diagnosis and decided to operate. When he opened the child's belly, the doctor realized that it was too late. The appendix had ruptured and infected the body. The rupture had been caused by the physical exercises forced upon the child.

Elli could not be saved. Shortly afterwards, he died.

The loss of Elli was a terrible blow for Uncle Joseph and Aunt Ruchel. He was their only child, and they adored him. They had been able to protect the child from deportation, but not from an incompetent doctor. Ruchel had a nervous breakdown from which she never completely recovered. At the funeral, seeing the tiny coffin lowered into the ground, I shed bitter tears. During his four years of life, I had become fond of Elli.

In 1944, as a result of the Soviet winter offensive, the front came close to Bukovina. The Jewish population of Czernowitz, as well as that of Transnistria, had mixed feelings about those events, and looked with apprehension at the developments on the front. Liberation appeared at hand, and years of suffering and oppression might soon come to an end. The proximity of the front, however, could also mean fighting and destruction in the city, more German troops in the area, and the imposition of German military rule. From BBC radio reports we knew that during their retreat on the Eastern Front the Germans used a scorched earth policy. They destroyed cities and villages before abandoning them to the advancing Red Army. Moreover, it was a real possibility that, once under German rule, those Jews who had survived so far would be liquidated by the SS. Both Jews and Gentiles watched the military development with trepidation. Uncertainty hovered over the city like a dark, threatening cloud.

It was at that time that we had an unexpected visitor. Mother was busy in the kitchen, and I was reading Jules Verne's *Voyage Around the World in Eighty Days*, when we heard a knock at the door. Since Father was in bed with pain in his legs, Mother and I went to see who it was. When we opened the door, a German soldier in green uniform, rifle hanging from his shoulder, was standing in front of us. Mother froze. I felt myself break into a cold sweat. My hand holding the book began to tremble, and I had to force myself to steady it. I had no idea that German troops had arrived in the city, and surely did not expect them at our door.

The soldier greeted us with a slight nod of his head and asked in a fairly polite tone, "Could I spend the night here? It would be just one night, no more."

Mother's face had turned white like a sheet of paper, but she quickly recovered from her initial shock. She had always been able to keep her cool, under any circumstances.

"We are Jews," she replied, "but you are welcome to stay in our apartment."

In the situation we found ourselves, to refuse the soldier's request would have been sheer lunacy. Nor could we deny that we were Jews. Once he moved in, he would have found out anyway.

"You are Jews?" he asked incredulous. He did not expect to find any Jews alive, especially Jews who spoke German fluently.

"Yes, sir, we are Jews," replied my mother, a light tremor in her voice.

She had taken a big risk by telling him the truth, not knowing what would follow. Would he curse us? Would he push us aside and enter our apartment? Would he take his rifle and shoot us?

"We have orders not to stay in Jewish homes," I heard him say. He paused, then added slowly, in a low voice: "It will be a tragic chapter in the history of mankind what Germany had done to the Jews." He turned and left.

Mother and I gave a deep sigh of relief. It was a frightening experience, and we had been very lucky. It was a narrow escape. He could have done with us whatever he wanted; he could have robbed us, beaten us, or shot us. Instead—surprisingly—he expressed regret for what the Germans had done to the Jews. Having fought on the Eastern Front, he obviously knew much more than we did about the crimes perpetrated by the Nazis against Jews, crimes we learned about only after the war. At that point we realized that there were still decent people in the German Army, people who felt embarrassed and ashamed by what their countrymen had done and were doing to the Jews.

In March 1944, the news spread that BBC radio had reported a major breakthrough by the Red Army. The radio report also said that in the southern region of the Eastern Front, which included our area, the Germans were retreating rapidly, to avoid being cut off by the advancing Soviets.

At the end of March, German supply convoys started to roll through the city, moving south, away from the front. From behind drawn curtains, I watched the columns of horse-drawn wagons filled to the top and covered with large, khaki tarpaulins. It was strange to see that the German army, in spite of the high level of mechanization, still used large numbers of horses in its supply convoys. For three days and nights the columns rumbled through the city, along the Russischegasse and towards the Tsetsina woods. A long column of mud-splattered military trucks, packed with grim-faced German soldiers, followed the supply convoys. Some of the trucks pulled artillery pieces behind them. The trucks raced through the city and disappeared in a cloud of dust. After the columns passed, several powerful explosions could be heard. The Germans were blowing up the bridges over the Prut. Then, an eerie silence settled over the city.

The next day, March 28, the first Russian patrols entered the city. In their green-gray helmets and gray military greatcoats, submachine guns at the ready, they advanced cautiously through the deserted streets. Moving close to the building walls in groups of three or four, they were eyeing rooftops and windows, looking for snipers. Isolated German stragglers, who were still on the streets, were cut down with short bursts of fire. Their bodies were left lying where they fell, while the patrols moved on. One of the German stragglers, apparently drunk, was shot while he tried to hide or break into our building. He lay in a pool of blood on the sidewalk, face down, until our doorman dragged him away.

Later in the day, Russian infantry entered the city in olive-green Jeeps and Studebaker trucks. We had been liberated.

When we realized that the Germans had left the city and that the Red Army had returned, we all felt enormous relief. Mother and sister embraced each other. Father, very agitated, kept saying with great satisfaction, "The Hitlerites are gone! The Romanians are gone!"

The anxiety and dread I felt from that awful day when the Germans and Romanian fascists entered our city had finally dissipated. It was as if an enormous boulder had been removed from my chest. We didn't have to fear for our life anymore. Still, our joy was tempered. The war was far from over. We lacked information from our loved ones who had been deported to Transnistria. We also knew that life under the Soviets would not be a bed of roses.

In spite of everything, our city and its inhabitants had been lucky. The

Germans and Romanians had abandoned the city without a fight, and in their hasty retreat had no time to destroy it. Only several fuel depots were burning, black plumes of smoke billowing into the sky; the railroad station and the airport were heavily damaged, but the city and its inhabitants were safe for now.

In the following weeks, the front moved further west and south, away from the city. At the same time, the Red Army occupied Transnistria and the northern part of Romania. The surviving Jews in the ghettoes and camps of Transnistria, nearly half of those deported, had been liberated.

The survivors began to return slowly to their former homes. They were a sorry lot. Emaciated from starvation and ravaged by disease, they were too weak to enjoy their freedom. Suffering was mirrored on their gaunt faces, in their slow movements, and in the gaze of their sad, mournful eyes. Dressed in rags and carrying their few belongings in small bundles, they came on foot, in horse-drawn wagons, and in empty Russian military trucks that picked them up on the road.

Some deportees had begun returning even before the arrival of the Red Army. Early in 1944, as the front moved closer to Transnistria, Antonescu issued an order allowing those deported to return to their place of origin. He realized that the war was lost, and hoped to save himself by showing some last-moment good will towards those he had cruelly persecuted.

We all waited for our relatives to return from Transnistria. We had not heard from them since they were deported in the summer of 1942. Mother waited for her three sisters, for Uncle Bernhard and for my cousin Gusta. I was especially eager to meet Gusta again, to hear her carefree laughter and to see her dark, sparkling eyes. Father waited for his relatives that had been deported from Suceava.

But nobody came.

One camp survivor, who knew Aunt Tzili and was able to escape across the Bug, returned to Czernowitz and told us that Tzili was still alive in the summer of 1943. She probably died in an *Aktion* later that year. The rest of the family probably perished earlier, in 1942.

Eddie wrote a brief letter from Tiraspol, Transnistria, informing us that his father had died, but that he had survived. Later we found out what happened in the camps across the Bug, where my mother's sisters had been sent. Before their retreat, the Germans murdered those who had not perished from disease or during previous German *Aktionen*. Only a handful of people had been able to escape across the Bug under cover of darkness, and survive.

The realization that our relatives, deported two years earlier, were no longer alive began slowly to sink in. The glimmer of hope that someday they would knock at the door, dressed in rags but alive, had flickered out. I realized that never again would I hear Gusta's carefree laughter or see her black, shiny eyes. That Aunt Tzili will never again bring me an orange when I am sick, or play on her mandolin. Hitler's executioners in collusion with Antonescu's underlings had murdered them, and dumped their bodies into some unmarked mass grave. Why had they been murdered? They had never done anything that could have harmed the German Reich or the Romanian Kingdom. Was Aunt Tzili, Aunt Jetty or Aunt Anna a threat to the Third Reich? Was little Gusta such a menace? There was no answer; there was no explanation of the murder of these defenseless, innocent people.

At night, alone in bed, I kept thinking about little Gusta. I tried to grasp what had happened. I couldn't. It made no sense, it had no meaning. Again and again I kept asking, why? I could not find an answer. Then, a crazy thought crossed my mind, like a falling star in the night sky. "What if little Gusta was still alive?" In the darkness of the night I pictured her walking into the room in her short, flowery dress, her eyes sparkling, her black curls bouncing around her head, a bright smile on her childish face. Then I shook my head: no, this isn't possible anymore. More likely, she would return with a torn coat caked with mud, her black curls covered with a worn cap, her black eyes contrasting with the pallor of her face. She would sit on the floor in front of me and ask, in a sad voice, "Do you want to play hide and seek?"

But reality kept coming back, and I cried. I tried to stop the tears, but they just kept rolling down my cheeks, and dripping onto the blanket. I wiped them away, but more took their place. No, Gusta will not return. She is now among the angels. I felt as if somebody had stepped on my heart and squashed it.

I tried to imagine how she died. Did she die from hunger because she did not have a crust of bread that would have kept her alive? Did she freeze to death because she did not have the blanket that the cruel janitor had grabbed from her mother's arm? Or was it a bullet from the pistol of a callous SS-man that had pierced her little heart? I did not know the answer. I only realized, again, how much cruelty and injustice there was in this world.

My grandparents were devastated by the realization that they had lost three of their daughters. Grandmother kept crying, and crying, and crying, until she ran out of tears. Her cheeks were sunken, her eyes were red, and her face was ashen. *"Far wos, far wos?"* Why, why, she kept asking, in Yiddish, with heartrending pain in her voice. Grandfather tried to console her. *"Der Oibershter,* God almighty, had willed it," he kept telling her, while tears were running down his cheeks into his gray beard. I added my own tears to their sorrow.

The awful strokes of fate had a crushing effect on my grandparents. Grandmother fell into a state of depression from which she never recovered. Grandfather became silent and withdrawn. Dark circles appeared around his eyes and deep furrows on his forehead. He walked bent forward, as if there was an enormous burden on his shoulders. Almost overnight, he added years to his age. He immersed himself more and more in the study of the holy books, as if he was trying to find a reason for this heartrending tragedy.

From survivors of the June 28 transport, we learned that Selma Meerbaum-Eisinger had been sent to the Mikhailovka camp and died of typhus in December 1942. She was eighteen. Her death was reported in the diary of the Jewish painter Arnold Daghani, who was in the same camp with her. He was able to escape over the Bug and published his diary after the war. Another survivor of that camp was able to save Selma's poems. They were published under the title *Blütenlese* after the war, in Germany and Israel. Some of her poems were turned into songs.

Recently I was able to acquire a collection of Selma's poems. They are filled with the delicate feelings of a young, romantic girl, expressed in beautiful poetic form. Some poems express longing, sadness and love (dedicated to her boyfriend, Leizer). Other poems, written in the ghetto or camp, express a feeling of foreboding and doom. For the sensibility of her feelings and the beautiful form in which she expressed them, she is often compared to Anne Frank. The fascists had deprived her first of her liberty, then of her life—a life that, like many others, was cut short when it was in full bloom.

Although we had been liberated, the war was far from over. It would take another three months before the Western Allies would land in Normandy; five months more before the Soviets would occupy Bucharest and most of Romania; another bloody thirteen months before Russian tanks would smash the defenses of Berlin and the Führer would put a bullet in his head. In the meantime, fierce fighting was taking place along the whole Eastern Front. Fighting an implacable enemy, the Soviet troops advanced toward Germany wading in rivers of blood. People were still dying en mass. They were dying on the front, in the concentration camps and in the bombed cities.

The Red Army had to replenish its ranks. The draft-age Jewish men liberated by the Soviets in Transnistria, although undernourished and emaciated, were promptly drafted into the army. Cousin Eddie was among them. After a few weeks of training, a long train packed with these draftees was sent to the front in Eastern Prussia. On the way to the front, however, near the city of Minsk, German bombers attacked the train. Racked with machine-gun fire and ripped apart by shrapnel from exploding bombs, hundreds of draftees were killed or maimed. Eddie survived. Sami, one of Bertha's friends, was on that train and was seriously wounded. He was pulled out from the wreckage, barely alive. After being treated in a military hospital, he was sent back to Czernowitz with both legs missing. He was 18 years old.

Now that Czernowitz was again under Red Army control and the front had moved away from the city, the Soviets reinstated civil administration. A series of orders were issued regarding blackouts, fuel and food rationing. A strict curfew was imposed. The city's inhabitants had to register with the civil authorities to receive new internal passports and food-rationing stamps. Draft-age men had to register with the military authorities.

Since Czernowitz was one of the few cities in the Western Soviet Union that had not been destroyed by war, it attracted large numbers of

Soviet civilians. People who before the war lived in Bessarabia, in Western Ukraine, or in Southern Poland came to settle in Czernowitz. Soon Russians and Ukrainians occupied every empty house and apartment abandoned by the fleeing Romanians. Many of the Jews returning from Transnistria found their apartments already occupied by Soviet civilians or military.

The Soviet authorities looked with suspicion at the local population. This was a population that had stayed under enemy occupation for almost three years and could not be trusted. The Soviet newcomers treated the *mestnyie* (locals) with a mixture of suspicion and condescension. Coming from totally devastated areas, the newcomers felt also a grudge toward those who had been able to live, throughout the war, in their homes and apartments.

Since Bertha had been active in an antifascist group, she was hired as a clerk by the newly established Soviet administration. One of the tasks of the new administration was to recruit a labor force for the factories and coal mines in the industrial region of the Ukraine. Most factory workers and coal miners had been drafted into the army, and there was a serious shortage of manpower.

The Soviets had effective methods to fill the quota of required manpower. Some of the men that came to the authorities to obtain new documents were detained. Other men were picked up on the streets by roaming patrols. Those detained were put under military guard and shipped eastward by train.

The authorities also needed manpower locally. The fast-retreating German and Romanian troops had left behind ammunition and military equipment scattered in barracks, school buildings, warehouses, and government buildings. These materials had to be collected, sorted, and turned over to the authorities. Furthermore, land mines had to be removed from a large area near the Tsetsina woods that had been mined by the retreating Germans. The task to do the job fell to the city's teenagers. Fifteen- and sixteen-year-old boys had to collect the scattered ammunition and remove the land mines. The boys who did this job were picked up at random on the streets. I was one of them.

On a sunny morning in early April, I decided to go to my friend,

Martin, to play a game of chess. I was cheerful and carefree. Since we had been liberated, I did not have to wear the yellow star anymore, did not fear to be beaten up by hoodlums, and, I thought, did not have to fear of being arrested. Well, on that last point I was wrong. When I passed a military patrol, one of the men in uniform stopped me.

"How old are you?" he wanted to know.

"Fifteen," I replied.

"Come with us," he said brusquely.

They took me to a building with a military guard at the entrance. It was the local Soviet administration building. I was led to a large room with wooden benches placed along the whitewashed walls. A picture of Josef Stalin in military uniform was hanging on the wall across the windows. There were about two dozen teenagers of my age, sitting on benches and on the floor. Periodically, the door opened and more teenagers were brought in. They had been picked up on the street and brought to this room. None of us had any idea why we were here.

By the end of the day, a Soviet officer came in and gave a brief speech.

"The Motherland," he said, "needs your help in the struggle against the fascist enemy. Your assignment will be to collect artillery shells, hand grenades, small arms and different explosives scattered throughout the city and cart them to collection centers." He then gave us the location of those centers.

The officer told us that we would also have to find and disarm land mines planted by the fascists. Before carrying out these tasks, we would be instructed how to proceed. Until the task was completed, we would stay in the Soviet administration building.

We spent the night sleeping on the floor on burlap sacks filled with straw. The next day was a day of instruction. We were shown and taught how to handle, pack and store different types of shells, grenades, rifles, and other military equipment. The instructor emphasized especially what *not* to do: we should not throw, play with or pull the safety pin of the egg-shaped hand grenades; we should not pull the string coming out of the wooden handle of the German hand grenades; and we should never drop or hit an artillery shell on its head. We were also taught about different types of land mines (anti-personnel, anti-tank), how to find them with mine detectors, and how to deactivate them. The lecture was followed by practical instructions, when we learned how to handle a land mine detector and different land mines. The instructor concluded the lesson with a warning:

"There is no room for error when you carry out this assignment. One mistake, and you lose a leg or you are blown to pieces." Such a warning really caught our attention.

For several days I collected German hand grenades and artillery shells left behind in schools and official buildings, where German troops had been briefly quartered during their retreat. I put them in crates and with other boys took them to the collection center. I was quite excited doing this job and felt proud of being given such an important assignment. How often was a youngster like me given the chance to handle so many live hand grenades and artillery shells? I worked with enthusiasm and dedication. We completed our assignment in three days.

The following morning the officer told us that we would start clearing land mines. I was one of several boys taken by truck to a field near the Tsetsina woods. The instructor who accompanied our group told us that the field had been mined by enemy troops before their retreat. Those were anti-personnel land mines, he said, and our task was to find and deactivate them.

We were divided into teams of two. In each team, one youngster had to detect the mines, while the other one had to deactivate them. I had to work with sixteen-year-old Rudi, a lanky lad with chestnut-brown hair, lively green eyes, and freckles sprinkled on his face. My task was to find the mines, while Rudi's task was to deactivate them. Then the instructor handed me a land mine detector. I already knew how the mine detector worked. When the hand-held detector came close to a buried land mine, the metallic part of the mine generated a signal which was transmitted to a headphone worn by the person holding the equipment.

The instructor assigned a stretch of the field to each team, reminded us again of the danger involved in this mission, and wished us good luck. Then we went to work. The area assigned to Rudi and me was a rectangular piece of land, about thirty meters long and several meters wide. The soil was partly covered with grass and partly bare.

I started my work at one end of the rectangle. I moved the minesweeper back and forth across the ground, listening intently for a signal. I was tense like a tight cord, and started to perspire. A mistake might cost me a foot or even my life. Concentrating on the task ahead, I watched the ground in front of me, and listened. Having searched about one third of my territory, I suddenly got a signal. I stopped instantly. My heart was pounding and my mouth felt dry. Buried in the earth was the source of the signal.

"Rudi, I have found a mine!" I yelled, full of excitement.

Rudi approached me slowly. There was a worrisome look on his face. He obviously was not thrilled to dig up land mines. Still, when he got next to me, he went down on his knees, took a small scoop out from his pocket, and started scraping the soil carefully over the spot I pointed at. He cautiously pushed aside the loose soil with his bare hands. I moved away to a safe distance. If the thing exploded, it was no point in blowing up both of us.

After about five minutes, that seemed to me an eternity, Rudi slowly removed from the ground the object that generated the signal. We stared at the object full of surprise. It was not a mine, but an old, rusty horseshoe. My detector had spotted a piece of metal in the ground and had generated a false alarm! Rudi and I had a brief, nervous laugh. The land mine detector obviously could not differentiate between a metallic mine component and an ordinary piece of metal.

The work had to go on. I picked up the mine detector and again resumed my work. When I came close to the end of the field, I got a signal again. This time I was less excited. I called Rudi and we started to joke. Did I discover another horseshoe, a worthless piece of metal, or was it perhaps a gold treasure? But this time what we had found was no joke. It was the real thing. Slowly, very carefully, Rudi deactivated the anti-personnel land mine. Then he removed it. It was a German "bouncing" mine. By stepping on such a thing, a spring would throw a shell into the air that would explode, causing mayhem and death. Just the thought that I could have stepped on this mine made a chill go down my spine. "So far," I thought, "I have been very lucky."

Another team of boys who searched for mines found and deactivated two anti-personnel land mines. There were no mishaps. At the end of the day, when we returned to our quarters, we talked, with excitement, about the events of the day. We were laughing about the horseshoe we found, but we all knew that our precarious assignment was no laughing matter. We were relieved to be alive, and proud of our accomplishments.

The next morning I was getting ready for another day of land mine clearing, when I had a surprise. One of Bertha's friends, Silva, also a former member of the anti-fascist group, worked in the same building where I was quartered. She had seen me and informed my parents about my whereabouts, and about my assignment. My parents were frantic since they did not know where I had disappeared. When they found out where I was and what I was doing, they implored Silva to do whatever she could to have me released. They realized the danger I was in, and Silva promised to do her best. She talked to the commander of my group and tried to convince him to release me, claiming that I was too young and too weak to clear mines. Indeed, at that time I was very skinny and looked more like a twelve-year-old. Since Silva had a key position in the city administration, the commander reluctantly agreed. Besides, the mine-clearing operation did not require as many people as the weapons collection. The commander told me to go home.

I had mixed feelings about the commander's decision. I would have liked to find more "bouncing" land mines, to feel the thrill of detecting and making harmless these small containers of death. It was much more exciting than playing chess or playing ball. I was doing the job of a man. But deep down I also felt some trepidation and anxiety. Branded in my mind were the words of my instructor, "If you do make a mistake, it will be your last one." The possibility of losing limb or life was, mildly put, not very appealing. However, my mixed feelings on this matter were irrelevant. Not surprisingly, my parents had made up their minds on this subject, and so had the commander. I went home, knowing that I had done something important, that I had made my contribution, albeit a small one, in the fight against the fascists.

More excitement was in store for us. In late May, while walking on the street, Shmuel was picked up by a military patrol. He was taken to a collection center, together with dozens of other men, caught in a dragnet set up by the authorities. The next day, those arrested were lined up into a column, and marched under military escort to the railroad station. They were supposed to be shipped to the industrial Donetz region in the Ukraine, to work in plants and coal mines.

Bertha found out about Shmuel's arrest from his friend Itzhak. He came over to our house very agitated, and told my sister that Shmuel had left in the morning and had not returned home. Through her connections with the authorities, Bertha found out where he was detained. She also learned that he was to be shipped out the following day. Bertha knew that once he was sent far away into Russia, she was not likely to see him soon, if ever. They had planned to go to Palestine together and to get married. Now that plan was threatened.

Bertha was not a person to remain passive in such a situation. During the night she came up with a plan. Next morning, as the column of those arrested was marched under military escort to the railroad station, Bertha approached the convoy and started talking to Shmuel. She was wearing the badge that identified her as an employee of the Soviet authorities. While talking to each other, Bertha and Shmuel slowed their pace until they were at the end of the column. The soldier guarding the rear saw my sister's badge and decided to ignore the two slow-walking people. After the column turned a street corner, Bertha and Shmuel, who had fallen behind, scurried through an open door into an apartment building. After awhile, they left the building and rushed home.

They knew that Shmuel's disappearance would be discovered, and that the authorities would be looking for him. He had to leave town. Bertha decided to join him. His two friends, Mordche and Itzhak, also decided to join him. My parents had strong misgivings about my sister leaving home for the unknown, but as usual, she was firm in her decision. Bertha and Shmuel had made a plan. They decided to move closer to the front, where there was no civilian administration. Under those conditions, it was less likely that Shmuel would be identified and apprehended. As soon as the Red Army occupied the rest of Romania, they planned to go to Bucharest. From there, with the help of the Zionist

Organization of Romania, they were hoping to reach Palestine.

Bertha filled her backpack with clothing and food, put on hiking pants, a sport jacket and hiking boots, embraced us, and said goodbye. It was an emotional farewell. Mother cried and even my father, who rarely showed emotions, had tears in his eyes. I also cried. I didn't want to see her go. I had gotten used to having her close to me, to help me with schoolwork, to bring me a good book to read. We all knew that the future was uncertain, that the war was still going on, and that the world was a very dangerous place. We also knew that we would not see Bertha for a long time. For my sister, this was only the beginning of a long and arduous journey.

In the fall of 1944, I went back to school. Not in hiding, in the private home of a teacher, but in a regular, public school. Although I had graduated from the 7th grade in the spring of 1941 under the Soviets, I was now accepted into the 9th grade due to my private studies at home between 1941 and 1944. As in 1940, the Soviets set up Russian, Ukrainian, and Yiddish schools. My parents sent me to the Yiddish school No. 18, since the school had very capable, local teachers.

Most of the teachers were Jewish, some from Bukovina and others from Bessarabia. Among those I admired the most was Professor Ginninger, for Yiddish language and literature. Gershon and Hersch Segal, who taught physics and math, respectively, were also among my preferred teachers. The males in our school liked Bella Gruenberg especially. She was a dark-eyed, very attractive, young woman from Bessarabia, with a charming smile and feminine demeanor. She taught Russian literature. Many of the male professors had a crush on her, and even we school boys were looking forward to having class with her. Not only was she attractive, but she was also a good teacher. With her guidance, I discovered many literary treasures. I was fascinated by Leo Tolstoy's *War and Peace*, captivated by Chekhov's plays, and read with interest Gogol's short stories. I also discovered the beauty of the poems written by the great Russian poet Alexandr Pushkin. In later years, I became a Dostoevsky devotee.

We had two non-Jewish teachers: a middle-aged, homely woman from

Kiev for Ukrainian language and literature, and a Soviet lieutenant as military instructor. The teacher from Kiev gave her lectures in Ukrainian, while the officer lectured in Russian. The lieutenant was a young Russian who had been wounded in the war and dragged his left foot when he walked. Unfit for the army, he became a military instructor in our school.

Some of the teachers were Party members and tried to show it at every occasion. This was the case with our history teacher, who never missed an opportunity to praise the Soviet Union and its leader, Joseph Stalin. We never found out if she was indeed a dedicated communist, or if she just wanted to give that impression. She never smiled, never joked, and always had a stern face. She also taught us the ideological course, the Marxist theories about economics and society. With anger in her voice she talked about the exploitation of the working people in the capitalistic countries, about the oppression of the colonial people. Then, with a voice vibrating with enthusiasm, she told us about the freedom all working people have in the Soviet Union under the genial leadership of the great Joseph Stalin. Every success, every victory, every achievement was the result of Stalin's wise leadership and inspiration. Our beloved leader was omnipotent and the party was infallible. She described the future communist society in rosy colors, as a classless society where private property will be abolished. Factories, businesses, buildings, the land—all will belong to "the people," to be shared according to need. General happiness will be a mark of that society.

The ideological lectures were followed by discussions that sometimes took a strange turn. One youngster wanted to know if, in a collectivist society, he would be allowed to keep his penknife (yes) or own his own house (no).

"Private property will be abolished. Except for minor personal belongings, the State will own everything," explained our teacher.

Another boy wanted to know if a man who had a wife or girl friend would have to share her with his comrades. That question caused a lot of giggling in the classroom, but the teacher did not smile.

"A wife or a girl friend are not objects or property," replied the teacher with a stern voice. Then she added with a straight face, "They would share only by mutual consent. All voluntary sexual relations are permissible in a communist society."

Needless to say that during the break, this aspect of the future communist society became an animated and amusing topic of conversation among us boys, an endless source of off-color jokes. Boys will always be boys...

Most of the teachers, however, avoided politics in their interaction with the students. The classes with Ginninger and Hersch Segal were especially interesting. These teachers had a wide horizon of knowledge that went far beyond the subject they were supposed to teach. In addition to the regular subjects, they taught us about the great writers and poets of universal literature, great philosophers, Jewish theatre, and about famous painters. Like a fish in water, they moved easily in the stream of world literature and art, while revealing its beauty to us. With their guidance, I developed a taste for literature, an ear for poetry, and an eye for line and color.

When discussing Yiddish literature, they compared the works of Yiddish writers with those of the universal literature. They pointed out the similarities and differences in the comedies of Sholem Aleichem and those of Molière, between the dramatic realism of Itzhak Peretz and that of Henrik Ibsen, between the fables of Eliezer Steinbarg and those of La Fontaine. In the process we learned much about both Yiddish and universal literature. They told us about the works of great Jewish thinkers of the past, such as Hillel, Maimonides, Spinoza, and Baal Shem Tov. They helped me discover a whole new world of thought. I am indebted to these great teachers for stimulating my intellectual curiosity for literature, philosophy and the arts at that early stage in my life. The interest in these subjects had stayed with me during my adult life. Although I lived as a teenager only for two years in their presence, they continued to live in me through my adult life.

In the class of military instructions, the lieutenant taught us about rifles, submachine guns and handguns. We learned how to take them apart and how to put them together. During training on a field outside the city, I learned how to hold a rifle, how to load it, and how to fire it. The rifle felt so heavy, I couldn't keep it steady. After loading, aiming and pulling the trigger, there was a flash of flame, a loud crack, and a strong kick into my shoulder. It was much harder to handle than it looked in the movies. My first shot was way off target. The following shots were somewhat better, but still off the mark. I was not a very good marksman.

We learned how to read a map and how to use it in conjunction with a compass. During classes in the field, I had to crawl, on my belly, in the dirt among a variety of obstacles, such as bushes, ditches, and discarded tires, while holding the loaded rifle and keeping it clean. The lieutenant was good-natured and was never too strict with us. We often saw that he had pain in his wounded leg, but he was kind to us. His experience on the front had taught him to take a more philosophical approach to life.

Occasionally, the officer would tell us about his encounters during the war. He had fought in an infantry unit that liberated many Russian towns and villages occupied by the Germans. Most of the liberated villages he had seen were almost totally destroyed, either during the fighting or deliberately blown up by the retreating Germans. In many of these villages, he had seen the corpses of civilians, men and women, executed by the Germans before their retreat. Grim faced, our instructor characterized, succinctly, those who had perpetrated those crimes: *"Ety ne liudy, ety zveriah"* (These are not people, these are wild beasts). When he heard us speak German to each other, he admonished us, "Don't speak German! This is the language of the Hitlerites" (he called them in Russian, *ghitlerovtzy*).

The class I attended was coed. About half the class was made up of girls. We were at an age when boys and girls pay attention to each other. It was nice to sit next to the girls, look at them, listen to them, even smell them, and sometimes talk to them briefly. Yet, I was not bold enough to court any of them. I felt we belonged to two different worlds.

At sixteen or seventeen, I was a teenager still shy in the presence of girls. I had difficulties even talking to a girl. At home most weekend nights, I would pass those evenings reading. I learned about romantic relationships between men and women from books, and about love and happiness or suffering that it caused. I read about the effect of sexuality on people's feelings and thinking. I may not have known how to engage a girl in small talk, but I had read about Freud's theories on sexuality.

Some of the girls excelled with their smarts, others with their physical features. There was one girl that we boys found extremely attractive. Her name was Evelyn. I often admired her—discreetly, from a distance. She was both brainy, and, what we would call today, sexy. Evelyn was well read—mostly in German literature and poetry—and did not hesitate to show off her knowledge. She had chestnut-colored, curly hair, milk-white skin, deep-brown eyes, and delicate hands. Hers were the hands of a piano player. Her legs were long and beautiful. I liked the way she moved, laughed, and the way her voice sounded. How I wanted her to notice me! I tried to talk to her—in class, naturally. But she didn't pay attention to me. She was interested in older boys. I was just a classmate to talk to occasionally, but no more than that. This was the extent of my "relationship" with Evelyn. Years later she married one of the older boys that had courted her in high school.

In my spare time I often went to the movies. We had no radio at home (we had turned over our radio to the Soviet authorities at the beginning of the war), and seeing a movie was one of the few forms of entertainment available. Some were historical movies from Russia's past, such as Eisenstein's *Alexander Nevsky*, about a Russian prince who defended his country against attack by German knights in the 13th century. Most of the movies, however, were patriotic war movies that glorified the Russian people in their struggle against the Nazi invaders. The films showed the heroism of the Red Army fighters and the barbaric behavior of the enemy. Occasionally, we also saw pro-Russian American movies, such as *Mission to Moscow* and *Song of Russia*.

Newsreels usually preceded the movies. They showed images from the front, from factories producing war materiel for the front, and the liberated territories devastated by the retreating German armies. I learned, for the first time, about the immense destruction caused by the Germans in occupied Soviet Russia. After the landing of the Western Allies in Normandy, the newsreels began showing battle scenes from Northern France. Occasionally they showed scenes from Italy, where American and British troops also fought the Nazis. The emphasis, however, was always on the Eastern Front.

In the summer of 1944, one of the newsreels showed 57,000 German prisoners of war that were marched through the Russian capital, with their generals in the lead. I watched that scene with fascination. What a miserable lot they were! An endless column of dejected, dirty, tired, unkempt, hollow-faced individuals, moving slowly in their tattered field-gray uniforms over the pavement of Gorky Street in central Moscow. Half a dozen sanitation trucks followed the column and washed the street clean—a sanitary as well as a symbolic act.

How different were those prisoners from the athletic, well-groomed, well-dressed and polished Nazi officers and soldiers that strutted around Czernowitz in the summer of 1941! Gone was their haughty arrogance, their air of superiority, their "superman" attitude. As prisoners, they did not look different from the Russian prisoners of war shown in the Nazi magazines *Signal* and *Das Reich*. The captive German "supermen" were now as wretched as the captive Russian "subhumans." I realized how easy it is to put man—any man—in circumstances that make him appear subhuman. These images also reminded me of the anti-Semitic pictures I had seen in German and Romanian magazines, showing dirty, ragged Jews in the ghettoes of Poland or Transnistria. Such pictures were designed to show the inferiority of these people, and to generate contempt for them. The captive Germans did not look much better.

The Yiddish theater was reopened in the fall. Artists from the Yiddish theater of Kiev, as well as local artists, started performing on a regular basis. I was a regular visitor at the theater, since actors and acting had attracted me from an early age. Tickets were cheap and when the theater was not full, teenagers could enter without tickets. The theater presented plays by Yiddish playwrights, such as Shalom Aleihem, Itzhak Peretz, and Soviet-Yiddish writers. Plays by Chechov, Gogol, and other Russian classics were also performed. Watching these plays, I began to appreciate their beauty and social meaning, as well as the diversity and complexity of the different characters portrayed. I felt more and more captivated by the theater, and only a few years later I myself began performing on stage.

In addition to the classics, the theater also presented contemporary plays that showed the barbaric behavior of the Nazis and the struggle against fascism. I recall how, in one of the plays that dealt with the struggle of Jewish partisans against the Nazis, the director put on the curtain the motto *Am Yisrael Chai!* (The Jewish people live!). This was a serious political mistake. Several months later, the director was arrested and accused of spreading Jewish nationalist propaganda. He was convicted and sentenced to spend 10 years in a labor camp.

Shortly after the arrest of the director, I had a very interesting experience in an area I least expected—in sport.

12. Adventures in Sport and the End of War

As a teenager, I was interested in sport. I often played soccer (we called it football) with other boys in the schoolyard or on an open field. I was good as goalkeeper and midfielder. On other occasions I played volleyball. I was also a good runner—the best in my class at 100- and 400-meter sprint. At sport competitions with students of my age from other schools in the city, I was among the three best sprinters. My physical education teacher, Mr. Stanger, trained me and helped improve my performance. He had good reasons to do it. Sport was highly appreciated and encouraged by the Soviets. Good sportsmen brought prestige to the school and to its physical education teacher.

Early in 1945, Mr. Stanger was given the task to prepare a sport team for the Spartakiade in Kiev, to be held in the summer of the same year. The Spartakiade was a sport competition somewhat similar to the Olympic games, held within the framework of each Soviet republic. The winners competed subsequently on a national level in Moscow. Since Czernowitz belonged to the Ukraine Soviet Republic, a selected team of its sportsmen, along with those from other parts of the Ukraine, participated in the competition in the republic's capital, Kiev. I was the best sprinter in my class and was selected to be a member of our school's team. Although I was good at running 100- and 400-meters, Mr. Stanger decided that I was to run in the 100-meter sprint competition.

For several months I trained intensively for the Spartakiade. I ran after school hours and on weekends at the school's sports stadium. Mr. Stanger was often present, with stopwatch in hand, instructing me and measuring my progress. I was very skinny—a result of the meager food rations received during the Romanian rule. However, due to frequent training, I gradually developed strong leg muscles. Perseverance and frequent practice paid off. Towards the end of training, Mr. Stanger told me that I was among the best 100-meter runners of my age in the city.

Five days before the opening of the games, our group embarked on a freight train for the trip. The freight car we occupied had bunks on two levels, covered with straw sacks. On these bunks we were supposed to rest and sleep, since the trip to Kiev was likely to last 3 to 4 days. Due to the chaotic situation created by the war, we did not know the arrival time in Kiev. We shared the freight car with sports teams from other schools, as well as with sportsmen from different factories and from the military.

The trip that, under normal conditions, would have taken no more than seven or eight hours, lasted three days. We passed through many towns and villages, and the train had to wait, often for hours, in small railroad stations before moving again.

On this trip I discovered the enormous devastation as well as the suffering caused by the war. The train hurtled through dead, ghost-like villages, bombed and burned into little more than rubble. I stared at the landscape of destruction, wondering what happened to the people that used to live in these villages. Houses that used to be inhabited by peasants were burned out shells. Rarely did I see any livestock. Most of the buildings in the small railroad stations were also burned out, with gaping holes where doors and windows used to be. In some of the stations, railroad personnel had restored only one or two rooms in the burned out buildings, to be used by the station master. In other instances, temporary wooden shacks had been installed.

I was most deeply impressed, however, by the human misery that I saw on the road. Through the open train door I looked at the changing scenery of hungry, degraded men, women and children, treading on dirt roads through burned-out villages. There were wounded soldiers, arms in slings, or with canes; some had stumps instead of legs, some with patched or empty eye sockets. Most shocking was the suffering of the countless orphaned homeless children that roamed in the devastated towns and countryside. They could be seen everywhere: in villages, hamlets, and in railroad stations. They wandered about bewildered, hungry, sick, barefoot; their frail tiny bodies were covered with rags.

I still remember the scene at the railroad station in Zhitomir, a town about 80 miles west of Kiev, where our train stopped for several hours. A crowd of civilians with small suitcases and bundles, as well as military personnel was waiting on the platform for a train. Some of the people were sitting or sleeping on the platform, while others were resting on their suitcases or bundles. Most of the suitcases were tied with ropes, to keep them from falling apart. Many of the civilians were wearing shabby military tunics or soldier overcoats. The strain and furrows on their drawn, gray faces spoke of a life of hardship and privation. The whole platform was enveloped in the odor of *makhorka*, the cheap tobacco that was rolled into pieces of newspaper and smoked by many of the waiting men.

Homeless children, boys and girls, were milling around in the motley crowd, begging. Dressed in rags and barefoot, with pale, drawn faces and big, sad eyes, with oversized *shapkas* (caps) on their heads, they stretched out their little, dirty hands, pleading for a handout. Sometimes the plea was accompanied by a single word, said almost in a whisper: *khleb* (bread). Some of the children walked in pairs: a little four- or five-year old led by an eight- or ten-year old, most likely an older brother or sister. These children were called *bezprezornye* (homeless or street children). They had lost both of their parents in the war; the father usually on the front, the mother most likely in one of the countless massacres carried out by the Germans.

Left alone, without care or supervision, these children survived by begging and stealing. They slept in railroad stations or in one of the numerous burned out, abandoned buildings. They often jumped onto passing trains, traveled hundreds of miles hidden in freight cars, got off in some faraway station, and started again looking for shelter and food. In this war-ravaged country, there was no other help available to them except for the kindness of some adult stranger, who himself lived on tight food rations. It was heartbreaking to see the suffering of these little ones, left at the mercy of a cruel fate. Mr. Stanger told us that there were millions of such homeless children all over the country. As I found out later, only gradually did the government build orphanages for these abandoned youngsters.

In some of the train stations, I saw long trains of flatbed rail cars loaded with machinery and equipment, waiting on sidetracks without cover or protection. Some of the machines had German inscriptions. These were the major components of German plants and factories, dismantled in Soviet-occupied Germany and shipped to the Soviet Union. Much of the machinery was already rusty. These trains were on the road many weeks and the equipment, unprotected from rain, had started to deteriorate. I was wondering, once it reached its final destination, how much of this machinery will still be of any use?

At the end of the third day of travel we finally arrived in Kiev. Like the rest of the railroad stations seen on our trip, Kiev's train station was heavily damaged. The main building was burned out, and the rebuilding of a new one had not yet started. The trains were run from temporary wooden shacks, set up next to the ruins of the main building. These shacks were also the living quarters of the station master and other railroad personnel. Only some of the railroad tracks had been repaired and were in use. Other tracks lay twisted and broken, torn up by bombs dropped during repeated air raids, or during heavy street fighting in the city. The platform was packed with people, some coming and going, others sitting and waiting. Most of them, men and women, wore military outfits. Among them were the always-present *bezprezornye*, the homeless children, milling around and begging.

Kiev is located near bluffs overlooking the Dnieper River. Large parts of the city had been destroyed during the war. Heavy fighting took place in and around the city, first when the Germans occupied it in September 1941, and again when it was liberated by the Soviets in November 1943. The retreating Germans had blown up many of the buildings that had not been destroyed during the fighting. Row after row of burned out or blown up buildings were standing in mute testimony to the destruction brought about by the savage clash between the armies of two implacable enemies. Some of the walls had collapsed and only the chimneys were standing erect and lonely, overlooking the bleak scenery. Detachments of German prisoners of war, guarded by armed Soviet soldiers, were cleaning the streets of the rubble of collapsed buildings. Other prisoners were pulling on cables attached to the still standing walls, to bring them down and make room for new buildings. The rubble-strewn streets were only just passable. Military trucks and pedestrians were picking their way, cautiously, among mounds of debris. The whole sight was that of terrible devastation.

We were quartered in tents near the stadium, where the sport competitions were to take place. The tents were comfortable, the food was good, and with mild weather, it felt like being at an outing. The following morning we started practicing in the stadium. We had one day of practice before the start of the Spartakiade. I ran the distance of 100 meters several times, with Mr. Stanger recording the time with his stopwatch. At the end of the day he was satisfied with my performance.

"You'll make it into the semifinals, and with luck, into the finals," he said with a smile.

I was in an upbeat mood, confident that I could beat most other competitors of my age. I was also proud of my new sport uniform the school had given me for this event: navy-blue shorts with a red stripe on the side, white jersey, white socks, and white running shoes.

The opening ceremony of the games took place the following morning. There were several thousand participants who came from all corners of the Ukraine. Teenagers and adults, men and women, all in sport uniforms, marched into the stadium in formation, to the music of a military band. Red banners fluttered all over the arena The participants paraded in front of a platform filled with government and party officials, then marched on to the center of the stadium. Once all participants were gathered in the stadium, the anthem of the Soviet Union was played, and the Soviet flag was raised. After several speeches, accompanied by the customary tribute to the great leader, Joseph Stalin, the games were declared open.

The competition started in the afternoon. While I was waiting, along with others, to be scheduled for the track and field competition, Mr. Stanger came over to me, red-faced and very agitated. A thin sheen of sweat covered his forehead.

"I have news for you," he said.

"What kind of news?" I was sure that Mr. Stanger had found out the schedule for my running.

"I just found out that you are not going to run in the 100-meter sprint."
I felt I was being hit over the head with a club. "Why?" I asked in amazement.

"The quota allocated to school children by the sports committee in the 100-meter sprint competition had been filled," he said, "and they do not accept additional competitors."

I was stunned. I had been betrayed. All these months of training and hard work had gone to waste because of a "quota." I knew I had a better running time than many of my competitors. Tears came to my eyes. Mr. Stanger understood my feelings and had a consolation prize for me.

"The quota for the 400-meter sprint has not been filled yet," he said, "and I have assigned you to participate."

"But I have not practiced the 400-meter run for this competition." I replied bewildered.

"Never mind; you have practiced enough in school." he replied. "Then we can report back home that you have participated in the games. Otherwise, we may have trouble justifying your trip to Kiev."

Dejected, I accepted my new assignment, and started to practice the 400-meter sprint. I had two days to practice. On the day of the competition I was able to pass the first tryouts, that eliminated half the competitors. However, I was eliminated during the second tryouts. I was dissapointed, but still pleased to have given a respectable performance at the 400-meter run.

After my return to school, my classmates treated me like a great athlete, like a star sprinter. Everybody congratulated me for participating in the games, and the girls gave me a lot of smiles. Gradually I began to feel better. The complements and the smiles had their effect. After all, I had participated in the games, hadn't I? I just did not compete in the area I had trained for. Moreover, Mr. Stanger had told me that with my running time, I would have qualified for the semi-finales in the 100-meter sprint competition. That made me feel good.

Thus ended my adventures in sport. However, it was the devastation and human suffering observed during my trip to Kiev that touched me deeply, and stayed in my memory.

In early May 1945, Berlin fell to the Soviets. On May 9, in the presence of representatives from the United States, the Soviet Union, Great Britain and France, Field Marshal Keitel signed the unconditional surrender of Nazi Germany to the Allies. Russian newsreels showed the signing ceremony, which ended with Soviet Marshall Zhukov showing Field Marshall Keitel the door. The bloodiest war in history had finally come to an end.

There was exuberant joy all over Czernowitz. The following day, the streets were full of people, celebrating. The city was festooned with flags, military bands played in parks, and people danced in the streets to the music of uniformed accordion players. Strangers embraced each other, or slapped each other on the back. Most Russians and Ukrainians celebrated as they usually did—with heavy drinking.

There was an unlimited supply of vodka. Never have I seen so many drunken people on the street. Some were too drunk to walk. After zigzagging through the cheerful, boisterous crowd, bumping into people and lampposts, feet shaking and out of control, the drunks eventually stumbled, dropped on the cobblestones, and promptly fell asleep. Others, staggering while holding on for dear life to more sober friends, meandered on the sidewalk on wobbly feet, trying to get home. Among them were many drunken women, some in military uniform, giggling and blabbering. Empty liquor bottles littered the streets. The air was filled with music, laughter, and the loud voices of the drunk. A heavy smell of vodka and tobacco hung in the air. In the evening, the sky was illuminated by multicolored fireworks and by moving searchlights.

The Jews of the city also celebrated, although they did it with less vodka than their Russian and Ukrainian neighbors. They had good cause to celebrate, for the simple reason of being alive. The celebration, however, was more subdued among the Jews, due to the losses that every family had suffered during the fascist rule. There was no Jewish family in Czernowitz that had not lost loved ones in Transnistria or during the massacres at the beginning of the war. At that time we did not know yet about the tragic fate of the Jews of Poland, where many of us had relatives. Nor did we know about the scale of Jewish extermination carried out by the Nazis all over Europe.

Now that the war was over, we were looking forward to hearing from Cousin Eddie. After surviving Transnistria and being drafted into the Red Army, we assumed that he was sent to the front. We did not know, however, what happened to him since. Several weeks after the war ended, Eddie wrote from Berlin, informing us that he was well. He would be stationed in Germany for the time being, serving as a translator. The Red Army put his knowledge of German to good use, since there was a serious shortage of people speaking both Russian and German, languages that Eddie spoke fluently. After spending another two years in the army, he was discharged and returned home. By the time Eddie arrived in Czernowitz, he found only my grandparents, since the rest of the family was no longer alive or had left for Romania.

Many years later, in America, Eddie told me the story of his life in Transnistria and in the Red Army. After being deported in the fall of 1941, he was sent to the ghetto of Moghilev. He arrived there sick and injured from repeated beatings by the gendarmes. In January 1942, he was separated from his father and sent to do hard labor in different labor camps. In those camps, he lived in barracks without doors in overcrowded, unsanitary conditions. During the day, in addition to doing hard labor, the guards constantly abused him and the other prisoners. At night, he had to fight off rats and lice. While in one of the labor camps, he fell sick with typhus. When he recovered he was sent back to work. He later learned from a fellow prisoner that his father had died.

After liberation in early 1944, he was drafted into the Red Army. After several weeks of training he was sent to the front. He was wounded twice, recovered, and was sent back to fight the Nazis. He fought all the way to Berlin, where he took part in the conquest of the city.

Eddie described to me an episode of that battle. During house-to-house fighting, he was cut off from his buddies and had to spend the night in a building that was partially occupied by enemy troops. Only a thin wall separated him from the Germans, who were unaware of his presence in their immediate vicinity.

In the wee hours of next morning, when the Soviets resumed their attack on the building, Eddie discovered that he was in a room behind the

Germans. He had two hand grenades and his submachine gun. He crawled through the rubble toward the room where the Germans were firing through the window, and lobbed one of the hand grenades through the open door. The firing from that room stopped. He then crawled to another room where the crackling of submachine gun fire could be heard. His second hand grenade quieted that room. For good measure, he then sprayed the room with bullets from his submachine gun. His action helped his buddies occupy the building. The end of the war found him among the ruins of Berlin.

Eddie was decorated with the Soviet medals "For Bravery," "For Military Valor," and "For Taking Berlin." I am very proud of my cousin for his accomplishments on the front. He had avenged the murder of his parents.

A few weeks after the victory celebration, a middle-aged man, with haggard face and dressed in shabby civilian cloths, visited my grandparents while I was there. At first, they did not recognize him. It turned out that he was a second cousin of my grandfather, who used to live in Zaleshchiky. The city, which used to belong to Poland before the war, was now under Soviet rule. The visitor told his story in rough, disconnected sentences. He used to own a small clothing and fabric store, and employed a couple of sales people. He had a wife and two small children. When the Soviets occupied the city in 1939, he was arrested as a capitalist exploiter and sent to a labor camp in the Komi Republic near the Ural Mountains. Later he was drafted into the Red Army. He spent the war years fighting on different fronts.

At the end of war he was discharged from the military and returned to Zaleshchiky to look for his wife and children. He could not find them. Nor could he find his parents, brothers, sisters, or any of his former Jewish neighbors. From a former Polish neighbor he learned that during the war, the Germans had rounded up the Jews of the city and shipped them to an unknown destination. Our relative remembered my grandfather, found out his address, and came to inquire if he knew anything about the fate of his family.

My grandfather had no idea what had happened to our family in

Poland, since we had lost contact with them during the war. Our relative left and we did not hear from him anymore. Later we learned that our family in Zaleshchiky had been sent to an extermination camp. It was an irony of fate (a prank of fate?) that the only family member to survive was the one deported by the Soviets to a labor camp.

I still remember my relatives in Zaleshchiky when I visited, with my mother, in 1938: their cheerful faces when we got off the train, the embraces and kisses, the sweets they gave me. I also remember the *cheder* next-door, the semi-dark room full of little, barefoot boys with side locks, sitting around the wooden table chanting together with the old, bearded *melamed.* That world had gone up in smoke.

Gradually, the enormity of the crimes perpetrated by the Nazis and their accomplices against the Jews of Europe began to emerge. Reality outdid the worst imaginable horror. We learned about the millions of innocent men, women and children whose lives had been blotted out by the Nazi "supermen." We found out that countless Jewish communities, which before the war had a vibrant, active life, had vanished. The hustle and bustle in the narrow streets of these communities, the *Chasidim* rushing to *shul* to pray, the Jewish housewives haggling in the market, the young Jewish mothers walking their little boys to *cheder,* the laughter of children playing in some backyard—all that had disappeared. The Germans had turned those people into smoke and ashes. We heard for the first time the names Auschwitz, Treblinka, Maidanek, Bergen-Belsen, Sobibor, and became familiar with the words "Nazi extermination camps."

In addition to the enormous loss of life, there was also a horrible loss of precious brainpower, knowledge and creativity. The loss in the areas of arts, science, medicine, music, literature and philosophy, areas in which Jews have been so prolific in the past, was immeasurable. So was the loss not only of the children that have been murdered, but also of the millions of children that were doomed never to be born. It was an incomprehensible monstrosity.

My father was terribly shocked by those revelations. For most of his life, the word "German" had been for him the epitome of culture, correctness, efficiency, discipline, and thoroughness. In many ways he felt and acted more German than Jewish. He had always seen the Germans as a people of culture, who had enriched the treasure of human knowledge with the output of their writers, philosophers, scientists, and composers. The wall-to-wall bookshelves of German literature in our house before the war were testimony of my parents' devotion to that culture.

One evening, after having read about a newly discovered atrocity perpetrated by the Nazis, Father put down the newspaper and asked Mother a rhetorical question. "How could the people who have given the world Beethoven, Goethe, and Schiller, fall under the spell of a criminal madman whom they called 'Führer'? How could they commit such monstrous crimes?" Mother didn't answer. Simply, there was no answer.

"How skillfully had a simple Austrian corporal," Father continued, "a painter without talent, without title and without wealth, but with an iron will and a fiery demagogic talent, been able to pervert a whole nation..."

He then read aloud a section of the newspaper article written by a well-known Russian-Jewish journalist. "Like a sculptor molds a dead lump of clay into a monster, so had Hitler been able to mold the minds of millions of Germans and Austrians. With his fiery speeches he convinced them to follow him with enthusiasm in the pursuit of his utopia of building a Thousand-Year Reich for the German "master race," and to save civilization from the 'Judeo-Bolshevik threat.'"

The article continued. "Enticed also by the demagogic speeches of fascist propaganda minister Dr. Göbbels and by the inflammatory articles in the fascist newspaper, *Der Stürmer* (the Soviets always used the term 'fascists" instead of "Nazis"), the self-appointed saviors of civilization wreaked havoc all over Europe. They caused enormous suffering and destruction, and murdered a whole people with Teutonic thoroughness and efficiency. How could this happen? Was this only an aberration during the Hitler era, a quirk of history, made possible by the blinding of the German people by a demagogic madman? Or was it something in the German character that had already been "set" long before Hitler, which was only kept in check by the norms of civilization? Was that sickening character trait let loose when Hitler discarded all rules of a civilized society and replaced them with those of Attila the Hun?"

Whatever the answer, the admiration for German culture and values quickly evaporated in our home. The word "German" was no longer associated with culture and orderliness, but with cruelty and barbarism. German "efficiency" and "thoroughness," much admired in the past by my father as positive values to be emulated, were now seen in a different light. He saw them in context with the way mass-murder of millions of defenseless and innocent people had been carried out. For my father, the most admired people in the past became the most hated.

The calamities of the war also brought other changes in my father's opinions. His past ambiguity about religion ended. Before the war, he went to Temple on the Jewish High Holidays and followed some of the Jewish rituals. Now, however, he started asking questions that were on everybody's mind. "Where was God when Hitler and his cohorts slaughtered the Jewish people? Where was God when over a million Jewish children were murdered by the German 'supermen'? Where was He?"

Considering what happened to God's "chosen people," my father began to question the existence of a loving, compassionate Divine Being. Was God dead, as the nineteenth century philosopher Friedrich Nitzsche claimed? Or was it a callous God, indifferent to human suffering?

From then on, Father never set foot in a synagogue. Mother, in turn, after losing most of her family in Transnistria and in Poland, became skeptical in her belief. She cooked the traditional meals on Jewish holidays, but did not attend any religious service.

The enormity of the crimes perpetrated by the Nazis and their accomplices also raised questions and doubts in my mind. After the Nazi genocide, one did not have to be a Marxist to wonder what had happened to God. How could one believe in divine justice, charity and kindness in the face of the methodical murder of more than a million innocent children? Why did so few, so precious few, Christians come to the aid of their fellow human beings? I could not find answers to these questions. I was puzzled and bewildered.

The events that later became known as the Holocaust also shook my faith in man. I became convinced that deep inside many people lurks evil. That, in a civilized society, evil is kept in check by the rules and laws of that society, hidden behind a veneer of civility. Haven't the great prophets and teachers, with their sermons and writings, tried to keep the evil in man under control? Hasn't Hitler's Germany shown that once people's dark instincts are given free reign against a certain ethnic, political or religious group, the otherwise "civilized" people will turn quickly into cruel and vicious creatures—or, at best, turn a blind eye toward the cruelty perpetrated in their midst? Freed of any constrains of civilized behavior, haven't the Romanian fascists in the first days of war behaved like wild beasts in our city, committing acts of murder and mayhem against defenseless men, women, and children?

Sure there were also decent, honorable people among the Germans and Romanians. They were, however, a small minority that in most instances remained passive or indifferent toward the rising tide of hatred and atrocities. Very, very rare were the cases when they tried to help or protect the innocent victims of persecution. Mayor Popovici was one such rare exception.

As on many subjects, my views with regard to religion have changed over time. Early influences and experiences, however, have left their imprint. During my mature life, when asked about my views regarding a Supreme Being, I reply that I am inclined to accept the opinion expressed by the 17th century Jewish philosopher Baruch Spinoza. Such a view has been concisely formulated more recently by Albert Einstein: "I believe in Spinoza's God who reveals Himself in the orderly harmony of what exists, not in a God who concerns Himself with fates and actions of human beings." In my opinion, the findings of science, from the Big Bang to the evolution of our species out of galaxies and exploding stars, suggest the existence of an ultimate, little-understood driving force in nature that shapes the world as we know it. But I doubt the existence of a merciful God concerned with the fate of each and every human being. The horrors that have occurred during my lifetime prevent me from reaching any other conclusion.

The German cultural graft in my heart began to give me great pain. I started to feel revulsion even for having a German-sounding family name.

"Father, why do most Jews have German-sounding names?" I wanted to know.

"In the eighteenth century," Father explained, "the Austrian Emperor Joseph the Second requested that all Jews living in his Empire Germanize their names. Since the Austrian Empire occupied a large part of Central Europe at that time and had a significant Jewish population, a large number of European Jews ended up with German names. Most of them kept those names even after they became citizens of other countries." Of course, those German names did not protect them from being murdered by the Germans during the Nazi era.

At school, the revelations of the atrocities committed by the Nazis and their accomplices against the Jewish people created shock and stupefaction. During recess, this subject became the major topic of conversation. Some of the "luminaries" in our class, with a philosophical bent, started discussing the subject of good and evil, of right and wrong. Among those most active in these discussions was Berty, our "philosopher" and "poet in residence." He believed in the ethical values expounded in the Hebrew Bible, was an idealist, and had written poems with a philosophical bent, in Yiddish and German. On several occasions he had run into trouble with some members of the party organization, due to his occasional use of Biblical quotes.

Then there was Tina, with a sharp mind and sharper tongue, a freethinker and good debater. She was often inclined to play the devil's advocate. During the many discussions in which she expressed firmly her opinions, we never knew if these were her personal convictions or if she just enjoyed contradicting the rest of us.

There was also Erwin, well read and smart, who was convinced that reason should shape people's beliefs and conduct.

I remember a debate, started during recess, in which Berty raised the question: what is good and what is evil? Who establishes the standards for good and evil? What is moral and what is immoral? Are these standards universal, are they permanent? The "luminaries" in our class (we called them *oiberchachomim*—Yiddish for super smart people) grabbed this subject like a dog grabs a juicy bone, and started a heated debate.

"There is no such thing as universal standards for good and evil, for morality and immorality," proclaimed Tina with conviction. "Each society has certain standards and most people in that society accept them."

"But who sets those standards for society?" inquired Erwin. "In an anti-Semitic society, such as Nazi Germany, beating a Jew on the street was acceptable, it was not an evil deed. In a democratic society, however, such behavior is considered evil and immoral. Who decides whose standards are right?"

Before Tina could respond, Berty intervened. "If you accept Tina's point of view, every society can set its own standards of good and evil. In a society ruled by a dictator, it is the dictator who sets the ethical standards. In the case of Nazi Germany, those standards led to the death of millions of innocent people. A modern, civilized society should base its ethical standards on the Bible, not on those of a dictator or of the dominant ideology. The values espoused by the Bible, such as the Ten Commandments, teach people how to live a decent, responsible life. 'You should not kill, you should not steal, you should not lie'—these are some of the standards to be used to decide what is good and what is evil."

"Are you saying that if somebody would have killed Hitler ten years ago it would have been an evil deed?" asked Erwin with an ironic smile on his face.

"No, I am not saying that. People should consider the consequences of their deeds when applying the biblical commandments," countered Berty. "One should look at the circumstances under which the commandment, 'You should not kill,' is applied. Since killing Hitler would have saved millions of people from persecution and death, such a deed would have been considered a good deed, a moral deed. Similarly, if a Christian family in Nazi dominated Europe hid a Jewish child and lied about it when questioned by the SS, such a lie would be a moral deed."

"If you are a religious person you may accept the morality taught by the Bible. Does that mean that an atheist or agnostic cannot be a good person?" inquired Tina.

Before Berty could answer, Erwin replied. "You don't have to be a religious person to know what is good and what is evil. There are many non-religious people who can differentiate between good and evil, and who live decent, responsible lives. Reason tells us that killing an innocent person is evil, while killing a mass murderer like Hitler is a moral act."

"With reason you can justify any deed," retorted Berty. "For those who accept Hitler's ideology, reason will tell them that concentration camps for 'undesirable elements' are necessary for the good of society. They could even rationalize the murder of those 'undesirables.' In a cannibal society it was 'reasonable' to eat the defeated enemy. Reason and morality have nothing in common. Reason is amoral. Only the values espoused by the Bible give people a moral compass that helps them decide what is good and what is evil, what is moral and what is immoral."

Now Erwin got really excited. "In that case you would expect that those people and institutions that are deeply religious and follow the moral percepts of the Bible will do good and moral deeds. But haven't the ancient Israelites slain the Amalekites in the name of *their* God? Haven't the Crusaders and the practitioners of the Inquisition killed tens of thousands of people, by sword or by fire, in the name of *their* God? Didn't the Moslems fight holy wars and kill thousands of 'infidels' in the name of *their* God? Do you consider these deeds moral?"

Tina replied before Berty could open his mouth—she was always eager to impose her point of view, "It is obvious that morality is a relative notion that changes from society to society and varies in time. There are no objective moral standards. Moral rules, like styles of dress, vary from society to society. What is acceptable as good and moral by one society is considered evil and immoral by other societies. What was considered moral in Spain 500 years ago—the burning of "heretics" on the stake—is not considered moral in our time. The Hindu custom to kill the wife when her husband dies and to immolate them together—a practice that prevailed in India until the early part of the nineteenth century—is no longer acceptable in that country. There still are Moslem societies where thieves have their hands cut off—a deed that, in our society, is considered cruel and evil. On the other hand, Buddhist and Hindu sects that are vegetarian consider the slaughter and eating of animals, as practiced in our society, barbaric and evil. All this proves that there are no absolute moral values. We accept as good and evil what we have been taught by our tradition, our parents and our teachers."

Berty did not give in. "But you can be taught the wrong values, as it happened in Hitler's Germany. We do need a moral compass to guide us. I do believe that moral principles espoused in the Bible can be used as a guide to differentiate between good and evil. I still believe that the tenet 'what is hateful to you, do not do to others,' or 'love thy neighbor as thyself' can be universal guidelines to lead an ethical life. Otherwise, what prevents a dictator, or even some individual, to set his own moral guidelines that fit his ideology or his needs? That can lead to untold suffering by other people, as we have seen in our own lifetime."

The bell rang and the discussion came to an abrupt end. As it happened often in such debates, non-of the participants changed his or her mind. I realized that the apparently simple question, "How to differentiate good from evil," does not have a simple answer. Then I thought of little Gusta with her bright eyes and crystalline laughter; of the little boys with torn pants and flying side locks running and playing cheerfully in a dusty yard in Zaleshchiky; of dreamy-eyed Aunt Tzili playing the mandolin with her long, delicate fingers. Those thoughts convinced me that in a civilized society, anybody with just a trace of conscience and a vestige of humanity would have no difficulty in deciding how the deeds perpetrated by the German and Romanian fascists against the Jews should be described.

After the war in Europe had come to an end, in the second half of 1945 and in 1946, there was a huge move of population all over the war-ravaged continent. Refugees who had fled the fighting and bombing were now returning home. Liberated slave laborers and concentration camp survivors, emaciated and dressed in rags, were trying to find the means to return to their countries of origin. Demobilized soldiers were returning to their families to start a new life as civilians. Prisoners of war set free were now returning home. It appeared that everybody was on the move.

A continuous flow of people made up of former concentration camp inmates, slave laborers and freed prisoners of war passed through Czernowitz. The concentration camp survivors came from Transnistria and some came from former Nazi camps in Poland. The slave laborers came from Poland and were trying to return to their country of origin. The freed prisoners of war came from the Soviet Union. They were from countries allied with Nazi Germany during the war and were now returning home. It was a motley crowd that stayed briefly in the city before moving on. On the streets one could hear a Babel of languages. In addition to Russian, Ukrainian, Yiddish and German spoken by the local population, one could hear Polish, Romanian, French, Dutch, Serb, Italian, Hungarian, Czech, and many other indistinguishable languages.

In that motley crowd there was also a group of former Italian prisoners of war. They had fought on the Russian front, had been captured by the Red Army, and had spent the rest of the war in Soviet prison camps. Now they had been released, and they passed through Czernowitz on their way back to Italy. In spite of the hardships they had experienced, many of them were cheerful, knowing that they were returning home. With their shiny black hair, dark eyes, and bright smiles, still wearing their military uniforms, they looked quite handsome. The girls of Czernowitz looked with friendly, shiny eyes at these handsome young men.

Which reminds me of Sophy. She was a young woman who lived not far from our house. She was attractive, intelligent, but aloof and very choosy with regard to the people with whom she associated. She also had very different ideas about life and marriage from those of other women. While most young women were eager to socialize with young men and eventually get married, Sophy saw life differently. She had concluded that marriage would be a burden for her, would limit her freedom, and decided not to get married. She wanted, however, to have a child; an attractive, intelligent child. Among her friends and acquaintances, Sophy could not find a man handsome and smart enough to deserve the honor of being the father of her child. She decided to wait until the suitable man came along.

She heard about the handsome Italians that were passing through town and resolved to take a closer look at them. Sophy saw a group of cheerful, noisy Italians walking through the center of the city, and noticed a dashing, young officer among them. She decided to approach him and become acquainted. After spending years in a prisoner of war camp, the officer obviously was more than eager to befriend this attractive young woman. They communicated in French, since both of them spoke the language fluently. Sophy invited him to her one-room apartment, and the following few days they had a good time together. Shortly afterwards, the officer left town with the rest of his comrades.

A few months later, Sophy's neighbors noticed that she had a bloated belly. When the time came, she gave birth to a charming little boy. She was a happy mother and very proud of her child, in spite of the snickering and gossiping that swirled around her. Sophy was a strong-willed woman who knew what she wanted, did not care much about other people's opinion, and had the courage to implement her plan. She was a woman far ahead of her time.

In the spring of 1946 I graduated from high school with straight As. With such grades, I could have enrolled at any university department, including medicine, without having to pass an admission exam. In contrast to prewar Romanian universities, attending a Soviet University or medical school was free—one of the positive aspects of life in a socialist society. Like most of my colleagues, however, I had not decided what career to choose. I was interested in both science and humanities, but I had to choose the career that would offer me a more promising future under the Soviet regime.

The school administration decided to help us. It organized visits for high school graduates to different factories, hospitals, to the university, to research institutions, and cooperatives. We were exposed to the "real world" environment, in which a diversity of people pursued a variety of productive activities. In this way we could learn about the work done in these enterprises, talk to the professionals there, and find out what occupation would be most interesting to each of us. It was a good idea that helped us choose our future careers.

Of all the visits, I found most interesting those at the university's physics department and at the city hospital. We visited each place with one of our teachers. At the university we attended a laboratory session on electricity and magnetism. I found the experiments fascinating: the electrical discharges in vacuum tubes, the generation of an electrical current by a dynamo motor and the formation of gases by electrolysis. I had not seen any of these experiments during my last two years of high school, since the school had non of the necessary equipment. I had a very good physics teacher, Gershon Segal, but his teaching was mostly theoretical. Still, I found his lectures quite interesting. My visit to the university lab stimulated my interest even more. The career of a physics professor or that of a scientist appeared quite attractive.

Another visit I remember well was one to the city hospital. (The hospital was conveniently located in the vicinity of one of the city's cemeteries.) First we visited the psychiatric ward, headed by my friend's father, Dr. Mayer. It was my first contact with mentally disturbed patients in a hospital, and it left a deep impression. Some patients were sitting and brooding, not aware of our presence. Others were wearing straight jackets and were tied down to a heavy, wooden bench. The doctor explained that these were the violent cases, and had to be restrained. The expression on each face was frightening: wild-eyed, red from the effort made to escape from the straight jacket, and they were screaming on top of their lungs. The room reverberated with their screams. Still, other patients were staring into the air or talking to themselves. There were others that were walking around freely, but had weird behavior and strange looks in their eyes.

In one of the rooms we saw a smiling, attractive young woman who fascinated the boys in our group. She was waiting for us to approach her. When we came close to her, she grabbed our guide, a middle-aged doctor, by the arm, pulled him over to her bed, and started to unbutton her dress. The doctor said a few quiet words to her, then pushed her gently away and walked to the next room. After we left the hospital, this event was an exciting subject of conversation among us teenagers.

We had several girls in our group who were interested in becoming pediatricians or gynecologists. They wanted to see the maternity ward and delivery room. At first, our guide was not inclined to take us there, since he felt that it was not appropriate for teenagers to see such a place. Eventually, the girls were able to convince him, and he took us to that section of the hospital.

We entered a large room, in which about a dozen women, lying on surgical tables, were in different stages of giving birth. With bloated bellies and faces contorted by suffering, the women were groaning and screaming in pain. Doctors and nurses, standing next to some of those screaming women, busied themselves helping with delivery. There was pandemonium in the room. The screams of the women in pain were mingled with the crying of just born babies. Bloodstained linen was lying on the floor in small piles. The white coats of the doctors and nurses were also blood-splattered.

The heavy smell of blood, sweat and urine in the room made me feel nauseated. I ran out into the hallway, pushed open a window, and took a deep breath of fresh air, just in time not to throw up. At that moment I made a decision: medicine is not for me. I just did not have the stomach for it—literally speaking.

While we toured the hospital, in addition to the doctor who guided us, a medical orderly accompanied us. His name was Paul. He was in his early twenties, had expressive dark eyes, and looked frail, like everyone in our group. The war years had left their mark on all of us. A colleague of mine knew Paul. During the war, he was drafted into a Jewish forced labor detachment. His parents were deported from Czernowitz to Transnistria. They died there. In 1944, Paul returned to Czernowitz and found a job as an orderly in the city hospital. In his spare time he wrote poetry in German, his native tongue. Years later I learned that Paul went to West Germany, where he had his poems published under the name Paul Celan. He became one of the most famous German poets of the post-war era. He was invited to literary meetings to recite his poetry, and schoolchildren learned his poems by heart. In 1970, while in Paris, he committed suicide. The terrible experience in the early stage of his life had taken its toll.

After visiting the different institutions and factories, I had to determine in which university department to enroll. Although I was interested in several areas of the humanities, such as arts and literature, I chose a career in science. I resolved to study physics, a field I found very attractive. Such a course was less risky than one in humanities, since it was less likely to be affected by changing political winds. Modern works of art, poems or novels that were considered valuable at one time, ran the risk of being considered later as mere products of bourgeois decadence. Those artists and writers who created these works, as well as those who wrote or spoke appreciatively of them, could find themselves, almost overnight, in deep trouble. This was less likely to happen in science—although it did happen, especially in biology.

At the end of August 1946, I enrolled at the physics department of the University of Czernowitz. After attending the first few weeks of lectures, however, my university studies came to an abrupt halt. The course of my life took a sharp turn.

13. "Repatriation" to Romania

During the spring and summer of 1944, the advancing Red Army had occupied most of Northern Romania. On August 23, King Michael decided to switch sides. He had Marshal Ion Antonescu, along with his foreign minister, arrested. He then ordered the Romanian Army to stop hostilities against the Soviet Union, and start fighting the German troops stationed in Romania. At the end of 1944, the Soviets entered Bucharest.

A succession of democratic coalition governments followed the Antonescu regime. With each new government, the power and influence of the Romanian Communist Party increased. The presence of Soviet troops on Romanian soil and the inaction of the Western Allies made free elections impossible. After a rigged election in March 1945, a coalition government that included the Communist Party took power under Prime Minister Petru Groza. It was well known that Groza was a stooge of the communists. Key positions in the government were now under communist control.

After Bertha and Shmuel left Czernowitz, they moved closer to the front that had temporarily stabilized in the region Dorohoi and Botosani, in the northern part of Romania. They spent several weeks in Dorohoi. After Romania switched sides in August 1944 and Soviet troops entered Bucharest, Bertha and Shmuel arrived there shortly afterwards. Their objective was to reach Palestine with the help of the Zionist Organization of Romania. Under the new regime, the organization had regained freedom of action, and was assisting young people to reach the Holy

Land. Considering their past Zionist affiliations, Shmuel applied to Bethar for assistance, while Bertha applied to Hashomer Hatzaïr. The Zionist Organization had received a number of immigration certificates for Palestine, issued by the British authorities. The certificates were part of the quota allocated by the British Mandate for Jewish immigration to that country. During the war, these certificates had not been used due to the military conflict. There were few certificates and the leaders of the Zionist Organization of Romania decided to give priority to refugees from Soviet territories. Shmuel received a certificate through the Bethar organization, in recognition of his many years of membership in that organization, and due to his flight from the Soviet Union. He boarded a ship in the Romanian port Constanta that took him to Haifa in Palestine.

Bertha encountered more difficulties in her effort to reach the Holy Land. She spent several weeks at a *hachsharah* camp of the Hashomer Hatsaïr organization, where she was trained for life in a kibbutz. After completing the training, she was given an immigration certificate for Palestine. She boarded a train to Bulgaria; from there she planned to travel through Turkey, Syria and Lebanon to her destination. Things, however, did not go as planned—they rarely do. When Bertha reached the Bulgarian-Turkish border, she was told that the immigration quota for Palestine had been filled. That meant the British authorities allowed no more Jewish immigrants to enter that country in 1944. It was a time when the British already knew that Jews were systematically murdered all over Nazi occupied Europe, and still refused to give them refuge. Bertha had to wait near the border several weeks, and only at the beginning of the following year was she able to continue her travel. She arrived in Palestine during January 1945, where she was reunited with Shmuel. They had finally achieved their goal.

After the Russians occupied Northern Bukovina and advanced into Romania, they reestablished the border of June 1941 between the Soviet Union and Romania. In the spring and fall of 1945, and again in 1946, the Soviets opened the border briefly, to allow former Romanian citizens to cross over into Romania. The process was called "repatriation." All that was needed to cross the border was a permit (*propusk*), readily issued by the Soviet authorities to Bukovina residents. The eagerness of the authorities to issue permits had a simple explanation. They needed every house and apartment that had not been destroyed during the war. "Repatriation" would go a long way to solve the housing problem in Czernowitz.

The Jewish residents of our city had to face an unusual situation. Until now, the authorities, either fascist or communist, had made most of the decisions concerning their life and existence. Now, for the first time in many years, they themselves faced choices and decisions that might drastically affect their future. It was not an easy decision. There was chaos and devastation in most of Europe, and the future of Romania, under Red Army occupation, was shrouded in uncertainty. Eventually, after pondering their options, most Jews of Czernowitz and of other parts of Northern Bukovina decided to take advantage of the "repatriation" policy and crossed the border into Romania. They settled in Southern Bukovina and in other parts of the country. Many of them were hoping eventually to emigrate to Palestine.

For my parents the decision to resettle was not an easy one. My father was advanced in age, weakened by the hardships endured during the war, and plagued by a chronic cough. He knew that he was too weak and ill to resume his practice of law in Romania. But he also knew that he could not practice his profession under the Soviets. Moreover, from the communist viewpoint, he—and implicitly his family—belonged to the capitalist class, and was, therefore, an "enemy of the working class." We all remembered very well how, in 1941, the NKVD men came in the middle of the night to pick up the "enemies of the people" and sent them to some distant labor camps. Those deportations were interrupted by the outbreak of the war, and now they might be resumed again. Indeed, we heard rumors that in other parts of the Soviet Union liberated from German occupation, thousands of people had been picked up by the NKVD and deported. Hesitantly, my father decided that we should leave.

Mother did not hesitate. Given the choice of living under a dictatorship or a democracy—which Romania still was at the time—she believed that life in a democratic country had a brighter future, especially for me. She felt that we would be able to make a better living in Romania.

Mother was convinced that I would be able to continue my studies in a democratic country and live a free life. She was also encouraged by the fact, related in letters from those who left for Romania a year earlier, that the "Joint Distribution Committee" (a Jewish-American charity organization) was assisting the newly arrived repatriates.

Bertha's departure from the Soviet Union contributed to Mother's decision. She did not want to be cut off from her daughter. Neither did she want to be cut off from Uncle Joseph and Aunt Ruchel, who had left for Romania a year earlier and were now living in Bucharest. Mother was firm in her decision to leave.

Initially, I had mixed feelings about moving. I enjoyed my university courses and would have liked to continue my studies. I also realized, however, that almost all our friends and acquaintances had left or were leaving. When Mother told me that I would be able to study in Romania, I accepted my parents' decision to leave.

In early September 1946 we applied for and received the required *propusk* for repatriation. Mother had no difficulty finding a buyer for our furniture and household goods that we could not take with us. The buyer was a young captain and his wife. By buying our furniture, the couple took also possession of our apartment—a precious commodity in a war-devastated country. They agreed to pay us eight hundred rubles for our belongings when we move out. To make sure that we didn't change our mind and that he would take possession of the apartment, the captain left his military coat on a hanger in the apartment before leaving.

We packed a suitcase of clothing for each of us, a bundle of bedding, and a large trunk with pots, pans and other kitchenware, including a wash board. I also packed several books and my small stamp collection. We were not allowed to take jewelry, money or art objects. Anything of value had to be left behind.

Mother arranged with a peasant to take us to the border in his horse-drawn cart. On the morning of our departure, the captain and his wife arrived to take over the apartment and its contents. After Mother gave him the keys, he told her to wait while he verified that everything we agreed to sell him was there. While the couple was in the bedroom, a heated argument started between the captain and his wife. Through the closed door we could hear snippets of what they were arguing about.

"These people are deserting the Soviet Union and therefore don't deserve to be paid anything," I heard the captain say in an irate voice.

"Decency and the word given by a Soviet officer require that the agreement be respected," countered his wife with anger. The arguing went on for awhile.

I looked at my mother. Her face expressed anguish and worry. I knew what she was thinking. We may have to leave without being paid anything for our belongings. We may not have enough money even to pay the peasant to take us to the border. And there was nothing we could do. We were at the mercy of the couple who were arguing behind the closed doors.

Finally the captain and his wife came out from the bedroom. Both were red-faced and irritated. The officer handed four hundred rubles to my mother, half of what was initially agreed. When mother pointed that out to the captain, he replied with annoyance that this was all the money he had, and that we should consider ourselves lucky to be paid at all. Since we were in no position to argue with him, we left. When we reached the waiting horse-drawn cart carrying our belongings, Mother gave the money to my father for safekeeping. At least we had some money.

I left the city of my childhood and early teens. I took a last look at the neoclassical buildings lining the Bahnhofstrasse and Hauptstrasse, and at the Ringplatz with the imposing city hall and clock tower. I remembered the statue of the crouching bronze soldier and the ice-cream cones my father had bought me on hot summer days in that square. I passed the lyceum "Aron Pumnul," now a Russian high school, where cruel, sadistic teachers had mistreated me during my early teens. I passed the *Volksgarten*, where I had spent many Sunday afternoons with my parents, listening to the music played by a military band. I left the city where I had lived under fascists and communists, seen NKVD troops and SS troops, seen mass murder committed by men in uniform against innocent civilians, experienced the beginning of war and the end of war. A city that had seen mass-deportations of thousands of its citizens to the freezing labor camps in the arctic north and to the deadly fields of Transnistria in the rugged east. I departed from a city that had left an indelible mark in my memory and on my soul.

After a two-hour ride on a bumpy, unpaved road, we arrived at the small, sleepy border town Siret, located near a shallow river with the same name. There we found other Jewish families who had decided to cross over into Romania. We had to wait for our turn. While we waited, we could see how the border control took place. After checking the documents, the Soviet border guards searched the baggage, and some of the people were submitted to body searches. They were looking for valuables, such as jewelry and gold coins, as well as foreign currency, primarily dollars. We had heard rumors that some families, after selling their belongings prior to departure, had used the rubles received to purchase dollars on the black market. The authorities, obviously, knew about these rumors and were determined not to let anything of value go through.

The search was thorough and without regard to damage caused. The border guard cut open pillows, tore apart the seams of padded clothing, ripped off the soles and heels from shoes. They even took apart washboards and split the walls of suitcases, looking for hidden precious stones, gold, and bank notes. Why should the guards be careful and considerate in their search? After all, here they dealt with people that were "deserting" the Soviet Union…

When our turn came, one of the border guards approached my father. The guard was a tall, strong man in gray uniform, rifle hanging from his shoulder. His face was grim.

"Your documents," he demanded with a gruff voice.

Father gave him our *propusk*. After examining the document, the guard ordered in a brusque tone: "Pay the driver!"

Father took out his wallet, where he kept all his money, to pay the peasant who had brought us to the border. At that moment, the guard grabbed the wallet, took out the money, gave a hundred-ruble note to the peasant, pocketed the rest, and returned the empty wallet to my father.

We were stunned. We had been robbed of all the money received from the sale of our household, as well as of all we had been able to save from the sale of goods in the flea market. We were left penniless.

Empty wallet in his hand, Father stared at the soldier. I looked at my father. Rage started boiling in him. His face turned deep red, his eyes bulged, the veins on his temples swelled, and his hands started to shake. He was tense like a taut string, but he suppressed his fury. I could see the enormous effort he made to control his rage. He felt humiliated and powerless. He knew well that we were at the mercy of those border guards. Any protest would have been useless. On the contrary, it could have been used as an excuse to prevent us from crossing the border.

On that occasion we found out that when it came to robbing Jews, the communist dictatorship had much in common with the fascist dictatorship.

The peasant who brought us to the border with his cart quickly unloaded our belongings in the middle of the road, turned the horse around, and left in a hurry.

Having taken all our money, the border guards didn't spend much time searching our baggage. True, they still went through each piece of luggage, took apart my mother's wash board, and tore up the pages of my stamp-collection album, searching for hidden foreign bank notes. But they didn't cut open the pillows or rip apart our clothes. They figured that somebody naïve enough to carry all his money in a wallet is less likely to smuggle valuables.

We finally came to the border. A heavy wooden beam, painted alternately in black and white, marked the border. The beam blocked the road connecting the two countries. It could be raised to let trucks or cars pass, but it was not raised for pedestrians. We had to drag our suitcases, bundles and Mother's trunk with kitchenware over a narrow walkway to the other side of the border.

On the Romanian side, the border guard glanced briefly at our document and waved us through. His face was morose and unfriendly. He was not happy to see all those Jews coming back to Romania.

On Romanian soil, peasants with horse-drawn carts were waiting for customers, to take them and their luggage to their destination. But we had no money to pay them. Who would want to take us and our belongings without being paid? While my father and mother were standing helpless, not knowing what to do, two well dressed gentlemen approached us. They were representatives of the "Joint" and spoke Romanian. They knew that the Soviets had left penniless everybody who crossed the border. They gave my father several hundred lei, so that we could pay for transportation and buy some food. My parents thanked them profusely. After being robbed by the border guards, we had finally encountered people willing to help us. Every family that arrived from the Soviet Union received some money from the two gentlemen. We rented a horse-drawn cart, loaded our belongings, and left for Suceava, my father's birthplace. Our destination was a two-hour cart-ride from the border. Thus began a new chapter in our lives.

Suceava is a small city in Southern Bukovina, located on the banks of the river with the same name, at the foot of the Carpathian Mountains. Next to it are the ruins of a fortress, built about five hundred years ago by the ruler of the Principality of Moldavia that is now part of Romania. Later, that area came under Ottoman rule. In 1774, Suceava was incorporated into Austria. At the end of World War I, with the collapse of the Austrian-Hungarian Empire, the city came under Romanian rule. More recently, Suceava was the administrative center of Northern Moldavia.

In 1946, Suceava was a small, provincial city. It had a main street lined with two-story buildings, most of them erected before World War I. At the ground floor of these buildings was a variety of small stores, while the upper floors were living quarters and offices. Several smaller streets branched out from the main street and ended in open fields. The center of the city was dominated by the town hall, a four-story building with a clock tower. Across the street from the town hall building was a small public park, graced by a bronze bust of the Romanian composer Ciprian Porumbescu. The city had numerous churches and monasteries, many of them built by Moldavian rulers centuries ago. With their beautifully glazed tile roofs and old frescoes, the monasteries attracted numerous visitors.

Before World War II there was a thriving Jewish community in Suceava. Jews were active mainly in the professions and in commerce. In 1940, when Czernowitz was occupied by the Soviets, Suceava remained under Romanian rule. After the invasion of the Soviet Union by Nazi Germany and its allies, the Jews of Suceava were deported to Transnistria, mostly to the villages of Shargorod and Murafa. The Red Army liberated the survivors in the spring of 1944 and let them return home.

My father had spent the early part of his life in that city. Although his family who used to live in Suceava did not survive the war, he still felt attracted to his place of birth. Father knew several Jewish families from the past, as well as some of the people who had come more recently from Czernowitz. For those reasons he decided to return to Suceava with his family.

When we arrived in Suceava, the city was extremely crowded. Some Romanians, who had fled Northern Bukovina, had settled in Suceava. Many of the Bukovina Jews who had returned from Transnistria also came to Suceava. They included Jews who used to live in smaller towns before the war. Those people decided not to return to the towns where many of their family members and friends had been murdered prior to deportation. The city had a number of Jewish families from Czernowitz, who had arrived there ahead of us.

The result of such overcrowding was a total absence of available living quarters. Every apartment, every house was packed with people. On the day of our arrival, my parents' frantic search for living space turned out fruitless. We had to settle in an abandoned warehouse, which contained empty wooden shelves along the walls and discarded, empty cardboard boxes on the cement floor. The room had two small dirty windows and a rusty iron door. The door did not close tightly, and there was a constant draft in the room.

The first night we slept on the cement floor on our own bedding. We took out all the blankets we had and spread them out on the floor over old newspapers. We put some down pillows and a down cover on top of them, and our beds were ready. It was a long, cold night. None of us could sleep. The cement floor was hard and cold, while the thin blankets we slept on provided little comfort. Father coughed continuously, and the constant draft made us shiver throughout the night. We could barely wait for daylight.

The following day we got some straw mattresses from the Jewish Community Center, as well as some warm food. My parents' search for a better place to live proved fruitless again. We had to stay in the same cold warehouse, without any furniture, without heat, and sleep on the cement floor.

A week went by before we were finally able to find a better place. It was in the house of an old lady, Mrs. Rachmut. Before the war, she and her husband occupied the whole house. When the war broke out, they were deported to Transnistria together with all other Jews of Suceava. Mr. Rachmut died in a labor camp, but his wife survived. When the war ended, she returned and took possession of her house. In her absence the house had deteriorated, and when Mrs. Rachmut took it over it was quite dilapidated.

Having no other source of income, she rented out each room in the house to a different family, leaving two rooms and a toilet for herself. My father had been a friend of Mr. Rachmut before the war, and he also knew Mrs. Rachmut. He remembered that they used to own a house, and went to see Mrs. Rachmut. He found her in a semi-dark room with peeling paint on the walls and a creaky, wooden floor. She wore a heavy, worn coat to protect herself from the cold draft that swept constantly the room. She was an older woman with snow-white hair, watery blue eyes and pale face crisscrossed by wrinkles. Father told us later that Mrs. Rachmut had once been a beautiful woman, and that she was actually younger than she looked. Obviously, Transnistria had not been a picnic for her.

Father described the desperate situation in which we found ourselves since the arrival in Suceava, and asked her if she could rent us a room. Since she had known my father as a friend of her husband before the war, she decided to let us have one of her two rooms.

To reach our lodging, we had to walk over a rickety, wooden veranda, enter a dark hallway, and pass through Mrs. Rachmut's room before entering our chamber through a tall, double door. The room was empty, except for a single light bulb suspended in the middle of the ceiling. There were two windows facing the street, and a small door leading to a storage area. The floor was made of worn-out, wooden boards. A coat of paint once covered the boards, but now only traces of paint could be seen on the floor near the walls. The room used to have a tile stove for heating. During the war, the tiles and the stove had been stolen, and all that was left was a black, round hole in the wall, leading to the chimney. There was no toilet or running water, and we had to use an outhouse. Water had to be brought into the room in buckets from an outdoor faucet.

Since we had been robbed at the border and had nothing of value to sell, we were totally destitute. We depended entirely on assistance from the local Jewish Community and Jewish-American charitable organizations. Father's health was deteriorating rapidly. The years of persecution, the extreme aggravation at the border, the sleeping on the cement floor in a warehouse, the despair brought about by penury and the inability to find a decent place to live—all these factors had a devastating effect on my father's health. It was at that time that he had a stroke, which paralyzed the left side of his body. Even with a cane he could barely walk, and his left arm had become useless. Incapacitated and unable to care for his family anymore, he fell into a state of deep depression.

Several weeks after we moved into Mrs. Rachmut's house, Mother was able to find a job. At the end of the war, "OSE" (Jewish-American children's rescue organization) set up in Suceava a canteen for children, under the management of Moshe Liquornik. Hundreds of Jewish children, many of them orphans, were fed at that canteen, mostly with canned food sent from America. Many Jewish families, being refugees or survivors from Transnistria, lived in abject poverty and were unable to feed their children. For those families, sending their children to the OSE canteen meant saving them from hunger and malnutrition. Mr. Liquornik needed a bookkeeper, and my mother was fortunate to fill that position.

Mother's job was a stroke of luck for the whole family. She received a modest salary that allowed us to buy some basic necessities. More important, as part of her compensation, she was allowed to bring home some food from the canteen daily, for Father and me. At that time there was an extreme shortage of food, and even with money it was difficult to buy foodstuff. I can still remember the delight I felt when eating canned apricots in their syrup for the first time. Mother brought them home from the canteen. After years of deprivation, it felt like feasting on ambrosia, the food of gods.

With the money earned by my mother, we bought a few pieces of furniture: three beds made of unfinished, unpainted wooden boards, an old cupboard, and a used table with four chairs. We also bought a wood stove for cooking and heating. Each of the beds was installed in one corner of the room. In the fourth corner, where the chimney sat, we installed the wood stove. The cupboard for our clothing and linen was set next to one of the beds, along the wall. A worn rug that we had brought from Czernowitz was placed in the middle of the room. On top of it we placed the table and chairs. This became our furnished living quarter. Nothing fancy, but much better than the warehouse with the cold cement floor.

I discussed with my parents the possibility of finding some work, to earn some money. However, both Father and Mother wanted me to continue my studies. They felt that only through a good education would I have a chance of a better life in the future. Once my parents decided that I should continue my studies, I focused all my efforts to prepare for the exams required for admission to the university. Considering the hardships my parents had already experienced, I did not want to disappoint them.

First I had to gain recognition of my Soviet high school certificates by the Romanian authorities. That was granted, but I had to take additional exams in Romanian literature, history and geography, subjects that I had not been taught under the Soviets. After studying intensively for several weeks, I was able to pass the required exams in the fall of 1946. Having taken all the exams required for graduation from high school, there still remained one more difficult exam: the baccalaureate.

The Romanian schooling system was similar to the one in France. After completing high school, one had to pass a difficult exam on several subjects—the baccalaureate—in order to be accepted by any university in the country. The required subjects were Romanian and French literature, math, physics, chemistry, history, geography, and philosophy. The exam had both a written and oral part and lasted for three days. The oral part of the exam took place in front of a commission of six professors. It was a grueling exam, since it covered material taught in the last four years of high school. The Ministry of Education sent the questions for the written part of the exam in a sealed envelope that was opened by the examining commission only prior to the test.

My proficiency in Romanian language and literature was limited, since

I had spent the last five years outside any school or in schools that taught in a different language. My knowledge of French language and literature, one of the subjects tested, was limited to what I had been able to learn during the war at home, a time when I was not allowed to attend school. In high school under the Soviets, I had selected German as the optional foreign language. The other required subjects I had studied in a haphazard, desultory way in the last five years. I knew I had to work hard to pass this exam.

I had two weeks to prepare, and went to work with vengeance. I had to make up for all those years I had been prevented from attending school. I received the necessary schoolbooks from the Jewish high school that had just been opened under the direction of Professor Isidor Schulmann. I studied twelve to fourteen hours daily. When the first day of exam arrived, by the end of October, I was ready. I passed the exam, finishing third best among seventy students.

A week later I was on my way to Bucharest, to register for admission at the Physics and Chemistry Department of the University of Bucharest. Mother had saved enough money to buy me a one-way train ticket to Bucharest.

When I arrived there, I went first to see Uncle Joseph and Aunt Ruchel. My uncle had started work in a small paper and cardboard business owned by his long-time friend, Mr. Biedermann. Before the war, Mr. Biedermann owned a stationery store in Czernowitz, under the name "Biedermann & Kindler." Uncle Joseph had worked for him before establishing his own business. When the Soviets occupied Czernowitz in 1940, Mr. Biedermann fled to Bucharest, and at the end of the war started a small stationary business. He then wrote to my uncle and convinced him to come to Bucharest and join him in his newly established company. My uncle and aunt left Czernowitz and settled in Bucharest.

At the end of the war the housing shortage in Bucharest was as bad as in Suceava. In 1940, many Romanian refugees from Northern Bukovina and Bessarabia settled in Bucharest. Another wave of Romanian refugees came from Northern Transylvania, when, under German pressure, Romania was forced to give it up to Hungary. The advancing Soviet armies brought a new wave of refugees in 1944. At the end of the war, some of the Jews returning from Transnistria also came to Bucharest. Since no new buildings had been erected during the war, the housing shortage in the city was extremely acute.

Uncle Joseph and Aunt Ruchel were able to find a one-room apartment on Aviator Drosu Street, in a nice, quiet section of the city, not far from Lake Herestrau. Their furniture consisted of a bed, a cupboard and a small table with chairs. Since there was no other place for me to stay in Bucharest, they accepted me into their tiny apartment. There was no room for a second bed, and I had to sleep on a mattress on the floor. In the evening I rolled out the mattress, and in the morning I rolled it up again. It was not a comfortable arrangement, but we had become accustomed to discomfort. From my childhood, I still remember how good and helpful Uncle Joseph had been to my mother and me. He again showed his kindness by sharing his small quarters with me so that I could attend the university.

Due to the chaotic situation in the country, the university opened late that year and I could still register in November. Because of my good baccalaureate grades I had no difficulties being accepted. Furthermore, in view of the persecutions suffered by the Romanian Jews under the Antonescu regime, the university administration was very accommodating when it came to Jewish applicants. Similar to the Soviet system, higher education was tuition-free.

I was interested in attending the lectures in physics that I had already attended in Czernowitz. At that time I was much less interested in chemistry. However, since physics and chemistry were taught at the university in the same department, I also had to attend lectures in chemistry. As it turned out, attending lectures and taking exams in chemistry resulted in an unforeseen change in my future career.

When I arrived in Bucharest at the end of 1946, the country was sliding deeper into chaos. During the last months of the war, the peasants had their grain confiscated or destroyed by the different armies that fought on Romanian soil. In the spring of 1946, there were not enough grain seeds left for cultivation, and most of the arable land remained fallow. The few fields that were cultivated were hit by a devastating drought in the summer of the same year. The consequences were disastrous. The peasants did not have enough food to feed their own families, let alone feed the population of the cities. There was famine, and many people, mainly the old and the sick, died from starvation. Improper transportation or storage spoiled some of the food, such as corn meal, sent from America by humanitarian organizations. Even the strict rationing of food imposed by the government did not help. Simply put, there was not enough food to feed everybody.

My parents were protected from the famine, since my mother had the good fortune to work in the OSE canteen. The "Joint" organization made sure that the canteen did not run out of food. Periodically, Mother sent me a package of canned food—vegetables, fruit compote, egg powder—which I shared with my uncle and aunt. Still, there were many days when we went to bed hungry.

There was also a serious shortage of fuel in the country. Many of the oil refineries had been destroyed or damaged during the war and had only been partially rebuilt. A large quantity of the oil produced was shipped to the Soviet Union as part of war reparations. When winter arrived, there was not enough fuel for heating and transportation. The lecture halls at the university were rarely heated, and both students and professors wore overcoats and gloves during the lectures. Buildings with central heating were allowed to use heating oil only several hours a day. At night, we slept under the covers, dressed in sweaters and wool socks, trying to stay warm. Transportation by bus was also hampered, due to lack of fuel and the breakdown of the machines. The collapse of the mass transit system forced people to walk long distances in freezing weather to and from work. I had to walk from my uncle's apartment to the university, a distance of several kilometers. That also meant awakening two hours earlier on a winter morning, in order to arrive at the lecture hall on time.

The political situation in the country was deteriorating. The democratic regime established shortly after the war was short lived. After the March 1945 elections, the political coalition set up by the communists under the name "The Block of Democratic Parties," headed by Prime

Minister Petru Groza, rapidly expanded its power and influence in the country. A new electoral law was passed that favored the communists. In the spring of 1946, Marshal Ion Antonescu was tried and executed. The communist-led Block was able to broaden its support in the country by promising the working- and middle-class, as well as the peasants, a series of appealing reforms.

At the same time, the "historic," traditional political parties—the National Peasant's Party and National Liberal Party—were struggling for their lives. In November of 1946, new elections took place. Like those held in 1945, these elections were also rigged. Although the majority of the population was strongly anticommunist, the presence of the Red Army in the country assured a communist victory. "The Block of Democratic Parties" won with 80 percent of the vote. The day prior to elections, members of the opposition National Peasant Party, who were supposed to observe the election process and participate in the vote count, were arrested on trumped up charges. Many voting places were staffed exclusively with communist-allied observers. Under those conditions, the outcome of the elections was predictable. It is said that Stalin once remarked, "Those who cast their vote decide nothing. Those who count the votes decide everything." This saying applied to the Romanian elections of 1946.

In some instances, the government used ingenious means to stifle the opposition. For example, in the village of Bosanci, near Suceava, which was known as a stronghold of the opposition National Peasant Party, the communist-controlled authorities discovered an "epidemic" in the days prior to the elections, and imposed quarantine. Naturally, on election day, the people of Bosanci could not vote. A few days after the elections, the same authorities discovered that actually there was no epidemic and the quarantine was lifted. Later we learned that such quarantines had also been imposed in other parts of the country.

To attract the Jewish vote, the Block of Democratic Parties accepted the Jewish National Block as a member of the coalition. This Block included Jewish organizations of every political stripe. Consequently, in the 1946 elections, the Block of Democratic Parties had strong support among the Jewish voters. The Jews believed the promises made by the

Groza government that their concerns would be addressed after the elections. Moreover, the Jews looked with suspicion at the National Peasant Party that had been joined by former members of the Iron Guard and of the Cuza-Goga party.

After the November elections, during the summer of 1947, the leaders of the National Peasant Party were arrested and the party dissolved. Later that year, the leader of the party, Juliu Maniu, and its vice-president, Ion Michalache, were put on trial and sentenced to life imprisonment. In the same year, Ana Pauker was named foreign minister and Emil Bodnarash was named minister of defense. Both were lifetime communists.

To increase its influence in the Jewish community, the Communist Party dissolved the Jewish National Block after the 1946 elections and created the Jewish Democratic Committee (*Comitetul Democratic Evreesc*, or CDE). This Committee served as a "transmission belt" from the party to the Jewish community. Its main purpose was to stir the Jewish political life in the direction set by the party, and to eliminate any non-communist ("bourgeois") political influences among the Jews.

Following the election victory of November 1946, the Communist Party adopted and implemented some Stalinist economic measures. The banks were nationalized, production plans and prices were set for different sectors of the economy, and raw materials were allocated to various industries.

Some larger enterprises tried to resist the government dictate. One of them was the company that ran the streetcars in Bucharest. The company had been prohibited from raising the ticket prices to keep pace with rampant inflation. At the same time, it was forced to continue operating the city's transportation system. When the company ran out of money, it stopped the maintenance work on the streetcars. As a result, the cars started to break down in their tracks. Those few that were still running had broken doors, missing windows, and peeling paint. They were packed to the limit with people, some standing on the buffers, and others hanging on the broken doors. I still remember how, on my way to the university, I was hanging from the fast-moving streetcar, clinging for life to the door, while risking any moment a fall under the iron wheels of the car. A year later, the company was nationalized, the former owners arrested, accused of sabotage, and sentenced to long prison terms.

The political tensions were also present at the university. There were student organizations that supported or sympathized with the Communist Party, while other organizations supported the "historic," nationalistic parties. Before the November 1946 elections there were frequent verbal clashes on campus between the two groups. The professors, most of them appointed under the previous regime, were mostly nationalistic, anticommunist and not friendly towards Jews. Some of them, like my physics professor, sprinkled the lectures with thinly-veiled, anti-Semitic remarks.

After the November 1946 elections, the atmosphere on campus changed. Members of the Communist Party and their allies were appointed to key positions in the university administration. Communist propaganda on campus intensified. Slogans were posted in the classrooms, in the hallways, in the auditorium. People finally realized that the communist takeover of the country was irreversible. Professors and students, who in the past openly supported the democratic parties, now kept their political opinions to themselves. The admission policies on campus also changed, to allow more members of the "working class," i.e. the sons and daughters of workers and poor peasants, to enter the university. At the same time, the number of accepted applicants that came from middle-class families was reduced.

The "social origin" of the applicant, not his or her grades in high school, became the decisive factor in the admission process. "Social origin" was a new term used to characterize a person, and to decide his or her position in the newly established communist system. Applicants from working class families were considered as having a "sound" social origin and were readily accepted. They received financial support, and were encouraged to join the Communist Party. Applicants from middle-class or upper middle-class families had an "unsound" social origin. Only a small number of openings were reserved for them, and only those with top grades were accepted.

The Communist Party directed and controlled all activities on campus. Political meetings, pro-government demonstrations, even social gatherings were all under party control. Party members decided who would speak at meetings, and what would be said. Student newspapers toed the party line. Professors who in the past had expressed nationalistic or anticommunist political opinions were gradually replaced. The newly appointed university professors were selected on the basis of their political orientation rather than on professional qualifications. This was the case especially in the departments for humanities, such as philosophy, linguistics, history and art, where the lectures often had a heavy ideological content.

Under the communists, not only was the present changed; the past was changed, too. The history of the country was rewritten, going back to ancient times. The Roman influence on Dacia (the ancient name of the land that was to become Romania centuries later) was minimized, the Latin roots of the Romanian people were ignored, and the influence of the benevolent Slavic neighbor in the East was emphasized and praised. The Latin origin of the Romanian language was discounted, while the Slavic influences on the same language were discussed in great detail.

This was the political situation in the country and on campus two years after the overthrow of the Antonescu regime. Communist dictatorship had replaced fascist dictatorship.

In the spring of 1947 I took my first exams. When the vacation started, I went back home to Suceava. The train that took me from the *Gara de Nord* rail station in Bucharest to Suceava was extremely overcrowded. I could barely move. The compartments and the passageways of each railcar were packed with people, suitcases and bundles. The travelers were a motley, smelly, noisy mixture of shabbily dressed city folks and peasants in sheepskin vests. There were old, frail women, their heads covered with dark kerchiefs, and younger women with crying, snotty babies. A heavy smell of tobacco, onion and perspiration hung in the air. Some people, who could not find room inside the train, traveled outside, sitting with their bundles on the running boards or on top of the railcars. When the train stopped at a rail station, there was pushing and shoving by people trying to get off the train against those trying to get on the train. Tempers flared. Some of the people who were not close to the door and tried to get off the train were unable to reach the door in time. They were cursing and arguing with those blocking their way. Eventually they were able to push their way through and get off the train at the next station. They were irate, disheveled and their clothing was torn.

When the train stopped in Pascani, a rail center in Northern Romania, a mass of people tried to get on the train, pushing against those who were trying to get off. There was a big commotion and tempers blazed. Men cursed, women yelled, babies cried. Among those trying to get on the train was also a group of Russian soldiers. Rather than push their way through the crowd, they found an easier way to get inside. They broke the window of a rail car with their rifle buts, and climbed inside through the broken window. I happened to be in the compartment with the broken window, and ended up with a lot of glass shards in my lap. Once inside, the soldiers demanded that the passengers make room for them, so that they could sit down. After all, they were the victors among the vanquished. Naturally, we all promptly complied with the request and traveled standing the rest of the trip.

The train ride that was supposed to last six hours took a full day. I arrived home tired and hungry, but was glad to see my parents. Mother had not changed much in the eight months since I left Suceava, except for her hair that showed streaks of gray. However, I was surprised and saddened to see how much my father's condition had deteriorated. The partial paralysis that struck him shortly after our arrival in Suceava had progressed. He could not walk without support, even from his bed to the table. He could not wash and dress himself. For months Mother had to wash, dress and feed my father every morning before going to work.

I realized soon that my vacation would not bring me much rest. While Mother worked in the OSE canteen, I stayed home with my father. Every morning I helped him get dressed, served him breakfast, and assisted him into a chair near the window. He sat there for several hours, almost motionless, looking at the people hurrying by, at the horse-drawn carts slowly climbing the steep road, and at the peasants cracking their whips. After awhile Father fell asleep in his chair. At noon I helped him to the table and we had lunch together. We ate whatever was left over from the food Mother had brought home from the canteen the previous evening. Afterwards I helped Father undress and climb into bed. He usually slept until Mother came home. Only after dinner did I go for a walk and enjoyed the fresh air. This became my daily routine, and only on Sunday, when Mother stayed home, did I have the whole day to myself.

As time went by, I found out more about the extent of the calamity that had struck the Jewish people of Europe during the years of Nazi rule. From newspaper reports, from radio commentaries and from the literature distributed by various Jewish organizations, I obtained more detailed information about the Holocaust. The trials of top Nazi war criminals at Nuremberg, described in detail by the Romanian press, revealed the enormous scale of murder and destruction perpetrated by the Nazis in their drive to become masters of the world. I learned that during the Nazi era the Germans had invented and perfected the mechanized obliteration of human beings, carried out with true Germanic thoroughness. Millions of defenseless and innocent men, women and children who had been labeled *Untermenschen* (sub-humans) had been turned into smoke and ashes with industrial efficiency.

I also learned about the attitude of the Western democratic governments, before and during the war, towards the European Jewry. I read about the refusal by American authorities to allow the ocean liner, *Saint Louis*, packed with German-Jewish refugees, to enter a U.S. port in 1939. I also read about the refusal by the U.S. government to approve a petition by Quakers and a group of clergymen to allow 20,000 German-Jewish children into the country. Only a few years later, many of these children would end up in Hitler's mass graves and gas chambers.

From Jewish newspapers I learned that the British displayed a similar "humanitarian" attitude toward the Jews. They closed the gates of Palestine to Jewish refugees, accepting only a trickle of immigrants based on their "quota" system. Hundreds of thousands of refugees that could have been saved in Palestine were left in Hitler's claws.

The same callous attitude towards the fate of the Jews persisted during the war. In 1944, while already aware of the genocide perpetrated by the Nazis against the Jews in the East European extermination camps, the Western governments ignored the pleas of American Jewish organizations to bomb the railroad tracks leading to Auschwitz. These were the tracks on which trains, packed with thousands of Jews, arrived daily in the camp. The cargo of innocent victims was delivered to the gas chambers and crematoria.

I also learned that during the Nazi era, Pope Pius XII, the Vicar of Christ, had made a "concordat," a peace pact, with the Nazis.

This kind of information convinced me, and many others, that the Jews had to have their own land, their own home, and could not rely on the good will of others to protect them. They had to have a land where they could defend themselves against any enemy trying to destroy them, a land that can become a haven for Jews persecuted in any part of the world. Never should calamities as those of the Nazi era strike the Jewish people again. Furthermore, there was also the urgent need to establish a Jewish homeland for the many thousands of stateless survivors of the Holocaust. I became convinced that the Zionist dream of a Jewish homeland had to be transformed into reality. I decided to make my contribution and became more active in the Zionist movement.

There was a Hashomer Hatzaïr organization in town, and I began to attend its activities in the evening. I remembered that organization from my childhood in Czernowitz, where my sister occasionally took me to the meetings. I found the activity interesting and stimulating. Having had little exposure to my Jewish heritage in the past, I became interested in Jewish history, in the history of Zionism, as well as in Jewish culture in general. I started reading Simon Dubnow's *Weltgeschichte des Jüdischen Volkes* (History of the Jews) and the work by Graetz on the same subject.

These subjects and others were discussed in small *kvutzot* (groups), led by a group *menahel* (leader). Some members of the organization were close to my age, but most were younger. We discussed the different ideologies within the Zionist movement, as well as left, center, and right wing ideologies that existed in society. These were intellectually stimulating debates. Singing and *horah* dancing followed the discussions.

We often made *tiullim* (excursions) into the hills surrounding Suceava or to the ruins of the old fortress. In the evening, we lit a campfire from dry branches, boiled some water, and served hot tea. Then we shared the food everybody had brought. After dinner we sat around the fire singing, chatting, and laughing. Dancing a *horah* around the campfire concluded the evening activities. When the fire had burned out, most youngsters withdrew to their tents. A few remained outdoors for awhile, admiring the star-studded firmament and listening to the noises of the night. Next day we returned to the city refreshed and full of energy.

During those excursions I learned Boy Scout skills, such as making a campfire, pitching a tent, and marking a trail. I also learned self-defense skills, using my hands, feet, and sticks. Periodically we organized a public *Oneg Shabat* with singing, dancing and recitation of poetry, to which parents were invited. We were boys and girls full of enthusiasm, happy to be together and to have interesting activities. For me it was also a welcome change from the depressing atmosphere at home.

When summer gradually turned to fall, I had to make a difficult decision: should I return to Bucharest and continue my university studies, or stay home and help Mother take care of my father? His condition had deteriorated to the point that he could not get out of bed anymore. His body had shriveled, his skin had become parchment like, and his ribs were clearly visible. He had become unable to turn in bed by himself. I had to turn him over in bed every hour since bedsores had appeared on his body. I had to help him with the urine flask and bedpan, since he could not get out of bed to perform basic bodily functions. The doctor who used to visit my father was sympathetic, but helpless. Then he stopped seeing him. Mother had to continue work at the canteen, to be able to bring home some food. Hiring somebody to stay with my father while Mother was at work was out of the question, since Mother's earnings were barely enough to pay for basic necessities.

At first I could not decide what to do, since I was reluctant to give up my studies. But then I realized that, in fact, I had no choice. Under the circumstances, I had to stay home and take care of my father while Mother was at work.

Once I decided not to resume my university studies, I used my free time—evenings and Sundays—to become involved in different activities. I spent more time at Hashomer Hatzaïr. I became a *menahel* and guided the discussions of my *kvutza*. The topics focused mostly on Jewish history and Zionism.

There was also a Yiddish Cultural Club in town that staged plays written by Yiddish playwrights. I decided to turn into reality one of my dreams of earlier years: play-acting. Guided by an older man with theatrical experience, I began playing roles in Shalom Aleihem's comedies and in Itzhak Peretz's tragedies. Occasionally, I sang and recited Yiddish poems by Soviet-Yiddish writers or fables by Eliezer Steinbarg, the Yiddish poet from Czernowitz. I took my acting quite seriously and put considerable effort and time into making each of my roles a success. I played them with zest and vitality. My acting ranged, as the play demanded, from delicate sentiment to deep emotion and tragedy, from gaiety to rage and despair, from naïveté to sophistication. The audiences liked my performances, and rewarded me with lots of applause. I was elated.

The elation, however, was not to last.

During the night of November 21, 1947, my mother awakened me. The light in the room was turned on, and I saw my mother's face bathed in tears.

"*Der Tata ist tod*" (Father is dead), she said with a wailing voice.

I looked in the direction of my father's bed. He lay there, his face to the wall, as if peacefully asleep. He had died in a simple bed made of ordinary wooden planks, in a cold and unfriendly world, surrounded by misery and poverty. The life of Joseph Scherzer, *doctor juris*, attorney at law, graduate of the University of Vienna, a man of integrity and honesty, thus came to an end, ignored by good fortune and fate. Death had come and claimed him.

Our neighbors, who had heard Mother's crying, came to our room. At dawn, one of them notified the *Chevrah Kadishah*, the Jewish undertakers, and the Jewish Community Center. Soon two bearded, old men arrived, wearing black hats and black overcoats. They were the *Chevrah Kadishah* men, who came to prepare my father's body for burial. According to custom, the funeral had to take place as soon as possible. The men in black went about their job in a business-like manner. They washed the body, put it on the floor in the middle of the room, wrapped it in a white shroud, then put potsherds over the eyes and mouth.

Mother and I sat down on footstools next to my father. A neighbor had been kind enough to bring us two low stools on which to sit, as required by tradition. As I looked at the motionless body lying on the floor wrapped in white, memories came back and images flashed in front of my mental eyes. Here was the body of the man who had scolded and molded me and taught me German grammar and Latin proverbs. I saw Father holding my hand when I was a little boy, walking with me on the *Ringplatz* on a balmy Sunday afternoon; treating me with a delicious ice cream cone when I came home from school with good grades. I saw him taking me to the lyceum *Aron Pumnul* to have me registered there. I remembered him on the day when he came home with tears in his eyes, telling my mother how he had been humiliated by an anti-Semitic judge in the courtroom packed with people. I saw his beaming face when he held in his hand the "Calotescu permit" that protected us from deportation. The image of barely controlled rage on his face when the Soviet border guard robbed him of all his money was very much alive in my mind. I also recalled the look of despair in his eyes when we arrived in Suceava and could not find a place to rest our tired bodies.

From a tender age, Father's life had been strewn with hardships. Raised by an aunt under difficult conditions, working hard and persevering, he had been able to finish the gymnasium and later to get a law degree at the University of Vienna. With his legal practice during the worldwide Depression years of the 1920s and early 1930s, he was barely able to earn a modest income to support himself and his family. But his later years became a real torment. He was tormented by his surroundings, by fate, cold, despair, bitterness, by a nagging cough, by his aching feet, and in the end by a paralyzing stroke. The world in which he had grown up had disintegrated and he did not know how to cope with the new reality. Deprived of the right to practice his profession by the communists and by the fascists, he had been plunged into a world without justice, without freedom, without security, a world of poverty, hatred and brutality. He had been tormented by his inability to find his way in this strange new world and by his failing health. In the end, he lived and died like a pauper.

My mother's subdued crying brought me back to reality. The shrouded body on the floor seemed much smaller than I remembered my father. Did death shrink his body? Was it the illness that did it, or was it my imagination? In any case, his suffering was now over.

After sitting on the footstool for several hours—not a comfortable position—I got up and walked to the window. Feeling drained, I gazed out through the dusty glass panes at the deserted street, and let my thoughts wander. There was a ray of sunlight on the window. Inside myself, however, there was only the darkness of death.

At noon a peasant brought a wooden casket on a horse-dawn cart, sent by the Jewish Community Center. The casket was a simple pine box with a lid and holes in the bottom, in compliance with Orthodox custom. The *Chevrah Kadishah* people put the body in the casket, closed the lid, and left it on the floor in the middle of the room. Mother and I sat on the footstools next to the casket. A few of our neighbors sat behind us, talking to each other in subdued voices.

The funeral took place later in the afternoon. The sky had turned cloudy, and cold air hung over the city. Shortly before the bleak ceremony, a fine rain started. Only a small group of people, holding up their umbrellas, followed the horse-drawn hearse. Our neighbors and some of my friends from Hashomer and from the Cultural Club were present. At the cemetery, the rabbi gave a brief speech, praising the deceased and evoking the suffering during his life. He hurried through his speech, since the rain was getting heavier. After I said *Kaddish*, the prayer for the dead, two bearded men from the *Chevrah Kadishah* lowered the casket into the dark, muddy grave. Mother and I threw each a handful of earth on top of it. That was the end of the funeral ceremony.

The people expressed their condolences to Mother and to me, shook our hands, then dispersed quickly to escape the rain. We walked home exhausted, without saying a word, each with our own thoughts and sorrow.

After sitting *shiva* for a week, I had to decide what to do next. Should I return to Bucharest to continue my university studies, or should I stay home with my mother? School had already started two months earlier, and it would have been difficult to catch up with lost lectures and laboratory work. Furthermore, I did not want to leave Mother all by herself so soon after my father's death. I felt I should stay with her for some time before leaving home. I was also deeply involved with the Hashomer organization, and was reluctant to abandon all the young people with whom I had established close ties in the past months. Considering all these factors, I decided to stay home for the time being, and to continue my activity in both the youth organization and the Cultural Club.

Now, having more free time, I performed more often on stage with my colleagues from the Club. I took on more difficult roles and took my acting very seriously. But most of the time I spent in the youth organization. I gave lectures on different subjects that varied from Jewish history to the evolution of the human society. I read some good books on these subjects, and came well prepared for the lectures. That reading also contributed to the expansion of my own knowledge and cultural horizon.

At that time I had my first girlfriend. Her name was Briana. She was one of the *tzofim* in the youth organization. Briana stood out among the other girls. She had big dark eyes with long black lashes slightly tilted at the ends, a finely chiseled face, and a perfectly shaped small nose. Her braided, shiny, black hair contrasted with her milk-white complexion. There was a touch of rosy-pink on her pale cheeks, and her full lips were cherry-red. A somewhat shy smile that exuded innocence enhanced her charm. She was endowed with long legs and shapely breasts that pushed against her tight blouse. Briana had a radiance—she simply glowed. People turned their heads when she walked on the street in the company of other girls, laughing carefree and showing her pearl-white teeth. She was fifteen at the time and many boys in their late teens courted her. Briana's mother, however, kept a close eye on her social life, and she went out only with the boys who had her parents' approval. Since her mother knew me from the youth organization as a fairly serious young man, she allowed Briana to go out with me.

Our friendship was innocent and platonic. Sometimes, when seeing her, I felt a gamut of deep emotions fill my heart. Were these the first stirrings of love? I don't know. Maybe at that time I didn't know what love was. But I know that we both were eager to see each other. We spent most of our time with the boys and girls in the organization. Then we went home together, since we lived on the same street. Occasionally, we went for a walk in the Central Park. We both were shy and did not talk much. Our closest contact was holding hands or putting my arm around her shoulders when we danced the *horah*. Sometimes we went to see a movie, and in the darkness I mustered the courage to give her a brief peck on the cheek. Briana, in turn, was lively when we were in a larger group, but became shy when only the two of us were together. We both didn't quite know how to deal with the opposite sex in an intimate situation. Still, we both felt attracted to each other.

Soon, however, we had to part company.

14. Romania becomes a People's Republic

While I was in Suceava, enjoying the company of my *chaverim* and performing on the stage of the Yiddish theater, significant political changes took place in the country. Towards the end of 1947, the communists had decided that the time had come to gain absolute power. After dissolving the opposition National Peasant Party and arresting its leaders, they dropped Gheorghe Tatarescu and his National Liberal Party faction from the government. In the fall of 1944, Tatarescu had split the old National Liberal Party, and his faction had joined the Groza government in March 1945. By joining the government, Tatarescu had hoped to moderate the communist influence in the country. The communists accepted the alliance with the Tatarescu faction in the Groza government, and used it to prove the "democratic" nature of that government. By the end of 1947, the communists had no more use for these fellow travelers and removed them from the government.

The Social Democratic Party suffered a similar fate. A splinter group of the party had joined the Groza government and was subsequently absorbed by the Communist Party. The communists later dissolved the remainder of the Social Democratic Party and arrested its leader, Titel Petrescu.

From the end of the war until the end of 1947, thousands of Jews left the country and tried to find their way to Palestine. Among them were many of those who had returned from Transnistria or had come from Northern Bukovina and Bessarabia, now re-occupied by the Soviet Union. They were paupers who saw emigration as the only way to a brighter future. The deteriorating economic situation in the country also drove many Jews to emigration.

Most of them crossed the border illegally into Hungary, and went on to Austria and Italy. Initially, the Romanian authorities did not prevent the clandestine crossing of the border, since it left fewer mouths to feed. By the end of 1947, however, the policy changed. People caught trying to cross the border illegally were arrested. The Hungarian authorities turned over to the Romanians those who were still able to reach Hungary. They were tried and sentenced to prison terms.

In November 1947, Dr. W. Filderman, who headed the Federation of Jewish Communities of Romania, found out that the government was preparing a "case" against him. Rumors had it that he was to be accused of being a British spy. He fled the country before he could be arrested. A month later, Chief Rabbi Dr. Alexandru Safran was expelled from the country, and replaced by the communist-approved Rabbi Moses Rosen.

By the end of 1947, the last bastion of the old regime still untouched was the monarchy. Since the fall of the Antonescu regime and the stationing of Soviet troops in Romania, King Mihai (Michael) had tried, in vain, to install a democratic government. Under relentless communist pressure, he lost more and more influence in matters of state. Eventually, his turn came. Having eliminated all opposition parties, the communists felt that the time had come to finally remove the monarchy.

On December 30, 1947, Prime-Minister Groza and First-Secretary of the Communist Party, Gheorghiu-Dej, requested an audience with the King. In polite terms they advised him that, for the good of the country, he should abdicate and leave the country. In return, the government would allow him to leave with a train of several railway cars filled with valuables from his palaces in Bucharest and Sinaia. Several hours later, realizing that the presence of the Red Army in the country would make any resistance on his part futile, the King signed the abdication. On the same day Romania was declared a People's Republic. The new name given the country was *Republica Populara Romana* (The Romanian People's Republic). The former King left the country by train for Switzerland on January 3, 1948,

A late-evening, special newspaper edition announced the abdication of the king. With huge letters the paper announced: "King Abdicates. Romania Is Now A Republic!" People on the streets of Bucharest grabbed the papers from the hands of the newspaper boys. Some could hardly control the shock and emotions they felt. Men and women on the street were crying. The King had been for many Romanians the last bulwark that could have prevented the takeover of the country by the communists. With his abdication, their last hope evaporated.

The Communist Party, until recently a minor, illegal fringe organization, had moved to the pinnacle of power. The population that for decades had been imbued with nationalistic and chauvinistic ideas about its own greatness, suddenly found itself under the rule of a dictatorship that acted in the name of an alien ideology. The new ideology of Marxism-Leninism went against the core of nationalistic feelings that the overwhelming majority of the Romanian people felt in their hearts.

Now that the monarchy had been removed, and the Communist Party had a monopoly of power in the country, the implementation of Stalinist economic principles was accelerated. The ultimate objective was to transform the country's economy into a socialist economy, using the Soviet model. Most major enterprises in the country were nationalized in 1948. The areas affected included heavy industry, mining, banks, and health institutions. The whorehouses in the Vacaresti section of Bucharest, which used to do brisk business, were closed down. Joint Soviet-Romanian enterprises, named Sovrom, were set up in key areas of the economy. In the name of paying war reparations, these enterprises siphoned off a significant amount of wealth from Romania to the Soviet Union.

The communists also began to implement Stalinist political principles. According to those principles, the class struggle had to be "intensified." The old bourgeoisie and landowner elite, as well as the intellectual elite had to be eliminated. To help implement these principles, the security police (*Securitate*) was created in 1948. A new constitution was adopted, following the model of the Stalinist Constitution.

In the name of intensified class struggle, repression spread to every segment of society. The "progressive" Stalinist method of forced labor was introduced and diligently applied to the "enemies of the people." Former owners and managers of large enterprises, land owners with large estates, spiritual leaders, top intellectuals and other old-time dignitaries were arrested and put in jails or labor camps. The purge of "unreliable elements" in the universities was intensified. Fear permeated all strata of society.

In addition to economic upheaval and political repression, the country was hit by a terrible drought in 1946 and 1947. That natural disaster created an acute shortage of food and subsequent starvation in many parts of the country. It also exacerbated rampant inflation and rapid devaluation of the leu, the local currency.

The communist-controlled government decided to fight inflation by implementing a monetary reform (*stabilizare*) in the summer of 1947. The government printed new money and allowed each person to exchange only a small amount of old money for the new one. After the monetary reform, the old money became worthless.

The reform had a devastating effect on the well to do and the middle class, whose money became worthless overnight. It also bankrupted most small businesses that were still in existence. The monetary reform was especially painful to the Jewish population, since Jews owned many of the small enterprises established after the war.

In our family, Uncle Joseph was hit hard by the reform. In the two years since he had come to Bucharest and worked for his friend in the paper business, he had been able to save some money. He worked twelve hours a day, lived frugally, and was trying to save enough to start his own business. The monetary reform wiped out all his savings. He never recovered from that blow. One year later the company he worked for was nationalized and his friend arrested. From that point on, his income barely sufficed to cover the cost of basic necessities for himself and for Aunt Ruchel.

During those turbulent and difficult times, while the communist dictatorship was tightening its grip on the country, news arrived that rekindled hope and brought joy to the Jews of Romania. The good news came from an unlikely place: the United Nations.

On November 29, 1947, The United Nations General Assembly voted for a resolution, partitioning Palestine into an Arab and Jewish State. Jews all over the world rejoiced. I was thrilled when I heard the news. The two thousand-year-old dreams of the Jewish people finally came true. In Suceava, the Hashomer, as well as all other Zionist organizations, organized meetings and festivities to celebrate this historic event. I led the discussion of this event with my *kvutza*. We talked about the historic importance of the United Nations decision, about the role of the *kibbutzim* in establishing "facts" on the ground in Palestine, about the *Haganah* (the Jewish defense force) that protected the kibbutzim from Arab attacks. We also talked about the Jewish *olim* (immigrants), detained by the British military in the camps of Cyprus, who would finally have their own home. At the end of the discussion we sang Hebrew songs and danced the *horah* late into the night. We were full of enthusiasm, looking forward to the establishment of the Jewish State.

A few months later, the British started to pull out their troops from Palestine, and on May 15, 1948, Ben Gurion declared the establishment of the State of Israel. The Jews of Suceava were overjoyed. They gathered on the streets, in synagogues, at the meeting places of the different Zionist organizations and discussed heatedly the latest news. Public meetings were organized to celebrate this event. In Suceava, like in many other cities and towns of Romania with a Jewish population, the Communist Party organized the meeting. The Romanian Communist Party, as did communist parties in other countries, supported the partition of Palestine and the creation of a Jewish State, since they saw this as a blow to British imperialism. The party invited the population of Suceava to participate at the meeting, and also decided who would speak. Two of the selected speakers were party members, and a third, a Jewish teacher, had no political affiliation.

The party also wanted a speaker from a Zionist organization, and invited me to speak at the meeting. Even the leaders of the local Communist Party realized that it would be outright ridiculous to celebrate the creation of a Jewish State in Palestine without having at least one speaker from a Zionist organization. Besides, the party still needed the support of the Jewish population, which they knew had strong, pro-Zionist feelings. They selected me as speaker, because I had a leading position in the left- leaning Zionist youth organization.

One day before the meeting, the speakers were invited to the office of the local party organization, and given an outline of the speeches they were supposed to deliver. The party wanted to make sure that "politically correct" speeches would be delivered.

On the day of the meeting, a large crowd gathered in the only open-air theater in the city. Most in attendance were Jews. Since the party had organized the meeting, leading local party and government members had been invited, and sat in the front row.

The regional party secretary opened the meeting. Then the other speakers stood up and spoke. Each followed the script received the previous day. Even the non-communist spokesman delivered his speech in accordance to the outline received from the party, since he did not want to jeopardize his job. Each speaker praised the Romanian Communist Party and the Groza government, thanking them for the freedom they had brought to the country and to its Jewish population. They proclaimed their dedication to the cause of socialism and vowed to work hard to build a socialist society in Romania. The creation of the State of Israel was mentioned only in passing, as if it had no relevance to the Jewish Community of Romania. The audience sat passively throughout these speeches and applauded politely at the end of each presentation.

I was the last speaker. At my request, the party representative allowed me to speak in Yiddish—the only Yiddish speaker at the meeting. I knew that most of the audience would prefer to hear the speech in *mame loshen*, rather than in Romanian. I decided to ignore the script provided by the party and prepared my own speech. I knew that I was the only speaker who could say something meaningful about the event we were supposed to celebrate. At that time I had no job to lose. I knew what was on the mind and in the heart of the Jewish audience gathered in front of me, what the people wanted to hear on this historic occasion.

When I rose, I spoke about the fulfillment of the two thousand-year-old dreams of the Jewish people, about the persecutions throughout the centuries, about Theodor Herzl and the *halutzim* who built the land. I talked about deserts and marshes turned into cultivated fields, about the struggle against British imperialism, about the survivors of the Holocaust in the "displaced persons" camps that finally would have a homeland.

"The murder of millions of Jews during the war had finally been given meaning by the creation of a Jewish State," I proclaimed with powerful voice. I had intended to conclude my speech saying something about the Jews of Romania and their gratitude to the party. However, I got carried away, forgot to praise the party, and concluded with "Long live the new Jewish State!"

It was a strong, eloquent speech, delivered with conviction and enthusiasm. While the other speakers read their party-prepared speeches with monotonous, unconvincing voices, I spoke freely, without script, and said what I felt the majority in the audience wanted to hear. It was a speech that came from my heart and was addressed to the hearts of the people.

I got a standing ovation. Even the non-Jewish dignitaries in the first row smiled and applauded, although they did not understand much of my speech in Yiddish. After the meeting, people who knew my mother embraced her and congratulated her for having such a "terrific" son. Others congratulated me for having the courage to express freely what many of them thought and felt in their hearts, but did not dare to say.

I felt very proud of myself after the meeting. Not only because I had pleased the crowd, but also because I had the courage not to give in to the dictates of the party. I had stood up to authority and expressed my own convictions. It was one of the best days of my life.

In the fall of 1948, at the beginning of a new school year, I had to decide whether or not to return to Bucharest and continue my university studies. It was not an easy decision to make. I had become accustomed to being together with my friends in the youth organization, to the interesting seminars and discussions we had, and to the excursions we made regularly into the surrounding hills and forests. Naturally, I enjoyed being with Briana and did not want to be separated from her. I had also grown accustomed to being active in the Yiddish drama club, to play the main roles in different plays we performed, and to enjoy the enthusiastic applause at the end of each performance. Furthermore, I knew that it was easier for Mother if I stayed with her. She still worked at the OSE canteen, but had no friends and few acquaintances. If I left, I knew she would be lonely.

I had to think, however, about my future. If I stayed with the organization, eventually I would have emigrated to the newly created State of Israel and, having no higher education or other skills, would have ended up in a kibbutz. I was also tempted to study drama to become a professional actor. But a stage director at the Bucharest Yiddish Theater, who visited Suceava, advised me against it. He told me about the hard work required to be a good actor, the tough competition that actors face, and the risk of an uncertain financial future. Moreover, the drastic political changes that took place in the country made the future for an actor even less predictable.

My heart told me to stay, but my head advised me to continue my studies. After careful consideration, I concluded that only by completing my university studies could I achieve a better future. Mother also encouraged me to continue my studies. I decided to return to Bucharest. I would have to part from my friends in the organization, terminate my theatrical activity in the Cultural Club, and return to the life of a student. My life was about to take another turn.

15. My Years at the University

I went to say goodbye to my friends in the organization and in the Cultural Club. They were disappointed to see me leave, but wished me luck. Then I went to see Briana. We had become close friends, had gotten used to meeting daily in the organization, laughing together, dancing the *horah* together, and taking walks in the park together. We had developed an emotional bond. Now we were to be separated. I told her about my decision to return to Bucharest to continue my studies, and promised to come back for summer vacation. I promised to write to her. While talking to her, I felt a knot in my throat. When we parted, I saw tears glitter on her eyelashes. I gave her a clumsy hug and a fleeting kiss on the cheek, turned around quickly and walked away. I didn't want her to see the tears in my eyes.

The evening before my departure I filled a small suitcase with a few of my belongings. I put a loaf of bread in my knapsack, half a pound of cottage cheese, a canteen with water, some dry egg powder, and two cans of fruit compote that Mother had brought home from her workplace.

The next day, after saying goodbye to my mother, I took the train to Bucharest. The train was packed with peasants, city dwellers, students, live chickens, bundles, suitcases, and an occasional goose. The smell of perspiration and tobacco engulfed the whole train. Through the din one could hear the occasional laughter of a peasant girl or the crowing of a rooster. After a full day of travel, squeezed between two peasants reeking of *tsuika*, I arrived at Bucharest's main rail station, *Gara de Nord.*. I spent the night at my uncle's place.

The following morning I went to the university to register for my second year of studies. When I arrive at what I thought was the Department of Physics and Chemistry, I had a surprise. I found out that the department did not exist anymore. It had been split into two departments: one for physics, and one for chemistry. A commission had been set up to divide the students between the two departments. Although I had interrupted my studies for one year, the commission accepted me. My case was not unique. Due to the chaotic situation in the country, many students had to interrupt their studies. Some returned to complete them, while others did not.

Although I pointed out that I was primarily interested in physics, I was assigned to the Chemistry Department. The commission, made up of party members, made the decision based on its own criteria, and that decision was final. Rumor had it that the quota set aside for students of middle-class origin like myself had already been filled in the Physics Department. Whatever the reason, my future profession was decided by the party, not by me. Although I felt little attraction for chemistry at the time, I accepted the commission's decision. Only during the following years did I gradually acquire more interest in this science, and eventually discovered its many beautiful aspects.

After registering at the university, I submitted an application to the Student Council in charge of student dormitories. The government had converted several nationalized buildings into dormitories for students who came from the provinces. These were people unable to find any accommodations in the city due to the severe housing shortage. I was accepted and assigned to a dormitory, not far from the university.

I was glad that I did not have to burden Uncle Joseph and Aunt Ruchel anymore. They had been very generous toward me in the past, and I didn't want to abuse their generosity.

The three-story dormitory had large rooms, each with eight or ten beds. There were a few smaller rooms, with two beds each, that were assigned to senior students and party activists. The hallways were long and smelled of cleaning liquid. I was assigned to a ten-bed room. It had bare whitewashed walls and two large windows facing the street. One electric globe hung from the ceiling. Five iron beds stood next to one wall, and facing them were another five beds along the opposite wall.

Each student was given a straw mattress, pillow and linen, as well as a small night table and chair. The students kept most of their belongings in suitcases under the bed. Shoes were placed next to the suitcases. There was one common closet in the room for overcoats and suits. Since most of the students smoked and changed their socks and underwear only once a week, the air was heavy with the smell of perspiration mingled with tobacco smoke. At night, in addition to snoring, one could occasionally hear strange noises, and indecent odors spread throughout the room. On those occasions, I got out of bed and opened a window to let in some fresh air, and let out some not-so-fresh air. Sometimes there was a whiff of *rakiu* in the air, when one of the students sneaked in a bottle of this stuff and decided to share it with his buddies.

The dormitory had a reading room for studying, a large shower room, and a cafeteria. The walls of the reading room were decorated with pictures of party and government leaders: Gheorghiu-Dej, Petru Groza, and Anna Pauker. There were also slogans on the walls, praising the "Romanian Workers' Party" (the new name of the Communist Party) and exhorting the students to build a socialist society.

The shower room had hot water allotted for only two hours each evening. Since there were several hundred students in the building, we had to wait in line before we could take a shower. Groups of two or three would cram under a showerhead so that we would be assured of warm water. That led to a lot of pushing and shoving under the shower. Occasionally the hot water stopped while we were covered with soap. Then we had to wash off the lather with ice-cold water. Not a pleasant experience, especially in the winter.

The cafeteria was a large room with whitewashed walls, decorated with the ubiquitous picture of party leader Gheorghe Gheorghiu-Dej and slogans praising the party. Long wooden tables, flanked with benches, filled the room. The benches were hard and uncomfortable. In the morning the room was cold. It gradually got warmer when the students filled the cafeteria at breakfast time. At noon the air was filled with the scent of food, that mingled with the odor of perspiration from the crowd. The students received three meals daily. The main meal, served at noontime, usually consisted of watery vegetable soup and a dish of boiled potatoes or cornmeal (*mamaliga*) with cheese. The food was far from sufficient, and each student had to supplement his diet or stay hungry.

My roommates were from rural areas, brought to Bucharest by the party for studies. They came from poor peasant families and had spent most of their lives working the fields. On Sundays, their major activity was drinking *tsuica* and talking about the latest soccer game. I had very little in common with my roommates. They kept to themselves and only occasionally did we talk to each other. We never talked politics, a subject all of us carefully avoided.

To have some pocket money and be able to buy additional food and clothing, I started to work at night at the railroad station. I unloaded freight cars of lumber, crates filled with machine parts, wooden boxes of furniture, sacks of potatoes or onions, and anything else that happened to arrive by the night train. Together with several colleagues, I worked three nights a week, from 8 p.m. until midnight. The pay was a pittance, and the work was backbreaking. Carrying a forty-pound sack of potatoes on my back, from the rail car to a waiting truck, felt like carrying a ton of rocks on my shoulders. Never before had I suspected that a sack of potatoes or a crate of onions could be that heavy. At the end of the night shift my back was aching, my shoulders were bruised, and I had to drag myself back to the dormitory for a few hours of sleep. The day following the night work I had to struggle to keep my eyes open during the lectures.

I worked at the railway station for several months. With the money earned, I was able to supplement my food during that time period, and saved enough to buy a warm jacket and pants for the cold season. When the end of the semester neared and I had to prepare myself for the exams, I gave up the night work.

The curriculum at the chemistry department was quite heavy. We had to take a variety of courses in chemistry—inorganic, organic, physical, analytical—as well as courses in physics and mathematics. None of these courses were easy; and they required long hours of study. Some of the courses, such as inorganic chemistry taught by Professor G. Spacu, required considerable memorizing.

There were long hours of laboratory work. The work involved precipitation, separation, fractionation, distillation, and crystallization. Other projects required synthesizing, purifying, analyzing, modifying, polymerizing, and measuring. There was lab work in inorganic chemistry, organic chemistry, analytical chemistry, and—in later years—physical chemistry. The work required patience, skill and tenacity. To complete an assignment, I often had to work late into the evening.

Sometimes an experiment I was attempting went awry. This happened usually in the evening, after a long day of work. Once a flask with a corrosive reagent slipped from my hand, dropped on the lab bench, and broke, spilling the liquid all over the bench, the floor, and on my lab coat. My misfortune caused amusement among my colleagues. Such accidents, in which nobody was hurt, were amusing—as long as they happened to others, of course (typical *schadenfreude*, glee at another's misfortune*)*.

In addition to science, all students were required to take ideological courses. I had to study Marxism-Leninism that included the history of the Communist Party of the Soviet Union, as well as the basic works of Lenin and Stalin. I also took a course in Dialectic and Historic Materialism.

Older professors with well-established reputations in their fields taught the science courses. These professors belonged to the old academic elite. The most prominent among them was Professor G. Spacu for inorganic chemistry and Professor E. Angelescu for organic chemistry. They had been professors under the old regime and, therefore, were not completely trusted politically by the new university administration. An exception was Professor C. Murgulescu for physical chemistry, a capable and experienced scientist, who was also a party member. He later became Minister of Education in the communist government.

A new breed of lecturers taught the ideological courses. They came from a completely revamped Philosophy Department, where young communist intellectuals had replaced the old-time philosophy professors. Many of those young intellectuals also occupied high positions in the party structure, and some of them were members of the Central Committee.

I spent most of my time studying. I attended lectures, worked in different chemistry laboratories, and spent the rest of the time in the university library. After a year of interruption, it took an extra effort to get back into the studying mode.

At least once a week we had political meetings in the evening. At these meetings, party officials gave presentations regarding national or international events. To avoid any misunderstanding, the officials gave the "proper" Marxist-Leninist interpretation of the news.

On other occasions, an editorial article in the party newspaper *Scanteia* was collectively read and discussed. After these discussions the party officials presented the audience with "resolutions" written in the name of the students and addressed to the party leadership or government. These resolutions gave enthusiastic support to the latest government or party decision, condemned some action by Western "imperialists," or expressed solidarity with those who were oppressed in foreign countries, and those who were struggling against capitalist exploiters. The students had to express their approval through applause or raising their hands. The approval was not 90, or 95, or even 99 percent. It was always 100 percent. Otherwise, the party secretary would have promptly questioned any student who would have dared to vote against a party resolution or who refused to vote. "You have a different opinion?" It would have been the last time that the student expressed his opinion or, for that mater, any opinion. He would be expelled from the university and eventually end up in a labor camp, where he could ponder the wisdom of not toeing the party line.

At that time there were three major holidays that were celebrated with great pomp at party-organized meetings and demonstrations. They were the May Day celebration, the festivities of the 23rd of August, and the 7th of November anniversary. The May Day, or First of May, celebrated the International Day of Workers' Solidarity and was observed in all communist and many non-communist countries. On the 23rd of August the country celebrated the day when Romania overthrew the fascist dictatorship of Ion Antonescu in 1944 and replaced it with an anti-Nazi government. The third major holiday, the 7th of November, commemorated the victory of the Bolshevik Revolution in 1917.

All three communist holidays were celebrated with mass demonstrations in front of party and government officials, demonstrations designed to express support for the party and its leaders, praise for the Soviet Union, and solidarity with the working people worldwide. The 23rd of August celebration was also accompanied by a military parade.

Most people looked forward to those holidays. Not because they were eager to demonstrate in front of the party leaders and to yell slogans dictated by the party organization; nobody enjoyed doing that. There was a much simpler reason. Several days before those celebrations, the stores—especially food stores—were stocked with items unavailable during the rest of the year: Russian red caviar, Norwegian sardines, Greek olives, American nylon stockings, Swedish razor blades, and Italian shoes. There were long lines for those items, since they were available only for a few days before a holiday. Once the holiday was over, the merchandise disappeared from the stores.

For those celebrations, the university students had to meet in front of the university early in the morning. Directed by party members, students and professors from each department were organized into columns, ten people abreast. In different parts of town other columns were formed by school children dressed in their "Pioneer" uniforms, sportsmen dressed in white, factory workers wearing their Sunday's best, and employees from almost every state enterprise in town. The atmosphere was relaxed. Since it was a day off and nobody took the whole thing too seriously, most people were in high spirits. We were given a variety of large pictures and red banners to carry during the demonstration. The pictures were those of Gheorghiu-Dej, Anna Pauker, Teohari Georgescu, and other leaders of the Romanian Workers' Party, as well as those of Joseph Stalin and other communist leaders. There was a sea of red flags. Red banners with slogans "Long live the Romanian Workers' Party," "Long live the eternal friendship between the Romanian and Soviet peoples" (that friendship was always described as eternal), and "Long live the international solidarity of working people," fluttered above the moving, compact crowd.

The different columns converged on Piata Aviatorilor (the Aviators'

Square), where a large official stand had been erected the day before. The stand was wrapped in red fabric and decorated with red flags as well as with Romanian blue-yellow-red flags. On our way to the stand we passed streets adorned with red and national flags, which were hanging from lampposts and windows. On many buildings there were red banners with political slogans praising the party and its leaders. Next to them were large posters of workers striking heroic poses. Pictures of Romanian communist leaders and of Joseph Stalin were everywhere: on buildings, in store windows, even on lampposts. The streets were lined with a thin crowd of onlookers, mostly elderly people who did not have to participate in the demonstration.

When our column finally reached the official stand, we saw it packed with party and government officials who had gathered to review the demonstration. While a military band played patriotic music, we marched in front of the stand with our banners and yelled slogans, while trying to get a glimpse of our leaders. They, in turn, smiled and waved at us. Everybody knew what to do: we had to show enthusiasm for the party officials, and they had to wave at us. Nothing was left to chance, to imagination. Everybody followed the script.

After the display of phony mass enthusiasm in front of the official stand, we tossed the pictures of our leaders, those of Stalin and the banners with slogans into a waiting truck, and the column disbanded. Finally we had some free time.

We spent the rest of the day with leisure activities. Some people went to a park; others took the bus to Lake Herestrau, while others went home to rest. The amount of liquor consumed on such holidays was quite significant. The smell of tobacco, of *rakiu,* and of beer was everywhere. Bands played, couples danced, youngsters shouted. After ingesting large amounts of alcohol, some fell asleep on a bench or on the grass in the park. During the evening, people who were still sober enough watched the fireworks. Young people found enjoyment in the darkness of the park. There were whispers, embraces, kisses and moving of hands on forbidden places. Still, most people controlled their behavior. They knew that "Big Brother" was watching.

I remember an episode from my student years that makes me smile even today. While doing some experiments in the laboratory, I often sang to myself even in the presence of other students. As a child, I picked up that habit from my mother, who sang while cooking or cleaning house. Although I was singing in a subdued voice, the assistant-supervisor of the lab enjoyed my singing. My colleagues working next to me usually made some ironic remark ("our Caruso is performing again"), but that did not bother me. I kept singing happily to myself.

There was one instance, however, when my singing almost affected the future of my career. During a mid-semester test I had to analyze the composition of a mixture of chemicals. The night before I had worked at the rail station unloading sacks of potatoes, and during the day I was dead tired. That, evidently, affected my ability to carry out the required analysis. After working for several hours at my laboratory bench, I handed over the results to the assistant-supervisor, an energetic and outspoken woman. She looked at the sheet with my results, compared them with the data she had in her notebook, and then turned to me. "The results of your analysis are not good, to put it mildly," she said. After a short pause, she continued, "You know, Scherzer, you have a nice and pleasant voice. Maybe you should consider studying canto instead of chemistry." She then turned and walked away.

I was shocked. I did not know if she was serious or sarcastic. In any case, I decided to do surreptitiously some inquiring. I went to the university's Music Department and talked to one of the canto teachers. I told him that I was a chemistry student and would like to know if I might have a more promising future by studying canto.

"I would have to test your voice first," he replied. We walked into an empty room in the department and the teacher said, "Sing a song for me. Any song." I chose a Russian song that I remembered from high school, a song that I always liked to sing. I liked its words and the tune.

After listening to me for about three minutes, the teacher stopped me.

"You have a nice voice," he said, "but you will definitely have a better future by studying chemistry."

I followed his advice and continued my studies in chemistry. I decided not to tell anybody about the supervisor's remark or about my meeting with the canto teacher. I also decided to get a good night's sleep before a test.

On Sundays I usually went to see a movie or visited Uncle Joseph, Aunt Ruchel, and my grandfather. After Grandmother died in early 1950, Grandfather left Czernowitz and moved to Bucharest. He was unable to find lodging and had to move in with my uncle and aunt in their one-room apartment. Whenever I visited them I found the room so cramped that it required the dexterity of an acrobat to move around without bumping into people or furniture. Still, I enjoyed my conversations with Grandfather and Uncle Joseph. During those conversations, Ruchel sat quietly on a chair, knitting a sweater or a pair of socks for Joseph, while listening to our talk. We talked about the political situation in the country and in the world, about the newly created Jewish State, about the outlook for Jewish emigration. It was one of the few occasions when I could express my opinions freely, without fear of informers.

With Grandfather I talked about the meaning of different Jewish holidays, about various Jewish traditions, about the Mishna, Gemara, and Midrash.

"For the last 2000 years," he said, "the great heroes of the Jewish people were not military commanders who distinguished themselves in bloody battles, but the sages of the synagogue, philosophers and men of letters."

Grandfather told me of the medieval Biblical commentators Rashi and Ibn Ezra, about the religious philosophers Maimonides and Ibn Gabirol, and of the 12th century poet Yehudah Halevi. He taught me that what is great and lasting in Jewish history is the spiritual wealth accumulated through the ages. He also told me the Chassidic legend of the 36 disguised righteous men *(lamed-vov'nicks)* that live in each generation, and who can be anybody—a laborer, a beggar, a peddler. The moral of that story is that one should treat all strangers kindly. At the end of my visit I was enthralled by grandfather's wisdom and knowledge. Even now I think of him with admiration and respect

My social life at the time was quite limited. I was just too busy with my studies to find time to socialize. Occasionally, on a nice sunny day, I took the tramcar to the Lake Herestrau, rented a boat, and spent some time on the lake. The rowing was good exercise, and the fresh air helped clear my mind. It also drove off the smell of chemicals that permeated my clothes and lingered in my nostrils after the long hours spent in the laboratory.

Sometimes I went to a symphonic concert at the Athenaeum Palace. The Athenaeum was a beautiful structure in the center of the city, facing the former Royal Palace. It was built in circular form in the classical style, with imposing Greek columns guarding the main entrance. The red, plush seats gave it an air of distinction. The interior frescoes that depicted scenes from Romanian history had been covered with red fabric, since some of the scenes showed Romanian royalty. Evidently such images could not be shown publicly in a proletarian society. People might get the wrong idea that Romanian royalty had played a positive role in the country's past.

Some of my fondest memories from those years are those of concerts attended at the Athenaeum Palace. The concerts took place Saturday evening and Sunday afternoon, and were usually sold out. The concert hall was one of the few places where people ignored the "proletarian dress code" and came well dressed, as in the old days. Clean-shaved men in dark suits, white shirts, and ties were sitting next to well-coifed women in dark dresses, silk stockings and high-heeled shoes. The musicians on stage were all dressed in black. Their dark suits contrasted with the bright-shining brass instruments, and the gloss of varnish on violins, cellos and basses. The atmosphere was festive. Once the concert began, the crowd turned totally silent. The seething turmoil of strings and winds, alternating with the soothing sounds rising from the same instruments, poured over the audience, filling ear and soul with magnificent beauty. I stared at the restless movement of the violin bows that drove obliquely downward, like the pelting streaks of rain in a summer shower. I watched the gamut of motions by the conductor from gentle to furious, who controlled the strains drawn from each instrument. I felt my heart soar with the sounds of this sublime music. It was an enchanting experience.

By attending these concerts, I became familiar with the classical repertoire. At the Athenaeum I heard for the first time the works of Mozart, Beethoven, and Tchaikovsky in live performances, with the well-liked Romanian conductors George Georgescu, Constantin Silvestri, and Sergiu Comissiona. Listening to Beethoven's *Choral Symphony* or *Emperor*

Piano Concerto, to Tchaikovsky's violin or piano concerti, I was transfixed by the depth and diversity of emotions expressed by the composers through their music. I was enthralled by the demonic energy of Beethoven's *Fifth Symphony*, by the sensuous beauty of Mendelsson's *Violin Concerto*, by the melancholy of Chopin's nocturnes, and by the romantic sweetness of Schubert's *Lieder*. Music touched my emotions more profoundly than words or pictures. For me, music became one of the best means of escape from the problems and worries of daily existence.

One of the most significant musical events took place in 1953 during an international youth festival organized in Bucharest. There was a remarkable gathering of glamorous performing talent, a group of musical genius and brilliance, from violinists Yehudi Menuhin and David Oistrach to pianist Sviatoaslav Richter. It was a true galaxy of stars. The Romanian Symphonic Orchestra performed Bach's concerto for two violins and orchestra with world-famous soloists David Oistrach and Yehudi Menuhin. In those days it was very rare for two renowned violinists to perform together. I was lucky to obtain a ticket to that concert. It was one of the finest musical performances I have ever heard. The public was ecstatic! I also attended concerts with pianist Sveatoslav Richter, violinist Igor Oistrach, and conductor Claudio Abbado.

From those concerts I learned that music transcends the confines of ethnicity, social structure, politics and religion. I enjoyed the music of a great German or Italian composer as much as that of a great Russian or French composer. The same applied to the great performers of classical music.

Sometimes, the unexpected happened in the middle of a concert. While conducting Antonin Dvorak's *New Wold Symphony*, the baton escaped from the conductor's hand and flew into the concert hall, hitting an elderly bald man on his shoulder. The audience laughed, the conductor turned and smiled at the public, then finished conducting the concert without baton. The man hit by the baton was amused. (Nobody was sued.)

In the summer of 1949, at the end of the school year, I returned to Suceava. I was glad to be back home and to see my mother. After eating watery soup and *mamaliga* with cheese for many months in the student cafeteria, I was looking forward to having some tasty food at home. Mother was happy to see me, and treated me with a lavish meal: old fashion borscht with sour cream and hot potatoes, fried chicken with vegetables, and delicious fruit compote, complements of the Joint. As a student who had been hungry more often than not, I surely knew how to enjoy a good meal.

Mother told me that the OSE canteen where she worked had been taken over by the government, and its management had been replaced. To have a private Jewish-American philanthropic organization run a canteen in the Romanian People's Republic was unacceptable to the government. Mother was kept on her job, but now she worked for the government. After the takeover, the quality of the food served in the canteen deteriorated, since most of the food sent from the U.S. was siphoned off to other organizations. Furthermore, having lost control of the food distribution, the Joint significantly reduced the amount of food sent to the canteen.

The second day after my return to Suceava I met Briana. We had exchanged letters during my stay in Bucharest, but during the last few months her letters were slow in coming. When I saw her, I was stunned by her looks. Last time I saw her she was a pretty girl—now she was a beautiful young woman. Her beauty stirred dormant feelings in my heart.

It did not take long, however, before I learned that she was going out with a number of young men, and that she had a new boyfriend. I was disappointed, but not surprised. I knew that a girl with her charm would have many suitors. I also knew that being far away for a long time made it difficult for both of us to maintain a close relationship. We remained friends, however, and were glad to see each other occasionally. She later married a young man from Suceava, who studied medicine. Her mother's dream to have a doctor son-in-law came true.

Still, I remember her as a flash of sunshine in my life.

Talking about the fair sex: it was at the Cultural Club that I met upon my return an attractive woman, whom I shall call Mira. She was in her early thirties, had dark curly hair, bright chestnut-brown eyes, and a delicately shaped mouth. Mira was an interesting, intelligent woman. She was originally from Balti, a small town in Bessarabia, where she had been married to a salesman. At the beginning of the war she and her husband were deported to Bershad, in Transnistria. Several months later her husband died of typhus. Mira survived by working in the fields, helping the local peasants with the harvest in return for food. After the war she came to Czernowitz together with friends she had made in Bershad. When the Soviets opened the border to Romania, she left Czernowitz and settled in Suceava. She found a job as an office clerk, and lived in a rented room with a Jewish family. Since she was interested in acting, she joined the Cultural Club.

The director of the club decided to stage a historical play, and assigned the main roles to Mira and me. I had the role of a military commander, and Mira that of a princess, the king's daughter. In the play, the commander and the princess fell in love with each other, but the king promised the commander the hand of his daughter only if he will be victorious in the upcoming battle. The commander returned victorious from the battle and married the princess.

There was, however, a problem with these roles: Mira was about fifteen years older than I was. The director of the play was hoping that the proper makeup would make the age difference less obvious.

Our group of actors met several evenings in Mira's room, sitting around the table and reading aloud the lines each of us was supposed to say. Since we did not have sufficient copies of the play, Mira and I sat near each other and read our lines from the same copy. On the second evening of reading Mira had moved closer to me, so that our thighs and elbows were touching. Since we were sitting very close, I detected her body's scent. She smelled fresh and clean; there was also the tinge of a disturbing fragrance that I attributed to the soap she used. The proximity of our bodies and her distinctive scent gave me a strange sensation, never experienced before. It distracted me from the lines I was reading and made my thoughts wander. I had to make an effort to concentrate on the text and on the role I was supposed to play.

Once we had become familiar with our lines, we began to act. There were several scenes just between Mira and me, and she suggested that the two of us rehearse these scenes separately from the group. I agreed and went to her place the following evening. She was waiting for me in front of the house, her figure defined by the light shining through the half-open door. The lamp opposite the door illuminated the white curve of her neck, lit up her dark hair, and brought out in relief her shapely body. She approached me with a big smile, put her arm around my shoulders, and guided me indoors. For some strange reason I felt my heart leap. Mira served me a cup of tea, then sat down next to me and we began rehearsing. I made an effort to collect my wandering thoughts and to focus on the play.

The rehearsal went smoothly until we reached the scene where the script required that I kiss her. In previous rehearsals, when other people were present, I kissed Mira on the cheek. Now, however, when I tried to kiss her on the cheek, Mira said with a smile:

"The play requires that the commander kisses the princess on her mouth, not on the cheek." I hesitated, since never before had I kissed a woman on the mouth. Then, with my lips pressed together, I touched her lips rather clumsily.

"Not that way," she said with a short laugh, "let me show you how to kiss."

She closed her eyes, and pressed her soft lips against mine. She wrapped her right hand around my neck and gently pressed my head towards hers, lips against lips. I felt a heat wave sweep my body. Never have I had a sensation of such intensity. I had seen people kissing in the movies, but had no idea what feelings a kiss could bring alive.

At first I was surprised and afraid. I did not know what to do, how to react. But as she pressed herself towards me, when I could smell her hair and feel the warmth of her body, I threw my arms around her body. She detached herself from me, and said with a smile:

"Wait. Let's make ourselves more comfortable."

Only then did I realize that she was wearing a house robe, not a dress or skirt. She took off first her robe, then her underwear, and stood naked in front of me, arms outstretched toward me. A vague, bold smile flickered on her face as she looked at me with her bright eyes. I was stunned. It was the first time that I saw a naked woman. I looked sheepishly at her shapely body, her milk-white skin, her full breasts.

"You are so beautiful!" I mumbled, overwhelmed by her naked presence.

"Get undressed," she said softly, the vague smile still on her face.

I undressed quickly. She took my hand and led me to the sofa. Without a word, she put her arms around me and drew me down on her in a mute embrace. I felt her bare breasts pushed against my chest, her smooth belly thrust against my belly, her strong thighs pressed against my thighs. Her body felt soft and warm, and seemed to melt into mine. Desire and happiness overwhelmed me, while my whole being was on fire. Every caress, every touch of her lips excited me.

When my excitement approached its peak, we made love. The sensation was overpowering. Never before had I imagined that such strong sensations exist. Afterwards, relaxed and satisfied, I laid next to her, deeply inhaling the smell of her hair and body. With my lips I touched the milk-white skin of her shoulder. I had lost my innocence. It was my first sexual experience, one of those exhilarating experiences in life that cannot be forgotten.

After that evening I felt the need to be together with Mira more often. When the other actors were present, we tried to keep the appearance of two people just interested in the play. In the absence of other people, we rehearsed and then made love. I felt drawn closer to her every time we were together. When I was not with her, I missed her. At night, alone in my bed, I thought of her shapely body, dreamed of it, desired and possessed it countless times in my imagination. I waited impatiently for the time when we will be together again, will embrace each other, will kiss each other, will make love, then rest for a while my head on her chest. I discovered that physical intimacy with the opposite sex could lead to emotions and feelings unknown to me until then. I discovered a new dimension of my inner life. Those were happy days for me, and most of the time I was in high spirits.

Finally, the day arrived when we had to perform the play in public. Before the performance I had some trepidation, but the performance went flawlessly. At the end the public applauded with enthusiasm. I was elated. The applause gave me tremendous satisfaction. At that time I realized how important and gratifying it is for an actor to see and hear the public applause. Mira was also very happy with the success of our performance. After the curtain fell, we embraced each other.

Several days after the performance I met Mira on the street. We spoke briefly about the success of our play, and then I asked her, in a somewhat awkward way, if I might visit her in the evening.

"I am now very busy at the office," she replied, "and have to work evenings, too."

From her tone of voice I realized that she had lost interest in seeing me. I was puzzled. Didn't she want to be intimate with me anymore due to my lack of experience? Or did she have someone else? I longed for her, for her kisses, for her shapely body. I missed the touching of her velvety skin, the smell of her body, the caresses of her gentle hands. Only several weeks later, when we left the theater together after another performance, did Mira explain her change in attitude.

"I like you very much, and I don't want to hurt you," she said, looking deep into my eyes and touching my cheek with the tips of her fingers. "I think it is better for both of us that we are no more intimate with each other."

She had realized that I was beginning to get emotionally involved with her. Since she was fifteen years older and had more life experience, she felt that it was best that we remain just friends. Reluctantly, I accepted her explanation. Our brief affair had come to an end. At night, I often thought of her. With my eyes closed I saw her smile, her lively dark eyes, her milk-white skin. It took a wile before my longing for her subsided.

Later on I realized that Mira had made the right decision. We remained friends and continued to perform on stage together. After I returned to Bucharest we exchanged letters occasionally. I wrote her about my life at the university, while she wrote me about the latest plays staged by the Cultural Club. A year later, when emigration became again possible, Mira left for Israel. I was told that she married there an immigrant from Romania.

There was considerable agitation in the Jewish community. Emigration to Israel was on everybody's mind. After the establishment of the State of Israel, the Romanian government changed its attitude towards emigration, and allowed the Jews to register with a government agency to obtain emigration passports. They could also apply for an immigration visa at the newly established Israeli embassy in Bucharest. As soon as the new policy became known by word of mouth—the government-controlled newspapers would never print such information—the Jews started lining up in front of government buildings to register for emigration.

In every city with a Jewish population, long lines of people could be seen waiting patiently to register. The intensive anti-emigration propaganda carried out by the communist-controlled Jewish Democratic Committee had little effect. The majority of the Jewish population was made up of small merchants, craftsmen, and intellectuals who were unemployed or had modest incomes. Many were leading a marginal existence. They were impoverished by years of fascist persecution and later by the monetary reform. Under those conditions, many Jews believed that they might have a brighter future in the newly established Jewish State. This applied especially to the Jews from Northern Bukovina and Bessarabia, who lived mostly in abject poverty.

Many Jews felt that a strong anti-Semitic undercurrent persisted in Romanian society. Officially, anti-Semitism had been prohibited. But many years of fascist and rightist rule had inoculated the poison of anti-Semitism into the Romanian masses, and their mentality could not be changed overnight. The fact that Jews occupied many key positions in the party also contributed to the resentment.

The activity of different Zionist organizations, which flourished in the years after the war, had a strong influence on the Jewish population, especially among the young. A significant number of Jews had become disillusioned with Romanian socialism, and became convinced that only a Jewish homeland could protect Jews from future persecutions. As a result of all these factors, in the years 1948 and 1949, the Israeli embassy in Bucharest was flooded with visa applications. Thousands of Jews received Romanian passports and left the country legally.

I discussed the subject of emigration with my mother. From Bertha's letters and from those written by newly arrived immigrants we knew that life in Israel was very difficult at that time. Bertha lived in a *tzrif* (wooden cabin) with Shmuel and her first-born child, Rachel. Shmuel struggled to support his family by working long hours. New immigrants had difficulties finding jobs and housing. The wounds from the war of independence were still fresh, and another war could break out any time. In view of this situation, Mother insisted that I finish my university studies before applying for an emigration visa. She assured me that she would also stay in Romania as long as I remained there. After considering the pro and cons, I decided to follow Mother's advice. We planned to apply for emigration visas to Israel only after I finished my studies, in two more years.

The lenient attitude of the Romanian government towards emigration, however, did not last. Stung by the failure of its policies among the Jewish masses and outraged by the large number of people that applied for emigration visas, the government reversed course. The Zionist organizations were accused of agitation and were disbanded. Leaders of Zionist organizations were arrested. An intense anti-Israeli propaganda campaign was started in newspapers and at meetings. Party activists replaced leaders of the Jewish communities. By the end of 1949, emigration to Israel had come to a halt.

The last two years of my university studies went by fast. In spite of hard work and difficult exams, I found time to make regular excursions into the mountains, mostly on weekends and during the winter vacation. At the university I met several students with whom I established close friendships. Some of them were my colleagues in the chemistry department, while others were from other departments. We made most of our excursions into the Bucegi Mountains, north of Bucharest.

The Bucegi are part of the Carpathian Mountain range that separates the "Old Kingdom" (what used to be Romania before World War I) from Transylvania. In the spring we went hiking there, and in the winter skiing. We took the train Friday afternoon and returned Sunday evening. The train ride from Bucharest to the mountains took about two hours. Occasionally, we would stop in Sinaia where there is a beautiful spired castle that once belonged to the royal family. Other times we stopped in

Predeal. These are two charming villages at the foothills of the mountains.

The Bucegi, located about 80 miles from Bucharest, are among the most beautiful mountain ranges in Romania. Omul and Caraimanul, two imposing, over 2000 meter peaks, offer a magnificent and picturesque view of the Prahova Valley. With their quaint mountain lodges and sparkling cold streams, the Bucegi had always been a major tourist attraction. There were numerous marked trails that were used in winter and summer. Upon climbing the slopes, the trails passed through forests of tall oaks and beeches, then through dark-green pine and fir forests, meandered among juniper shrubs and ended next to majestic rocks near the peak. There were also steep slopes where we inched our way along narrow ledges, dislodging pebbles with our feet and letting them tumble down the face of the slope. The falling pebbles produced an echo that reverberated through the transparent atmosphere.

In the spring, lively colorful mountain flowers embellished the slopes, while in the fall the changing leaves turned the mountains into a symphony of colors. The air was cool and fresh—a welcome change from the dirty, stifling air of Bucharest. Often I left the mountain lodge very early in the morning, climbed to the peak, and waited for the sunrise. Low clouds surrounded the peak and wrapped the scenery in a milky embrace. Then, by and by, the first rays of the rising sun pierced the dense mist and lifted the clouds a little. While wisps of fog swirled around me, the beam of light projected my shadow on the dissipating clouds like that of a giant. The grandeur and beauty of the scenery, the ever-changing play of light and shadow stirred my deepest emotions. It felt like being in the midst of a fairy tale.

In the evening, sitting on a weatherworn bench in front of the cabin, I inhaled the smell of nature and watched the majestic mountain peaks sparkle in the last rays of the setting sun. I listened to the silence, and felt immersed in undisturbed serenity rarely experienced in the city. After dark, I sat on a log outside the cabin and watched the black, star-studded sky or the bright moon darting in and out between the clouds. The night seemed wrapped in an eternal magic. The bright canopy of stars, the vast, cold silence of infinite space filled me with the uplifting sensation of unlimited tranquillity. In the midst of such natural beauty my spirits soared, and all my worries were temporarily removed. The charm of nature gave me a liberated feeling.

A major attraction for tourists was *Pestera* (The Cave). It was a huge cave carved out by nature on the western slope of the mountain. Inside there was a small monastery, built centuries ago and served by a handful of monks. They had built a small lodge for visitors next to their living quarters. The rooms were austere. They held only a simple bed with straw mattress, a table and two chairs. The monks served the tourists hot *mamaliga* with feta cheese. After a long day of hiking, it was a good place to rest.

In winter we went skiing and rode sleds in the Bucegi. I was not a good skier. I started out on the beginner's slope, where I took my first lessons and first falls. My ski instructors were colleagues that knew only slightly more about skiing than I did. I had long, heavy wooden skies that were difficult to handle on the slope. I had my share of falls, and by the end of the day I returned to the cabin with quite a few bruises. Still, I enjoyed it.

Sled riding was also fun. We pulled the sled to the top of a hill not far from the village of Sinaia and sledded down the snow-covered slope. Gradually we picked up speed, glided easily over the white, glistering surface, negotiated turns, dodged trees, outran hikers and arrived in the valley in no time. It was an exhilarating experience.

In the evening, we sat together in the lodge around a big fire in the fireplace, warming our hands and feet, commenting about the day's events, while our wet socks, boots, and clothing were drying next to us. The place was warm, noisy and lively. The atmosphere was clammy, and permeated with the odor of dried clothes and socks. Occasionally, a whiff of freshly boiled soup came from the adjacent kitchen, and made my mouth water. Some of the mountain lodges, such as the one at peak Omul, had only one large room, with bunks on two levels near the walls and a large iron stove in the middle. At night the air was heavy with the smell of sweat and wet clothing, but it was warm and cozy. The memories of those excursions into the Bucegi Mountains are some of the few pleasant memories from my past.

In the spring of 1951, I graduated from the University of Bucharest. To receive a diploma, I had to pass a special exam at the end of the four years of study. The exam was taken in front of a commission that consisted of professors who taught the major subjects in the Chemistry Department. The commission also had a professor for Marxism-Leninism, Leonte Rautu, who was a member of the Central Committee of the party. To prepare for the exam, I had to review many of the subjects studied from the first to the fourth year. I also had to write a research paper (its title: "A Comparative Study of Different Theories of Catalysis"). It was a heavy load, but I passed the exam with good grades (mostly A, one B). I received the degree of *Diplomat Universitar* in chemistry. That is more than a bachelor's degree but less than a master's degree granted by a Western university.

The government assigned jobs to most graduates, while a small number of them tried to find employment through their own connections. Many of my colleagues were sent to the provinces as chemistry teachers, while others were assigned to chemistry laboratories in factories, hospitals, and research institutes.

Shortly after graduation, I was called to the Polytechnic Institute of Bucharest to have an interview with Professor Peter Spacu, who chaired the Section for Inorganic and Analytical Chemistry. He was the son of Gheorghe Spacu, professor of inorganic chemistry at the University of Bucharest. Peter Spacu was a polite, affable gentleman in his forties, whose friendliness and warm voice made me feel at ease. After a brief conversation, he asked if I would be interested in the position of assistant in his section. Naturally, my reply was an enthusiastic "yes." He smiled, said that he would recommend me for that position, but that the personnel department would make the final decision. When we parted, he shook my hand and wished me good luck.

Several days later I received a call from the *Serviciul de Cadre* (the personnel department) of the Institute. Most people dreaded to deal with the *Cadre*, as they were called, since they decided the hiring and firing of personnel. They kept a file for each employee of the institution, and that file followed an individual wherever he applied for a job. With a "bad" file that person had no chance of getting a promotion or, if fired, of finding another decent position. The file followed the person everywhere for the rest of his life.

When I arrived at the *Cadre*, I was asked to fill out a six-page questionnaire. Besides the usual personal questions (name, age, address, degree) there were questions regarding the occupation of my parents, about my own and my family's present or past association with political parties, arrests in the family and assets owned before 1947 (the year of the King's abdication). I had no problem answering the questions about political associations, since nobody in my family had belonged to a political party. With regard to assets, the Antonescu regime and the Soviets had taken care of those. The only "dark" spot in the questionnaire was my father's profession that put me in the category of those with an "unsound" social origin.

About ten days after my visit to the personnel office, I received a reply from the Polytechnic Institute. I had been accepted for the position of assistant for inorganic and analytical chemistry. I was overjoyed. I was offered one of the most coveted positions for a university graduate: work at an academic institution.

As I found out later, there was a serious shortage of well-qualified graduates. Very few party members who graduated with me were professionally well qualified. At the same time, the number of students admitted by different institutions of higher learning had increased drastically. Most of the newly admitted students, who represented the future communist intelligentsia, were of working class and poor-peasant origin. They were lacking proper education and needed qualified professional guidance and assistance.

The task of providing such guidance was given to the assistants at the institutions of higher learning. Having graduated with very good grades and having an "apolitical" past, the *Cadre* found me acceptable for the position of assistant, in spite of my social origin. My work at the Institute consisted in supervising the laboratory work in analytical chemistry done by freshmen students, and in conducting seminars in inorganic chemistry. The seminars were based on the lectures in inorganic chemistry given by Professor Spacu.

On that occasion I found out that I had pedagogic talent. I was able to explain often-complex phenomena and theories in a way that made them easily comprehensible to my students. I also found that in order to conduct a seminar on a certain topic, I had to have a thorough understanding and knowledge of that subject; otherwise, the students very quickly discovered the gaps in my knowledge, and did not hide their findings from me. It reminded me how, as a child, I enjoyed embarrassing my teachers. But I liked my work, took it seriously, and got used to it. My work with students was a rewarding experience. Later on, I also gave lectures in analytical chemistry.

Peter Spacu liked the way I worked with the students, and informed his father, Gheorghe Spacu, about my performance. As a result, at the end of the first semester, I received an offer from the university to work part time as an assistant to Professor Gheorghe Spacu at the Department of Chemistry. I accepted the offer, although I already had a full workload at the Polytechnic Institute. My job was made easier because the two professors taught similar courses. The laboratory requirements were also similar. Together with other assistants, I held seminars and guided the laboratory work at both institutions of higher learning. On the average, I worked twelve hours a day, six days a week.

While my work at the two institutions was similar, the personalities of the two professors couldn't have been more different. While Peter Spacu was friendly with his subordinates, always making them feel at ease in his presence, Gheoghe Spacu was quite the opposite. He had studied in Germany and acquired the manners and customs that prevailed in German universities at the beginning of the century. He was authoritative, very demanding towards his subordinates, and intimidating to his students. He was distant and unapproachable, but of impeccable integrity. Gheorghe Spacu was a highly esteemed member of the Academy of Science and known abroad for his scientific work. He was stout, heavy build, with a round full face and sharp, penetrating ice-blue eyes. He wore a small pince-nez for reading. His soft, white hair was always combed carefully to cover the bald spot on his head. He dressed impeccably, always wore dark suits, with the corner of a white handkerchief sticking out from his breast pocket. The onyx on his tie clip matched those on his cufflinks. His personality inspired respect.

Everybody knew that the exam with Professor Gheorghe Spacu was the most difficult one in the Department of Chemistry. There were students who tried twice or three times until they succeeded in passing that exam. He was strict, but objective in his judgement. Professor G. Spacu also ignored the tacit understanding among most faculty members that students with a "sound" social origin—sons and daughters of poor peasants and workers—should never flunk an exam. Every student, regardless of social origin, had to work hard for this exam in order to pass it.

After starting work at the Polytechnic Institute, I had to leave the student dormitory and find a new place to live. At that time my friend, Hardy, lived with his parents in a nice section of Bucharest on Jules Michelet Street, near the British Embassy. When his father, a doctor, was arrested because of some of his activities in the past, his family became afraid that they might lose their apartment. Therefore, when I started looking for living quarters, they were more than happy to rent me a room. It was a large room, but the family had to walk through it to reach the kitchen. When the doctor was released and returned home, I had to move into a tiny room in the same apartment.

When I say tiny, I mean it literally! It was a former servant's or storage room, and I felt like a sardine in a can. I had more privacy, but very little space to move. It could accommodate only a narrow iron bed and a very small table; not even a chair could be squeezed into the small space. I had to sit on my bed to write or read at the table. Since there was no closet, I kept my things in a suitcase under the bed. Whenever I wanted to pick up my shoes or socks from the floor, I had to open first the door to avoid hitting it with my head or back. To move in that room required the skill of a contortionist. Nowadays, a convict has more room in a jail cell than I had in my tiny room.

I tried desperately to find another room to rent, but was not successful. At that time, finding living quarters in Bucharest was extremely difficult, and having a room—any kind of room—was considered acceptable. I spent most of my time at work and came home to my "sardine can" only to sleep.

I worked a full year at both the Polytechnic Institute and at the University of Bucharest. I had a full time position at the institute, and worked part time at the university. After the first year, Professor

Gheorghe Spacu asked me if I would be willing to give up my position at the Polytechnic Institute and take a full-time position in his section at the university. The number of students had increased, and he needed an additional assistant. He also wanted his assistant to carry out scientific research.

I accepted the offer. I gave up my position at the institute and took a full-time position at the university. Considering how demanding Gheorghe Spacu was, I knew that working for him full time would not be easy; however I wanted to do research, and I could do that only at the inorganic section of the university. Furthermore, working for Gheorghe Spacu was a highly prestigious position.

Giving up one of my positions didn't gain me any free time. On the contrary. I worked with the students daily, doing seminars in inorganic and analytical chemistry, and supervising their work in the laboratory. After the students left, I went back to my laboratory and did research until late into the night—except for those evenings when we had political meetings. The days were long, the work was tedious, the pressure constant. The party organization pressured the assistants to work harder with the poorly prepared students of "sound" social origin, while the professor insisted that we spend more time in the laboratory doing research. I found myself in the proverbial position "between a rock and a hard place."

Sometimes the professor walked into the laboratory during the evening and inquired about my progress. After I brought him up to date, he suggested a series of additional experiments that required five or six hours of work. Next morning, at nine o'clock, the professor was back in the lab and wanted to know what I had accomplished since our last conversation. At my reply that I had barely started the work, he frowned and walked away, mumbling something about not having done it the night before. Under those conditions, there was not much time left to do anything else but work, work, and more work. Still, I was happy with my academic activities. I liked working with the students, and I liked doing research. Both activities gave me great satisfaction.

The professor gave me an office on the third floor, not far from the laboratory of inorganic chemistry. It was a small room, where I prepared myself for work with the students and for my research. The office, however, had a problem. Next to it was a door identical to the one that led into my room. Behind it was the students' toilet. There was no sign on either door to distinguish the two rooms. That confused some people. It happened frequently that a student entered abruptly my office, his hand on the zipper, ready for action. My sight startled him. He stopped, mumbled an excuse, turned quickly, and left, closing the door behind him. My repeated requests to the building's administration to put up the proper signs on the two doors were ignored. After awhile, I got used to these uninvited visitors.

After leaving the Polytechnic Institute, I decided to supplement my income by doing translations of scientific books and articles from Russian and German into Romanian. I worked mostly on weekends, and submitted the translated material to *Editura Technica*, the Romanian publishing house for scientific literature. I dictated the translated text to a private typist, named Sandra. She was a pretty woman about my age, whose husband had been convicted and sentenced to hard labor for having belonged to the "exploiting class." He had been sent to the Danube—Black Sea canal to "build socialism." Left on her own, Sandra supported herself by typing for a variety of private clients. Besides being pretty, Sandra was intelligent, well-read, and had a pleasant personality. During breaks in our work we talked about music, books, theater plays, but never about politics. We both knew that politics was a topic to be strictly avoided. I enjoyed working with her, and, as time went by, we became friends.

My work with students put me sometimes into ticklish situations. One such situation occurred during my first year as full-time assistant to Professor Gheorghe Spacu. It happened during the year-end written exam in inorganic chemistry taken by the second year students at the Department of Chemistry. It was a difficult exam that required memorizing a large amount of descriptive chemistry and numerous chemical equations.

Several weeks before the exam, one of the students, Claudia (not her real name), came to my office with questions regarding a subject discussed by the professor. Claudia was one of the prettiest young women among the second year students. With her long, dark-brown hair, large hazel-colored eyes, porcelain-white complexion, shapely body and long legs, she attracted the glances of both students and professors. I had been told that Claudia had a very active social life, and that she spent much more time socializing than studying chemistry. She was also very skillful in using the physical assets she was endowed with to her advantage. Rumor had it that she had been seen repeatedly in the company of one of our younger professors, who was known to like cold beer and hot women. He also happened to be secretary of the party organization.

I explained to Claudia the subject she had difficulties understanding. She listened attentively, thanked me politely, and gave me a charming smile before leaving. Several days later she returned to my office with more questions. While I explained the subject she was referring to and wrote several chemical equations on a sheet of paper, she stood very close to me—I would say too close. I could smell the perfume she was wearing. I was surprised, because the party discouraged the wearing of perfume by students. The fragrance was disturbing and distracted me. I suspected that the perfume was a French import to be found only in stores accessible exclusively to the party elite. Claudia was not a party member, but obviously she had the right connections. When I finished my explanation, she thanked me with a charming smile, and lightly touching my arm with the tips of her fingers. She left, looking at me with her smiling, bright eyes—a look that lingered just for a second too long. Was she flirting? Was she making advances? I had to be on guard. Not being a party member, I had to be very careful in my attitude toward students. A *faux pas* on my part could have cost me my job.

Eventually, the day of exam arrived. About fifty students sat in a large classroom on short school benches, two on each bench. Professor Spacu entered the room, dictated the questions and left the room, leaving me in charge of supervising the students for the next two hours.

There was perfect silence in the room. Only occasionally could one hear the rustling of paper sheets shifted or turned. The students were deeply immersed in their work. I walked slowly among the benches for about ten minutes, then sat down at the lecturing table near the blackboard. I pulled a newly purchased chemistry book from my briefcase and started leafing through it, glancing occasionally at the classroom.

About an hour had gone by when I glanced in the direction of Claudia. She was sitting in the third bench near the window with her legs crossed. For this exam, Claudia had come elegantly dressed: pale-beige, semi-transparent silk blouse with embroidery, black wraparound skirt, nylon stockings, and shiny, black shoes with high heels. Claudia was determined to take the exam by whatever means necessary. She had spent time preparing herself for the exam, although not in the same way as other students. When I glanced at Claudia, I noticed that she had turned over one flap of her wraparound skirt and was looking at paper slips pasted inside the skirt. She was cheating.

I closed my chemistry book, got up, and started walking slowly through the classroom. The moment I got up Claudia flipped the skirt back into normal position, making the paper slips disappear. She seemed to be aware that I had noticed what was going on, since she looked at me with big, frightened eyes.

While I was pacing slowly among the students deeply involved in their work, I was thinking. What should I do? I now realized that Claudia's visits to my office and her flirtatious behavior had been part of a strategy to gain my goodwill, since she knew that I would supervise the students during the exam. If I exposed her, not only would she flunk the exam, but she would also be in deep trouble with the party organization. The cheating would be recorded in her personal file, and would remain there even after graduation. On the other hand, it was not fair to the other students who had worked very hard for this exam, to let someone pass it by cheating. Should I ask her to unwrap her skirt and expose the paper slips hidden underneath? Or should I myself turn over the end of her skirt and reveal the chemical equations and formulas? Doing that would expose more than the slips of paper and would get me into deeper trouble than her. I could see the headline in the student newspaper: "Faculty member forces female student to undress in public!" or "Faculty member peeks under student's skirt!" I saw myself in a faculty meeting being harshly criticized by a prudish party member for my immoral, "bourgeois-decadent" behavior. Claudia's cheating would be ignored, and I would be treated as a villain. I knew that some of my colleagues would take great pleasure in turning me into a verbal punching bag. Exposing Claudia's cheating would also get me in trouble with the party secretary. He would not look kindly at what I had done to his close friend.

Then I thought of all those inept students who were given passing grades by different professors because of the students' "sound" social origin or because of their political activity. Wasn't that cheating—by the faculty and by the institution that tacitly encouraged them to act that way?

I decided to compromise: I will not have Claudia lift her skirt for me, will not create a fuss and disrupt the exam, but will prevent her from further cheating. For the rest of the exam—nearly one hour—I paced close to Claudia's bench, or stood next to her. She did not fidget anymore with her skirt, but neither did she write much from that point on. At the end of the exam, I collected her paper together with those of all other students, and turned them over to Professor Spacu. I did not mention the incident to him. Three days later the professor announced the results. Claudia had passed the exam, barely, with grade 5, corresponding to C-. She had written enough during the first hour of the test to get a passing grade.

Somehow, I was glad that she did not flunk the exam. I would not have liked to see tears in those big, beautiful eyes...

While I was busy with my professional activity, significant changes had taken place in the country. My personal life also underwent a significant change.

16. Travel in the Communist World

At the end of the 1940s and the beginning of the 1950s, the Romanian Workers' Party continued to implement Stalinist principles in the political, economic and cultural life of the country. Having crushed the non-communist parties and keeping with the Stalinist dogma of "intensification of the class struggle," the communists continued to use ruthless methods to consolidate their power in the country. The communist system was imposed at every level of society.

An intense campaign of ideological re-education was carried out throughout the whole country. Party organizations in every village, every factory, every school and every cooperative organized meetings, delivered speeches and gave lectures designed to prove the superiority of the new economic and social system. The Land Act of March 1949 enforced the collectivization of farms without compensation to landowners and farmers.

Hundreds of thousands of people, considered hostile to the "people's democracy," were arrested. A careless, ill-chosen word, a critical remark, a derogatory comment, or an inappropriate joke, was sufficient reason to be denounced, arrested and convicted to years of prison or hard labor. Workers and engineers in plants, factories and in a variety of nationalized enterprises who were unable to achieve the goals set by unrealistic official economic plans, were arrested and accused of sabotage. They were accused of being "wreckers," put on trial, and sent to do forced labor at the Danube—Black Sea Canal.

When the collectivization of agriculture began in 1949, the ranks of those arrested were swelled with tens of thousands of peasants who resisted collectivization. They were also sent to the canal. The slave laborers at that project formed a motley mix: legionaries, Zionists, former members of the democratic parties, war criminals, intellectuals, peasants, army officers, workers, students and businessmen. Unable to cope with the hard labor under the burning sun or in freezing weather, mistreated and fed a starvation diet, tens of thousands of political prisoners died over the years at the canal.

The implementation of Stalinist political principles also involved a drastic change in the country's history and culture. The old history books were withdrawn from schools, libraries and bookstores, and replaced with party-approved books. The new books gave a Marxist interpretation to the country's history. They described it as a struggle between the working masses and the ruling classes. Kings and aristocrats were the villains, workers and poor peasants—the heroes. In modern times, the country's history was primarily a struggle between the exploited working class and the domineering capitalist class of industrialists, bankers, merchants and big landowners.

While restructuring the country's economy, culture and history, the party touted the successes of the socialist enterprises. Production had been increased, goals had been achieved, then surpassed. Reality, however, was quite different. The accomplishments of the collective farms as claimed by the newspaper "Scanteia," the consistent "surpassing" of the goals set by the state plan for industrial production— were mostly fictitious and had little to do with reality. Nobody bothered to verify the accuracy of the reports. It would have been a risky enterprise. Certain "difficulties" (read failures) in the economy that were too obvious to hide were blamed on "wreckers" and "class enemies."

Out of the huge accumulation of blunders, miscalculations, unrealistic plans, phony enthusiasm, and planned slave labor, the socialist society emerged gradually, cemented with the suffering of millions and held in check by the iron grip of the party and its institutions of repression.

While repression went on throughout the country, a struggle developed between different factions within the party. The winning faction branded the losing one "deviationists," or simply "lackeys of the imperialists." The losers were forced out of their positions of power, put on trial, and sentenced to long jail terms. Some were executed. In 1948, Lucretiu Patrascanu, representing national communism, was accused of "national chauvinism" and expelled from the party. He was later put on trial and executed.

In 1952 we learned about the arrest, trial and execution of a group of prominent Jewish writers in the Soviet Union. They had been accused of being "bourgeois-nationalist traitors and enemies of the people." Following the Stalinist example, the first-secretary general of the Romanian Workers' Party, Gheorghe Gheorghiu-Dej, accused a group led by Ana Pauker, Teohari Georgescu, and Vasile Luca (the so called Moscow Faction) of "right wing deviations." The group was blamed for many failures of the system and was expelled from the party.

A campaign of "unmasking deviationists" followed, drawing ever-wider circles of the population into an orgy of denunciations and counter-denunciations. Deviationist sinners were sent to do penance at the Danube—Black Sea Canal for 25 years.

The expulsion of Ana Pauker, a Jew, from the party, as well as Stalin's public anti-Semitic remarks during the last years of his life, had a chilling effect not only on the Jewish population in general, but also on the Jewish party members. Some of them, mostly intellectuals, were accused of being "deviationists" and were demoted or expelled from the organization.

The political repression in the country was accompanied by cultural repression. In the late 1940s and early 1950s, the cultural Stalinization of the country reached a fever pitch. A new ideological witch-hunt started among the party intellectuals. Their perceived crime was "cosmopolitanism." Whenever real or imaginary Western influence was perceived in the work of an artist, writer or composer, he was accused of the crime of "cosmopolitanism." Those accused were usually removed from their posts and expelled from the party.

The Romanian Academy was reorganized and filled with docile party appointees. The new academics rewrote not only the country's history, but also its cultural history. The writings of many respected cultural personalities of the past and present, such as Nicolai Jorga, Titu

Maiorescu, and Lucian Blaga, were characterized as "bourgeois" and their books removed from bookstores and libraries. The writings of other Romanian classics, such as Mihai Eminescu, Vasile Alexandri, and Gheorghe Cosbuc, were published in a censored form. Bookstores were flooded with the works of Marx, Lenin, and Stalin, as well as with Romanian translations of numerous Russian and Soviet authors. Writers, poets, and artists were forced to submit to the demands of "Socialist Realism," the prevalent Stalinist cultural doctrine. The works of Romanian authors who toed the party line, such as Mihai Sadovianu, Tudor Arghezi, and Mihai Beniuc, were widely distributed. These writers and poets were rewarded by the regime with praise and a comfortable life. Those who refused to submit to the party dictate had their creative voices silenced.

The study of the Russian language in high schools and universities became compulsory. At the same time, the cult of Stalin's personality reached a fever pitch: songs, wall posters, street slogans, radio programs, films—all had to sing his praises. The slogans that glorified the Great Leader were everywhere: on buildings, on lampposts, in schools, in factories and in offices. "Hail to the genial Joseph Stalin!" "Praise to the great leader Joseph Stalin!" "Long live our beloved Father Generallissimo Joseph Stalin!" People read the slogans, heard the slogans, and applauded them at meetings, but few believed them. They knew, however, even great men don't live forever.

In early 1953, the newspapers reported that a new "plot" had been discovered in the Soviet Union. A group of Jewish doctors was accused of planning to kill top party and government leaders, supposedly by poisoning them. The doctors were arrested and sent to the LiubliTina prison. A trial against them was being prepared.

While people were discussing the implication of the doctors' arrest, an unexpected event occurred that was to change the course of history.

On a sunny day in early March 1953 I went to the university to do my research work in the laboratory. When I arrived, I found an unexpected commotion. People were standing in small groups, talking in subdued voices. The telephone kept ringing, but nobody answered it. Some of the female party members had tears in their eyes.

"What happened?" I asked, intrigued.

"Haven't you heard?" one of my colleagues replied. "Stalin has died."

It was stunning news. Everybody was taken by surprise. There had been no reports in the press or on the radio that Stalin had any health problems. Some people, mostly party members, looked bereaved. The atmosphere of grief was mixed with an air of uncertainty. What will happen next? Nobody knew the answer. One thing we all knew: an era had come to an end. We also knew that whatever happened in the Soviet Union would have a strong impact on our country and our lives.

Soon the buildings were festooned with red flags bearing black pennants. Stalin's pictures appeared in the store windows draped in black. A hush settled over the city. In many enterprises work was suspended, and shops closed down. At the university all classes were suspended.

The following day a meeting was called at the large university auditorium. The hall was packed with students and professors. People sat in silence, many with a somber expression. First, the party secretary of the university spoke, then the rector, then several professors and students. In speech after speech, Stalin was eulogized as a great leader, great teacher, great military commander, great philosopher, and as a man who had brought happiness to hundreds of millions of people. Listening to those speeches, one would have concluded that Stalin was the greatest man that had ever lived.

Looking at the audience, I wondered how many people in that auditorium believed the pompous words of praise heaped on the deceased. At the time, nobody knew about the horrible crimes Stalin had committed against his own people during his rule, crimes that were exposed only a few years later by his successors.

During my years of employment by the University I had to work not only with freshmen, but also with senior students. At that time I met Susana ("Suzi") Latter. She was a senior student, and did work in the laboratory of inorganic and analytical chemistry where I had been assigned as an assistant. Before meeting her as a student, I had met her socially through Hardy. I also had met Rita, who later became Hardy's wife. Together with other friends

(Adrian, Dodi, Key) we formed a small group that met on weekends, and occasionally took joint hiking or skiing trips.

Suzi was a tall young woman, slim, with curled black hair and dark-brown eyes, an attractive face and intelligent expression. Her smile showed a row of regular, white teeth. At that time we had many things in common: we had similar cultural interests (classical music, opera, theater), and we loved mountain climbing. Those common interests and her pleasant personality attracted me to her and brought us closer together. My prestigious position at the university may have contributed to her interest in me.

Gradually, an emotional bond developed between us. We spent more and more time together. We went to the movies together, enjoyed a concert or opera together, and on weekends we hiked in the Carpathian Mountains together. While maintaining our ties to the rest of the group, we became close friends.

We got married on March 26, 1955. The wedding took place in the apartment of Suzi's parents. They had a large apartment on Roma Street, a nice tree-lined street in a quiet section of town. An Orthodox rabbi celebrated the wedding ceremony under a *chuppah*, according to the Orthodox tradition. There were about two dozen people in attendance. My family was fairly small: my mother, who came from Suceava for the occasion, Uncle Joseph, Aunt Ruchel, and my grandfather. Suzi's family was slightly larger; besides her parents, Andy and Renee Latter, and her sister Gherda, in attendance was Andy's brother Shoni with his wife, Renee's sister Dora, and Suzi's grandfather (Renee's father). There were also several friends of the Latter family, as well as Suzi's and my friends. The brief ceremony was followed by a buffet meal. My grandfather read a beautiful poem he had written in German for the occasion. It expressed deep human feelings about love, devotion and happiness. The poem brought tears to my eyes. It revealed, for the first time, my grandfather's poetic talent, and made me feel proud of him.

Suzi and I were given the room formerly occupied by Suzi in the Latter apartment. The Latters occupied what used to be the master bedroom. Suzi's grandfather lived in the small room next to the kitchen that used to be the servant room (After his death, Renee's sister Dora moved into that room.). Another room in the apartment had been given up to a Romanian family. This was the result of a new law that allowed only a specific number of square meters per person as living space. Any excess living space had to be given up. There was only one kitchen, used by all families in the apartment. To take turns in the kitchen, a schedule was worked out. There were two bathrooms. The Latters, Suzi and I shared the same bathroom. Suzi and I had to walk through my in-laws' bedroom to reach the bathroom. Obviously, it was not a comfortable arrangement, but there was no alternative.

The Latter family had been fairly well off before the war. The family members came from Timisoara, formerly a Hungarian part of Romania, and spoke Hungarian, as well as German, at home. Andy Latter had worked in the import-export business, and had made a good living. The war, however, and later the communist regime, had destroyed that business. Under the communists, the Latter family had a meager income earned from Andy's translations from Hungarian and German into Romanian. Andy was a tall, slim man, slightly stooped, with bright brown eyes and a pleasant personality. He was intelligent, well read, and sociable. His wife, Renee, was diminutive, attractive and usually friendly. I was told that in her youth she had been very pretty. Besides Suzi, they had a younger daughter, Gherda. Shortly after my marriage to Suzi, Gherda got married. After being married for about one year, she had a son, Victor.

In the first years after graduation, Suzi worked as an assistant in the Department of Chemical Engineering at the Polytechnic Institute of Bucharest. She was assigned to the Chair of Physical Chemistry, where she held seminars or worked in the lab with undergraduate students. A few years later, she was forced out of her job, and replaced by a party member. She found a new job at the Patent Office in the center of Bucharest, where she worked until we left Romania.

Following the death of Joseph Stalin, the political atmosphere in the country underwent a gradual transformation. The sudden, unexpected change of leadership in the Soviet Union and the uncertainty with regard to the future course of events convinced our communist leaders to relax their grip on Romanian society. One of the consequences of that relaxation was the inauguration of limited tourism between communist countries. Of course, such travel could be done only by organized tours, in which the guide would lead the group to specified locations and could keep a watchful eye on the travelers. We all knew that the political relaxation might be of short duration, and that traveling to another country could be curtailed at any time. We decided to take advantage of this window of opportunity

In the summer of 1956, Suzi and I traveled together to Hungary. The university organized a trip to the capital, Budapest, combined with a short side trip to Lake Balaton. The trip was part of an exchange between the faculties of the universities of Bucharest and Budapest. We were quite excited. Traveling to a foreign country, even to a communist country, was rare in those days, and a privilege usually reserved for party members. Suzi was especially excited about the trip, due to her Hungarian background. About a dozen people joined us. They were faculty members from different departments, some with spouses.

We boarded the Russian-made plane at the Bucharest Airport. I had never flown on an airplane before, and for me it became an exciting experience. With engines roaring, the propeller-driven plane sped down the runway at what seemed to me a dizzying speed. The force pushed me back into my seat. With trepidation, I held on to the arm supports with all my strength. After gaining more speed, the plane climbed rapidly. We were aloft.

We reached some disparate clouds and kept climbing. I saw the Romanian countryside far below. It was a strange feeling to see the fields, the tiny houses, and the ant-like cars moving slowly on the winding roads. Throughout the whole trip I stared out the window. Transfixed, I watched the diversity of shapes and sizes of the clouds we passed, sometimes flying above them, other times diving into them. I watched the rugged mountain peaks parading deep under the plane, admired the silvery streams and rivers snaking through green valleys, and looked at the tiny villages surrounded by cultivated fields. How different the world appeared from that high altitude! Now I knew what the world looked like to a flying bird...

Upon arrival in Budapest, we were received by a Hungarian delegation from the University, put on a bus, and quartered in a student dormitory. The following day we started touring the city by bus, with a guide provided by the university. It was my first visit to a major Western city. Its beauty fascinated me. Located on the shores of the Danube, the city is divided in two parts: on the western, hilly bank of the Danube is Buda, while on the eastern, flat bank of the river is Pest. Half a dozen bridges, some of them quite impressive, connect the two parts of the city. In the middle of the river there is a small island, called Margaret Island.

Having been the seat of kings for many centuries, the city has numerous palaces, majestic buildings and countless monuments. We walked through the Castle District in Buda; passed the thirteenth century Matthias Church with its imposing "Bela" tower, visited the Fishermen's Bastion with its intricate stairways and terraces, and admired the equestrian bronze statue of St. Stephen, the founder of Hungary. We learned that almost every house in Buda has several levels of cellars underneath, consisting largely of caves and passageways formed naturally in the limestone rock. They served as bomb shelters during Wold War II. Now, the caves and passageways are used as wine cellars. Lovers, who do not want to be disturbed in their activities, also use these underground facilities. Cheaper than a motel room!

After visiting the site of the Royal Palace and its fortification—where the guide gave us a brief history of Hungary's past—we were taken across the Danube to the Inner City or Pest. Most of the buildings in this area are in neo-classical style. I was impressed by the nineteenth century Opera House, admired the Millennium Monument built to commemorate the 1,000th anniversary of the conquest of Hungary, and stood in awe in front of the Parliament Building with its Gothic arcades and imposing dome.

Wherever we were in the city, we could see the huge monument on top of a hill in Buda. It dominated the city. The main figure in the monument is that of an enormous woman holding aloft a palm branch, the symbol of freedom. It was dedicated to the Soviet soldiers who liberated the city during World War II. The damage and destruction caused by heavy street fighting during the war was still visible. Many buildings were pockmarked by bullet holes, while other buildings, heavily damaged by the fighting, had not yet been rebuilt.

Compared to drab Bucharest, Budapest was a much livelier city. The stores displayed a variety and, what appeared to me, an abundance of merchandise that I had not seen in Bucharest. I was also surprised to learn that some of the smaller stores were still privately owned. But what impressed me the most was the nightlife in the city, which contrasted with austere Bucharest that had practically no nightlife. On Margaret Island there were several nightclubs with colorful lights, lively entertainment, and young people crowding the dance floor. It was the first time that I went to a nightclub. The loud, Western music, bright lights, and lively, carefree atmosphere was dazzling. This was one aspect of the liberalization introduced by Premier Imre Nagy in Hungary.

We came home from our trip full of enthusiasm. Budapest had left a strong impression on me, since it was the most beautiful city I had seen so far. The freedom and prosperity that I had noticed in Hungary gave hope that Romania might follow the same path in the near future.

Events, however, took a different turn. One month after returning from our trip, in the summer of 1956, a revolution broke out in Hungary. We listened with trepidation to the BBC reports on London radio about the bloody events on the streets of Budapest. The Soviet Union sent its tanks into the city, removed the liberal leadership of the Hungarian Communist Party from power, and replaced it with a more conservative, Soviet-oriented leadership. The Hungarian liberalization had been crushed.

As expected, the Romanian newspaper *Scanteia*, the mouthpiece of the Romanian Workers' Party, expressed the Soviet point of view about these events. The leadership of the Hungarian Communist Party that had liberalized the regime prior to the revolution, was accused of treason, and the paper expressed its support for the Soviet armed intervention in Hungary. At that point we realized that the prospects for more freedom in any Soviet block country had been dashed.

In the fall of the same year we took our first cruise on the Black Sea, on the Romanian ship *Transilvania*. It was a 5,000-ton cruise ship, one of the few Romanian passenger ships traveling on the Black Sea. Our cabin was very small. It consisted of two bunks, a wash basin, a shower, and a porthole. The cruise started at the Romanian port Constanta, with stops and visits at the Soviet ports of Odessa in the Ukraine, Yalta in the Crimea, and Sochi at the foot of the Caucasian Mountains. While the sailing on the Black Sea was rough and often made us sick, the visits on land were most interesting.

The first stop was in Odessa. When the ship docked, we rushed off with the rest of the passengers, down the gangway, only too delighted to have a chance of spending a few hours on land. The water was a dirty gray, smudged with rainbow-hued oil slicks, and had a pungent smell of kerosene. Several large commercial vessels were anchored in the harbor, while smaller boats and barges moved lazily among them. Sailors, soldiers, and civilians mingled on the shore, looking busy and surly. In the city that had seen a lot of destruction during World War II, we walked on acacia-lined Primorsky Boulevard overlooking the port. Some imposing wooden houses, build in the turn-of-the century style, lined the boulevard. From our guide we learned that the buildings had been destroyed during the war and had been rebuilt afterwards. Some of the streets had been named after the 18th century French founders of the city—Richelieu and Langeron. On top of the Potemkin Steps there was also a monument of Duke de Richelieu .

We arrived at the Potemkin Steps that became famous through Eisenstein's movie about the mutiny on the battle ship Potemkin during the 1905 revolution. On these steps, the czarist troops massacred a large crowd of terrified civilians. Eisenstein staged and filmed the event in 1925. The sight of the long row of steps descending to the sea brought back memories of scenes from the movie that I had seen years earlier. I recalled the scene in which a civilian man was shot through his eyeglasses, of the mother shot dead on top of the stairs, of the baby carriage rolling down the steps with the screaming baby. The movie *Potemkin* had some very powerful scenes and had become a classic in the annals of movie history.

After visiting the *Potemkin* Steps, we walked to the entrance of the Odessa catacombs, quarried out in the 19th century. The catacombs are a labyrinth of intersecting tunnels, several hundred kilometers long, in which it is easy to get lost. During World War II, the catacombs were used as a hiding place by Soviet partisans.

While walking in the port, shabbily dressed Russian civilians approached us and inquired if we were willing to sell the jackets and sweaters we were wearing, as well as the plastic baskets and handbags we were carrying. These items had recently become available in Romania. Some of the people literally pulled at the sleeves of the clothes we were wearing, as if to test the quality of our garments. At the same time they kept asking *skolko?* (how much?), trying to convince us to sell the clothing on our backs. We realized that in spite of the shortages experienced in Romania, we were still much better off than the people of the Soviet Union.

The highlight of the cruise was the visit to Yalta, a small resort town located on the southern shore of the Crimea peninsula, on a cypress-strewn strip between the Crimea Mountains and the Black Sea. The scenery of the South Coast of Crimea was of a picture-postcard beauty— a land of vineyards and cypresses, of fruit trees, lilacs and bougainvillea. Prior to the revolution, Yalta and its environs had been the summer residence of the czar and of the aristocracy. Famous Russian writers, such as Leo Tolstoy and Anton Chechov, also spent time in Yalta.

After the revolution, many of the aristocratic estates had been converted into sanatoriums for workers, while *dachas* (summer cottages) were built for the party elite. Several stately mansions could be seen on the surrounding hills. The beach was pebbly and narrow, with beach goers lying on wooden pallets and trying to catch some sun rays (foam pads or air mattresses were not available at that time). Palm and cypress trees dotted the landscape.

We took also a short trip west of Yalta, to a magnificent place called Swallow's Nest. It is a castle perched on the top of a steep cliff, lonely and majestic, overlooking the vast sea. While standing on top of the cliff, I looked at the glistering sea stretching to the distant horizon, stared at the silver foaming of the surf washing gently over the pebbles on the shore, and watched the seagulls circling overhead. I smelled the salty air, and felt the cool breeze caressing my face. It was a magnificent experience.

The most famous place we visited near Yalta was the palace where F. Roosevelt, W. Churchill, and J. Stalin held the conference in February 1945. Czar Alexander II had built the palace at Livadia, near Yalta, as his summer residence. After the revolution it was used for rest and recreation by the party and government elite. Located on the bluffs high above a narrow rocky beach, the palace oversees a vast stretch of sea and a large coastal area.

We visited the room where the delegations of the three major allies held their conference. It is a large, palatial room, with tall windows overlooking the sea; heavy crystal chandeliers hang from the decorated ceiling, and tapestries with mythological themes decorate the walls. The shiny, polished parquet floor is partially covered by a huge Persian rug. In the center of the room is a large, wooden round-table, surrounded by a dozen upholstered chairs.

As I looked at the room with its large table and empty chairs, I realized the historic importance of this place. This was the room where the fate of post-war Europe had been decided. It was here that the "spheres of influence" of the major powers had been established, a decision that resulted in Soviet control over most of Central and Eastern Europe for nearly half a century. Standing in that room, I wondered if the amiable Western delegates at the conference knew what the consequences of their decisions would be for the over one hundred million people affected. Not likely.

From Yalta we sailed to Sochi. We arrived there on a quiet, sunny afternoon. The town, located not far from the Turkish border, rests at the foot of the Caucasian Mountains near the sea, in the midst of luxuriant vegetation. It is both a summer and winter resort. As the ship approached the coastline, our view was one of breathtaking beauty. With binoculars we could distinguish the great variety of vegetation that covered the mountain slope, from the seashore all the way to the mountain peak. At the foot of the mountain there was an abundance of palms, cypresses and magnolia trees, alternating with luxuriant, blooming hibiscus and oleander shrubs. Higher up we saw oak, birch, and maple trees, while above them were fir and pine trees. Closer to the peak, hidden among large boulders, were small, hardy juniper shrubs, and finally, at the top, there was the rugged, snow-covered crest of the majestic mountain. The whole impressive scene was mirrored in the unusually quiet sea. It was a view to remember.

The morning after our arrival we boarded a bus, and were taken on a tour of the city and its environs. The major street, Kurortny Prospekt, runs north—south, close to the beach. Several side streets branch out from the main road, leading to the mountain. The streets are lined with magnolia trees, and whitewashed, two- and three-story houses. Although it was early autumn and the water was cool, the pebbly, narrow beach was crowded with people lying on wooden pallets, trying to catch some of the weak sun rays. Several boats were bobbing sleepily in the gentle waves. Nearby, a few snack bars were offering *pirozhki* and cold drinks. The fragrance of the salty sea permeated the balmy air. The sound of an accordion came from the distance. From the beach one could see ferries arriving or leaving for Sukhumi, Batumi, and other resort cities on the Black Sea.

Not far from the beach, nestled in the foothills, were rest homes, among them the *Metalurg* and *Ordzhenikidze* sanatoriums. Selected workers from across the Soviet Union were sent to Sochi to spend their vacation. Many of them, such as miners and steelworkers, performed heavy-duty work most of the year. Others came from the northern, freezing areas of the country, such as the Arctic Region of northern Russia and Siberia. There were also workers from various plants and factories. The sanatoriums were for those who suffered from tuberculosis or other pulmonary diseases.

People were milling around on the streets or sitting on park benches among blooming hibiscus and oleander shrubs. They were talking, smoking or reading the newspaper, *Pravda*. For people who spent most of the year in the depth of a coal mine or in the dark, frozen tundra of the arctic region, being in sunny Sochi one or two weeks must have seemed like being in paradise. It was not, however, enough to wipe away the furrows and gloom from their faces. What a contrast between the fresh, lively colored hibiscus flowers and the pale-gray, wrinkled faces of the visitors! Nature radiated beauty, freshness, energy and youth at its prime, while the downcast, drawn and pale faces expressed hardship and afflictions of those whose prime and youth were long gone.

A winding road led to *dachas* perched on the mountain slopes. The cottages were hidden by oleander and hibiscus shrubs, or, higher up on the mountain, by birch and oak trees. Many of the *dachas* were protected from prying eyes by tall stone walls. These cottages were mostly for the party and government elite. Men in uniform guarded some of the *dachas*, suggesting the presence of high-ranking *apparatchiks* behind the high walls. Obviously, the Soviet elite felt it necessary to protect itself and its turf from the run-of-the-mill comrades.

Next day we left Sochi and sailed home. In the morning the sky was clear. I sat on the deck in a folding chair, watching the peaceful scenery. A breeze made gentle ripples on the surface of the sea. Diamonds of sunlight danced on the water, while I stared at their nimble movements. The waves were slapping gently against the bow of our ship. Beautiful white-gray clouds were hovering over the dark-blue sea. I smelled the saltwater that embraced our ship. I felt the sun on my skin and the warm breeze. The wind whipped through my hair. It was a magnificent feeling and a glorious sight.

Soon, the wind picked up and whipped foamy crests over the water. The waves grew mightier. Dark clouds appeared as if from nowhere, and quickly covered the sky. The sea turned ink-black, its surface lashed by an increasingly furious wind. Tall, powerful waves began to rock our ship, lifting and dropping it like a yo-yo. The tossing and bobbing journey across the sea went on for hours—or, at least, that was my impression. Then it began to rain. It was one of those rainstorms for which the Black Sea had been known since ancient times, and which gave it its name. The rain came down in sheets and slapped furiously the ship's deck. The wind blew the rain sideways. With trepidation, I listened to the maddening howling of the endless gale, to the crashing of furious, towering waves against the ship's hull. The tempestuous sea seemed ready to swallow the ship and its terrified passengers at any moment. Many people became seasick. They vomited, as if in competition with each other. I was no exception. My stomach was moving around as if it was at the center of the storm. I felt a constant urge to vomit, long after my stomach had disgorged all its contents. We had no anti-sea sickness medication, nor did the crew of the ship have any. I tried to escape the nauseated feeling by lying down in my cabin, which was close to the engine room. The constant thud of the engines, however, as well as the resulting vibration of the cabin, combined with the sickening smell of oil fumes from the diesel engines, made me feel even more miserable. In those moments I would have given all my earthly possessions to be again on solid ground.

Toward the evening, the storm subsided, the sea gradually calmed down, and so did my stomach. The dark clouds began to dissipate and patches of blue sky appeared. When darkness fell, the sea was almost still and stable. The breath of a light breeze came now and again across my face. Shadowy and silent, the ship moved in the light wind like a phantom. It glided smoothly over the ink-black sea, enveloped by the enormous dome of the star-studded sky.

After another day of sailing on fairly peaceful waters, we finally returned to the port of departure, Constanta. I was glad to be back on solid ground. Still, the magnificent scenery of the Crimean and Caucasian resorts, as well as the palaces near Yalta left a deep and lasting impression.

After the Hungarian revolution of 1956, the Romanian Workers' Party, led by the general-secretary Gheorghiu-Dej, started talking about a Romanian road to socialism. What would have been considered Marxist heresy during the years of Stalinist dictatorship, became official policy. The Romanian government resisted pressure from the Soviet Union and other socialist countries to accept economic specialization within the Socialist Block. Such specialization would have relegated Romania to a raw material supplier and primarily agricultural country, while the more developed socialist countries, such as East Germany and Czechoslovakia, would have emphasized industrial production and development.

Following the withdrawal of Soviet troops from Romania in 1958, the Romanian party leadership introduced a certain degree of economic liberalization in the country. That resulted in increased trade with the West, and the increase of imports from capitalist countries. Most imported consumer goods were available in special stores, accessible exclusively to the party elite. Some Western products, however, such as French perfume, Swedish razor blades, Italian leather goods, and American nylon stockings began to appear in stores open to the public. In spite of the high price of these imports, they were bought up quickly by a population starved for quality merchandise. Western machinery was also introduced in some factories and plants.

Along with the machinery came Western technicians who installed the new equipment. These technicians had a field day in Bucharest. Carrying dollars or German marks in their pockets, Kent cigarettes and a variety of "gifts" in their briefcases, they were often seen in the company of the prettiest Romanian girls. The new "boy friends" could provide the girls with a bottle of Channel eau de Cologne, a pair of nylon stockings, or a pack of Western cigarettes. The pretty girls, in turn, could offer the technicians a good time. Both sides benefitted from this friendship. The rest of us looked at these Westerners as people descended from another planet, one that remained inaccessible to us.

In the fall of 1958, my grandfather died. He was in his mid 80s. The last six years of his life he lived in the same small, crowded room with Uncle Joseph and Aunt Ruchel. He spent most of his time sitting at the little worn table in the middle of the room, studying a volume of Talmud borrowed from the local synagogue, reading from Goethe's *Werther* in German, or translating poetry from Russian into German. His mind and memory were sharp and clear to the end. He died at home, in his bed. In the twilight years of his life he carried a deep wound in his soul, caused by the loss of his wife and three children. He rarely talked about it, but we knew the wound was there.

While I was sitting next to Uncle Joseph on a footstool, looking at the body of my grandfather wrapped in a white shroud, memories came back from past years. I remembered him on Friday evenings, dressed in a black *caftan*, white shirt, and black hat, walking solemnly to the synagogue, prayer book and *tallit* under his arm. In my memory I saw him instructing me for the Bar Mitzvah and showing me how to put on the *tfillin* on my forehead and on my left arm. I also remembered him reading to me, in German, poems by Friedrich Schiller and Heinrich Heine. He always pointed out the meaning and beauty of those poems: the charm of the scenery depicted, the human feelings described by the poet, the moral message. He told me enchanting Chassidic tales about angels, miracle-makers, and princes. I remembered the story about the pious rabbi, who ordered that his cat have socklets put on its feet on Passover eve, lest it bring into the house a crumb of unleavened bread. How I savored those stories! I will never forget the beautiful poem he composed for my wedding.

From my early childhood on I had the highest respect and admiration for my grandfather. He was knowledgeable in matters of Torah and Talmud, often explaining to others some obscure passage. Having grown up in Austria and attended Austrian school, he also showed erudition in German literature, an erudition that my mother inherited. He was a *Talmud-chochem* (Talmudic expert) and a secular intellectual at the same time—a rare combination for Jews of his generation. It is an irony (or tragedy?) of fate that this kind, wise and enlightened man, who was so knowledgeable and attached to German culture, had three of his daughters and their families murdered by those who claimed with arrogance to be the standard-bearers of German culture and civilization. Grandfather also had to suffer the loss of his wife eight years before his death. He always treated her with kindness, while she, in turn, treated him with the love and respect he deserved.

Grandfather was buried at the Jewish Cemetery in Bucharest. At the gravesite, Uncle Joseph shed bitter tears of sorrow—he had lost a father he loved and respected.

Shortly after the death of my grandfather, during the Jewish High Holidays, the Romanian government sprang a surprise on the Jewish community. Rabbis and community leaders announced in the synagogues during services that whoever wanted to emigrate could file a petition with the authorities. It seemed that the government had again changed its policy toward Jewish emigration. The news created a lot of excitement in the Jewish community. People made all kinds of assumptions, trying to explain the government's decision. Was it an attempt to improve relations with Israel? Was it the result of pressure from Western governments or organizations? Only a few key Jewish party members knew the real reason behind that decision.

In the second half of the 1950s, a new Romanian intelligentsia graduated from the universities and polytechnic schools, an intelligentsia with a working class or poor-peasant origin, educated by the party and eager to take up positions in the government, party, and in the economy of the country. There were, however, only a limited number of positions available. The situation was exacerbated by the acute shortage of housing, mainly in the larger cities. Letting some Jews emigrate was seen by the government as a partial solution to this problem. Emigration would open up jobs, would result in many vacated homes and apartments, and would allow the new class of intellectuals to buy goods at bargain prices from the emigrating Jews. It would also deflect, at least temporarily, the discontent that had built up in the population due to persistent shortages.

Shortly after the announcement was made, a silent, subdued multitude of people lined up in front of the Police Headquarters in Bucharest to apply for emigration visas. As the days went by, the lines grew longer and longer. Similar lines could be seen in front of police headquarters in many provincial cities with a Jewish population.

We had lengthy discussions in our family, to decide what to do. Suzi had already lost her job at the Polytechnic Institute. Eventually, she found a job in the Patent Office. Although I still had a prestigious position at the university, I could see the writing on the wall. Not being a party member, having a "bourgeois" family background, and being Jewish, I knew that sooner or later I would also be replaced by a Romanian party member from the new intelligentsia. Suzi's parents wanted to leave, since their own future in Romania looked bleak. I talked to my mother repeatedly by phone, and she told me that she would do whatever I decided with regard to emigration.

In the end, we decided to apply for exit visas. On a cold October morning we went to the Police Headquarters. It was five in the morning, but people were already standing in line. The office opened at eight. By that time a long line had formed, and snaked around the building, reaching into the next street. I stood close to the building wall, attempting to hide from the view of passerby. I hid my face behind a newspaper like a felon trying to avoid arrest, pretending to be engrossed in reading about the latest achievements of our socialist economy. If somebody from the university had walked by and recognized me, he would have informed the party organization, and I would have lost my job.

Around noon we finally entered the visa office, filled out a form requesting emigration to Israel, signed it, and left. Both Suzi and I took a great risk by applying, since our jobs were now in jeopardy. But we had to take the risk if we wanted to emigrate and have a better life.

Several weeks after the announcement was made during the High Holidays, more than half of the Jewish population of Romania had applied for exit visas. Now it was the turn of the authorities to be surprised. They had not expected that such large masses of people would apply to emigrate. Moreover, many Jewish party members, disappointed with the system and fearing for their future, were among those who had applied. The mass registration was clear proof of the total failure of the government and party policies towards the Jewish population. It was a slap in the face of the party leadership. Moreover, the Soviet government was displeased with this new emigration policy. Arab governments, fearing a massive influx of Jews into Israel, logged energetic protests with the Romanian government.

The party and government had to take action. After handing out several hundred visas, no more visas were issued. Some people had their passports confiscated. Jewish party members who had applied for emigration visas were harshly criticized at party meetings, accused of lack of loyalty to the regime, and expelled from the party. They also lost the key positions they occupied in the institutions and enterprises where they worked. Jews who were not party members and occupied important economic or administrative positions, were fired or demoted if they applied for exit visas. Even Jews who had not applied for exit visas and occupied key positions were gradually replaced. At the same time, a campaign began against Israel, which was accused of carrying out subversive activities in the country and misleading the Jewish population of Romania. Some Romanian Jews were arrested as Israeli "agents," and several Israeli diplomats were expelled.

In the past, when the Jews did not have a country of their own, Romanian nationalists and anti-Semites used to scream at them: "Go to Palestine!" Now, when Jews finally had their own country and wanted to go there, the Romanians were telling them: "We are not going to let you go. You will stay here, with us!" How times have changed...

Neither Suzi nor I lost our jobs. We assumed that our positions were not important enough to make it necessary for the government to inform the personnel departments of our institutions. Or was it a bureaucratic oversight? In any case, the personnel department of the university was not aware that I had requested an exit visa. They caught up with me later, however, in a way I could not have expected.

On January 4, 1959, Gabi was born in the Central Hospital of Bucharest. I felt great joy to have a little boy, and was proud to have become a father. After bringing Gabi home, we rearranged the furniture in our room, and set up the crib not far from the stove. We wanted to make sure that the child would stay warm in the harsh winter months. We also had to rearrange our lives. During the first few months, neither Suzi nor I got enough sleep. For that matter, neither did my in-laws. Every night they could hear the baby cry, since the thin wall that separated us did not make the rooms sound proof.

Before Suzi returned to work, we hired a young Hungarian girl, Anush, to take care of Gabi in our absence. Anush was about fourteen years old, came from the Hungarian region of Transylvania, and spoke only a smattering of Romanian. It was mostly Suzi and my in-laws who communicated with her, in Hungarian. Since my knowledge of Hungarian was practically nil, I communicated with her by using a selected few words she understood, or by using sign language. Gabi, however, who at that time did not speak either Romanian nor Hungarian, was able to express his wishes quite clearly, mostly by crying or by pointing with his little finger at things he wanted.

Time went by and Gabi turned from a baby into a toddler, and then into a little boy. He was lively, cute, playful and loved by everybody in the family. At the age of three or four he was a chubby boy with pink cheeks, curly soft hair, and lively, brown eyes, always ready to run and play. He loved to sit in the bathtub and splash around in the soapy water, or let his rubber duck float on the water.

For the adults, who lived and worked under constant pressure and uncertainty about the future, there were few occasions for relaxation and enjoyment. For me, one of those few occasions was when I came home after a long day at work, to see Gabi running towards me with open arms to embrace me. After spending the whole day with Anush, he was happy to see me. We played together, laughed together, rolled on the floor together. He liked to play "horsy" with me. In that case I had to get down on my hands and knees while he climbed on my back and drove me around the room, calling out *ghio, ghio* as if enticing a horse.

On Sundays we went to visit Uncle Joseph or took a walk in the park. In the summer, we often went to Lake Harastrau where I rented a rowboat. We climbed into the boat and I started paddling over the smooth, glittering surface of the lake, with Gabi facing me and holding on firmly to his seat. He watched with fascination the boat gliding over the blue-gray water, the waves generated by the oars plunging into the water, and the occasional fish swimming briefly near the boat and then disappearing in the depth of the lake. These were enjoyable times for both of us. We came home refreshed, in good spirits, and hungry.

There was one experience that Gabi had in his early childhood that left its mark on him for the rest of his life. In the summer of 1962, when Gabi was about three-and-a-half years old, my mother-in-law Renee sent Anush to the market to buy a chicken. In those days it was common to go to the open-air market and buy a live chicken from a peasant. The bird was taken home and kept in a cage or in the courtyard until its owner decided to make a meal of it. Anush brought home a chicken and put it in the small courtyard behind the house. The feathery animal fascinated Gabi, who saw a live chicken for the first time. He watched the bird, fed it with corn kernels, and sometimes chased it.

After about a week, the day came when Anush took the chicken to the ritual slaughterer (*shochet*), then brought home the dead chicken, cleaned it, cooked it, and served it to the family for dinner. Gabi, who had not seen the chicken the whole day, wanted to know where the chicken was. Unaware of the sensitivity of a small child, Anush pointed to Gabi's plate and said with a smile, "Here is your chicken." Gabi started to cry bitterly, and it took a long time to quiet him down. Since that evening, Gabi refused to eat meat. He became a vegetarian, and remained one even as an adult. This event showed me how a relatively insignificant event in early childhood can leave its mark on a person's adult life. It also reminded me how certain events in my childhood had left their mark on my life.

In mid 1950s, the University of Bucharest introduced a PhD program. At the Chemistry Department, the program required completion of a scientific research project in a specialized area of chemistry: inorganic, organic, physical, or industrial chemistry. Once completed, the project was to be presented before a commission, consisting of the senior professors in the department. Additionally, the candidate had to pass exams in Marxism-Leninism, in Materialism Dialectic and Historic, as well as an exam in a foreign language to be chosen from French, German, English, and Russian.

I decided to start working towards a PhD degree in inorganic chemistry, an area in which I had worked for many years. I chose my subject in the field of "complex compounds:" the synthesis and characterization of a series of complexes containing chromium and a variety of amino acids. My scientific advisor was Professor Peter Spacu. He had taken over the chair for inorganic and analytical chemistry at the university in 1955, after his father, Gheorghe Spacu, who headed the chair until then, died. As I already knew from past experience at the Polytechnic Institute, the personalities of father and son could not have been more different. While Gheorghe Spacu had been very energetic and extremely demanding, Peter Spacu was placid and quite lenient towards his assistants and students. He let me do my work without interference or pressure; only at the periodic review meetings of our group did I report my progress.

In 1958, I completed the scientific project and wrote my dissertation. The exams in ideological subjects (Marxist philosophy) and in foreign language (I had chosen German) went without a hitch. It gave me great satisfaction to have passed these tests with flying colors. For the presentation of my thesis I prepared a series of graphs, tables, and charts that I did draw myself on large sheets of paper. (Making slides and using a projector for the presentation involved a technology one could only dream about at that time.) On the day of my presentation, I mounted the sheets with data on the walls of the auditorium where I was facing the examining commission. I was very excited, and eager to present the results of tedious research work to the top professors of the department. I was looking forward to this presentation, which I felt would be the crowning of years of my effort. It was an important moment in my life.

The meeting was open to the public, and many faculty members of the department, students, as well as my family gathered in the spacious room to listen to my dissertation. Assisted by the data on display, I gave a good presentation. I felt this subject in my bones. I expected that after a few questions, designed to clarify some points in my thesis, the meeting would come to an end with the approval of the dissertation. The members of the commission had been given copies of my thesis several weeks earlier, and none of them had made any critical comments in writing prior to the meeting.

I was, however, in for a surprise. After my presentation, a heated debate started between two members of the examining commission. They differed in the interpretation of some of the data I presented. One of them agreed with my interpretation, while the other one gave a different interpretation. Such discussions and differences of opinion were common at scientific meetings, but not at the presentation of a dissertation. Except for one, all other professors on the commission agreed with my interpretation of the experimental data. Somewhat embarrassed by the behavior of one of their colleagues, they approved my thesis without delay.

Only later did I find out that there was more to it than a simple difference of scientific opinions. The one member of the commission who disagreed with my interpretation of the scientific data did raise his objections at the instigation of some of my younger colleagues. They were members of the new intelligentsia, party members with a "sound" social origin, unable to get a Ph D degree, but eager to get a fast promotion. They could not accept that a Jew—and a non-party member to boot— would received an advanced degree and become a potential competitor for them in the future. They also intended to tarnish the image of my scientific adviser, Professor Spacu, in order to facilitate his replacement by a party member.

The professor they had approached for that purpose was a leftover from the old, fascist regime, anxious to keep his position. He also had a history of anti-Semitic remarks, and was more than happy to comply with the request of my younger colleagues. Fortunately, the objectivity and integrity of the other members of the commission prevailed. Several months later I published my thesis as a series of articles in the *Zeitschrift für Anorganische und Allgemeine Chemie*, a scientific journal in East Germany. After publication, I received requests for reprints of my articles from all over the world.

The incident at the presentation of my thesis left me disappointed. It also taught me a lesson: there was no future for me in the university system. The events that occurred in the following months proved me right.

So far, I have not described my marriage to Suzi. In spite of the excitement generated by our trips and joint attendance of cultural events, the relationship between us became gradually strained. Disagreements became more frequent. Irritation crept into our conversations. There was not much laughter anymore when we were together. The smile that Suzi displayed so often before our marriage had been replaced by a frown. We had frequent disagreements on how to manage our limited budget, what to buy for the house, how to spend a free evening. I remember the row we had because I had purchased a French art book about the Dresden Art Gallery, which had exquisite reproductions and commentaries. Suzi complained, even to her parents, that I was squandering money for such "things."

The tensions and aggravations accumulated during the day on the job also had a negative impact on the atmosphere in our home. Even now, remembering the events that occurred in my life in the late 1950s and early 1960s, brings back pain and sorrow. In hindsight, I realize that neither of us knew how to handle our marriage. Moreover, the pressures experienced on the job, the oppressive political environment we lived in, the countless hours spent standing in line to purchase items such as sugar or toilet paper—all that exacerbated the tension. The crowded quarters we had to share with Suzi's family and later with our child, the total lack of privacy, further increased the stress in our relationship. As time went by, our marriage deteriorated.

I started thinking about a divorce, but rejected the idea for two reasons. First and foremost, I did not want to break up our family for

Gabi's sake. It would have been a traumatic experience for such a young child to be removed from one of his parents. Another reason was the extremely severe housing shortage in Bucharest. To obtain an apartment or even a room in an apartment required special connections, which I did not have. As a result, Suzi and I continued to stay under the same roof. Besides Gabi, we had little else in common.

At the beginning of the 1960s, the tensions in my family were further exacerbated by an unexpected upheaval that turned my life upside down.

Gabi at age 2

17. Trading Jews for Dollars. Arrest and Retribution

In the early 1960s, following its zigzag policy towards Israel and "the Jewish Problem" in Romania, the government's policies took a new turn. Eager to show its independence from Moscow and to polish its image in the West, the Romanian government improved its relations with Israel. That improvement took different forms: the government sent about 2,000 Torah scrolls to Israel, taken from the numerous synagogues shut down, first by the fascists and later by the communists; Jewish emigration resumed, although at a very slow pace, mostly for the elderly and people without useful skills. At the same time, the government continued to arrest and persecute those it accused of spreading Zionist propaganda or being Israeli "agents."

In order to gain hard currency, the government set up, in secret, a barter system for Jews wanting to emigrate. Through various intermediaries placed in different Western capitals, people living in the West or in Israel would pay a certain amount of dollars or other hard currency into an escrow account. In return, the government would discretely issue exit visas to their relatives in Romania, and collect the money. The prices varied by profession and degree of relationship. For a university graduate, the price was $5,000 a head. For a doctor the price could be as high as $20,000. The state was selling its Jews!

When we heard about the new "trading" practiced by the Romanian government, we decided to explore the new route. We had relatives in Israel who could possibly help us. Andy had a brother and I had my sister and brother-in-law there. We did not know their financial situation, but we were hopeful that they could help us. We wrote to them and asked that they contact one of the foreign intermediaries. We wrote in a roundabout way, to avoid problems with the Romanian censors, who routinely opened letters sent to foreign countries. After awhile our relatives replied that they would explore the possibilities we suggested. And then— silence. Months went by and our relatives did not mention that subject in their letters anymore. We were puzzled. Were they unable to help us? Had they written to us on this subject and the censors had confiscated the letters? We were in the dark, and our hopes dimmed.

Early in 1962, Andy, Renee, and Dora received a brief official notice, requesting that they appear at Police Headquarters at a specified office the following Monday. No reason was given for the request. The letter caused anguish and worries in our family. Dealing with the Romanian authorities had always been an intimidating experience. Being called to Police Headquarters with no reason given was quite upsetting. Would it result in arrests? One never knew the outcome of such an invitation. After all, Andy had been a businessman before the war; therefore he was a member of the exploiting class. Some of his former business friends had been arrested and sent to the Danube-Black Sea canal to do hard labor. Dora's husband had also been a businessman. Moreover, the Latters and Dora were considered "unproductive elements" by the regime, since none of them worked for a state enterprise. Were they called to be evicted from their apartment, to make room for a party bureaucrat brought in from the provinces? We knew of several such situations, and we were worried.

On Monday, Andy, Renee, and Dora went to Police Headquarters with trepidation and anxiety. Before leaving, they told Suzi and me what to do and whom to contact in case they didn't return. At Police Headquarters they had to wait over an hour in a dimly lit hallway before being admitted into the office. After showing their identification papers, a sullen police officer informed them that they had been granted exit visas for Israel. They had to leave the country within a week.

The Latters and Dora came home very agitated. The news was unexpected and left them with mixed feelings. They did not understand why exit visas had been granted to them. Had they been "bought out" by their relatives in Israel, or had the government granted them exit visas because they were "socially unproductive" elements? As they found out later, they had been "bought out." In any case, having been given permission to leave the country, they felt that their wish had become reality. But the Latter's excitement was tempered by the awareness that they had to leave their children and grandchildren behind. Gherda and her family had no intention of emigrating, while Suzi and I had no idea if or when we would receive exit visas.

The thought of having to start a new life in a country with a different culture, a different social system, and a different language, made the Latters apprehensive. The fact that they were already in their fifties, an age at which making a new start is not easy anymore, was not comforting either. In the end, optimism prevailed. Andy felt he had enough energy to begin a new life, and that his relatives in Israel would be helpful. Renee felt the same way, but was worried about those of us left behind. Dora was most eager to leave, since she had no family to leave behind and was looking forward to being with her relatives in Israel.

After selling a few of their belongings and dividing the rest between Gherda and us, the Latters and Dora left for Vienna. It was an emotional separation, marked by an uncertain future. None of us knew if or when we would see each other again. After the airplane left, we returned home in a somber mood, each with our own thoughts. I realized how limited our choices were regarding our lives and our future. I felt that we were like nutshells tossed around by the waves of a stormy sea, totally at the mercy of pitiless political forces. We were at the mercy of a government that decided if we might or might not leave the country, keep our jobs, or keep our apartment. The same government decided if we could benefit from the very limited freedom it granted its subjects, or if we were to be branded "enemies of the people" and arrested. As I was to find out soon, the government had a nasty surprise in store for me.

On a sunny morning in early 1962, I stepped out of the house and crossed the street to walk to the bus stop. I had no students that morning and intended to take the bus to the university to do research work in the laboratory. Suzi was out of town on one of her business trips, and Anush stayed home with Gabi. As I crossed the street, two men approached me.

Each of them grabbed one of my arms, and continued to cross the street with me. I looked at them with surprise, while they smiled at me and said, "Let's walk together." For a moment I thought they were two of my former colleagues, whom I did not recognize anymore. Indeed, any passer-by would have thought that we were friends, judging by the smiles of the two individuals. When we reached the sidewalk, before I realized what was going on, a speeding, unmarked car came to a screeching halt next to us. The doors sprang open, and my two companions pushed me into the backseat. Then they jumped into the car, one to my left and the other to my right. They slammed the doors shut and the car took off. All this happened in less than one minute, and none of the people waiting for the bus noticed anything unusual.

While the car sped away, one of the men said to me in a commanding voice: "Bend forward, head close to your knees, and don't move." I finally realized that the *Securitate* (secret police) had picked me up. It was obvious that they did not want me to see where they were taking me.

My heart started pounding; I could feel the blood pulsing in my ears. The position in which I was sitting was far from comfortable. I realized, however, that I must keep my cool. I had to control my emotions and think fast. While I was staring at the spotted car floor between my knees, arms crossed under my chest, thoughts started to race through my mind. It was clear that I had been arrested. Why? Maybe it was a mistake. Maybe they wanted to arrest someone else and picked me up instead. In that case I would clear it up as soon as I could talk to someone in charge. If it was no mistake, however, what did they have against me? I racked my brain, but could not come up with an answer.

I tried to figure out in what direction we were going. At the beginning I could hear the traffic noise from passing cars and the screeching wheels of tramcars. I knew we were in the center of the city. But then the traffic noise subsided, and only occasionally did I hear a passing car. We were now driving in a much quieter part of town, possibly in a suburb. The air also felt cleaner and fresh. Then the car slowed down, made a turn, and came to a stop. The driver talked briefly to somebody in a subdued voice, and then I could hear the screeching sound made by the opening of a heavy gate. The car moved slowly and came again to a halt. I heard the gate closing behind us with a thud. We had arrived at the destination. Only then was I allowed to raise my head.

I got out of the car into a paved, enclosed courtyard. Still flanked by the guards, I walked toward a tall wooden doorway. I could hear our footsteps reverberating off the walls surrounding the courtyard. We entered a long, dimly lit hallway, with white-painted doors on both sides. One of the guards opened one of the doors and gestured to me to follow him. I stepped over the threshold and looked around quickly. The whitewashed walls of the room we had entered were bare, and a single light bulb was hanging from the ceiling. The windowpanes were painted white—evidently, to prevent people like me from looking outside, as well as outsiders from looking inside. In the middle of the room there was a heavy wooden desk, with a chair next to it. Along the wall opposite the window was a wooden bench. The atmosphere was unfriendly, chilly. I felt as if I had entered a crypt.

One of the guards, who appeared to be senior in rank between the two, ordered with a brusque voice, "Empty your pockets and put the content on the desk."

Out came my wallet, handkerchief, a few coins, keys and address book. The junior guard checked my pockets, to make sure that I did not try to hide anything. The senior one looked into my wallet, but apparently did not find anything of interest. Then he went through my address book. That attracted his attention, since he sat down and started to read carefully page after page. When he finished reading, he put it in his pocket. From his blank face I could not tell whether or not he had found what he wanted. He then returned the rest of my belongings.

I heard him say, "Sit down on the bench and wait until we call you."

"But why am I here?" I wanted to know.

"You'll find out," was his snappy reply. He and his partner left the room, closing the door with a thud.

I sat on the bench and started thinking feverishly. Why did they arrest me? What did I say or do that could be perceived as anti-socialist or subversive activity? I tried to remember the people I talked to over the last few weeks, but nothing suspicious came to my mind. Have I been falsely accused by one of my colleagues or by a disgruntled student? Many scores have been settled over the years by false accusations. Or was it a neighbor who wanted our apartment? I knew that they would interrogate me. I would have to be very careful with my answers, not to incriminate my family, my friends, or myself.

Hours went by. I became more and more nervous. How long are they going to keep me here? Why do they make me wait so long? Is this their method to let me "boil in my own juices," to soften me up before interrogation? I kept repeating to myself: be calm and stay alert. This is what I must do under these circumstances.

Finally, the door opened. The senior guard stood in the doorway. With a brief "come" he told me to follow him. I got up and walked out the door quickly. We walked down the hallway until the guard stopped in front of a tall, wooden door. He knocked, and when the reply came, "come in," we entered the chamber. We were in a room similar to the first one. The walls and windowpanes were also painted white. A large picture of Gheoghe Gheorghiu-Dej, the secretary general of the party, hung between the windows. Underneath the picture, sitting behind a desk with a folder in front of him, was a man in civilian clothes. The guard put my address book on the desk and left the room without saying a word.

The man I was facing was short, stocky, and middle-aged, with carefully combed raven-black hair slicked back with oil. He had sharp, penetrating, black eyes that focused on me with a stern glance. He wore a dark gray suit, white shirt and red tie.

"Sit down, Mr. Scherzer," he said in a crisp, cold voice. I was not surprised that he did not address me "comrade Scherzer." I knew that those arrested were always addressed "Mr." and not "comrade." They were no longer worthy of being members of the community of "comrades."

I sat down in a chair facing him. It was one of those hard, wooden chairs with a straight back, not very comfortable to sit in. The man took out a blank form from the folder and put it in front of him. He picked up a pen and began the interrogation.

Last name? First name? Year of birth? Place of birth? Present address? Place of work? While I was answering the questions, my interrogator made notes on the blank form. These questions were a simple formality, since I was sure that he already had that information. Then he asked me if I had applied for an exit visa to Israel.

"Yes," I replied. He recorded my answer.

Then the unctuous, little man opened the folder, took out a picture, and showed it to me. It was a group picture of ten people, Suzi and me among them. The others were Hardy and Rita, our friends Adrian and Suzy, Key with his girlfriend, Dodi, and a male friend of his. I recognized the picture immediately. It had been taken New Year's Eve at a mountain cabin in the Bucegi, where we had spent a few days of winter vacation. At the cabin we met Dodi and his friend, whom I did not know. We had asked somebody to take a picture of our group.

The interrogator asked me where and when the picture was taken, and the identity of the people in the photograph. I told him about the location, about the occasion of our gathering, and gave him the names of the people in the group. I could not remember the name of Dodi's friend. He then asked me to give detailed information about each person in the picture: how long I had known them, their occupations, how often and where we met, what we discussed during those meetings, and if I knew which one had applied for an exit visa. I tried to answer carefully all the questions, aware that a careless answer could mean serious trouble for my friends. Then the interrogator asked if any of the people in the picture had encouraged me to apply for an exit visa.

"No," was my prompt reply.

At that point I began to suspect what he was after. Someone in this group was suspected of Zionist propaganda, and he was looking for potential witnesses. He took my address book, browsed through it, and questioned me about some of the people listed there. After I told him that they were friends, relatives, or colleagues, he did not show any interest in them. Apparently, he had not found any of the names or addresses he was looking for.

Only later did I find out that several days before my arrest, Dodi and his friend had also been arrested. They were accused of being Zionist "agents," of spreading Zionist propaganda, and of enticing people to emigrate to Israel. During the search of Dodi's apartment, the police had found the picture taken on New Year's Eve. Dodi had to identify each person in the picture.

The interrogator returned to the subject of my exit visa.

"Have you notified the university, your work place, of the application?"

"No," I replied.

"Do you know what would happen if the university found out about your application?"

"I would lose my job," I answered. He nodded, then closed the folder and leaned back in his chair.

He took out a pack of cigarettes from his pocket and offered me one. When I declined, he lit one for himself. After a few puffs on his cigarette, he suggested a deal. "I have a proposition for you to consider. We are willing not to inform the university about your visa application, about your intention to leave the country. In return, we want you to work with us. We want you to meet periodically with one of our men and have a conversation with him. To tell him what was being discussed among your colleagues and friends; what their opinions are with regard to the party and government policies; if they make any political jokes or derogatory remarks about our leaders; if they listen to or discuss radio broadcasts from the West. You give our man this kind of information, and you don't have to worry about your job."

Then he added, "Money would not be a problem. Whatever expenses you would incur during these activities, you would be fully reimbursed. For example, if you invited some people to a good restaurant and order food and drinks for everybody—especially lots of drinks to loosen their tongues—you should not worry about the cost. My man would take care of the bill."

I now realized that this was another objective of my arrest: to blackmail me into becoming an informer. I knew that people had been forced to become informers by threatening them with arrest or loss of their jobs. Other people had become informers for the money, while some did it out of conviction or opportunism. But it had never occurred to me that I could be blackmailed into becoming an informer.

In addition to the loss of my job, there was another threat that my interrogator did not mention or was not aware of: the loss of my doctoral degree. I did not yet have the doctoral diploma, and I knew that the Ministry of Education would issue it in the next several weeks. If the

Ministry found out about my visa application, I could have said "good bye" to my diploma.

I had to reply to the proposal made by my interrogator. Do I accept or reject the deal he was offering me? I felt instant revulsion against snitching on my friends and coworkers, of betraying their friendship and trust. I knew that I would not ruin their lives and careers in order to save my job. If I did such a despicable deed, I would be disgusted with myself for the rest of my life. I also knew that sooner or later the university would find out about the visa application and that I would lose my position. But I wanted at least to save my diploma. I had earned my doctoral degree through many years of hard work, and I was not going to let it slip away. Whatever the future had in store for me, I knew that I would be better off with a doctorate than without one. I had to find a way to convince my interrogator not to inform the university at least in the next few weeks, until I got my diploma.

"I accept your proposal," I told him.

He seemed to be pleased to have achieved his objective, to turn me into an informer.

"Very good. You made the right decision. One of our men, by the name of Peter, will contact you by phone," he said, "and arrange a meeting soon. Furthermore, I advise you not to talk to anybody about today's events, not even to your family."

He then returned my address book and rang a bell. One of my guards appeared and led me out into the hallway. We walked to the car and drove off.

It was already dark and I could not make out where we were driving. When the car stopped, the guard told me that I was free to go. I was in the center of the city, near the university. I stood on the sidewalk for a few minutes, inhaling the fresh evening air. I was free again. Or was I? Suddenly I felt very hungry. Since morning I had not had anything to eat. I walked quickly to the bus stop and went straight home. I didn't tell anybody what happened, what kind of day I had. That night I tossed and turned in bed, unable to sleep. I wished there was a caring shoulder to lean on. But there was none. I felt lonely and miserable.

In the days that followed I avoided seeing any of my friends. I tried to avoid a situation in which I would have to listen to some derogatory remark about our political system, the latest jokes about some party leader, or comments on the latest news broadcast by BBC radio. In the past we freely discussed these topics, since we knew each other for many years and trusted each other. But now I was scared. What if someone else in our group had been forced to become an informer? What if somebody in our group tells a joke about one of our leaders, and I don't report it? Will someone else report it? I had heard that the *Securitate* often uses one informer to check on another one. I suddenly realized that I couldn't trust even my closest associates anymore. How terrible it is to live in a system in which you cannot trust even your best friends!

Two weeks later I got a call from "Peter." He called me in the evening, at home, and asked me to meet him. He gave me an address, as well as the date and time of our meeting. We met in a private apartment, not far from the university. Peter was waiting for me. He was a short, skinny individual with gypsy features. His face was pockmarked, his eyes dark, and his complexion swarthy. His heavily pomaded black hair was shining and sticking to his scalp. He wore an ill-fitting, dark-gray suit, white shirt, and blue tie.

After exchanging greetings, he got directly to the point. "So, tell me about your friends and colleagues. Have you discussed with them the latest political events in the country, the latest decisions taken by the party and government? What was their attitude, what political remarks did they make? Any political jokes? Did any of them discuss news or comments heard on Western radio stations?"

"I have not seen any of my friends lately, since I'm very busy with my work and family," I replied. "Nor did I have time for discussions with my coworkers."

Peter was not pleased. He instructed me to find time to meet my friends, to lead my conversation with them to political topics. He wanted me to find out their opinions about the latest party and government decisions, about the situation in the country and in the world. I should also try to listen to the conversations of my colleagues at my work place. At the end, he requested that we meet again in two weeks.

To improve my chances of getting my doctoral diploma, I tried to gain time. I suggested that we meet in three weeks, since this would provide me with more opportunities to speak to my friends and colleagues. Peter agreed.

After that meeting, my decision was final. I would not stoop to the level of a snitch; I would not denounce and betray my friends and coworkers, regardless of the price I would have to pay. I could not act against my conscience. Preserving my dignity and self-respect was very important for me. These were some of the few aspects of my life over which I still had control.

The next morning I went to the university's office for advanced degrees to inquire about my diploma. The secretary said that several diplomas had arrived, and that they would be distributed in the following days. Indeed, a week later I was called by the university administration, and the secretary handed me my doctoral diploma. There was no ceremony, no speech by the rector. I received the document with a deep sigh of relief. After years of hard work, obstacles and uncertainties, finally I had the coveted diploma in my hand.

For my next meeting with Peter I came prepared. I told him again that I had been much too busy to meet with my friends, that I have had no opportunity to listen to or to engage in conversations with my colleagues, and that I had nothing to report. I made it clear to him that I was unable and unwilling to inform on my friends and colleagues. Peter frowned, but said nothing. He understood. We parted without shaking hands.

It is in times of crisis and despair that the traditional values, which my parents instilled in me during my childhood and adolescence, were put to the test. I had to choose between decency, dignity and fairness on one hand, and selfishness, immorality and betrayal on the other. I chose the former, well aware that I would have to pay a high price for that choice. In retrospect, in spite of the hardships that followed, I am proud that I had the moral strength to pass this test. I had discovered strength I did not know I had until the day I needed it.

Three days after my meeting with Peter, I received a phone call. The rector's secretary was on the line. She informed me that the rector wanted to see me the following morning. I was not surprised. After my last encounter with Peter I expected that phone call. Next morning I presented myself at the rector's office. Although I had seen him at meetings, I had never met him in person. He was a tall man, with dour blue eyes and neatly combed white hair. He was well dressed and had an imposing figure. I knew that he was an old party member, a communist intellectual, who had spent years in jail under the old regime.

Our conversation was brief. He told me that he had been informed that I applied for an exit visa, that I want to leave the country. "Is it true?" he asked.

"Yes," I said, "it is true." I knew the consequences of my answer.

"In that case," the rector replied with an icy voice, "you cannot keep your position at the university any longer."

As of that moment, I was fired. He also told me not to return to my office anymore. I was not allowed to pick up even my teacup from the office. I left without saying a word.

Thus, my career at the University of Bucharest came to an end. It was spring of 1962.

Almost overnight, my life had taken a sharp turn for the worse.

The loss of my position at the university came as a shock. Although it was not unexpected, the loss of my job was a financial and psychological blow. Over the years I had grown accustomed to working with students, to doing scientific research in the lab, to preparing lectures and seminars. Suddenly I was cut off from that world and left with no income. That reality sank in very slowly.

I began to search for another job. Wherever I applied, I had to state my last place of work and the reason for leaving. As soon as the personnel department found out the reason for losing my position at the university, my application was rejected. I knew that my file at the university would follow me, that I could not hide my visa application anymore. I felt as if I had been branded with a mark of Cain. Weeks went by without success. Eventually I realized that my only chance to get a job was to accept the position of an unskilled worker, of a laborer.

Finally, a chemical factory, located in a remote suburb of Bucharest, hired me. The factory manufactured paints and varnishes, and had a small analytical laboratory for the analysis of its products. I was hired in the position of "laborant," a kind of assistant to a laboratory chemist. A "laborant" usually cleans reaction vessels and test tubes, wipes the lab benches clean, and occasionally mops the floor. My salary was close to that of a laborer. It was quite a change from my previous position of university assistant.

There were four chemists in the laboratory, doing chemical analyses for the factory. The head of the laboratory was Maria. She was a middle-aged, dark-haired woman-chemist, with wide, deep-brown eyes, pale skin and attractive features. She was a party member, but not a firebrand communist. Like many others, she had joined the party to be able to get a better position in the factory and a faster promotion. She treated her subordinates, including myself, in a gentle, friendly manner. She knew what my previous position had been, knew why I had lost my job, and showed a certain understanding for my predicament.

After I had worked in my new position for a month, cleaning glassware and mopping the floor, Maria approached me one morning. She said that a large number of analyses had to be completed within the next few days, and she did not have enough manpower to do the job. She asked me if I would like to help the chemists with laboratory work.

I accepted the offer immediately. I was glad to work again as a chemist, instead of doing the work of a housemaid. The work was very simple compared to the research work I had done in the past. I felt a certain joy putting on a lab coat and working again with chemicals, beakers, distillation equipment, and a variety of instruments. I carried out my new assignment almost with no effort.

After I completed the analyses in record time, Maria decided to talk to the factory party secretary on my behalf. It was a total waste of my experience and knowledge, she told him, to use me as a laborant. I would be much more useful to the factory if I worked as a chemist in the laboratory. The secretary of the party organization agreed. Even he realized how absurd it was to let me work as a laborant, and instructed Maria to assign me the work of a chemist. In the personnel department, of course, I would continue to be listed as laborant and continue to be paid accordingly. I was quite pleased when Maria brought me the news. At least I could work in my profession, even if the pay was that of a laborer.

The winter of 1962/1963 proved to be difficult for me. It was a harsh winter, accompanied by storms and heavy snow. The city's streets were cleaned only sporadically, and transportation became chaotic. There were food shortages, and gas for heating was provided only several hours daily. To get to work, I had to take first a bus, then the tram to the last stop, and then walk a mile over an open field to reach the factory. The bus and tramcar were without heat and each was packed with people wrapped in heavy winter coats. Most of the time an icy wind blew over the open field I had to cross on foot. After a heavy snowfall, the streets became impassable. Either the buses or the tramcars stopped running. In that case I had to walk several miles, often through deep snow, to reach my work place. During the winter months I left home at 5 a.m. It took me two to three hours to reach the factory. When I finally arrived at the laboratory, I was shivering and exhausted. A cup of hot tea and a ten-minute rest restored some of my energy. Only then could I start my work.

Suzi had kept her professional position at the Patent Office, while I had the position and income of a laborer. The loss of my academic position, the temporary unemployment, and my job as a laborant proved to be the last straw. Our marriage was at the breaking point. Now that I had lost my prestigious position, Suzi displayed, more and more often, an attitude of contempt towards me. She started to come home late in the evening, without explanation. Soon I learned that what I had suspected for a long time was true: she had found solace outside the family.

It takes sometimes years of cohabitation to discover in a person character traits whose existence one does not suspect. Unusual situations drive often these features into the open. Under difficult circumstances, my spouse displayed a very disturbing behavior that tore apart the already frayed bond between us. She had no interest anymore in maintaining that bond.

We divorced in March 1963. As expected, Suzi was granted custody of Gabi.

For me, the divorce was devastating. After the blow I had suffered in my professional life, I now had to cope with a serious blow to my personal life. I felt that fate had turned against me, that my life had reached a low point. What pained me most was the harm the divorce was doing to Gabi.

He was only four years old, and his innocence would not save him from suffering the consequences of the break up of our family.

As if these upsetting events were not enough, more excitement was in store for me.

18. Redemption

Three weeks after the divorce, the police notified us that we had been granted exit visas. Since our papers had been processed prior to our divorce, the visas were granted to the three of us as a family. At the same time, my mother was also granted an exit visa in Suceava. We knew that the families in Israel—my sister and Suzi's parents—were working intensely to get us out of Romania. Only later did we find out that they had deposited a large amount of money, through an intermediary, in an escrow account in London on our behalf. My mother was included in the deal. Once we left Romania, the money was supposed to be transferred to a bank account of the Romanian government.

There was, however, a problem with the entrance visa. To obtain the exit visa from the government, we needed to have an entrance visa from another country. To avoid frictions with Arab countries, Romania refused to grant exit visas to Israel. Another country had to be found. After a frantic search, the intermediary that had made the financial deal eventually made the visa arrangements. We were granted entrance visas by the British embassy in Bucharest, with the understanding that the British visas would be valid only to leave Romania. Once we arrived at our first destination, Vienna, we had to make further travel arrangements to Israel or another country, but not to Great Britain. The Brits did not want us.

When I went to Maria, my supervisor at the factory, and told her that I was resigning from my job and leaving the country, her first reaction was surprise. She did not expect to see me leave that soon. Then she grabbed my hand and congratulated me. Her face expressed joy, but also envy; the envy that I was able to leave a drab, difficult life behind and start a new life in a better world. I saw a similar reaction in the faces of my other colleagues, when I said good-bye to them. In spite of the intense communist propaganda that described Western countries as lands of oppression and exploitation, most people perceived life in the West as being much easier and happier than their present lives.

We had to dispose of most of our belongings. We were allowed to take only a wooden trunk filled with clothing and kitchen utensils, weighing no more than 60 kg. Nothing of value could be taken. Paintings, silverware, jewelry, artwork had to be left behind. Photographs, including family pictures, were not allowed. Nothing made of paper, such as notebooks, diaries, address books, or newspapers could be taken out of the country.

You may ask, why couldn't we take anything made of paper? The answer is simple: our rulers treated us as potential spies and traitors. They suspected that some of us would write state secrets on paper with invisible ink, smuggle them out of the country, and deliver them to the imperialists. Therefore, we were allowed to carry only the emigration documents. Other papers, such as birth certificates and school diplomas, could be taken only after they had been examined by a police officer and had received a stamp of approval. Books could be sent separately by mail, after censors carefully screened them. Many of the more valuable books we sent, such as the four volumes of the Encyclopedia Judaica (in German), never arrived at the destination. They were stolen. We were not allowed to take any money with us, Romanian or any other kind of currency. We had to leave the country with empty pockets.

Some of the valuables, such as paintings and silverware, we divided between Uncle Joseph and Gherda. The rest, such as furniture and household goods, we had to sell at ridiculously low prices. The buyers knew that we had to sell our belongings, and therefore we would accept any price. Besides, since we could not take money with us, we would have to leave it behind anyway, with relatives. What we could not sell, we gave away. Most of the money we made from the sale was spent to purchase airline tickets for the flight to Vienna.

Uncle Joseph went to Suceava to help my mother pack her few belongings, and sell or give away whatever she was forced to leave behind. Unfortunately, among the items discarded were our family pictures, including pictures from my childhood. There was not sufficient time to obtain government approval to take those pictures with us. When the packing was completed, Mother and Uncle Joseph took the train for Bucharest.

But things rarely go without a hitch. The moment the train left the station, Mother happened to look out the rail car window and noticed that her trunk had been left behind on the station's platform. She and Uncle Joseph got off at the next station and took a return train to Suceava. As it turned out, paying the shipping fee to the station master had not been sufficient to have the wooden trunk put on the train. Several other people had to be bribed to do the job. After paying the bribes, the trunk was loaded on the next train, and Uncle Joseph and Mother eventually arrived in Bucharest with Mother's belongings.

We left Bucharest in April 1963 on a Tarom (the Romanian airline) flight to Vienna: Mother, Suzi, Gabi, and myself. Uncle Joseph, Aunt Ruchel and Gherda accompanied us to the airport. It was an emotional, tearful parting. Saying goodbye to loved ones, not knowing if it will be the very last time we will see them, was not easy. I felt that I might never see my uncle and aunt again. Indeed, I never did.

After armed border guards checked our documents, we boarded the plane. I had a window seat and could still wave to my relatives left behind. Shortly thereafter, the plane took off. I felt physically and emotionally exhausted. I realized that another chapter of my life had come to an end, and I faced a new beginning, where new challenges and new uncertainties awaited me.

It was a cloudy day and the plane quickly disappeared among the dark-gray clouds. Looking out through the window, I could not see the landscape of the country I was leaving. All I could see was the cloud cover that stretched all the way to the horizon. When we flew over the Carpathian Mountains high above the clouds, I could see only some of the taller mountain peaks piercing the cloud cover. They looked like dark, rocky islands floating on a white sea of foam.

I leaned back into my seat, closed my eyes, and let my thoughts drift into the past. I had left behind the country where I had spent 35 years of my life. Those years, lived under different dictatorships, had been difficult years. I grew up in an increasingly hostile and abusive environment, from which my parents were unable to protect me. I had witnessed many outrages and swallowed many insults. The taunting and beating in elementary school, the cruel and despotic behavior of some of my teachers in lyceum, the years of anguish—with the fear of beating, fear of arrest, fear of deportation—all had left deep scars on my psyche.

I had experienced dictatorships of the right and the left, from the fascism of Cuza-Goga and that of the Antonescu regime, to the communist dictatorship of Gheorghe Gheorghiu-Dej and acolytes. I had seen that country's anti-Semitism in its most brutal forms under the fascist regimes, and in a more subtle form under the communists. I felt that the persecutions I had been exposed to prior to and during the war had robbed me of my childhood. They had hampered my ability to form close personal relationships with others and had created difficulties in my social life. The unpredictable life under communism, the constant uncertainty of what tomorrow might bring, the fear of expressing my own thoughts and opinions even to my closest friends, the gloomy outlook for the future—all these had brought little joy into my adult life. A broken marriage did not help either.

Reviewing the past, I remembered the saying of the ancient philosopher Heraclitus, that "Everything flows, nothing remains unchanged. Everything moves, nothing is still. Everything passes away, nothing lasts." How well this profound truth applied to my own past, to my own experiences! How often did I have to start life all over again! Stability had been as elusive in my life as peace of mind.

Episodes from my past flashed before my mental eye. The image of a column of miserable men, women, and children under military guard, trotting on cobble stones towards a cattle train to be deported. The anguished waiting in the middle of the night, to hear the knock at the door by the NKVD men. The experience of being grabbed on the street and hauled off to a secret place for interrogation by the Romanian secret police. Such events cannot be forgotten, regardless how much time had passed. I had learned that life is fragile and full of unpredictable cruelties. I had found out that brutality and inhumanity perpetrated by the extreme left can be as painful and outrageous as that perpetrated by the extreme right. I had learned that exceptional circumstances bring out the best and the worst of human nature. Some people turn into vicious beasts, others show unscrupulous greed and selfishness, while still others rise above depravity to maintain dignity and humanity. I had discovered that "civilized behavior" is often only a thin and fragile veneer. When social restraints are removed, that veneer is readily discarded and replaced by atavistic brutality and unscrupulous selfishness.

Looking back into my past, I realized that through most of my life, I had been treated like a second class human being. Under the fascists I was "the Jew," the *"jidan"* that can be spit on, kicked, and mocked at will by every hoodlum. Under the Soviets I was one of the *mestnye*, one of the "locals" that had lived under capitalism and therefore could not be trusted. Under the Romanian communists, I was the offspring of a bourgeois family, a person with an "unsound" social origin. True, I had been given a good position in the academic world, but that was at a time when the university was desperate for qualified personnel to teach and train the new, communist intelligentsia. I knew that I had no future in academia, and that soon I would be replaced.

Now, I would have to start over again. How often did I have to give up everything my family and I had accumulated over time with hard work! How often had I been forced to start from scratch! The fascists and the communists, the Russians and the Romanians had been quite effective in depriving my family and me of our belongings. Joseph Stalin, Adolf Hitler, General Antonescu, Ana Pauker, Gheorghiu-Dej—they were all effective in raising the level of misery in my life. At the age of 35, all I had in my possession was a crate of old clothes and used kitchenware. But I had one valuable asset: I had an education! I had knowledge! That, nobody can take away from me. It will be the foundation on which I will build my new life.

I was shaken from my thoughts by the jolt of the plane landing at Schwechat Airport near Vienna. After taxiing briefly on the runway, the plane stopped, the door opened and I stepped down on Austrian soil. I had stepped out from behind the "Iron Curtain," and entered what, in the

West, is called the "Free World." As I set foot on solid ground, I felt a tingle of anticipation. What will life be like in this new world?

Mother and I entered the airport terminal on our way to passport control. We walked in a restricted area along with the passengers who had just arrived on other flights. A thick glass wall separated that area from the visitor section. Great was my surprise when I saw, behind the partition, about two dozen pretty young girls smiling, jumping, and frantically waving at me, some with flowers in their hands. I could also hear muffled screams of joy coming from behind the glass wall. First I thought that all visitors arriving in Vienna get such a warm welcome. I quickly became aware, however, that all those pretty girls were smiling and waving only at me, and paid no attention to the other passengers. Realizing that, I was first astonished, then extremely flattered. What a great reception! I felt like a star, without knowing the cause of that adulation. Only the following day did I find out from the Hias people what actually happened at the airport, and the reason for my enthusiastic reception.

Shortly before our plane landed, a British rock-and-roll band had arrived from London on another plane. The band was well known from its recordings, and a large group of girls was waiting for the players at the airport. The girls apparently did not know what the band members looked like, but knew that they were eccentric types. When I walked through the restricted area of the airport, I was wearing the hat and coat that I brought with me from Romania. My clothing was completely outmoded, compared to the fashion worn in the "Free World." I wore a wide-brimmed hat, compared to the narrow-brimmed hats worn in the West at the time; my coat was long and had wide lapels, while Western coats were much shorter and had narrow lapels. Seeing me dressed in clothes that people used to wear before those teenagers were born, the young girls concluded that I was one of those eccentric band players. Therefore, they all smiled and waved at me. It was a case of mistaken identity. Realizing that all those cheers were for somebody else, my ego quickly deflated like a punctured balloon. I was disappointed, but briefly I had my moment of glory.

After going through passport control and customs, we were received by two well-dressed gentlemen. They were the representatives of Hias, the Jewish-American aid organization. They told us that we would have to spend some time in Vienna, until our immigration into the country of our destination could be arranged. In the meantime, we were to live in an apartment in Vienna, paid for by Hias. Since they knew that we had arrived with empty pockets, they gave us some Austrian Schillings, the local currency.

Mother and I were given a room in a modest apartment in the center of the city, on Mariahilfer Strasse, not far from the Ring. The apartment belonged to a Mrs. Hammerl, an elderly widow who supplemented her pension by renting out rooms. Suzi and Gabi got a room in another apartment.

The following morning we met again with the representatives of the Hias. After filling out a series of forms and giving them information about my education and qualifications, they told me that I could choose from several countries. I could go to Israel, in which case I could leave within a few days, either directly or via Rome. I could also go to other countries, such as the United States, Australia, or Brazil. In that case, the processing of the immigration papers would take several months. My mother can join me, they said, as long as I take the responsibility to support her. Suzi and Gabi, however, will have to go to Israel, since her parents lived there.

It was the first time that I was given a choice regarding my future. It was a dizzying feeling. I suddenly became aware that I could break free from the constraints that have held me captive in the past, so that the future can become a world of my own choosing. It was not a political party, a government, or my parents who decided my future, but I, myself, had to make that decision. I was able to decide how and where to live the rest of my life.

I was overwhelmed. Having lived under totalitarian regimes, completely isolated from the West, I knew very little of life in those countries. Should I go to Israel, the country I dreamed of in my early youth? Or should I go to America? In my childhood, the kids used to say that in America the streets are paved with gold; but they also told stories about Al Capone and the Chicago gangsters. Should I go to Brazil, with beautiful Rio de Janeiro and its fascinating women? I was in a quandary. The Hias people knew that such decisions are not easily made, and gave me several days to think it over.

I began to inquire about the outlook in different countries for people with my qualifications. In Israel, I was told, there was a surplus of scientists and professionals, and that it would not be easy for me to find a job in my profession. In America, however, I was told that the situation was different. It was the post-Sputnik era, and the U.S. government and industry were pouring large amounts of money into scientific and technical research. The people from Hias assured me that I could easily find a position, either in the academic field or in an industrial research laboratory. There was also a demand for scientists and engineers in other countries, but not to the same extent as in the U.S.

The decision came down to choosing between Israel and America. It was not an easy decision. My sister and her family in Israel wanted us to join them. Gabi would also be living in Israel. But the outlook for a good position was slim. In America, I could readily obtain a position of my choosing in my profession. There, however, I had only a few friends, among them Hardy and his family. They had arrived in that country a year earlier. I also learned that no other country offers the "freedom of choice," how to live one's life, to the extent that America does. I discussed with Mother, with the people from Hias, and with several acquaintances the choices available to me and asked for their opinion. Mother left it up to me to decide. The Hias people and my acquaintances told me that if I decide to settle in America, I could travel to Israel to visit my family any time; or, if I wanted, I could later settle in that country. My youthful Zionist idealism, quenched by the realities of life, gave way to a down-to-earth decision regarding my future. I decided to go to the U.S. with my mother.

I informed the Hias of my decision, and was told that it would take several months to process my papers. They promised to pay the rent until the day of our departure, then gave us some money for food and local transportation.

Several days later Suzi and Gabi left for Israel. It was a tearful good-by for me and for Gabi. I promised to come and see him as soon as possible. It was the first time that I was separated from my son, but I knew that I would see him again, soon.

With time on my hands, I started exploring Vienna. It was my first contact with a major city in the "Free World." I knew about the city from stories my parents told during my childhood. Father had been there during World War I, and had studied law at the Vienna University. It was the city of the Hapsburgs, where Empress Maria Theresa and a row of emperors held court, the city where Mozart, Beethoven, Schubert, and Strauss composed some of the finest music the world had known. My parents had always described the city as a major cultural center located on the shores of the blue Danube. It had been the capital of the Austrian-Hungarian Empire until 1918, when the empire collapsed. I still recall the admiration felt by my parents for its last Emperor, Franz-Joseph. Now I was finally able to see this historic, famous city.

I went sight seeing with a vengeance. I visited the Hofburg, with its luxurious imperial apartments, and goggled at the imperial treasures; descended into the underground, somber *Kaisergruft* (Capuchins' Crypt), where an array of emperors and empresses lay peacefully in their embellished, metallic caskets; relished the dancing and jumping of the white Lippizaner horses at the Spanish Riding School; admired the resplendent palaces of Schönbrunn and Belvedere, and their magnificent gardens; visited twice the *Kunsthistorisches Museum* (Museum of Fine Arts); and was fascinated by the huge collection of Italian, Flemish, Dutch, and German artworks assembled by the Hapsburgs over the centuries. I left the museum elated by the experience of having seen such a magnificent collection of famous works of art.

While walking along the Ring, I stopped in front of the Burgtheater, the most famous theater in the city. Looking at the classical façade and imposing colonnade, I remembered the story my father had told me about the death of his father. My grandfather traveled frequently to Vienna, where he regularly visited the Burgtheater. During a visit to that city, in 1895, he disappeared. At the time of his disappearance, a fire had broken out at the theater during a performance. People panicked and tried to leave the building through the main doors. The frantic mass pushed toward the exit but could not open the doors. To their horror they discovered that these were inward opening doors. Hundreds of people were trapped and died in the fire. My grandfather was among them.

Following this tragic accident, the Viennese building codes were changed. All buildings where large numbers of people gathered—theaters, opera houses, concert halls, restaurants, dance halls—had to have outward opening exit doors. These building codes were soon adopted across Europe, and later, across the globe. Looking at the Burgtheater, I thought that the death of my grandfather in this building—and that of a few hundred other people who perished in that famous fire—had saved countless lives in subsequent fires around the world.

From the Burgtheater I walked to the State Opera, then turned into the glitzy Kärntnerstrasse and walked to the ancient *Stephansdom* (St. Stephen's Cathedral). I watched the well-dressed people walking leisurely on the streets, or enjoying coffee and pastry at an outdoor café. I admired the opulence on display in the windows of elegant stores. I felt like a child let loose in a candy store. Day after day I walked from morning till evening, and by the end of the day I could barely stand on my feet. I wanted to make up for all those years I had spent behind the Iron Curtain.

I stopped in front of the *Sacher* coffeehouse. I knew the name of this famous place from my parents. It was filled with well-dressed elderly gentlemen and elegant, jewelry-bedecked ladies. They were sitting at round, white-linen covered tables, conversing quietly or reading a newspaper, while enjoying a cup of coffee and a slice of pastry. Crystal and silver glistened. I looked at the *Schokoladentorten* (chocolate cakes) covered with *Schlagsahne* (whipped cream) on display. The aroma of chocolate and freshly baked pastries that drifted through the open door made my mouth water. How tempting, how enticing! Tempted as I was, I resisted the siren call. With the few Schillings received from the Hias I had to buy a loaf of bread and a package of butter that Mother had asked me to bring home. I had to satisfy myself inhaling the aroma of pastries and freshly brewed coffee that tickled my nostrils.

What impressed me the most was the calm, relaxed attitude of the people on the street. In Bucharest, under the communists, the pedestrians usually were grim faced, tense and always in a hurry. In Vienna, everybody appeared relaxed. I learned later that the leisurely attitude of the Viennese was called *"Gemütlichkeit."*

Walking on the streets of Vienna brought back old memories. I recalled Austria as the birthplace of good and evil in central Europe. It was the birthplace of Wolfgang Amadeus Mozart and Johan Strauss, but also the country where Adolf Hitler and Adolf Eichman had grown up. I recalled the famous Jewish writers who had lived in Austria in the second half of the nineteenth century and in the early part of the twentieth century. Most of them had lived and written their most important works in this beautiful city: the novelists Arthur Schnitzler, Stefan Zweig, essayist Felix Salten, and poet Hugo von Hofmannsthal. They had made a very significant contribution to Austria's literary life.

Before the war we had many works of those writers in our house. I had a strange, elevated feeling when I realized that I was walking on the same streets on which they had walked, and occasionally sipped a cup of hot mocha coffee in one of the cafes where they had heated literary debates.

I also recalled Sigmund Freud, who had lived in Vienna. Many of his theories were and still are a subject of debate, but the Nazis proved one of his theories correct. Before the war, Freud had been criticized for denying the supremacy of culture over instinct. However, his opinion that the barbaric instinct in man cannot be eradicated, regardless how cultured man is, had been confirmed in the most terrible way during the Nazi-fascist rule over Europe.

Walking the streets of Vienna I made some surprising discoveries. At the newsstands there were numerous magazines with glossy pictures of beautiful women on display, many of them scantily dressed. Some of those pictures appeared to me outright indecent. Most of the articles printed in these publications had a salacious character and appealed to the erotic imagination. Even many of the books on display in bookstores were filled with strongly erotic content.

I was not prepared to find in Vienna such an abundance of magazines and books focused on sexuality and lust. Neither in communist Romania, nor in the Soviet Union, had I seen such magazines or books. Erotic novels and magazines were not published in communist countries. Their import or distribution was strictly prohibited, since they were considered a form of "bourgeois decadence." Anybody traveling in a Western country and returning to Romania with such publications had them promptly confiscated at the border. On the streets of Vienna, however, sex was touted on the covers of magazines, and nobody seemed to care. In a more seedy part of the city, in the Seventh District, I found a whole street where sex was for sale. Women past their prime, wearing heavy makeup and deep-cut necklines, were walking up and down the street, looking for customers. I had discovered the spicy side of life in the West.

Browsing through the magazines on the newsstands (obviously, I had to satisfy my curiosity stirred by the novelty of this discovery), I discovered that the German language had been enriched with words borrowed from English, words with which I was not familiar. I found out that the word "Job" was not referring to the ancient biblical figure, but had the same meaning as the English word "job." That "Hamburger" was not an inhabitant of the city of Hamburg, but a kind of sandwich. I also leaned another German word of English origin: the word "sexy." I had to look at the picture of the person the word was referring to get its meaning. I found out later that these words had entered the German language after the war, as a result of American influence.

Another novelty I discovered in Vienna was commercial advertising. Mrs. Hammerl had a small black-and-white television set in her living room and I sat sometimes in front of it and watched a program. That was where I saw, for the first time, televised commercial advertisements. Under communism there were no commercials on television. In Romania there was always a shortage of good merchandise, and people bought everything of acceptable quality without any advertising. When a store received Italian shoes, French eau-de-cologne, Hungarian textiles, or Russian caviar, it was amazing how quickly a line formed outside the store without any prior publicity. The goods were sold out in no time. No advertisement was necessary. The information was spread by word of mouth.

In Vienna, however, advertisement was everywhere: on television, on the radio, in newspapers, in magazines, in store windows, on billboards, even in public restrooms (there they advertised a certain brand of condoms). Some of the advertisements had an erotic bent, implying that the use of a certain product will result in success with the opposite sex.

While for people who had grown up in the West these advertisements had become part of their daily life, for me it was a totally new experience.

I also learned that some of these advertisements had to be taken "with a grain of salt."

During my stay in Vienna I visited the local Jewish Community Center several times. I discovered a small library there. One of the books that caught my eye was *The Jewish Contribution to Civilization* by Cecil Roth, written in English. In communist Romania, books on such a subject could not be found in any library. They were considered nationalistic and subversive. I read the book, eager to familiarize myself with a subject of considerable interest. Although my knowledge of English was far from perfect, with the help of a dictionary I was able to understand most of what I read. The book was an eye opener. Besides the familiar names of Sigmund Freud, Karl Marx, and Albert Einstein, were those of novelists Marcel Proust, Franz Kafka, Emil Ludwig, Franz Werfel, and Heinrich Heine; of philosophers Maimonides, Baruch Spinoza, Moses Mendelssohn, and Henri Bergson; and of painters Camille Pissarro, Mark Chagal, Amedeo Modigliani, and Max Liebermann. Among composers were the names of Felix Mendelssohn, Jacques Offenbach, Gustav Mahler, George Gershwin, and Arnold Schönberg. Among conductors, the names of Bruno Walter, Otto Klemperer, and Pierre Monteux. There were the virtuosi Artur Schnabel, Arthur Rubinstein, David Oistrakh, and Isaac Stern. Among medical researchers were Paul Ehrlich and Jonas Salk. There were the physicists Lise Meitner, Max Born, and Albert Michelson. The chemists Fritz Haber and Richard Willstaetter; and a host of other writers, artists, composers, scientists, statesmen, and philanthropists. I discovered that many famous writers, philosophers, doctors, scientists and musicians I had heard about in the past, were Jews. Many of them became Nobel-prize winners.

Cecil Roth's book opened my eyes. It made me aware of the enormous Jewish contribution to Western civilization and culture in different lands and times. It made me proud to belong to a people who had made such an important contribution to human civilization. It also made me aware that the Holocaust perpetrated by the Nazis and their collaborators was not only a calamity for the Jews of Europe. By destroying the genetic pool from which so many brilliant minds had risen in the past, the Holocaust was also a huge loss for Western culture.

During the second week of my stay in Vienna, I met Felix, a mathematician from Romania, who was also waiting for his immigration papers to be processed. We knew each other from Bucharest, where we had met occasionally. He suggested that I try to earn some money while I was waiting for my visa by getting a temporary position at the University of Vienna. I thought it was a good idea, since I did not know how long it would take to get my immigration papers for the U.S.

The next day I visited the Technical University, and asked to see the head of the inorganic chemistry chair. That is when I met Professor Victor Gutmann. He was a gentleman in his forties, with sharp features and thin nose, polite manners and friendly attitude. I told him where I came from and of the likelihood of spending several months in Vienna. I described my education and experience at the University of Bucharest, and showed him my Ph.D. diploma together with a list of my scientific publications that I had put together from memory. I then asked him if it would be possible for me to do research work in his laboratory, until the immigration papers arrived.

First he expressed surprise that I spoke German; he did not expect that people coming from Romania who were not of German extraction would speak that language. He then said that he would be glad to accept me, since there was a shortage of research personnel in his department. My fluency in German probably also contributed to his decision. The salary was modest, but for me it was sufficient.

Two days later I started work at the laboratory for inorganic chemistry. Since it was summer time, students and assistants were on vacation, and I spent most of the time by myself, working on my project. The assignment from Professor Gutmann was to develop a polarographic method to measure the concentration of a certain organic compound in solution. I was familiar with this method from my work in Bucharest and was able to make progress without much effort.

Occasionally, one or two graduate students appeared in the lab, worked for a day or two, and then disappeared for the rest of the week. There was also an assistant, whose preferred topic of conversation was boxing and horse racing. He also spent a good deal of his time at these events. The Viennese *Gemütlichkeit* was quite noticeable at the university, especially during the summer.

In my spare time I continued to explore Vienna. I started also to study English, to prepare myself for the U.S. In mid September the Hias informed me that the preparation of the immigration papers for the U.S. was nearing completion. It would take another month until we will be able to leave for America.

In the next few weeks, I completed my work at the university. I wrote a detailed report about the work done and handed it to Professor Gutmann for publication (it was later published). I also told him that this would conclude my research in his laboratory.

"Dr. Scherzer, are you leaving already?" he asked with a frown. (In Austria, people who were not close, were highly formal and addressed each other by title and last name)."You have done good work in the laboratory and been able to generate a publication in a very short time. I was hoping you would stay with us longer. I am very sorry to see you leave."

He paused briefly, and then made me an offer. "If you decide to stay, I can give you a permanent position in this department. Your fluency in German would allow you to teach, and we could continue to do scientific research work together." He assured me that the university administration could obtain, from the Austrian authorities, a permanent resident permit for me.

Naturally, I was very pleased and flattered to hear such words of praise. The offer of a position at the prestigious Technical University of Vienna was quite attractive. Never before had anybody expressed appreciation for my professional performance or offered me such a good position. I thanked Professor Gutmann and told him that I would consider the offer, and that I would inform him of my decision within the next few days.

During the few months spent in Vienna, I had time to learn more about the Viennese and the Austrians in general. The initial awe inspired by the glitzy shops on Kärntnerstrasse, the imperial palaces and majestic monuments, as well as by the relaxed, comfortable lifestyle of the Viennese, had given way gradually to a more realistic appraisal. I began to realize that many of the city's buildings, even some historic buildings, had not seen a fresh coat of paint for many years. I also found out that the beautiful but expensive merchandise on display in the stores on Kärntnerstrasse was not accessible to everybody. As my landlady, Mrs. Hammerl, explained to me, this was not because the people who did not belong to the political party in power were prohibited from shopping in those stores, as was the case in Romania. It was because for many, the merchandise was too expensive.

In Romania, money had played a somewhat minor role in life, since even with money the average citizen could not buy much. In Vienna, however, I learned that money played a key role in everybody's life, and that people were often measured by what they owned and the money they earned.

By talking to different Viennese during my stay in Vienna—to colleagues, neighbors, and the landlady—I learned that most of them were far from happy. To the customary greeting, "*Wie gehts?*" (How are you?), the usual answer was a deep sigh and a litany of complaints: about arthritis or some other health problem, about the lack of money, about high taxes, and, in general, about the miseries of life. Many older Austrians talked with nostalgia about the "good, old days" under Emperor Franz Joseph, when Austria was a mighty empire and life apparently was wonderful. My initial impression of general contentment soon evaporated.

Other discoveries I made during my stay in Vienna were even more disappointing. In the few months I spent in the city, I discovered that many of the polite, neatly dressed middle-aged and older people had been enthusiastic supporters of Adolf Hitler. From the local newspaper, *Der Kurier*, I learned that several former commandants of concentration camps were on trial in Vienna. Eventually, the Austrian judges acquitted them. Under the Nazi regime, many Austrians had held high positions in the SS, in the Gestapo, and in the *Wehrmacht*. After all, the Führer himself was Austrian. I learned about the Austrian Ernst Kaltenbrunner, one of the top Nazis convicted and hanged at Nürenberg for crimes against humanity. I heard of the horrible deeds perpetrated by Franz Stangel, the infamous Austrian Nazi commandant of the Sobibor and Treblinka extermination camps. By talking to local Jews, whom I met on Saturdays at the synagogue, I learned that anti-Semitism was still alive and widespread among Austrians, although it was usually hidden behind a veneer of cold politeness.

All that information about the Austrians led me to conclude that, given a choice, this was not an environment in which I would like to spend the rest of my life. Although the academic position at the Technical University was attractive, I decided not to accept it. I returned to Professor Gutmann, told him that I had decided to emigrate to the U.S., and thanked him again for his offer and assistance during my time at the university. We parted on friendly terms.

In October, Mother and I prepared for our trip to the U.S. We packed our few belongings in the same trunk we brought from Romania. The clothing, shoes, and a few pots and pans fitted easily into the crate. The Hias had given us the necessary documents, including the American visas. We departed from Schwechat airport on October 21, 1963, in a propeller-driven plane, chartered by several immigration organizations. Hias was one of them.

The plane carried immigrants of different nationalities, religions, and cultures, speaking a variety of languages. Most of the passengers had come from countries that were under communist rule and from which they had been able to escape. The plane was buzzing with conversations in Hungarian, Romanian, Polish, Czech, Slovenian, Yiddish, Ukrainian and other undistinguishable languages. Indeed, it was a modern version of the Tower of Babel. There were bespectacled intellectuals in rumpled coat and tie, laborers with caps, wool sweaters and rugged worker's pants, peasant women with flowery scarves on their heads and crying babies in their arms, bearded, Orthodox Jews dressed in black, and a motley mixture of noisy children of all ages. Still, in spite of their diversity in origin, education and culture, the immigrants had one thing in common: the wish to live in America.

As soon as the plane took off, many of the passengers, who were not used to flying, became sick and started vomiting. It wasn't a pleasant scene. A pervasive, acrid smell spread through the plane, and stayed with us for the rest of the flight. Children began to cry and held onto their parents. Only gradually did they quiet down and fall asleep. Most of the passengers also fell silent, immersed in their thoughts about the life they left behind and the one on which they were embarking.

While looking out through the window at the cloud cover that stretched all the way to the horizon, I started thinking about the past, about the twists and turns of fate. I left behind a continent that, in this century, had been drenched in an ocean of blood and seen mountains of corpses. I left behind countries where war, hatred and prejudice had left deep scars on people's souls. My youth had been a cloudy episode in my life, during which the bright sun of joy and happiness only rarely shone through. I had never felt secure or fully at home. Repeatedly uprooted, I had been an outsider all my life, even in my own birthplace. I was neither Austrian, nor Romanian, nor Russian, nor Ukrainian.

The feeling of being an outsider was reinforced when I spoke. As soon as I opened my mouth, the accursed accent gave me away. Whatever language I used, I was told by the natives that I spoke "with an accent." Even in Vienna, where I talked to the Austrians in my native tongue, in German, they told me that I speak with a "foreign" accent. My accent was hard to place—a little German at the vowels, a little Romanian in the consonants, with a pinch of Russian for intonation—a reflection of the different languages and cultures I had been exposed to during the early part of my life. I was and remained a foreigner, an outsider. I knew that even in America I would speak English with an accent. At my age, it wasn't possible to speak a new language without an accent. But I knew I was going to a country of more opportunities and fewer prejudices than there were on the continent I was leaving behind.

It was a long flight. Day turned to night, but at first I was too excited to sleep. Thoughts and images from the past were washing through my mind. The plane refueled at Shannon Airport, Ireland, before starting to cross the Atlantic. After leaving behind the lights of the airport, the plane flew through total darkness. Turning to the window, I could see only the small flashing red light at the tip of the plane's wing, immersed in complete blackness. Finally, enticed by the hypnotic humming of the plane's engines, I fell asleep.

I must have slept several hours, and when I awoke, a new day was dawning. Through the window I could see the crimson aura rising at the horizon, but the ocean was still black beneath the plane. As the veil of night dissipated and darkness gave way to daylight, I saw the shimmering ocean stretch out beneath us. At a distance, I could see the contour of land. At that moment the pilot announced, over the intercom, that we were entering Canadian airspace over Newfoundland. We had reached the New World! Fourteen hours after leaving Vienna, the plane touched down at Idlewild Airport (later renamed John F. Kennedy Airport) near New York. We had arrived in America, the new land of milk and honey.

After getting off the plane and setting foot on American soil, my mother exclaimed with enthusiasm, "We are now in the land of unlimited possibilities." She remembered the description of the United States given by one of her teachers, when she was a young girl in middle school. How right she was!

Epilogue

This is a brief synopsis of my life in America. It is not part of my narrative.

After our arrival in the U.S., Mother and I spent several months in Boston, while I was looking for a job. I accepted the position of research associate at the Chemistry Department of Brown University in Providence, Rhode Island. We moved to Providence, where we rented a small apartment. I also found a part time job in a local metal plating company. After three years at Brown University, I took the job of research scientist at the Research Center of the W.R.Grace Co. in Columbia, Maryland. We moved to Baltimore in 1966, and later to Columbia, Maryland, where I purchased a house. I also got a dog, Wendy. While working at the Grace Co., I started attending evening classes at Johns Hopkins University. In 1975 I graduated with a Master of Science degree in Environmental Engineering.

In Baltimore, we met several Romanian families, with whom we became friends. Over the years, I made several trips with my mother to Israel to visit Gabi and my sister's family. In the summer of 1967, Gabi came to visit. Together, we made several trips, including one to my relatives in Montreal. These trips left a deep impression on Gabi. He visited again in 1970 and 1973, and in 1974 he returned to attend the last two years of highschool in Columbia. He then went back to Israel to fulfill his military duty.

In 1974 I was able to bring my cousin Eddie with wife and two sons from the Soviet Union to Baltimore, where they settled in our neighborhood.

In 1978 I was offered a better job. I moved with my mother to Anaheim, California, and started work in the Research Laboratory of Filtrol Co., a company that made certain products (catalysts) for the oil industry. After a few years of work at Filtrol, I was promoted to the position of Director of Research.

When Filtrol Co. was purchased by another company in 1983, I had to change jobs. I took the position of senior research scientist at the Research Center of Unocal, a large oil company, in Brea, California.

Gabi returned in 1982 and attended the University of California in Riverside, from which he graduated cum laude. He continued his studies at the University of Chicago, and in 1987 earned a Master degree in Business Administration. Afterwards, he went to work for American Airlines at their headquarters in Dallas, Texas.

In 1984 we learned that Uncle Joseph had died in Bucharest. A few years later, in 1988, Aunt Ruchel also died. Both have had a very difficult life under the communist regime.

In early 1994, my mother died at the age of 96. Her loss was a severe blow for me. It took me a long time to recover. In 1995, following a company restructuring, I retired from Unocal. During the next two years, I worked as a consultant for several oil companies. I retired completely from my professional activities in 1997.

During my career, I had written two scientific- technical books, had my name on more than 50 patents, and published over 40 scientific articles in different journals. In 1990, I received the Grand Prize for Creativity from Unocal's top management.

In 1999, Gabi got married and settled in Seattle. He made me the grandfather of three lovely boys: Benjamin, Daniel, and Michael.

Over the years I had several friends, traveled often, visited family, attended artistic performances and wrote this autobiographical narrative. America had been good to me. It gave me opportunities that an immigrant cannot find easily in other countries.

Attachments

Die Räuber
(Parodie von Schillers "Die Bürgschaft")

Das Oranienburger Lager
Der Führer just inspiziert,
In einer Zelle grad'
Ein Sozialist Schillers Werke studiert.
Drauf bleibt der Fuehrer erstaunt stehn
Und spricht zum Sozialisten:
"Hast endlich doch eingesehn
Dass wir Nationalsozialisten sind,
Trotz aller Gegner gross' Geschrei,
Die einzig richtige Partei."
Worauf der Sozialist sich erhebt
Und lacht ihm ins Gesicht;
"Schiller Nationalsozialist?
Das glaubst Du selber nicht!"
Darauf der Führer wutentbrannt:
"Das wagst du mir zu sagen!?
Dafür wird dir von Henkers Hand
Noch heut' der Kopf abgeschlagen!"

"Ich bin," spricht jener, "zum Sterben bereit,
Doch bitt' ich gewähr mir drei Minuten Zeit,
Bis ich Dich vom Wahne befreit,
Und Dir bewiesen—trotzdem's mir fatal ist,
Dass Schiller international ist.
Er schrieb als internationaler Mann
Für Frankreich 'Die Jungfrau von Orlean,'
Er schrieb, wie Dir wohl bekannt,
'Maria Stuart' für England,
Er schrieb, das weiss jedes Kind bereits,
'Wilhelm Tell' doch für die Schweiz;

409

Und ist Dir unbekannt geblieben
Was für Italien er geschrieben?
Ich las heut' früh in aller Ruh
'Die Braut von Messina' und 'Fiesko' dazu;
Ich las heut' früh in der Burg von Oranien
Dass Schiller geschrieben 'Don Carlos'
für Spanien."—
"Halt!" schreit der Führer krebsrot im Gesicht,
"Und für Deutschland, Schurke, schrieb
Schiller nichts?"
"O doch, mein Herr, gewehrt mir die Bitte,
Für das heilige Deutsche Reich das Dritte,
Wo tausende Gelehrte emigriert,
Wo tausende Menschen sterilisiert,
Wo gottverlassene braune Horden
Tempel schänden und Juden morden,
Wo auf der Flucht erschossen man
fand ihre Leiber,
Dem Lande schrieb Schiller das Drama
'Die Räuber'."

The Robbers
(Parody on Schiller's "The Bail")
English translation

The infamous camp of Oranienburg
The Führer came to inspect,
There, an inmate, leaning on a pillar,
Was avidly reading the works by Schiller.

The Führer stopped before the man
And smugly tells a subordinate:
"This man has finally seen the light,

The works of Nazis he recognized."

At this the man rose from his place
And laughed the Führer in his face.
"Schiller a Nazi? You must be mad!
Even you could never believe that."

At this the tyrant flew into a rage:
"How dare you say to me such outrage,
For this insult, without delay,
With your own head you'll have to pay!"

"I am," said the inmate, "ready to die,
But grant me three minutes for a reply,
So I can free you from your fixations
And prove that Schiller wrote for many nations.

He wrote as international man
For France 'The Maiden of Orleans'*,
He wrote, as you may know first-hand
'Maria Stuart'* for England;

He also wrote, on the other hand,
'Wilhelm Tell'* for Switzerland,
Remember for Italy what he begot?
'The Bride of Messina'* and 'Fiesko'* on top.
With open mind, without disdain
Schiller had written 'DonCarlos'* for Spain."

"Stop!" yelled the tyrant, as if snake-bitten,
"And for Germany, scoundrel, had Schiller
not written?"
"Oh, master, allow me to tell you what I have heard,
What Schiller had written for the Reich, the Third,
Where thousands of innocents are beastly brutalized,

411

Where God-forsaken gangs have temples vandalized,
Where desperate thousands have emigrated,
And defenseless Jews are denigrated,
Where those were shot who tried to escape -
To that country, 'The Robbers'* did Schiller dedicate."

* marks the title of a play by Schiller

Bibliographical Note

The interested reader can find more details about the historical events described in this narrative in the following publications (these are only some of the books available on these subjects):

I.C. Butnaru, *The Silent Holocaust. Romania and its Jews,* Greenwood Press, New York; 1992.
Encyclopedia Judaica, Jerusalem.
Vlad Georgescu, *The Romanians. A History* (transl.), Ohio State University Press, Columbus, Ohio, 1992.
Alexander Werth, *Russia at War,* Caroll & Graf Publishers, New York, 1964.
Julius Fisher, *Transnistria: The Forgotten Cemetery,* Thomas Yoseloff Publ.,1969
Jean Ancel, *Transnistria,* Israel, 1998.
Mihail Sebastian, *Journal 1935—1944. The Fascist Years* (transl.), Ivan R. Dee Publ.,2000.
Radu Ioanid, *The Holocaust in Romania,* Ivan R. Dee Publ., 2005

GLOSSARY
of Yiddish/Hebrew terms used in this narrative

Afikoman: piece of matzo concealed by the head of household during the Seder meal; child who "steals" it gets a reward

Aleph-Bet: Hebrew alphabet

Apikores: non-believer

Bar Mitzvah: religious ceremony celebrating the turning of a boy into a man at age 13

Caftan: long, black outer garment worn by many East European Jews

Challah: traditional Sabbath egg bread

Chalutzim: pioneers, youthful agricultural settlers in Palestine

Chametz: food prepared with leaven (not to be eaten on Passover)

Chanukkah: festival commemorating the defeat of Syrian Greeks by Maccabees in 165 BCE and rededication of desecrated Temple in Jerusalem

Charoset: mixture of ground apples, raisins, almonds, cinnamon, and wine; one of the symbolic foods used during the Passover Seder

Chassid: pious Jew that stresses religious fervor and good deeds

Chaver: comrade, friend

Chazzan: cantor; leader of congregational prayer

Chevrah Kadishah: group providing ritual burial to Jewish dead

Cheder: elementary Jewish religious single-room school

Cholent: Dish cooked on Friday and kept warm for the Sabbath noon meal

Chossen: groom

Chuppah: canopy under which pair stands at wedding ceremony

Gemara: rabbinical comments on the Mishna; part of the Talmud

Git Yomtov! : have a good holiday! (Greeting on Jewish holidays)

Grogger: noisemaker used by children during Purim festival

Hamantaschen: triangular Purim cakes with a honey, raisins, and poppy seeds filling

Hachsharah: agricultural training camp for working in kibbutz

Horah: folk dance in a circle

414

Kaddish: the mourner's prayer
Kaizelach: pancakes made of matzo meal or potatoes
Kashern: process of rendering eating utensils ritually pure
Kashes: questions; refers to the traditional four questions asked during the Seder on Passover
Kibbutz: agricultural collective farm
Kiddush: blessing over wine, preceding Sabbath or festival meal
Kittel: white robe worn on High Holidays
Klotzkashes: outlandish questions
Kneidlach: dumplings made of matzo meal, eggs, onions, cheese, potatoes and fat
Kosher: pure; refers to foods permissible under Jewish law
Kugel: potato or noodle pudding
Kultusgemeinde: Jewish Community Center
Kvutza: group, collective
Latkes: potato pancakes
Leidiggaiers: people with nothing to do
Mame-Loshen: mother tongue (meant Yiddish)
Matzo: unleavened bread eaten during the Passover festival
Mechitzah: partition that separates men from women in a synagogue
Melamed: teacher, usually of young children
Megillah: scroll, referring to the Book of Esther
Menahel: group leader (in youth organization)
Mezuzah: small roll of parchment inscribed with biblical text and the name of God; put in case and attached to door post of house
Midrash: rabbinic commentary on the Bible
Minyan: quorum of 10 males over the age of 13, required for religious service
Mishna: compilation of legislation based on Torah principles; part of the Talmud
Oiberchochem: supersmart person
Oneg Shabbat: 'Sabbath delight;" social gathering on Sabbath
Passover: 8-day spring festival commemorating the Exodus from Egypt
Purim: festival celebrating the rescue of the Jews of Persia from planned destruction by prime-minister Haman, through the

intervention of Jewish Queen Esther with King Ahasverus(4th or 5th century BCE)

Rosh Hashanah: New Year celebration, as part of the High Holidays

Seder: ceremonial meal conducted on the first and second night of Passover

Shtetl: Jewish village in Eastern Europe

Sheitl: wig; worn by married women over their cropped hair

Shivah: seven days of mourning for the dead, immediately following the funeral

Schnapps: strong liquor

Shtreimel: black hat trimmed with velvet and edged in fur, worn by Chasidim

Shein Yingahleh: nice little boy

Shochet: ritual slaughterer

Shvitzbood: steam bath

Shul: house of prayer and study

Sukkah: booth in which observant Jews eat during the Sukkoth festival

Sukkoth: Feast of the Tabernacles; seven-day fall harvest festival

Tallit: prayer shawl

Tallit katan: short jacket-like garment worn by Orthodox men under their coat

Talmud: collection of ancient Jewish civil and religious laws; consists of two parts: Mishna (text) and Gemara (commentaries)

Talmud chacham: a person knowledgeable in matters of Talmud

Tefillin: phylacteries; are worn on the forehead and arm while reciting the Morning Prayer

Torah: generally referred to as the Five Books of Moses; broadly used for the whole Bible

Tzaddik: righteous man

Tzimmes: combination of vegetables and/or fruits usually served with the main course of a meal

Tzitzit: ritual fringes of twine cord at the four corners of the prayer shawl

Tzofim: scouts